BLACK DANCE

IN THE UNITED STATES
FROM 1619 TO 1970

LYNNE FAULEY EMERY

with Foreword by
KATHERINE DUNHAM

 National Press Books

Library of Congress Catalog Card Number:
79–187213
International Standard Book Numbers:
0–87484–202–6 (paper)
0–87484–203–4 (cloth)

Manufactured in the United States of America
National Press Books, 850 Hansen Way, Palo Alto, California 94304

MINSTREL MAN

Because my mouth
Is wide with laughter
And my throat
Is deep with song,
You do not think
I suffer after
I have held my pain
So long?

Because my mouth
Is wide with laughter
You do not hear
My inner cry?
Because my feet
Are gay with dancing,
You do not know
I die?

—LANGSTON HUGHES
The Dream Keeper

CONTENTS

FOREWORD
Until the publication of Lynne Emery's fascinating book, *Black Dance in the United States,* there has been in this country no comprehensive study of the dance forms of people of African origin. Considerable original material exists: French, Portuguese, English, Spanish and American sailors, doctors, tourists, slave owners, and priests over the past four hundred years have described, often in tantalizing detail, what they have seen in Africa, the West Indies, and the Americas. But in this country little has been published beyond occasional articles and treatises, and these have only hinted at the profusion of material available.

Now Lynne Emery, a social scientist and historian with a thorough knowledge of dance, has written the first truly comprehensive book on black dance. The scope and interest of her work are enormous. She analyzes the entire complex of black dance, traces its origins, and describes with remarkable lucidity and conciseness its social meaning in the areas where it has been performed. Her generous quotations from long unavailable source material are fascinating in themselves, and her extensive bibliography alone merits publication for its contribution to the study of black culture.

Aside from her incomparable research effort, one of Mrs. Emery's most important contributions is her analysis of the place of dance as a fundamental element of African aesthetic expression, impossible to separate from African music, poetry, and oral literature. There is no doubt that, in Mrs. Emery's phrase, the heart and soul of Africa is, in effect, a gigantic drum, and that the rhythms of its dance are basic to social cohesion, ritual observance, the maintenance of tradition, preparation for war, autohypnosis, the expression of grief and joy, and the satisfaction of play and sexual selection instincts. Mrs. Emery cites many examples of all of these functions. Early in the book she makes the point that slaves both aboard ship and on plantations were often forced under the lash to dance "for reasons of health" and to give the impression of well-being and contentment. On the other hand, the dance by and large has been an instrument of black survival under the most depressing economic and social circumstances, and continues to be so.

In the latter half of the book Mrs. Emery has brought to life many pioneering artists now almost unknown or long forgotten. It is refreshing to find the names of Asadata Dafora Horton, Noble Sissle, and Eubie Blake, in addition to the more familiar Florence Mills and Josephine Baker, to name but a few. She deals in detail with the Negro renaissance of the forties and fifties, and extensively with those dancers and teachers of today who have already achieved regional, national, and international recognition.

In these times it may be surprising to many that Mrs. Emery is not black. She has written, however with both care and dignity, and without exploiting the material she has uncovered for effect in the manner rather commonly practiced by white chroniclers of black fact.

Since Mrs. Emery has quoted so liberally from my own book *Dances of Haiti*,[1] I want to congratulate her for her singular appreciation of that pioneering work. Indeed, she has taken over where I left off. Of course her book will serve as a ready and authoritative reference for dancers. anthropologists, and students of black studies, but it is so rich in human interest and so clearly organized that it should fascinate a far broader public. By the finish of the book we are acquainted not only with the history of black dance, but we also know much more about the enslaved and the enslavers, the psychology of colonialism, and the nature of those who have danced their way out of poverty and racial prejudice into the opera houses and concert halls of the world.

Katherine Dunham, Director
Performing Arts Training Center
Southern Illinois University
East St. Louis, Illinois 62201

[1] Dunham, Katherine, *Dances of Haiti: An Analysis of Their Form and Function*. Mexico: Bellas Artes, 1946; and Paris: Fasquell, 1948. Not published in the United States.

PREFACE

Seemingly insignificant experiences sometimes change the course of one's life; and it was just such an experience which led to the writing of this book. It is hard to believe that the reading of a single book could produce such change, yet *The Autobiography of Malcolm X* was no ordinary book. I had noticed the startling lack of dance literature with which my black students could identify and nebulous thoughts which had been floating through my mind suddenly fell into place and became concrete ideas. *Malcolm X* provided the inspiration which eventually grew into *Black Dance in the United States,* and I will always be indebted to him for the understanding and insight I have gained.

The purpose of this book is twofold. Basically, it was written to provide a documented, historically accurate account of the dance performed by Afro-Americans in the United States. Its second purpose is to serve as a guide or basic reference source for in-depth research in the areas covered.

Black Dance is intended not primarily for dancers but for everyone interested in the contributions of the Afro-American to the cultural development of this country. It could certainly serve, for example, as a supplementary reference for classes in the history of dance and perhaps for certain music and Afro-American history courses. The contribution of the Afro-American to the dance of the United States has been immense and a source of great pride.

Because this book is limited to black dance in the United States, there is little reference to the dances of Africa as such. However, the relative proximity and the great exchange of people between the American mainland and the islands of the West Indies necessitated the inclusion of a chapter dealing with dance in the Caribbean.

When dealing with contemporary black dancers (1930–1970), the focus of this book is on concert dance only. It is in this area that the black dancer has met with the greatest resistance and prejudice. Yet it is also here that the Afro-American dancer has become an artist of the first magnitude.

Rather serious limitations in the literature reviewed became apparent as research for the book progressed. Most of the existing literature on the early Afro-American in the United States and West Indies was written by Caucasians and reflects characteristic biases. Many accounts were written by slave owners, while wealthy travelers were responsible for much of the rest. The fact that the majority of authors describing the dance of the blacks were neither dancers nor dance enthusiasts proved a further limitation. The descriptions of the dances recorded by these writers frequently lacked both clarity and detail.

In addition, many of the older traditions, customs, and dances of the Negro have been lost because of rapid acculturation, the influence of the church, and the failure to preserve historical materials. Any history, of course, is bound to suffer in accuracy and completeness from such loss.

So many people have cooperated and assisted me in writing this book that it is impossible to mention them all by name. I must extend special thanks, however, to the librarians of the following libraries for their assistance: the Pasadena and Los Angeles Public Libraries; libraries of the University of Southern California, University of California at Los Angeles, and Claremont Colleges; the Henry E. Huntington Library; and the Dance, Theatre, and Schomburg Collections of the New York Public Library. The Dance Collection, in particular, possessed a wealth of material. Special thanks must also be given to Dr. Lois Ellfeldt of the University of Southern California for her continued support, encouragement, and belief in my work and to Drs. Eleanor Metheny and Earl V. Pullias, also of the University of Southern California, for their constant enthusiasm and encouragement.

I am further indebted to Misses Katherine Dunham and Pearl Primus and Mr. Alvin Ailey for their generous gifts of time and wisdom. Above all, I am obligated to Mr. Thomas Hamilton, whose continuous encouragement, prodding, patience, tolerance, and understanding made the book possible.

August, 1971   Lynne Emery
Pasadena, California

1

THE SLAVE TRADE

▟▞▟▞ The gigantic drum that was Africa's heart and soul throbbed and pulsated. Many years before, they had entered Africa and taken her people, and now, in the fifteenth century, it was beginning again. Even though sanctioned by Pope Felix V, this rape of Africa was no different from the others, except in the larger numbers of people taken away.

The drumbeat quickened and grew wilder as thousands upon thousands of people were sold into slavery. And at the end, the beat—heaving, sighing—softened to a mere whisper: nearly a sob, as from a grieving mother.

The slave importation to the New World in the seventeenth century was not the first incidence of enslavement in Africa. Africans had been enslaved by Europeans before the sailing of Columbus. The Portuguese, in fact, had begun the African slave trade in 1441 as an element of national commercial expansion.[1] Over the next century the slave trade grew from a mere trickle until a gigantic flood of black bodies poured out of Africa. As early as 1518, slaves were being imported to the West Indies, particularly to the island of Hispaniola (Haiti). By 1540 ten thousand Negroes a year were being imported, and, according to one estimate, by the end of the sixteenth century there were already nine hundred thousand black slaves in the West Indies.[2]

From what area did the thousands of slaves come, and what sort of people were they? A review of the evidence presented by Elizabeth Donnan[3] shows that most of the Africans taken as slaves came from the Gold Coast-Niger area. Reports of slave coffles traveling a thousand miles of the coast before embarcation have been shown to be false.[4]

Were these slaves indeed totally devoid of a native culture? Were they savages with no knowledge of their ancestry? Some earlier American scholars believed this and developed theories based on what was later shown to be ignorance and bias.[5] Further study has demonstrated that the Africans of the slave areas did, indeed, have a cultural background, and a highly developed one at that.[6]

A rich African mythology developed through the centuries and was spread by word of mouth from generation to generation. Folk tales, riddles, proverbs, and poetry were examples of the African heritage. The graphic and plastic arts were highly developed in the Gold Coast-Niger area also. Included were arts such as wood and iron working, weaving, sculpting, and mask making. Music was one of the most highly developed of the arts and the complexities of African rhythmic structure have yet to be equalled.

A fundamental element of African aesthetic expression was the dance. Music and mask making were incorporated into the wide variety of religious dance forms. Dance could also be of a recreational or secular nature and in one form or another pervaded all of African life.

Slaving captains, ashore to bargain for slaves, were sometimes entertained by native slave-traders. Such an event was related by Captain Theodore Canot, who, as a guest of the mulatto trader Mongo John, observed that:

> . . . a whirling circle of half-stripped girls danced to the
> monotonous beat of a tom-tom. Presently, the formal ring was
> broken, and each female stepping out singly, danced according

to her individual fancy. Some were wild, some were soft, some were tame, and some were fiery. After so many years I have no distinct recollection of their characteristic movements.[7]

John Barbot, on one of his many trips to the African coast, described a dance which he witnessed in Nigeria in the early 1700's:

> . . . they sit up and dance. . . . Their dances are commonly in a round, singing the next thing that occurs, whether sense or nonsense. Some of them stand in the middle of the ring, holding one hand on their head, and the other behind their waist, advancing and strutting out their belly forwards, and beating very hard with their feet on the ground. Others clap their hands to the noise of a kettle, or a calabash fitted for a musical instrument. When young men, or boys, dance with maidens, or women, both sides always made abundance of lascivious gestures; and every now and then each takes a draught of palmwine to encourage the sport.[8]

Again and again we will find the elements of dance described by Barbot: the circle, the clapping, the stamping of the feet. These characteristics traveled from Africa to the West Indies and eventually to the plantations of the southern United States.

Nicholas Owen, an English slave dealer, while ashore procuring slaves in the mid-1700's, made the following observation on the life of the Sherbro, a West African coastal tribe:

> Their chief deversions [sic] is playing upon a certain instrument of wood which sounds like a bad fidle [sic]; this instrument is called a BANGELO; they have likewise drums and other games or exercises of deversion.[9]

Dance was used, in some cases, to entice the native Africans to board the white man's ships. Thomas Johns, an ex-slave living in Texas, was ninety years old when he was interviewed in the 1930's:

> My father's name was George and my mother's name was Nellie. My father was born in Africa. Him and two of his brothers and one sister was stole and brought to Savannah, Georgia, and sold. Dey was de chillen of a chief of de Kiochi tribe. De way dey was stole, dey was asked to dance on a ship which some white men had, and my aunt said it was early in de

John Barbot visiting the king of Sestro to procure slaves, from
Churchill, *A Collection of Voyages and Travels,* . . . (1732)

mornin' when dey foun' dey was away from de land, and all dey could see was de water all 'round. She said they was members of de file-tooth tribe of niggers.[10]

Most slaves, however, were not *enticed* on board ship but were bought from slave-dealers, captured as prisoners of war, or abducted singly or in pairs by slave traders both white and black. They were then taken to the slave "factories" near the water's edge and held there, awaiting the arrival of a slave ship. In his travels on shore, Captain Canot developed a kind of storage place for slaves while awaiting a full shipment. He described these slave-pens, or barracoons, as follows:

> The entrance of each slave-pen was commanded by a cannon, while in the centre of the square, I left a vacant space, whereon I have often seen seven hundred slaves, guarded by half dozen [*sic*] musketeers, singing, drumming, and dancing, after their meal.[11]

Each slave trip fell into three distinct parts: the procurement of a full cargo of slaves on the African coast, which could take from as little as a month to nearly a year; the Middle Passage, or voyage from Africa to the New World, which took from fifteen days to four months; and finally, the landing and disposal of the slaves. The life and work of slavers on the African shore has been widely documented, but there are fewer accounts of the tragic Middle Passage, the horrors of which have nevertheless become well-known.

Most students of slaving know, for example, that heads were shaved and all clothing removed, for the sake of health, before sailing, They are also aware of the tremendous death rates from disease, filth, and suicide; the shackling of the men while the women roamed free at the mercy of the sailors; the small device used to pry open the mouths of slaves who refused to eat; the screaming and howling in the airless holds; the savage beatings administered to those who attempted suicide by jumping over the railings; and the sharks which followed each slave ship, waiting for its human cargo. Even in descriptions of the Middle Passage, however, there is mention of dance.

Slave ships built to carry a crowd of four hundred people often actually transported more than six hundred. This overcrowding resulted, of course, in a high death rate: a slaver was considered fortunate to arrive in the New World with a loss of only one quarter of his cargo. Usually he lost up to one-half during the voyage.

A slave ship diagram was developed by Thomas Clarkson and a committee created for the abolition of the slave trade in England.[12] The diagram of the packing of the slaves in the hold was based on the dimensions of the *HMS Brookes*. With conditions so crowded that slaves were forced to lie front to back in order to sleep, it is obvious that dance could not have taken place in the hold. However, according to Dr. Thomas Trotter, a surgeon on board the *Brookes* in a 1783 voyage, there was a ceremony held immediately following the morning meal called "dancing the slaves. Those who were in irons were ordered to stand up and make what motions they could, leaving a passage for such as were out of irons to dance around the deck."[13]

"Dancing the slaves" on board ship was a common occurrence. It was encouraged for economic reasons; slaves who had been exercised looked better and brought a higher price. Getting slaves on deck also afforded time to clean out the holds below. Such dancing was usually encouraged by a cat-o-nine-tails.

> Music was provided by a slave thumping on a broken drum or an upturned kettle, or by an African banjo, if there was one aboard, or perhaps by a sailor with a bagpipe or a fiddle. Slaving captains sometimes advertised for "A person that can play on the Bagpipes, for a Guinea ship."[14]

James Arnold, testifying before the Parliamentary Committee for the Abolition of Slavery stated:

> In order to keep them [the slaves] in good health it was usual to make them dance. It was the business of the chief mate to make the men dance and the second mate danced the women; but this was only done by means of a frequent use of the cat. The men could only jump up and rattle their chains but the women were driven in one among another all the while singing or saying words that had been taught them; — "Messe, messe, mackarida," that is: — "Good living or messing well among white men," thereby praising us for letting them live so well. But there was another time when the women were sitting by themselves, below, when I heard them singing other words and

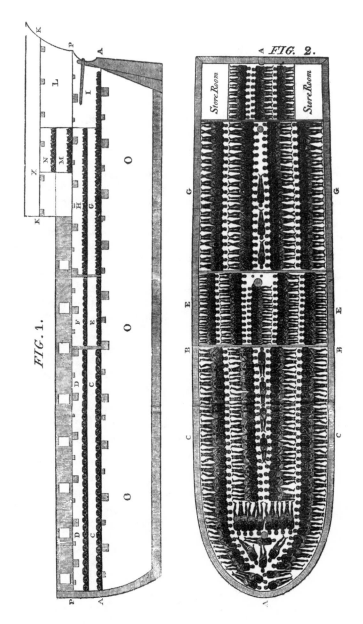

Plan for loading slaves on HMS *The Brookes*, from
Abstract of the Evidence. . . . (1791)

then always in tears. Their songs then always told the story of their lives and their grief at leaving their friends and country.[15]

Arnold also stated that, "if the sea was rough the slaves were unable to dance and whenever it rained hard they were kept below."[16]

Alexander Falconbridge, in his book, *An Account of the Slave Trade on the Coast of Africa,* said essentially the same thing as Arnold. As a surgeon on a slaver, he wrote:

> Exercise being deemed necessary for the preservation of their [the slaves'] health, they are sometimes obliged to dance, when the weather will permit their coming on deck. If they go about it reluctantly, or do not move with agility, they are flogged; a person standing by them all the time with a cat-o-nine-tails in his hand for that purpose. Their music, upon these occasions, consists of a drum, sometimes with only one head; and when that is worn out, they do not scruple to make use of the bottom of one of the tubs. . . . The poor wretches are frequently compelled to sing also; but when they do so, their songs are generally, as may naturally be expected, melancholy lamentations of their exile from their native country.[17]

In his testimony before a select committee of the British House of Commons in 1791, Falconbridge reported, "After meals they [the slaves] are made to jump in their irons. This is called dancing by the slave dealers."[18] In every ship on which Falconbridge served, he had to flog such slaves as would not jump.

The same committee also heard the testimony of another slave-ship surgeon, a Mr. Claxton:

> The parts . . . on which their shackles are fastened, are often excoriated by the violent exercise they are thus forced to take, of which they made many grievous complaints to him [Claxton]. In his ship even those who had the flux, scurvy, and such oedematous swelling in their legs as made it painful to them to move at all, were compelled to dance by the cat.[19]

Since many of the captains also owned stock in the slaving companies, they were reluctant to say anything derogatory about the trade even after retirement. It should be noted that the treatment of seamen was often nearly as brutal as that of the slaves, and that the murder of many such seamen was disclosed in the hearings for the abolition of the British slave trade. Nevertheless, if a seamen wished to sail safely on another slaving expedition, he kept his mouth shut. Despite this, several accounts taken from journals of such seamen and captains are in existence.

One of the earliest accounts is found in *A Journal of a Voyage Made in the Hannibal of London* by Thomas Phillips. On May 21, 1694, the following entry was made in Phillips's journal:

> We often at sea in the evenings would let the slaves come up into the sun to air themselves, and make them jump and dance for an hour or two to our bag-pipes, harp, and fiddle, by which exercise to preserve them in health; but notwithstanding all our endeavour, 'twas my hard fortune to have great sickness and mortality among them.[20]

John Barbot, who had observed the dance of the Nigerians, also made some general observations on the management of slaves aboard ship. He wrote:

> Towards the evening they [the slaves] diverted themselves on the deck, as they thought fit, some conversing together, others dancing, singing, and sporting after their manner, which pleased them highly, and often made us pastime.[21]

Richard Drake spent fifty years in the slave trade, all of them after the official abolition of the trade in England. At the age of twelve he left England for Boston, and from 1807 to 1857 he was engaged in the slave trade. He joined his American uncle, and the two of them passed themselves off as Spaniards so that they could continue buying and selling slaves. Drake carried slaves to Brazil, Honduras, and Florida, where they were "seasoned" and then smuggled into the United States for work on cotton plantations.

While Drake's autobiography, *Revelations of a Slave Smuggler,* must be approached with caution as an authentic account of the slave trade, many of the incidents reported have been verified by witnesses. One of his first entries deals with a voyage from Africa to Brazil at the outset of his life in the slave trade:

> May 10, 1808: Today has been a busy day. The slaves are all below, and the *Coralline* sails to-morrow for the Indies. I think the arrangements for the slaves are excellent. My uncle tells me they are to get two meals a day, of boiled beans or rice, each has a light wooden dish and spoon tied about the neck, and every gang is to be allowed a pipe and tobacco once a day, to

pass around. Besides this, my uncle says, the gangs are to come
on deck, in fine weather, to dance and enjoy themselves. So the
poor people will take a good deal of comfort. This slave trade
is not such a bad thing after all. My uncle says it is a necessary
evil. I think he is getting rich.[22]

On a later voyage, after five years in the trade, Drake reports
more fully the evils of the trade. He had left the company of his
uncle and was on a voyage to the Floridas. While the slaves who
died during the voyage were thrown overboard, frequently those
who became ill were removed from the hold and placed in a
small room under the supervision of the ship's surgeon or knowledgeable seaman. In charge of the makeshift hospital on this
voyage was a crewman named Pedro.

November 2, 1812: Pedro, my assistant, reports one of our
patients blind. We had half the gangs on deck to day [sic] for
exercises; they danced and sung, under the driver's whip, but
are far from sprightly. Captain Leclerc says he never knew such
a sluggish set; yet they all appear healthy.[23]

The blindness mentioned by Drake was a common occurrence on slave ships and was highly dreaded by all. The disease
was called opthalmia, and on some ships affected every person
aboard. Temporary blindness occurred; if it did not disappear
within ten days, it became permanent.

On an undated voyage aboard the *Miranda,* Drake reported
that:

Our blacks were a good-natured set, and jumped to the lash so
promptly, that there was not much occasion for scoring their
naked flanks. We had tamborines on board, which some of the
younger darkies fought for regularly, and every evening we
enjoyed the novelty of African war songs and ring dances, fore
and aft, with the satisfaction of feeling that these pleasant
exercises were keeping our stock in fine condition, and, of
course enhancing our prospect of a profitable voyage.[24]

Conditions varied from ship to ship and the circumstances
aboard the Brazilian brig *Gloria* appeared to disgust even Drake.

Once off the coast, the ship became half bedlam and half
brothel. Ruiz, our captain, and his two mates, set an example
of reckless wickedness, and naught but drinking and rioting

could be seen among the men. They stripped themselves, and danced with black wenches, whilst our crazy mulatto cook played the fiddle. No attempt at discipline; but rum and lewdness seemed to rule all.[25]

George Pinckard, a London physician, hearing of the evils of slavery, decided to see for himself the conditions of the slavers and slaves, and secured permission to board a ship which had just anchored in Barbados.

Their sleeping berths were the naked boards. Divided into two crowded parties they reposed, during the night, upon the bare planks below—the males on the main deck—the females upon the deck of the aft cabin. In the day time they were not allowed to remain in the place where they had slept, but were kept mostly upon the open deck, where they were made to exercise, and encouraged, by the music of their loved banjar, to dancing and cheerfulness.[26]

Pinckard continued his description with a vivid if inexact picture of the dance aboard a slave ship:

We saw them dance, and heard them sing. In dancing they scarcely moved their feet, but threw about their arms, and twisted and writhed their bodies into a multitude of disgusting and indecent attitudes. Their song was a wild yell, devoid of all softness and harmony, and loudly chanted in harsh monotony.[27]

Another observer, Sir William Young, saw a slightly different picture of life aboard a slave ship than that presented by Pinckard. After a visit to St. Vincent's Island in the Caribbean he recorded the following observation on December 16, 1791.

Three Guinea ships being in the harbour, full of slaves from Africa, I testified a wish to visit the ships previous to the sale. I would have visited them privately and unexpectedly, but it was not practicable. Everything was prepared for our visit, as the least observing eye might have discovered: In particular I was disgusted with a general jumping or dancing of the negroes on the deck, which some, and perhaps many of them, did voluntarily, but some under force or controul [sic]; for I saw a sailor, more than once, catch those rudely by the arm who had ceased dancing, and by gesture menace them to repeat their motion, to clap their hands, and shout their song of Yah! Yah! which I understood to mean "Friends."[28]

So it went, and so they came, a black stream from Africa to the Americas. The African was forced to dance in bondage and under the lash. He danced because the white ruler wanted his stock in good condition. He danced not for love, nor joy, nor religious celebration, nor even to pass the time; he danced in answer to the whip. He danced for survival.

The Africans danced in a ring; they danced in their shackles; they jumped up and rattled their chains; they writhed and twisted in "disgusting and indecent attitudes." This they did to the accompaniment of a drum—sometimes a broken drum or kettle and sometimes even a relief pot. The beat of the drum followed the captives across the Atlantic to their home in the New World.

▯▯▯▯ NOTES FOR CHAPTER 1

1. Saunders Redding, *They Came in Chains* (Philadelphia: J. B. Lippincott Company, 1950), p. 11.

2. Daniel P. Mannix and Malcolm Cowley, *Black Cargoes: A History of the Atlantic Slave Trade, 1518-1865* (New York: Viking Press, 1962), p. 5. See also John Hope Franklin, *From Slavery to Freedom. A History of Negro Americans*, Vintage Books (3d ed.; New York: Random House, 1969), pp. 62-63.

3. Elizabeth Donnan, *Documents Illustrative of the History of the Slave Trade to America* (4 vols.; Washington, D. C.: Carnegie Institution of Washington, 1931), I-IV, *passim*.

4. Melville J. Herskovits, *The Myth of the Negro Past* (Boston: Beacon Press, 1958), pp. 46-53.

5. The most frequently read scholars on American slavery—Phillips, Tillinghast, and Weatherford—have all included deprecating statements later shown to be false. See Ulrich B. Phillips, *American Negro Slavery. A Survey of the Supply, Employment, and Control of Negro Labor as Determined by the Plantation Regime* (New York: D. Appleton and Company, 1918), pp. 4-8; Joseph Alexander Tillinghast, *The Negro in Africa and America*, a publication of the American Economic Association; (3 vols.; New York: Macmillan Company, 1902), pp. 29f.; and Willis D. Weatherford, *The Negro from Africa to America* (New York: George H. Doran Co., 1924), pp. 20f.

6. Herskovits, *Myth of the Negro Past*, chap. III.

7. Theodore Canot, *Adventures of an African Slaver. Being a True Account of Captain Theodore Canot, Trader in Gold, Ivory and Slaves on the Coast of Guinea: His Own Story as Told in the Year 1854 to Brantz Mayer*, ed. by Malcolm Cowley (New York: Albert and Charles Boni, 1928), p. 73.

8. John Barbot, *A Description of the Coasts of North and South Guinea;*

and of Ethiopia Inferior, Vulgarly Angola: Being a New and Accurate Account of the Western Maritime Countries of Africa, cited by Awnsham Churchill, A Collection of Voyages and Travels, Some Now First Printed from Original Manuscripts (6 vols.; London: 1704, 1732), V, 53.

9. Nicholas Owen, Journal of a Slave-Dealer, A View of Some Remarkable Axcedents in the Life of Nics. Owen on the Coast of Africa and America from the Year 1746 to the Year 1757, ed. by Eveline Martin (London: George Routledge and Sons, Ltd., 1930), p. 52.

10. Thomas Johns, interviewed in Texas by the Texas Writers' Project in Federal Writers' Project, Slave Narratives. A Folk History of Slavery in the United States from Interviews with Former Slaves (17 vols.; Washington, D.C.: Typewritten records prepared by the Federal Writers' Project, 1936-1938), XVI, Part 2, p. 201.

11. Canot, Adventures of an African Slaver, pp. 310-11.

12. Thomas Clarkson, The History of the Rise, Progress, and Accomplishment of the Abolition of the African Slave-Trade by the British Parliament (2 vols.; London: R. Taylor and Co., 1808), I, 111.

13. Minutes of the Evidence Delivered Before a Select Committee of the Whole House . . . to Whom it was Referred to Consider of the Slave-Trade (4 vols.; British Sessional Papers, 1731-1800), cited by Mannix and Cowley, Black Cargoes, p. 114.

14. Ibid.

15. Report to the House of Lords on the Abolition of the Slave Trade (2 vols.; London: 1789), cited by George Francis Dow, Slave Ships and Slaving (Salem, Mass.: Marine Research Society, 1927), pp. 177-78.

16. Ibid., p. 178.

17. Alexander Falconbridge, An Account of the Slave Trade on the Coast of Africa (London: J. Phillips, 1788), p. 23.

18. An Abstract of the Evidence Delivered Before a Select Committee of the House of Commons in the Years 1790 and 1791, on the Part of the Petitioners for the Abolition of the Slave Trade (Printed at the Expense of the Society in Newcastle for Promoting the Abolition of the Slave-Trade, 1791), p. 39.

19. Ibid.

20. Thomas Phillips, A Journal of a Voyage Made in the Hannibal of London, Ann. 1693, 1694, From England, to Cape Manseradoe, in Africa; and Thence Along the Coast of Guinez to Whidaw, the Island of St. Thomas, and so Forward to Barbados, cited in Churchill, A Collection of Voyages and Travels, VI, 230.

21. Barbot, Description of the Coasts of North and South Guinea, cited in Churchill, A Collection of Voyages and Travels, V, 547.

22. Richard Drake, Revelations of a Slave Smuggler: Being the Autobiography of Captain Rich'd Drake, An African Trader for Fifty Years—from 1807 to 1857; During Which Period He Was Concerned in the Transportation of Half a Million Blacks from African Coasts to America (New York: Robert M. DeWitt, 1860), p. 44.

23. *Ibid.*, p. 49.

24. *Ibid.*, p. 59.

25. *Ibid.*, p. 88.

26. George Pinckard, *Notes on the West Indies* (2 vols.; 2d ed.; London: Baldwin, Cradock, and Joy, and L. B. Seeley, 1816), I, 102-03.

27. *Ibid.*, I, 103.

28. William Young, *A Tour Through the Several Islands of Barbadoes, St. Vincent, Antiqua, Tobago, and Grenada In the Years 1791 and 1792,* in Bryan Edwards, *An Historical Survey of the Island of Saint Domingo, together with an account of the Maroon Negroes in the Island of Jamaica; and a History of the War in the West Indies, In 1793 and 1794* (London: John Stockdale, 1801), p. 268.

2

BLACK DANCE OF THE CARIBBEAN, 1518-1900

⬛⬛⬛⬛ The beat of drums in the distance broke the stillness of the warm, starlit Caribbean night. Through the darkness, the deep voice of the large drum played by bare black hands sounded against the staccato of sticks on the smaller drum. The rhythm was complex— four or five patterns played against one another—but most of all, it was exciting, stimulating.

The African heritage is obvious today in the West Indies. French and Spanish slave owners were more liberal than English and Americans in allowing the native Africans to retain their own culture. According to Harold Courlander, the survival of African heritage in Haiti, for example, was due to the relatively liberal attitudes of the first French and Spanish rulers and the Catholic Church. The main objective of the Church was salvation of the soul:

[The] church did not insist on washing out of the African mind everything that was there. The Catholic Church regarded every slave as a soul to be saved, as a complete and finished man except for salvation.[1]

In the West Indies the African was generally considered a human being, whereas in the United States the slaves were frequently considered non-human, and Protestant denominations were more repressive than the Catholics. Wherever the Catholic Church was powerful, as, for example, in Louisiana, Mexico, and South America, Africanisms were retained in greater number.

Because of the great interchange of slaves between the West Indies and the mainland, consideration of Negro dance in the Caribbean is basic to discussion of Negro dance in the United States. According to historian John Hope Franklin, many Africans debarked first on one of the West Indian islands for a process termed "seasoning." The slave "was regarded as seasoned within three or four years and was viewed by mainland planters as much more desirable than the raw Negroes fresh from the wilds of Africa."[2]

During the 1803 overthrow of the white ruling class in Haiti, white planters and their slaves flocked to Louisiana and particularly to the New Orleans area. After the Civil War there was a further exchange between the areas. The large West Indian population in New York City and the large number of Cubans in Florida are current evidence of a continuing process.

▣⫶▣⫶▣ MUSICAL INSTRUMENTS OF THE BLACK WEST INDIES

The dance of the West Indian black was based on rhythm, and movement was frequently controlled by percussion instruments, usually the drums. The complexity of the rhythmic patterns of the music led to a similar complexity in the structure of the dance; the feet might follow one rhythm while the hips moved to a second and the arms and head to a third and fourth. A brief look at the instruments found in the New World may lead to a clearer understanding of black West Indian dance. Several early accounts of dance accompaniment demonstrate the resourcefulness of the transplanted Africans.

Sir Hans Sloane, a medical doctor, visited the islands of Madera, Barbados, Nieves, St. Christopher, and Jamaica in the late 1600's. In a memoir published in 1707, Sloane wrote that the slaves of Jamaica "are much given to Venery, and although hard wrought, will at nights, or on Feast days Dance and Sing; their Songs are all bawdy, and leading that way."[3]

Sloane then described some of the musical instruments used by the Jamaican Negroes.

> They have several sorts of instruments in imitation of Lutes, made of small Gourds fitted with Necks, strung with Horse hairs, or the peeled stalks of climbing Plants or Withs. These instruments are sometimes made of hollow'd Timber covered with Parchment or other Skin wetted, having a Bow for its Neck, the Strings ty'd longer or shorter, as they would alter their sounds.[4]

This same stringed instrument was familiar to William Beckford, who lived in Jamaica from 1764 to 1777. Beckford called this instrument a "bonjour," which he described as "a kind of Spanish guitar."[5]

The bonjour was called a "banza" by Moreau de St.-Méry, who described it as "a sort of large guitar with four strings."[6] Still another name for the same instrument was given by Bryan Edwards, who called it a "banja" or "merriwang." According to Edwards, the instrument was "an imperfect kind of violincello [sic]; except that it is played on by the finger like the guitar; producing a dismal monotony of four notes."[7] Whether called a bonjour, banza, or banja, the instrument described is, in fact, the banjo which Thomas Jefferson later called the only instrument of African origin to find its way to the United States.

Another instrument frequently described was a rattle similar to the present-day maracas. Moreau de St.-Méry described this instrument as a gourd or calabash "filled with pebbles; these gourds are pierced lengthwise by a long handle by which they are shaken."[8] Matthew Gregory Lewis called this rattle a "shaky-sheky," which consisted of "a bladder with a parcel of pebbles in it."[9]

The most important instrument, however, was the drum. In his early account, Hans Sloane wrote that at one time the Negroes were allowed to use trumpets and drums made of hollow logs with skin stretched across one end. However, "making use of these in their Wars at home in Africa, it was thought too much inciting them to Rebellion, and so they were prohibited by the Customs of the Island."[10] While it appears that the drum was banned in some areas as early as 1700, most authors writing on black West Indian dance spend some time describing this important instrument. A vivid and often plagiarized description of the drums used by the transplanted Africans was given by Père Labat in his book published in 1724:

> . . . they [the Negroes] use two drums made of two tree trunks hollowed to unequal depths. One of the ends is open, the other covered with a sheep skin or goat skin, without hair, scraped like parchment. The largest of these two drums which they simply called the "big drum" may measure three or four feet in length with a diameter of fifteen inches. The smaller one, which is called the "baboula" is of about the same length with a diameter of eight or nine inches. Those who beat the drums to mark the beat of the dance put them between their legs or sit on them and strike them with the flat of the four fingers of each hand. The man who plays the large drum strikes it deliberately and rhythmically, but the baboula player drums as fast as he can, hardly keeping the rhythm and, as the sound of the baboula is much quieter than that of the big drum and is very penetrating, its only use is to make noise without marking the beat of the dance or the movements of the dancers.[11]

Moreau de St.-Méry's often-quoted description of West Indian drums is very similar to Labat's. Beckford gave names to the types of drums, calling one type a "cotter, upon which they beat with sticks," and the other "a gomba, which they strike with their hands."[12] Edwards also wrote of the gomba, calling it a "goombay" which "is a rustic drum; being formed of the trunk of a hollow tree, one end of which is covered with sheep skin."[13] Lewis called this drum a "gamby" and indicated that it was a drum of the Eboe tribe.[14] Another type of drum, corresponding to Beckford's "cotter" was called the "kitty-katty" by Lewis, who described it as "nothing but a flat piece of board beat upon by two sticks. . . ."[15]

"Manner of Playing the Ka,"
a large drum played with
hands and heels of feet;
probably the same drum
called by many the "gomba";
from Hearn, *Two Years in the
French West Indies* (1890)

West Indian "Carib Drummer"
from *Theatre Arts Monthly*
(January, 1933)

Accompanied, then, by a banja (or banza, bonjour, or home-made banjo), a calabash or gourd filled with pebbles, and a baboula (or goombay, gomba, cotter, or board played with sticks or hands)—and sometimes a jawbone rubbed by a stick or bone—the Negro slaves sang, clapped, and danced.

▐▌▐▌ DANCES DONE BY THE WEST INDIAN BLACKS

That the black slaves of the Caribbean danced there is no doubt. Nearly every author writing of life in the West Indies before 1900 mentioned the dance. Many of these descriptions are scanty, but it is certain that the blacks did dance. Speaking of the slaves, Sloane observed that "their Dances consist in great activity and strength of Body, and keeping time, if it can be."[16] Eighty-three years later, Beckford wrote:

> Their style of dancing is by no means ungraceful. . . . They generally meet before their houses, and sometimes in the pastures . . . where, if allowed, they will continue their favourite diversions from night to morning.[17]

Writing of the slaves of Barbados in 1816, George Pinckard stated that they were "passionately fond of dancing" and that

> . . . they undergo more fatigue, or at least more personal exertion, during their gala hours of Saturday night and Sunday, than is demanded of them in labour, during any four days of the week.[18]

The most complete account of the dance of the Negro in the New World was given by Moreau de St.-Méry. Born in Martinique in 1750, he lived there until he was twenty-two, when he moved to Santo Domingo. He obviously knew more of Negro dance than those who were just visiting or touring the islands. His writings, and particularly his book, *Danse*, have been quoted extensively because of their wealth of descriptive material.

One of St.-Méry's favorite theories was that people born in the lush, hot tropics have a passion for dance and that the degree of passion decreases as one moves north to colder climates. Since the climate of the West Indies was similar to that of Africa, St.-Méry felt that "the Negroes bring with them their passion for the dance and are able to conserve it."[19] He felt that the black interest in dance was

> so strong that a negro, no matter how tired he may be from his work, always finds the strength to dance and even to travel several leagues to satisfy his passion.[20]

He also wrote that:

> The Negroes of the Gold Coast, warlike, blood thirsty, accustomed to human sacrifice, know only dances that are ferocious like themselves, while the Congolese, the Senegalese and other African shepherds and farmers, enjoy dancing as relaxation, as a source of sensual pleasures.[21]

While St.-Méry's theory on climate and dance has been disputed, specific tribes did seem to prefer certain types of dances. Yet even among the wide variety of tribes brought together in the Caribbean, some dances were enjoyed by nearly all the slaves: the Calenda, Chica, Bamboula, and Juba.

Calenda

The Calenda seemed to be the favorite of the blacks. Most white observers thought it indecent. Labat believed that the Calenda came "from the coast of Guinea and, by all indications, from the Kingdom of Arda."[22] By 1724, when Labat's book was published, the slaver owners had banned the Calenda, partly because of its immodesty and partly because they feared uprisings among large gatherings of blacks. Labat wrote that this prohibition was no small matter since the dance was such a favorite that the blacks "would willingly pass entire days at this exercise."[23]

Labat's description of the Calenda is the earliest found and is here given in its entirety.

> The dancers are arranged in two lines, facing each other, the men on one side and the women on the other. Those who are tired of dancing form a circle with the spectators around the dancers and the drums. The ablest person sings a song which

he composes on the spot on any subject he considers appropriate. The refrain of this song is sung by everyone and is accompanied by great handclapping. As for the dancers, they hold their arms a little like someone playing castagnettes. They jump, make swift turns, approach each other to a distance of two or three feet then draw back with the beat of the drum until the sound of the drums brings them together again to strike their thighs together, that is, the men's against the women's. To see them it would seem that they were striking each other's bellies although it is only the thighs which receive the blows. At the proper time they withdraw with a pirouette, only to begin again the same movement with absolutely lascivious gestures; this, as many times as the drums give the signal, which is many times in a row. From time to time they lock arms and make several revolutions always slapping their thighs together and kissing each other. It can readily be seen by this abridged description to what degree this dance is contrary to all modesty.[24]

Even though the dance was considered indecent by some, it was adopted by the Spanish Creoles and proved to be one of their favorite pastimes. While opinions differ regarding the name of the dance performed by the nuns, Labat wrote that in the churches of the Creoles:

. . . the nuns don't miss the opportunity to dance it [the Calenda] on Christmas Eve on an elevated platform in the choir, behind the grill which is left open so that the people may take part in the joy which these good souls demonstrate for the birth of the Saviour. It is true that no men are admitted to dance such a devout dance. I am willing to believe that they do this dance with the purest intentions, but how many spectators are there who would not be as charitable as I in their judgement?[25]

This same Calenda was described somewhat differently by St.-Méry, who called it the Kalenda. It must be remembered that St.-Méry was writing nearly seventy-five years after Labat, which may account for the apparent changes in the dance. At no time did St.-Méry call the dance indecent. As he described it:

One male and one female dancer, or an equal number of dancers of each sex push to the middle of the circle and begin to dance, remaining in pairs. This repetitious dance consists of a very simple step where, as in the "Anglaise" one alternately extends each foot and withdraws it, tapping several times with the heel and toe. All one sees is the man spinning himself or swirling around his partner, who, herself, also spins and moves about, unless one is to count the raising and lowering of the arms of the dancers who hold their elbows close to their sides with the hands almost clenched. The woman holds both ends of a kerchief which she rocks from side to side. When one has not witnessed it himself, it is hard to believe how lively and animated it is as well as how the rigorous following of the meter gives it such grace. The dancers ceaselessly replace each other, and the blacks derive such pleasure from this entertainment that they must be forced to stop.[26]

Even though officially prohibited, the Calenda was frequently performed through the years. The naturalist Descourtilz, in Haiti from 1799 to 1803, reported that the blacks would not stop dancing the "indecent Calenda" until they were "exhausted with fatigue and love by the lewdness of their movements."[27]

In describing the following dance done by the slaves in Barbados, Pinckard was probably referring to the Calenda:

The dance consists of stampings of the feet, twistings of the body, and a number of strange indecent attitudes. It is a severe bodily exertion — more bodily indeed than you can well imagine, for the limbs have little to do in it. The head is held erect, or, occasionally, inclined a little forward; the hands nearly meet before; the elbows are fixed, pointing from the sides; and, the lower extremities being held rigid, the whole person is moved without lifting the feet from the ground. Making the head and limbs fixed points, they writhe and turn the body upon its own axis, slowly advancing towards each other, or retreating to the other parts of the ring. Their approaches, with the figure of the dance, and the attitudes and inflexions in which they are made, are highly indecent.[28]

Attesting to the long life of the Calenda was an account of a "genuine" Negro dance seen by Charles Day in 1852 on the island of Barbados. While Day called the dance the "Joe and Johnny," his description was much like that given by St.-Méry of the Calenda.

The first movement was an *en avant* by both, the feet close together toeing and heeling it very gently, the *retirez* the same; then the feet were straddled in a somewhat indecorous manner for ladies. . . . I must not omit to remark that the feet did *not* take the most active part in the dance, as that was executed by a prominent part of the person, commonly understood to be that peculiarly African development on which "Honour holds her seat." That wriggle transcends description: none but itself could be its parallel.[29]

Another author described the Calenda and yet called the dance the "Joan-Johnny." Writing in 1833, James Alexander said that a couple "would twist their bodies, thump the ground with their heels, and circle round one another . . . . "[30]

That the Calenda exists even in modern times can be observed in Katherine Dunham's description of a dance she called the Congo Paillette, in which "practically the only movement is in the rapid agitation of the extended haunches, accomplished by a rapid shuffling motion of the feet."[31]

The Calenda, according to most accounts, had certain general characteristics: it was performed by one or more couples encircled by a singing, clapping ring; the movement of a couple consisted of a rather shuffling advance and retreat, with most of the movement originating in the hips, while the limbs played a very small part in the dance. Except in the description given by Labat, there was no physical contact between dancers.

One further passage describes a Calenda entirely different from the others. Lafcadio Hearn described a "Caleinda" as a dance done "by men only, all stripped to the waist, and twirling heavy sticks in a mock fight."[32] Stick dances did exist in the Caribbean; perhaps the names of various dances became confused, leading Hearn to identify the dance he observed as the Calenda.

Chica

Another popular dance which eventually reached the mainland and New Orleans was the Chica, known under that name, according to St.-Méry, in both the Windward Islands and Santo Domingo. It was thought by one writer that the Chica eventually became the modern West Indian dance called the Shayshay.[33]

St.-Méry described the Chica as being peculiar to the Congolese and performed as follows:

When one wants to dance the Chica, a tune, especially reserved
for that type of dance, is played on crude instruments. The beat
is very pronounced. For the woman, who holds the ends of a
kerchief or the sides of her skirt, the art of this dance consists
mainly in moving the lower parts of her loins while maintaining
the upper part of her body practically immobile. Should one
want to enliven the Chica, a man approaches the woman while
she is dancing, and, throwing himself forward precipitously, he
falls in with the rhythm, almost touching her, drawing back,
lunging again, seeming to want to coax her to surrender to the
passion which engulfs them. When the Chica reaches it most
expressive stage, there is in the gestures and in the movements
of the two dancers a harmony which is more easily imagined
than described.[34]

It was the Chica which was danced by the nuns at Christmas,
according to St.-Méry. Perhaps in the passage quoted earlier
Labat was in fact describing the Chica and mistakenly calling
it the Calenda. It is unlikely that the church women would adopt
two African dances as a part of the religious service. In any case,
St.-Méry insisted that the best dancers of the Chica were the
black women of the Dutch island of Curaçao. Upon watching
them dance he wrote:

It is difficult to conceive of the refinement which they have
applied to this dance. They go so far that their breasts seem to
be independent of their chests, which they shake with such
vigor that it is tiring even to watch.[35]

Whether the dance described by Labat was the Chica or
Calenda is relatively unimportant. What is important is that a
dance much like the one described by St.-Méry was found
throughout the Caribbean. In 1774, Edward Long described a
dance done by the Jamaican blacks:

The female dancer is all languishing, and easy in her motions;
the man, all action, fire, and gesture; his whole person is
variously turned and writhed every moment, and his limbs
agitated with such lively exertions, as serve to display before
his partner the vigour and elasticity of his muscles.[36]

In 1851, while on a tour of Cuba, Fredrika Bremer saw a
dance performed on a plantation in Serro. She described the
dancers in these terms:

. . . she turning round on one spot with downcast eyes, he surrounding her with a vast many gambols, among which are most astounding summersets and leaps, remarkable for their boldness and agility.[37]

Bremer saw the Chica performed on various plantations in Cuba and at La Concordia, where she observed that "in the centre of the ring two or three dancing couples flourished about, leaping and grimacing, the men with much animation, the women sheepishly."[38]

In 1889, Spenser St. John wrote a controversial book about Haiti. In addition to mentioning cannibalism and apparent hearsay which he recorded as fact, St. John noted the Chica, which he said was popularly called the Bamboula. Rather than describing the dance himself, St. John quoted St.-Méry's French account of the Chica. St. John added that the Bamboula was so lascivious that no modest woman would perform or be seen at such a dance, and yet said that the young black women of his acquaintance delighted in performing it.[39] St. John recorded that "the dance grew fast and furious; . . . and . . . all are said to give themselves up to the most unreserved debauchery,[40] a statement that makes it questionable whether he saw the dance he described.

The main characteristic of the popular Chica appears to have been the rotation of the hips with an immobile upper body. The role danced by the woman was apparently one of coquetry, while the man pursued and enticed. Perhaps elements of the Chica appeared in the much later Rumba and Mambo.

Bamboula

One of the drums used to accompany the Chica was known as the baboula. The dance called the Bamboula undoubtedly received its name from this drum. This dance is discussed by a few authors, but a careful examination of the descriptions leads to the conclusion that the Bamboula is in fact another name for the Chica.

In his 1823 book J. Stewart wrote of a dance performed by a man and woman inside a ring. "When two dancers have fatigued themselves," he said, "another couple enter the ring."[41] According to Stewart's account, the Jamaican slaves were so fond of this dance that they would continue for days and nights without stopping if permitted. Stewart, however, did not name the dance, nor does his description provide many clues as to its nature.

Besides St. John's report of the Chica being popularly called the Bamboula, the only other mention of the Bamboula in the Caribbean was by Henry Breen in 1844. Breen merely indicated that the term Bamboula designated a dance held out of doors, while any dance held inside was termed a ball.[42]

Neither in the West Indies nor on the mainland of the United States does the Bamboula appear as a separate dance. It seems instead to be the same dance as the Chica. The one remaining dance, the Juba, could not have been confused or mistaken for any other dance since it had a style all its own.

Juba

Dunham, studying West Indian dance in the late 1930's, wrote that the Juba or Jumba dance was "primarily a competitive dance of skill."[43] These competitive or challenge dances appeared throughout the islands of the Caribbean and spread to the southern United States, where the Juba was a well-known dance.

In 1844 F. W. Wurdemann vividly recalled a dance done in Cuba by Negro slaves:

> Presently a woman advances and commencing a slow dance, made up of shuffling of the feet and various contortions of the body; thus challenges a rival from among the men. One of these, bolder than the rest, after awhile steps out, and the two then strive which shall first tire the other; the woman performing many feats which the man attempts to rival, often excelling them, amid the shouts of the rest. A woman will sometimes drive two or three successive beaux from the ring, yielding her place at length to some impatient belle, who has been meanwhile looking on with envy at her success. Sometimes a sturdy fellow will keep the field for a long time, and one after another of the other sex will advance to the contest only to be defeated; each one, as she retires, being greeted by the laughter of the spectators.[44]

"Negro Dance on a Cuban Plantation," from *Harper's Weekly* (1859)

Charles Edwards wrote of the same type of dance performed in the Bahamas, except that his account dealt with a dance done by men only. "Some expert dancer 'steps off' his specialty in a challenging way,"[45] while the rest of the men keep time by clapping, stamping, and slapping their thighs. (This accompaniment was called "patting Juba" in the United States.)

> All applaud as the dancer finishes; but before he fairly reaches a place in the circle a rival catches step to the music, and all eyes are again turned toward the centre of attraction. Thus goes the dance into the night.[46]

The same type of dance was reported by L. D. Powles in his *Land of the Pink Pearl.* Because a fire was built to warm the drum heads, Powles termed the dance the "fire dance,"[47] although the movements he recorded were those of the Juba.

Labat's Dance of the Congolese

One other dance remains distinct from those previously discussed. Labat alone describes it. He notes that the movements are quite the opposite of those of the Calenda and that it was performed only by the Congolese blacks:

> The dancers, men and women, form a circle and without moving about they do nothing else but to raise their feet in the air and strike the ground with a sort of cadence, holding their bodies bent toward the ground, each in front of the other. They intone some story that one of their number tells, to which the dancers respond with a refrain while the spectators clap their hands. There is nothing shocking about this dance, but neither is it very entertaining.[48]

No other account of this particular dance has been found. Either it disappeared or Labat happened upon a dance not seen by other diarists.

The Congolese ring dance reported by Labat, the Calenda, the Chica-Bamboula, and the Juba dance comprised but a small part of the dance activities in the Caribbean. Much dance was done, for example, as a part of the religious ceremonies of Voodoo or Shango groups. Special occasions such as weddings, funerals, and holidays also provided great opportunities for the slaves to dance.

John Canoe

One of the most intriguing Caribbean traditions is called John Canoe, and persists, it is said, even to the present day in the New Orleans Mardi Gras.[49] The term John Canoe is applied to the groups of specially costumed dancers who appear at Christmas time. Formerly in the West Indies, the thwank, slap, slap of the gombay drum heard for several weeks before Christmas announced that soon the John Canoe[50] dancers would be coming into town to perform and parade through the streets.

The origin of the John Canoe custom is obscure but Long gave a feasible explanation most frequently quoted by other authors:

> This dance is probably an honourable memorial of John Conny, a celebrated cabocero at Tres Puntas, in Axim, on the Guiney coast; who flourished about the year 1720. He bore great authority among the Negroes of that district.[51]

Long described the John Canoe dancers as tall and well-built men, dressed in peculiar clothes, carrying wooden swords, and followed by a group of drunken women. On the head of each John Canoe dancer was "a pair of ox-horns, sprouting from the top a horrid sort of vizor, or mask, which about the mouth is rendered very terrific with large boar-tusks."[52] This man, according to Long, danced at every door "bellowing out 'John Connu!' with great vehemence."[53]

There is another possible origin for John Canoe, however. Sir William Young described a phenomenon named Moco Jumbo, whom he considered to be the Mumbo Jumbo of the Mandingoes described by African travelers. Young saw this Moco Jumbo on the island of St. Vincent on December 26, 1791, and wrote that:

> Returning to the villa, we were greeted by a party which frightened the boys. It was the "Moco Jumbo" and his suite. The "Jumbo" was on stilts, with a head mounted on the actor's

"Jaw-Bone or House John-Canoe," from J. M. Belisario's *Sketches* in Lewis, *Journal of a West Indian Proprietor* (1929)

head, which was concealed: the music was from two baskets, like strawberry baskets, with little bells within, shook in time. The swordsman danced with an air of menace, the musician was comical, and Jumbo assumed the "antic terrible," and was very active on his stilts.[54]

The fact that the Moco Jumbo appeared at Christmas, wore a mask, and brandished a sword makes him appear quite like the John Canoe described by Long. Perhaps John Canoe originated among the African Mandingoes rather than as a memorial to a man named John Conny.

Whatever its origin, the John Canoe custom was a reality. As the John Canoe walked through the streets he was followed by groups of drunken women. The origin and composition of these groups of women is most interesting. At some obscure point in time the women divided themselves into rival factions, frequently called the Reds and the Blues, according to the color of clothing worn. In 1816 Monk Lewis wrote:

> It seems that many years ago, an Admiral of the Red was superseded on the Jamaica Station by an Admiral of the Blue; and both of them gave balls at Kingston to the "Brown Girls"; for the fair sex elsewhere are called the "Brown Girls" in Jamaica. In consequence of these balls, all Kingston was divided into parties . . . eventually spreading through the whole island at Christmas.[55]

Whether this was the case, or whether, as Beckwith stated, the "Reds and the Blues were distinguished for their allegiance to English army or Scotch navy,"[56] makes little difference. The fact remains that the black and Creole girls were divided into two rival groups, each led by a queen, wearing clothing of the same color, and carrying parasols. Each group of women was called a "sett." In 1827 Alexander Barclay described them as they paraded through the streets.

> They have always with them . . . a fiddle, drum, and tambourine, frequently boys playing fifes, a distinguishing flag which is waved on a pole. . . . A matron attends who possesses some degree of authority, and is called Queen of the Sett, and they have always one or two Jon-canoe-men. . . .[57]

Many authors writing of the Christmas festivities in the West Indies mention the sett girls and John Canoe men.[58] It is interesting to note the evolution of the costume worn by the John Canoes. From the late 1700's, when Long described the mask of the John Canoe as having ox-horns and boar-tusks, to 1816, when Monk Lewis was writing, the costume became much more sophisticated. Lewis said that "The John Canoe . . . dressed in a striped doublet, and having upon his head a kind of paste board house-boat, filled with puppets. . . ."[59]

The houseboat headdress remained the trademark of John Canoe, although, according to Beckwith,[60] the animal masks have continued in many of the secluded areas of Jamaica. Beckwith also stated that in St. Elizabeth, the entire John Canoe proceedings were connected with the practices of Obeah, a form of religion, concerned primarily with charms, curses, and poisons. The ceremony accompanying the construction of the elaborate headdress was explained to her by a priest of Myalism (a type of religion concerned with destroying the curses of Obeah) named White:

> Before building the house-shaped structure worn in the dance, a feast must be given consisting of goat's meat boiled without salt, together with plenty of rum. As the building progresses, other feasts are given. On the night before it is brought out in public, it is taken to the cemetery, and there the songs and dances are rehearsed in order to "catch the spirit of the dead," which henceforth accompanies the dancer until, after a few weeks of merriment during which performances are given for money at the great houses and at village crossroads, it is broken up entirely. For "as long as it stays in the house the spirit will follow it."[61]

This is the only reference found relating John Canoe to Obeah or any religious practices. Beckwith stated that the connection of John Canoe with Obeah was admitted only in St. Elizabeth and was stoutly denied by Jamaicans of other districts.

The actual dance done by the sett girls and John Canoe men has not been clearly described. Most authors say that a gamboling type of movement was used in parading from one place to another, with John Canoe gyrating as much as possible in his elaborate costume. The purpose was apparently to get money from the spectators to pay for the final feast of the holiday season.

Cyric Williams, touring Jamaica in 1823, gave perhaps the most complete description of the John Canoe ceremony:

First came eight or ten young girls marching before a man dressed up in a mask with a grey beard and long flowing hair, who carried the model of a house on his head. This house is called the Jonkanoo, and the bearer of it is generally chosen for his superior activity in dancing. He first saluted his master and mistress, and then capered about with an astonishing agility and violence. The girls also danced without changing their position, moving their elbows and knees, and keeping tune with the calibashes filled with small stones. One of the damsels betraying, as it seemed, a little too much friskiness in her gestures, was reproved by her companions for her *imperance* [*sic*]. . . . All this time an incessant hammering was kept up on the gombay, and the cotta (a Windsor chair taken from the piazza to serve as a secondary drum) and the Jonkanoo's attendant went about collecting money from the dancers and from the white people.[62]

Usually accompanying the John Canoe was a drum called the gumbé. This drum was perhaps the one that Edwards called the goombay and Lewis termed gamby. Helen Roberts said it was

. . . square and resembles a milking stool not a little except that it has four legs. . . . The player holds it slanting away from him . . . and thrums it with slaps of his broad palms . . . or . . . with his fingers and broad splay thumbs. . . .[63]

Perhaps it was this same gumbé drum which gave its name to the Bermuda Negro Gombay dancers.

Gombay Dancers

Appearing primarily in Bermuda during the Christmas season were the Gombay dancers. Composed only of men and boys, the groups paraded through the streets accompanied by drums, triangles, tambourines, and pennywhistles.

According to one early observer of the Gombays, the men were "masked, bearing on their heads the heads and horns of hideous-looking beasts . . . as well as beautifully made imitations of houses and ships. . . . The houses are known as gombay houses."[64]

The masks of houses and ships are reminiscent of those worn

by the John Canoe men. In the beginning the Gombays wore masks of animal heads quite similar to those of the early John Canoes. Over the years the masks changed until they became "transparent masks . . . worn over the face. And there is an elaborate head-dress surmounted by tall waving peacock feathers."[65] The Gombays also carried weapons.

The dance of the Gombays was described as follows by Bolton: "As the men approach the houses, the group, sometimes twenty in number, dance a break-down, and shout: — 'Gombay, ra-lay; Gombay, ra-lay.' "[66] Hansford gave a clearer description of the actual dance:

> The dance is an odd series of movements, following to some extent the stamping steps seen in American Indian War Dance. . . . The movements are confined to a circle, around which the chief dancers move to the incessant beat of the drums. . . . At the climax the chief dancers throw themselves about in a masterly manner, with great physical ease, even falling to the ground in a sort of ecstasy of rhythm, the drums and fife going like mad all the time.[67]

Observing the Gombays as late as 1956, Lythe DeJon wrote:

> The complex syncopated rhythms accompanied dexterous and intricate foot movements, while the torso swung violently from side to side. The Chief blew a shrill whistle. The circle of dancers continued their stampings. The Captain moved into the center, engaging each in turn. It was obvious that a dance play was being enacted. The gyrations of the dancers became fantastic as each endeavored to excel. The jungle-like drummings rose to fever pitch. Jumps developed into amazing leaps as, with a wild shout, the descending Gombeys executed knee slides. . . .[68]

The costuming of the Gombays seen by DeJon was the same as that observed by Hansford, and the authors seemed to agree that the Gombay dances were influenced by the importation of other West Indian Negroes into Bermuda. DeJon tried to differentiate between Gombay and John Canoe dances, saying that:

> The emphasis on foot and leg movements characteristic of West Africa's Gold Coast, and the pirouettes and splits of the Gombeys help distinguish them from other dances of the West Indies.[69]

While pointing out that the Gombay had little in common with the shuffled Johnny Canoe dances of Nassau, DeJon also wrote: "It should be noted the term 'goombay' is still used there [in Nassau] to denote Calypso rhythms."[70]

Since the Gombay dancers are mentioned by so few authors, it is impossible to draw any definite conclusions about their origin. It would appear that the Gombays were an outgrowth, however changed, of the West Indian John Canoe customs.

Other Christmas Season Dances

Describing the Twelfth Day celebration in Cuba, Wurde-mann wrote of the liberty given to the Negroes on this day and of the parade and dancers, who seem to resemble those of the John Canoe festivities closely.

> Each tribe, having elected its king and queen, paraded the streets with a flag. . . . The whole gang was under the command of the negro marshall, who, with a drawn sword, having a small piece of sugar-cane stuck on its point, was continually on the move to preserve order in the rank.
> But the chief object in the group was an athletic negro, with a fantastic straw helmet, an immensely thick girdle of strips of palm-leaves around his waist, and other uncouth articles of dress. Whenever they stopped, their banjoes struck up one of their monotonous tunes, and this frightful figure would commence a devil's dance, which was the signal for all his court to join in a general fandango, a description of which my pen refuseth to give. Yet when these parties stopped at the doors of the houses, which they frequently did to collect money from their inmates, often intruding into the very passages, the ladies mingled freely among the spectators.[71]

The famed Cuban scholar, Fernando Ortiz, writing of the Cuban Twelfth Day, or, in his words, the "Day of Kings" said that on that day all of the Negroes in the *cabildos* (assembly halls or club rooms)

> . . . thronged into the street and there they performed the most typical dances of their remote countries with complete liberty. It was that day when all of the transplanted African groups allowed their little devils to be seen on the streets of Havana.[72]

Ortiz described a dance which was performed on the Day of Kings and during other street fiestas. This dance was called *matar la culebra*, or "kill the snake." In colonial Havana, according to Ortiz,

> . . . the dance, "kill the snake," was very popular among the negroes, so much so that the writers of the day say that it was "the dance of the mob." One dancing group of negroes jumping, dancing and singing, carried on their shoulders a huge artificial snake several meters long through the streets of Havana, stopping in front of the large houses where they gave them gifts. The Day of Kings, after travelling through all of Havana, such a pantomime was done in the patio of the captain generals, before the supreme authority. In the songs and gestures the terrible characteristics of ophidian [snake] are referred to:
>
> And looking at his eyes, they seem to be candles;
> And looking at his teeth, they seem to be needles.
>
> Someone pretended to kill the snake, and with him sprawled on the floor, they danced around him singing to him.[73]

The Cuban Day of Kings celebration and the customs of John Canoe and Gombay were markedly similar in that the purpose was dancing for money or gifts. Each dance centered around an object either carried or worn. However, because the object carried in the Cuban celebration was a snake, it is doubtful that the customs had a common origin. The snake or serpent was a well-known religious symbol among many black West Indians. Snakes were particularly important in the religions of Voodoo and Nañigo, a fact which suggests then that the Day of Kings celebration developed from sacred rites and beliefs.

Most of the West Indian plantation slaves were customarily given a three-day holiday at Christmas and at New Year's. During these days many dances were held for the plantation slaves as well as those from neighboring plantations. The literature is full of descriptions of the clothing worn by the slaves and the music accompanying the dancing, and yet little is reported on the dances performed.

Mrs. Carmichael, who owned the Laurel-Hill plantation in Trinidad, described a Christmas dance given by her slaves. After discussing the surroundings and clothing of the slaves, she said that "many dances of all kinds were performed: among the most interesting a *pas de deux*, by the two oldest negroes present."[74]

Describing the plantation slaves' dance on the evening of Christmas day, Williams wrote that:

> They [the slaves] . . . assembled on the lawn before the house with their gombays, bonjaws, and an ebo drum, made of a hollow tree, with a piece of sheepskin stretched over it. Some of the women carried small calabashes with pebbles in them stuck on short sticks, which they rattled in time to the songs, or rather howls of the musicians. They divided themselves into parties to dance, some before the gombays, in a ring, to perform a bolèro or sort of love dance. . . . Others performed a sort of pyrrhic before the ebo drummer, beginning gently and gradually quickening their motions, until they seemed agitated by the furies. . . . The entertainment was kept up till nine or ten o'clock in the evening, . . . and at last retired, apparently quite satisfied with their saturnalia, to dance the rest of the night at their own habitations.[75]

Whatever form the dance might take—the John Canoe and sett girls, the Gombays, the festivities of Twelfth Night, or the plantation dances of the slaves—it appears that the Christmas season in the West Indies began and concluded with a dance.

Other Holiday Dances

The pre-Lenten carnival or Mardi Gras appears at a later time in the history of the West Indies than the period now under discussion. Little reference is made there to any form of Easter carnival or dancing during the seventeenth, eighteenth, and nineteenth centuries.

Gardner, in his history of Jamaica, stated that "two or three days were given [to the slaves] at Christmas and also at Easter, which the slaves called pickaninny Christmas. What holidays the slaves had were usually spent in dancing. These dances were almost invariably of a licentious character."[76] Gardner also stated that at Easter and Whitsuntide, "groups of people often danced around the American aloe, . . . familiarly known as the Maypole."[77]

One of the popular New Orleans holidays, St. John's Day, was known as San Juan's Day in Cuba. A religious holiday celebrated on June 24, it was described by a former Cuban slave, Esteban Montejo:

> It was the custom at fiestas to dance the *caringa*, which was one of the white man's dances. It was performed by couples holding handkerchiefs, and whole groups used to dance it in the parks and in the streets. It was amusing to watch because the people used to leap about a lot to the sound of accordions, gourds and kettle-drums. . . . They danced the *zapateo* as well, the traditional Cuban dance, and the *tumbandera*. The *zapateo* was very graceful, and not so indecent as the African dances.[78]

The Tumbandera, according to Montejo, was a popular dance. "The whites didn't dance it because they said it was a vulgar Negro dance. . . . The *jota* was more elegant." However, the Tumbandera was more like the Rumba: "very lively and always danced by a man and a woman. It was sometimes danced in the streets and also in the Negro clubs."[79]

Wedding Dances

On many of the plantations in the southern United States there was no formal or legal marriage ceremony for the slaves. The fact so little mention is made of wedding festivities in the West Indies indicates that the same was apparently true for the slaves there.

The few Jamaican wedding ceremonies described seem to have followed English customs. Beckwith described two which she witnessed. One was a morning church wedding followed by a breakfast with a huge cake and the drinking of many toasts. "The afternoon is spent in games, songs, dancing and riddling, or there may be a formal dance given in the evening."[80]

A Maroon wedding was the second described by Beckwith. After the church wedding and breakfast:

> The Colonel donned ceremonial suit of white duck, and the whole population turned out, the horn man with his conch in front, the rest following in pairs to the tune of a lively marching song. On the parade ground it was pretty to see elderly dames and young girls joining in the old English dances, withered little old women carrying off the palm for stately grace. They

took hands at the far end of the level and advanced dancing and singing up its entire length. Afterwards the men played athletic games.[81]

The Maroons lived in the mountainous regions of Jamaica, and were descendants of slaves who had escaped to the mountains during the Spanish rule of Jamaica. This revolt occurred approximately in 1690, and the descendants have been living as free men ever since. According to Dunham, who lived among the Maroons for a period of time, many of the old formal dances of the whites have been retained among them.[82]

In the following passage Pinckard indicates that the acculturative process evident in black Jamaican weddings was also active on the island of Martinique.

> They [the slaves] danced, in large groups, upon a spacious green, in front of their owner's dwelling; and never was a happier crowd assembled. Great agility was displayed, and, compared with the rude motions and savage gestures of the slaves in the Dutch and British settlements, their steps might be considered as graceful.
>
> Besides the happy party upon the green, the inferior orders of the gang were seen at the negro-huts of the estate, footing it merrily, to the simple sound of the banjar; nor even among these, did we observe those disgusting attitudes and movements which constitute so great a part of the common, hideous dance of the Africans.[83]

Acceptance of the wedding festivities of the whites may have been due to the fact that slave weddings were so rare. The only slaves able to afford a formal wedding were probably the house servants, and those festivities were undoubtedly promoted and sponsored by the white slave owners, who thereby influenced the ceremonial customs among the Negroes.

Funeral Dances

Extensive literature exists on the rites of death performed by the West Indian Negroes. In any culture in which the spirits of the departed ancestors are worshipped, elaborate funeral rites are necessary to appease these spirits in order to assure their good will. According to Joseph Howard, such appeasement was the underlying tenet of the African death rites brought to the New World.[84]

In discussing Haitian funeral dance, Dunham stated that the Banda was utilized as a "dance to give pleasure to the spirit of the dead so that it will depart soon and [be] well entertained."[85] The Herskovitses acknowledged the same function for the Bele dance of Trinidad when they wrote that in that dance "the dead are feted to assure their continuing benevolent surveillance over their descendants. . . ."[86]

The dance is expressive of sorrow as well as joy. Discussing the funeral dance in Haiti, Dunham wrote:

> The funeral dance serves to release the feeling of personal injury which friends and relatives are apt to feel at the loss of a loved one, and to furnish the mourners with a common means of expression; a common release mechanism. True, they may also weep, but at sometime during the period of the wake, there will be rum drinking, story telling and erotic dancing. Regular rhythmic activity serves the function of an immediate emotional release, especially when accompanied by music and song and when, as in the maison, emphasis is on that section of the body which connotes sexual stimulus and release.[87]

Dunham saw just such a sexual funeral dance on one of her trips to Trinidad. Hearing the sound of drums, she happened upon a circle of boys beating bamboo sticks together, surrounding a man and the widow, who were dancing in the center. This dance was a shuffling kind of movement in which

> The shuffle would take them clockwise, then, as if by mutual consent, they would shift into a pattern of low second position interrupted by cross-kicks with right and left leg alternately. Then they would shuffle again, and spurred by remarks from the sidelines, the center couple would come closer and the emphasis would move from the feet well into central torso, becoming unmistakeably sexual in intention.[88]

The life of the slave on the plantations of the New World was not an easy one and many times slaves looked forward to death as a relief from bondage. This anticipation was reinforced by the belief that the souls or spirits of the dead would return to their native Africa by flying. The Cuban ex-slave, Montejo, stated that the belief that the dead flew back to Africa was held by many, but he thought the idea silly.

> Some people said that when a Negro died he went back to Africa, but this is a lie. How could a dead man go to Africa? Holy Moses, dead men don't fly! It was living men who flew there, from a tribe the Spanish stopped importing as slaves because so many of them flew away that it was bad business.[89]

Writing in 1790, Beckford stated that the

> . . . principal festivals [of the slaves] are at their burials. . . . Their bodies lie in state; an assemblage of slaves from the neighborhood appears: . . . When the body is carried to the grave, they accompany the procession with a song; and when the earth is scattered over it, they send forth a shrill and noisy howl, which is no sooner re-echoed, in some cases, than forgotten. . . . After this ceremony . . . the affected tear is soon dried, the pretended sigh is soon suppressed, and the face of sorrow becomes at once the emblem of joy. The instruments resound, the dancers are prepared; the day sets in cheerfulness, and the night resounds with the chorus. . . .[90]

In 1816, Pinckard witnessed the preparation for a slave funeral, saying that it was conducted

> . . . not with the afflicting solemnity of the Christian rites, but with all the mirthful ceremonies of African burial, forming a scene of gaiety, which consisted of music, dancing, singing, and loud noise. They all seemed to rejoice more in his escape from pain and misery, than to sorrow for his loss.
> The body being put into the coffin, and everything made ready for proceeding to the grave, the corpse was taken . . . into the yard, and placed very carefully upon the heads of two robust negroes, who carried it as far as the house, and then, halting under the window of the manager's room, they set the coffin upon the ground, and the whole gang of slaves danced and sang, and played their music around it, in loud gambols, for nearly two hours; beating at intervals, with great violence, against the door and window shutters, and threatening vengeance upon the murderer of their companion. . . . They at length concluded their dance, then replacing the coffin upon the heads of the two negroes, and observing much ceremony as to the

position of the corpse, they proceeded towards the place of interment . . . [the manager] exerting his influence to appease them, led them away, when they proceeded, dancing, singing, and beating their music, to the place of burial.[91]

The custom of carrying the corpse and lowering and raising it three times during its journey to the grave is African in origin. That such customs have been retained in the New World has been documented by Joseph Williams in his book, *Psychic Phenomena of Jamaica.*[92]

Describing a dance done at the burial of a respected or aged Negro, Edwards wrote that the slaves "exhibit a sort of *Pyrrhick* or warlike dance, in which their bodies are strongly agitated by running, leaping, and jumping, with many violent and frantic gestures and contortions."[93]

In many of the writings dealing with black death rites, the fact that most of the funerals were conducted at night is cited as evidence of barbarism. One fact, however, was not clarified by these authors: these slaves had to work from sun-up to sun-down, and few white owners would allow time off for a burial. Therefore, only the night was left for these ceremonies. According to Gardner, the death rites in Jamaica became so wild in the early part of the nineteenth century that "in 1831, night funerals were prohibited by law: owners permitting them were liable to a penalty of 50 pounds, and slaves attending them to a whipping of thirty-nine lashes."[94]

Many contemporary authors have also observed the funeral services of West Indian Negroes. Beckwith, for example, said that the wake for the dead "is probably the most strictly popular of all Jamaican festivities and the one most closely approaching old African customs."[95]

There is a belief held by some Negroes that the soul or spirit of the dead returns to his former home from the grave at some time between the third and ninth night after death. This spirit, now called a "duppy," must be appeased so that he will return to the grave. If he is not pleased, he must wander over the earth forever, frequently doing evil deeds. Friends of the dead person, therefore, congregate at his home during these nine evenings to eat, talk, sing, play games, and dance, in order to lay the ghost to rest.

In Zora Neale Hurston's report of one of these nine-evening wakes, she stated that dance often led to a form of religious ecstasy or possession of the dancers by the spirits.[96] Courlander, observing a Haitian wake, wrote that it was

> . . . the occasion for rather simple, though gay, dances. . . .
> The younger people, gather outside . . . to sing, tell stories, and dance. It is believed that such gaiety is pleasing to the soul of the dead person. Some of these dances involve moving in a circle around a hat on the ground, to the accompaniment of singing and handclapping, . . . Sometimes there is a stick dance. . . .
>
> Nine or ten days following the burial of a dead person, there are more rites in his honor, and more dancing. On the habitation of the family there will be dancing of the Juba or Martinique, which is specially reserved for such occasions. Every few years a family may give a feast for the dead (mangé morts), and here again the Juba or other steps will be danced.[97]

The Herskovitses, when describing the Bele dance of Trinidad as a wake dance, believed that in other West Indian islands the same dance was called the Juba.[98] Paraphrasing the conversations concerning wakes which they had with the natives of the village of Toco, they wrote that:

> He [the Tocoan] refers to the bele songs, calling the dance for which they are intended the belier, or Congo or juba dance as well, and adds, "We dance it because the dead people like it too much." He names the calenda, or stick-play songs, the bongo songs that accompany this wake dance, and the cheer-up songs that go with a Grenada dance "near to calenda."[99]

Attending a wake in Toco, the Herskovitses stated that:

> Nearby a game of "high-low" was in progress, and another somewhat farther away, while behind the kitchen a Bongo dance was in full swing. Here, in the main, were younger people, formed into a ring about the dancers, only two of whom performed at any one time. The dancers were principally men, though several times young women, or an older, more experienced matron would enter the ring to dance intricate steps forward, then backward, to the complex rhythms.[100]

Dunham, having studied Voodoo practices, believed with Hurston that funeral dances were frequently religious or an element in cult worship. She summed up the function of dance in funeral rites in Haiti when discussing the Banda dance:

> The like emotions of anger and grief seem best relieved either by violent or by rhythmic motor activity; rather than tear his hair, beat himself and roll in the dirt, as is the customary expression of grief with some peoples, the Haitian peasant dances. The dance may serve as direct externalization, or it may go the round about way of hypnosis and auto-intoxication. In either case the end is achieved, and the Haitian peasant funeral wake is apt to take on many of the external attributes of the bamboche even to the free distribution of clairin. That the funeral dances are sexual is an aid to a quicker, more complete externalization and re-direction of energy. A re-affirmation of community solidarity is one of the sociological functions of the funeral dance, while often cult participation is also evidenced in song and dance.[101]

Crop-Over Dances

The final dance to be discussed is that held at crop-over, or harvest-home. When the last of the crop was cut and brought in, most plantation owners allowed their slaves to celebrate by having a dance. The actual dances done on this occasion did not differ significantly from others done throughout the year. The main social difference was the intermingling of the races on these occasions.

Writing in 1825, Barclay, who lived twenty-one years in Jamaica, stated that

> . . . in the evening, they assemble in their master's or manager's house, and, as a matter of course, take possession of the largest room, bringing with them a fiddle and tambourine. Here all authority and all distinction of colour ceases; black and white, overseer and book-keeper, mingle together in the dance. About twenty years ago, it was common on occasions of this kind, to see the different African tribes forming each a distinct party, singing and dancing to the *gumbay*, after the rude manners of their native Africa; but this custom is now extinct. Following the example of the white people, the fiddle, which they play pretty well, is now the leading instrument; they dance Scotch reels,

"A Negro Festival drawn from Nature in the Island of St. Vincent,"
in Edwards, *The History . . . of the British West Indies* (1819)

and some of the better sort (who have been house servants) country-dances.[102]

On St. Vincent's Island, according to one observer:

> There is a regular contention who is to cut the last cane, and when this is done the rest of the day is spent in mirth and jollity. The male boys dress themselves in ribbons, and as there is generally a fiddler upon the estate, he leads the procession up to the proprietor's, or if absent, the manager's, who provides wherewithal to make them merry. The women, who are well dressed, dance before the door, singing their wild choruses of joy at the last cane being cut. The evening is ended by a general dance; . . .[103]

Richardson Wright and W. J. Gardner[104] have short discussions of crop-over festivities in their books, but these appear to be based on Barclay's writings on the subject and present no new material.

Vincent Briggs of Barbados, quoted by Beckwith, stated that "at crop-gathering time the people [of Barbados] danced in couples, men and women dressed in 'Sunday best,' in figures the steps of which resembled a 'cake-walk.'"[105] This was the first mention of any dance resembling a Cake-Walk found in the literature of the West Indies. Perhaps this crop-over dance was the origin of the dance so popular in the United States.

Dances of the "People of Color"

There was a great distinction made in the West Indies among the Negroes or blacks, the "people of color," and the whites. The people of color, or mulattoes, did not associate with the Negroes, but neither did the whites socialize extensively with the mulattoes. This in-between group had more privileges than the Negroes, yet not so many as the whites; and at no time could there be intermarriage between people of color and whites.

Many alliances were made, however, between white men and mulatto women. Since marriage was not sanctioned, the woman usually served as the "housekeeper" or mistress of the man. In order to meet the white men, the women of color would frequently arrange public balls, from which the men of color were excluded.[106]

According to Stewart, who wrote in 1823, the people of color "feel a kind of pride in being removed some degrees from the negro race, and affect as much as possible the manners and customs of the whites."[107] Among the things imitated were the dances of the whites: the minuets, quadrilles, waltzes, and polkas.

This tendency to imitate the whites and their customs eventually reached the blacks through mulatto influence. Many of the old African dances began to disappear or go underground. There was another, stronger influence on the West Indian Negro: the Christian church. Mrs. Carmichael summed up this influence well as she described the effects of Methodism on the Negro:

> The Methodists I fear have done harm; . . . it would be much better, if the negroes were taught that lying, stealing, cruelty . . . were sins in the sight of God, rather than level their anathemas against dancing—the favourite, and let me say, the innocent recreation of the negroes. . . .[108]

When questioning a Methodist missionary regarding the confusion of both the St. Vincent and Trinidad Negroes regarding the position of the church on dancing, Carmichael wrote:

> I stated this to Mr. Goy, telling him that some of the negroes said the Methodists forbade their communicants dancing at all; that others said they only forbade the drum, and not the fiddle dance; while others said it was only the African dances that were disapproved of. I asked whether any of these accounts were correct,—but Mr. Goy, and afterwards Mr. Stephenson, heard me in silence, and made no answer of any kind.[109]

With the condemnation of dance by the Protestant church and the trend toward imitating the stiff and formal dance of the whites it was no wonder that many of the uninhibited old African dances were hidden from view. Many of these old dances became ritualized and were incorporated into secret religious services, as the only link remaining with the African homeland. The dances discussed to this point have been secular dances, but the largest African dance heritage is in those dances considered sacred.

▉:▉:▉ SACRED DANCE

The sonorous sound of the mama, largest of the sacred drums echoed for miles, accompanied by the pulse of the seconde and the boula, the smaller drums. Somewhere close by there was a ceremony continuing through the night. The voices were those of the Voodoo drums.

The sacred or religious dances of the West Indies were probably more involved with myth than any of the other dances. There were the Voodoo ceremonies of Haiti; the Shango rites which were prevalent in Trinidad; the Obeah of Jamaica; and the Nañigo of Cuba. All of these religions were similar, all of African origin, and all included dance in their rituals.

Voodoo

Voodoo—Vodun, Vaudoux, Vodu: mysterious orgiastic rituals, cannibalism, black magic, sorcery, drums throbbing, naked bodies gleaming in the fire light. Never has so much been written with so little understanding and truth.

Just what is Voodoo? Where did it come from and how did it develop in the islands of the West Indies? What was the dance— the dance of the Voodoos? Was it nothing more than a sexual orgy or was it part of a meaningful religion?

Slaves were brought to the New World primarily from the western region of Africa and included the Ashanti, Congolese, Dahomean, Ibo, Koromantyn, Yoruban, and similar tribes. To understand the development of the religions of the West Indies, something of African religion must be known.

The religion of western Africa, with variations from tribe to tribe, had three primary characteristics. First the religion was a part of living—a part of the daily routine of life and not something to be attended to on Sunday and forgotten the remainder of the week. Secondly, religious practice included much ritual, which in some instances was strictly set while in others improvised. Thirdly, this ritual was primarily carried out through song and dance; the end result—the supreme experience—was "possession." Possession was the ultimate religious experience; to be possessed by a god who spoke through one was the aim of the drumming and dancing.[110]

Many of the slaves imported into the West Indies were priests and religious leaders, and a number of surviving rituals have been shown to be similar to those performed in Africa. Since the slave owners rationalized their position by bringing Christianity to the heathen Africans, the slaves were introduced almost immediately upon their arrival to the Christian—and usually Catholic—doctrine. Catholicism, more lenient in its view of the slaves than the Protestant denominations, was assimilated with African beliefs. This syncretism of Catholic dogma and African beliefs led to Voodooism.

According to the *Dictionary of Folklore, Mythology and Legend*, the word "Vodu" is the Dahomean term for deity.[111] Herskovits wrote the section on Voodoo in the *Dictionary of Folklore* and stated that in Haiti the word Voodoo is spelled "Vaudou" and "is the name of the African-derived popular cults that comprise the religious belief systems of a large proportion of the people. . . ."[112] Erika Bourguignon, in an excellent article, wrote that the word "Vodun" meant "ancestor or ancestral spirit" and the religion was "centered about the worship of these ancestors."[113] George Simpson[114] believed that Voodoo became standardized in Haiti somewhere between 1750 and 1790. In any case these Voodoo rites were well-developed by the time they were described in the 1790's by St.-Méry.

> On Santo Domingo, and particularly in the western, French portion, there has existed for a long time a type of dance called "Vaudoux" which requires two or four people and which is characterized by movements where it seems that the upper part of the body, the head and the shoulders all move on springs. This dance is also accompanied by the drum, the hand clapping and the chanted chorus. I have no idea where it got its name, but it has such an effect on the blacks that they sometimes faint from dancing it.[115]

The dance described by St.-Méry, as shall be seen, was the Zépaules, a dance done with the shoulders, as the French name implies, and one of the dances of the Voodoo rites.

Voodoo, then, was a series of elaborate rituals of song and dance with the ultimate experience being possession by one or more gods, or, in this case, loa. Loa is the term for god used in

Haitian Voodoo, the chief loa being Damballa, or the serpent god. Interestingly enough, these loa, while mainly of African derivation, have their counterparts in Catholic saints and all can be identified in pictures of the saints. For example, a picture of St. Patrick leading the snakes out of Ireland was used to represent Damballa, the serpent god. Writing in 1797, St.-Méry asserted that the Aradas blacks were the true cultists of Voodoo and according to them "Vaudoux designates an all-powerful, supernatural being upon whom all the events which take place on this globe depend. This being is the non-poisonous snake. . . ."[116]

Dunham reported three main divisions within Haitian Vaudun; these "are the 'true' vaudun or Rada-Dahomey, the Petro, and various divisions of Congo."[117] Herskovits, clarifying the statement, wrote in the *Dictionary of Folklore* that Rada was the

> . . . term for a group of Haitian deities of the *vodun* cult who themselves comprise one pantheon, others being the Petro, Congo and Ibo gods. The word is a contraction of the name of the old capital of the Dahomean kingdom of West Africa, Allada (or Arada). This derivation is confirmed by the fact that the majority of the Rada deities are of Dahomean origin.[118]

Each of the divisions has its own type of drums, songs, dances and loa. Thousands of loa exist, since each family can incorporate its dead ancestors into the form of a loa, much as Catholic saints become cannonized. Alfred Metraux, discussing the loa, said that "Man has always made his gods in his own image and this is strikingly true of Haiti: the *loa* have the tastes of modern man, his morality and his ambitions."[119]

Possession, as stated previously, is the ultimate religious experience; when a person is possessed by a loa, it is said that he is being ridden or "mounted" by the loa. The possessed person no longer has his own personality, but becomes the loa who has mounted him. Since he is being ridden by the loa, he is therefore termed the "horse." He is the vehicle through which the loa speaks and makes his wishes known.

Voodoo is complex and quite elaborate in its rituals. Many books have been written on the subject.[120] One of the first writers on Voodoo dance was St.-Méry. Following his description of the dance called Vaudous he continued with a description of a Pétro or Don Pédro dance:

> As with the voodoo, the dance . . . consists in the shaking of the shoulders and head, but this shaking is extremely violent, and to accent it further, the blacks guzzle brandy with which they have thought to mix gun powder, well pulverized. The effect of this drink, hastened and intensified by their movements, is so great on them that they enter into a veritable fury with real convulsions. As they dance, they make the most horrible contortions to the point where they finally collapse in a sort of epileptic fit which bowls them over; they enter a state which seems close to death.
>
> It was necessary to prohibit strictly the dancing of the Don Pedro because it caused great disorders and inspired ideas contrary to the public tranquility. Be it prohibition or electrical effect, the spectators themselves shared the ecstasy and instead of stopping their chanting when the frenzy began, they redoubled the level of their voices, accelerated the beat and precipitated the critical moment, sharing in it up to a certain point.[121]

Obviously St.-Méry was here describing possession, which he attributed to the brandy and gunpowder. The fact that this "epilepsy" as he called it, could be attributed to the dance rather than drink apparently did not occur to him. Since the state of possession was desired, it was natural that the spectators would redouble their efforts when possession was imminent.

St.-Méry was the first of many writers who looked on the Voodoo rites with horror and who attributed cannibalism, among other practices, to the influence of Voodoo. Ignorant or imaginative later writers linked Voodoo with savage rituals involving black magic, sorcery, human sacrifice, and the eating of human flesh. Research by reputable scholars and long-time residents of the West Indies has left unsubstantiated the claims by these sensationalistic writers.

One of the most questionable of the writers about Voodoo was Her Majesty's Consul-General in Haiti, Spenser St. John, writing in 1889.[122] An anonymous article in the *New York World* also contributed to the atmosphere of horror. The opening paragraph of the article "Cannibalism in Hayti" stated:

Some months ago the statement was made to *The World* by a reputable resident of Hayti that human sacrifices to the god Voodoo are of frequent occurrence in that Republic; that the practice is well-known to the Government and that the sacrifice is almost always followed by a cannibal feast.[123]

As late as 1929, with the publication of W. B. Seabrook's *The Magic Island*,[124] these errors and fictitious views were still being projected onto the white American public. Richard Loederer, whose *Voodoo Fire in Haiti* was published in 1935, still credited the concept of human sacrifice, as recounted in the story of "Congo bean stew."[125]

The previously mentioned authors dealt with Voodoo dance as a wild, stimulating orgy, leading up to the culminating event, the sacrifice of the "goat without horns," or human sacrifice. The Voodoo dances seen by modern anthropologists, sociologists, and ethnomusicologists, however, bear little resemblance to those wild orgies set down in the past as true occurrences.

The instruments used for the sacred dances were mainly percussive, and included sacred drums, rattles, bamboo tubes, and an iron plate or hoe blade, called an ogan, which was struck by another piece of metal. The drums were considered sacred, baptized in a formal ceremony, and never used for any other than sacred dances. According to Dunham, the standard sacred drum or Rada was used in indivisible sets of three, including the mama (largest), seconde, and boula or kata (smallest). She also wrote that "the form and style of the rada was imported intact from Africa."[126]

The Petro drums, usually two to a set, were played by the hands. In the Petro rituals, the dance was performed around an iron pole approximately three feet high which was centered in the fire.[127]

During the ceremonies, the drummers appeared to control the proceedings. While they followed the movements of the dancers, they still set the tempo of the ceremonies and took breaks at times they felt necessary. Maya Deren stated that upon the drumming falls the burden

. . . of integrating the participants into a homogeneous collective. It is the drumming which fuses the fifty or more individuals into a single body, making them move as one, as if all of these singular bodies had become linked on the thread of a single pulse.[128]

The priest (hounsi) or priestess (mambo) led the rituals and nearly always underwent possession, while the drummers rarely became possessed.

Herskovits believed that the vodun dance functioned in many ways:

> Above all, it is an integral part of the worship of the *loa*, and as such is marked by repeated possessions which indicate the presence of the gods. Yet it also offers an important opportunity for recreation. . . . by no means do all who go to a dance become possessed, for of one hundred to 150 persons present, no more than twenty or twenty-five will come under the power of their gods.[129]

There are various kinds of religious or sacred dances. According to Dunham, these may be performed to honor the ancestors or to call the loa in order to feed and expiate them; or they may be possession dances in which the dancer is possessed by the loa, who dances through his "mount."[130]

Herskovits, who further analyzed various types of dances within Voodoo, wrote:

> Of *vodun* dances there are the *avalou*, or *yanvalou*, a word meaning supplication in the speech of Whydah; the specialized steps for the various Rada and Petro gods; . . . for the Congo, Ibo, and Nago *loa*; the *mazon*, as an interlude dance between possessions; and steps of the *asagwe*, or salute to the gods. . . .[131]

The *Yanvalu*, described by Metraux,

> . . . is danced with the body leaning forward, knees bent, and with undulations which seem to spread from the shoulders all down the back. Movement is effected by sliding the feet sideways with a pause on the fourth beat. The undulations of the *yanvalu* are much more pronounced in the *yanvalu-dos-bas;* to such an extent, indeed, that it is taken for an imitation of waves or a serpent. Thus it is often danced in honour of Agwé or Damballah-wédo. In this dance the body is considerably bent and the dancer goes gradually lower until he is virtually squatting with hands on knees.[132]

Describing a Voodoo ceremony in which she participated, Dunham stated that Damballa was chosen as her loa because she was skilled in dancing the Yonvalou.

> Once in a long while a Petro or Congo god would join the Arada-Dahomey ceremonies, and these occasions I loved for a change of pace. I particularly loved to dance the various congos. But it was while dipping and swaying, knees close-pressed, bent back undulating in the yonvalou as seen in Dahomey today, in obeissance to Damballa, the serpent, that Teoline had decided on my loa.[133]

Describing her feelings while dancing the Yonvalou, Dunham continued:

> During the yonvalou we gravitated to partners, outdoing ourselves in undulating to low squatting positions, knees pressed against the knees of someone else without even realizing the closeness, each in his own transported world. I would faint and realize that I had danced with [a man named] 'ti Joseph. . . . I would salute the drums, then begin again the serpent movement that had brought under its hypnosis all whom the peristyle would hold, as well as bystanders outside . . . , and the ki-ki-ki, ric-tic-tic, and tongue-whirr of the serpent god cut through the drumming, singing, and heavy breathing . . . ; I felt weightless . . . but . . . weighted; transparent but solid, belonging to myself but a part of everyone else.[134]

Courlander, in contrasting two sacred dances, wrote that "the steps and postures vary with the type of dance performed"[135] and gave as examples the Zépaule, in which the dancers stood erect and used mostly shoulder movement, and the Petro, which consisted of constant, almost agitated movement of the feet. Courlander stated that the Zépaule was also called the Yenvalo Debout or the upright Yenvalo. In comparing the Zépaule to the Yenvalo he said that "the only differences are in position, body movement, and drum rhythm. The shoulders are here free, the back unbent; hips, too, are less restrained, and footwork is faster. Like Yenvalo Jenon, however, it is delicate and digni-fied."[136] Metraux, describing the Zépaule, stated that

> . . . another version of the yanvalu is the yanvalu-debout or Dahomey-z'epaules which, as its name indicates, is a dance characterized by the play of the shoulders. The dancer, body

upright, rolls his shoulders ever more rapidly following the beat of the drums.[137]

Another dance mentioned by Courlander was the Danse Nago which is characterized by

. . . pirouetting, swaying, and fast footwork. It is in the Nago that relaxation, one of the primary qualities of the Haitian dances, conspicuously manifests itself. Without muscular relaxation the difficult combination of shoulder movement (forward and backward), loin movement (side to side), knee bending, swaying, and pirouetting would be physiologically impossible.[138]

Of the Danse Nago, Metraux wrote:

The *nago-chaud* is particularly for warrior-spirits. It is akin to the *yanvalu* but distinguished by its rapidity and violence. The steps are short and hurried, the pirouettes numerous, the shoulders seeming to be shaken by a continuous trembling accompanied by a certain swinging of the hips requiring an unbelievable muscular suppleness.[139]

Each of the families of loa has its own drum rhythms and distinctive dances. This does not mean, however, that Rada, Congo and Ibo loa cannot be present in the same ceremony, and most frequently they are. One is able to discern which loa has mounted a possessed one by observing the dance being done. As already described, the Yanvalou is one of the dances done for Damballa, the serpent god and for Agwé, the loa of water. One possessed by Damballa may also writhe, twist, and turn on the ground in serpent-like movements or slither up a tree.

Another of the loa with specific characteristics is Legba, who is, among other things, the guardian of the crossroads. Legba is the first of the loa called upon in a religious service. According to Courlander:

When a person is mounted by this loa one of the things he may do is to go about limping, since Legba is thought of as an old man with one lamed leg. . . . Sometimes a person mounted by this deity may dance or spin around with a kind of cane-crutch called a Legba-stick, around which he twines his leg. Under conditions of possession, the spinning and twirling often become a true acrobatic feat.[140]

The dance of Agwé, the loa of the sea and water, has movements which are flowing, representing the movements of the waves. As previously stated, the Yanvalou may be used by the loa Agwé. Deren viewed the dance to Agwé and reported:

> Before me the bodies of the dancers undulate with a wavelike motion, which begins at the shoulders, divides itself to run separately along the arms and down the spine, is once more unified where the palms rest upon bent knees, and finally flows down the legs into the earth, while already the shoulders have initiated the wave which follows. The eyes are fixed on the ground and although the head is steady, the circular movement of the shoulders seems to send it forward, to draw the body after it, over and over; and as the bodies, which began in a posture almost erect, bend toward the earth, the undulation becomes more and more horizontal, until all figures blend into a slow flowing serpentine stream circling the centerpost with a fluency that belies the difficulty of the movement.[141]

Perhaps Deren is describing the Yanvalou, but she saw the dance directly in connection with the loa Agwé.

During her initiation into Voodoo, Dunham watched the mambo (priestess) and two of the initiates in a simultaneous state of possession by the loa Erzulie. Regarding the dance of those possessed by the goddess Erzulie, she wrote:

> Erzulie's dance has always intrigued me; still, it is something that is hard to define choreographically. It is more an attitude, an atmosphere than a dance. They moved, these three, with feminine grace, gliding, eyes downcast, in a world of their own. In Africa . . . only among the royal dancers of Dahomey have I seen . . . the flowing arm movements, the extreme femininity of wrist and hand, the sinuous movement emanating from the vertebral column and sending its flow into the far corners of the room. The salutations were repeated frequently, Téoline always imperious, head slightly inclined, the true Virgin Mother with a secret all her own.[142]

The dances of Asaka, the loa of mountain and field, usually included some characteristics and physical attitudes of that god: for example, bending low as if hoeing and planting.[143] Deren wrote that Asaka (or Azacca), upon arrival at a Voodoo ceremony, asked the drummer to play "a Martinique or a Juba dance."[144] Courlander, commenting on the Juba, wrote that "Haitians who know about such things say it was one of the first African dances in the New World. . . . In certain parts of Haiti Juba, with the other dances of its group, is more popular than Pétro and Vodoun."[145] More will be heard of the Juba in the section on the dance of Negroes in the United States.

One more loa deserves attention here: Guede (sometimes spelled Gede), frequently known as Baron Samedi—a favorite character of West Indian dancer Geoffrey Holder.

> The only dances which are frankly obscene are those carried out in honour of the Guédé or by devotees possessed by them. The rhythm is brisk and gay and the dancers sway their hips as much as they please. The dance of the Guédé-fatras was the speciality of the *hungan* [priest] Tullius. Wearing a police hat and leaning on a *coco-macaque* (walking stick), bent double, he rolled his buttocks in time to the drum-rhythm. Then he raised and lowered his head mechanically with an idiotic smile. Sucking in his cheeks to give his face an even sillier aspect he threw the upper part of his body backwards and danced rapidly throwing up his legs as high as possible. He was accompanied by the *hunsi* [initiates] who weaved their bottoms in and out and sang an improper parody of a Catholic psalm.[146]

In describing the dance during her initiation into Voodoo, Dunham summed up the uses of dance in the Voodoo rites:

> We danced, not as people dance in the houngfor [Voodoo temple], with the stress of possession, or the escapism of hypnosis or for catharsis, but as I imagine dance must have been executed when body and being were more united, when form and flow and personal ecstasy became an exaltation of a superior state of things, not necessarily a ritual to any one superior being.
> There is something in the dance of religious ecstasy that has always made me feel that through this exercise man might come into his own, be freed of inferiority and guilt in face of whatever might be his divinity.[147]

Courlander made the point that it was not easy to determine if a dance seen was sacred or profane. The distinction, he felt, lay in the attitude of the people gathered; a sacred dance was characterized by a feeling of humble entreaty and an awareness of supernatural forces.

> The gathering may have many of the earmarks of a purely social gathering, which of course it is in large part. But the dance

"The Voodoo Dance" by E. W. Kemble, in *Century Magazine* (1887)

steps are different. There is a sense of discipline. There is authority. The po-teau or centerpole is far more significant than in secular dancing. The dancers move close to it. It is the entrance way of the loa. Perhaps a drummer will come forward from the drummers' bench to touch his instrument against the pole, calling it to the attention of the vague force known as the hountor, spirit of the drums.[148]

The dances normally seen by outsiders are the pleasure dances, or Bamboche. The sacred ceremonial dances are rarely observed even today. "Gradually," said Joseph Williams, "it was found desirable to cloak the real Voodoo rites by holding in advance a public dance."[149] As early as the 1790's, the Voodoo rituals were conducted in secret. St.-Méry related that "the meeting for the real voodoo . . . is held only in secret . . . [at] night . . . in an enclosed area protected from all profaning eyes."[150] Deren stated that the purpose of ritual dance was to

. . . affect the participant; to create a particular psychic state. This dance is a meditation of the body, so that the entire organism is made to concentrate on a concept . . . inaccessible to verbal articulation.[151]

In the Voodoo ceremonies, dance was the means of achieving ecstasy. While each of the more than fifteen types of Voodoo dances had its own specific purpose, collectively the functions of the sacred dances included:

. . . ritual; establishing contact between the individual and the deity; inducing or breaking hypnosis; and the establishment of cult solidarity by motivation and direction of religious ecstasy through dance.[152]

Shango

Closely related to Voodoo is the religion known as Shango. Shango is the Yoruban god of thunder and is "found in those portions of the New World where Yoruban cults have persisted, notably Brazil, Cuba and Trinidad."[153] Like many African gods, Shango is also known as a Catholic saint. He is known as Santa Barbara in Cuba and St. John the Baptist in Trinidad.[154]

Shango and Ogun, who is associated with St. Michael, are

the two main gods of the Shango cult. While Shango is the god of thunder, lightning, and sunlight, Ogun is the god of iron and war and supposedly has the power to cure illnesses.

The Shango ritual is similar to Voodoo in that the main function is to induce possession by the gods. The initiation into Shango consists of washing the head, which must be prepared to receive the god during possession. Each person to be initiated either chooses or is chosen by one particular god and then follows the prescribed routine set forth for his god. There are certain days of the week sacred to each god and the initiate must observe his sacred days and also obtain the objects sacred to his god.[155]

Many of the gods of the Shango group have certain paraphernalia associated with them. These objects are used when the dancer is possessed by that god. For example, Shango is associated with a shepherd's crook, Ogun with a sword, and Ajaja, who is the African deity for Saint Jonah, with a harpoon. These pieces of equipment, along with other sacred objects, are kept in the chapelle or Shango shrine.[156]

The drums used in the rituals are called omele drums and include

> . . . three medium-sized drums of a battery of eight used in rites of the Shango cult. The drums are of European type and played with sticks. The two large drums, named for Ogun . . . and Shango . . . , call upon the gods. Devotees in a state of possession address the drums speaking the rhythms of the different gods, each selecting one for special homage. Of the three small drums, one is named for Ogun and the other two are Congo drums.[157]

Certain ceremonies must be completed before and during the dance. According to the Herskovitses, the dancers move with

> . . . skill and control that marks this cult group as one where excellence in dancing is valued. This was made evident when the priestess herself became possessed. Though a large woman, she danced with consummate artistry, an artistry, in fact, characteristic of these large women, who astonish the more by their lightness of foot, and their supple use of body.[158]

During the dancing many spectators gathered around and the priest moved about in this group and "corrected those who sat with crossed legs, for anything 'crossed' will keep the 'saints' away."[159] The act of maintaining the legs and feet in an un-crossed position during a religious ceremony was carried to the mainland and will be reported in the description of the "praise-meetings" or "ring-shouts" in the United States.

The god Asharoko made an appearance at a ceremony which was observed by the Herskovitses.

> The next one possessed was a woman, another "strong" dancer, who signalled for something which she described in gestures. A goblet with a green ribbon about its neck was brought to her, and this she placed on her head and began to dance. Without a headpad to steady it, and without spilling any of its contents she danced vigorously for thirty-five minutes. Opposite each of the possessed men, then toward the four corners of the "tent," back into the center again, and repeating the dance to the four corners, she continued, with only short interludes of pacing about the dancing space. It was evident that among both cult members and spectators there was admiration for this performance of Asharoko, who chose to manifest himself so exuberantly that night.[160]

A similar dance was performed on many southern planta-tions. Many dances of possession occurred during the Shango rituals which were designed to lead to the ultimate experience of possession by a god.

Obeah and Myalism

In 1823 Stewart mentioned Obeah in his book on Jamaica, saying that it was the "most dangerous practice, arising from superstitious credulity" and a "pretended sort of witchcraft."[161] Stewart further described Obeah as involved with charms and fetishes, spells and poisons. "The negroes practising obeah are acquainted with some very powerful vegetable poisons. . . ."[162]

Hesketh Bell, in his book entitled *Obeah, Witchcraft in the West Indies,* described the ceremonies as accompanied by prayers, incantations, and animal sacrifices, and completed "by an African dance to the inspiriting sound of the tom-tom, lasting till daylight, when all would peaceably return to their avoca-tions, and would, most likely, be seen next Sunday hurrying to their church. . . ."[163]

It is difficult to gain any real insight into the Obeah ceremonies from the above descriptions. Herskovits, in the *Dictionary of Folklore*, wrote that Obia or Obeah was:

A term used by Negroes of the English-speaking islands of the Caribbean and of English and Dutch Guiana to denote various forms of supernatural power. In the islands it is officially regarded as a term for evil magic and its use is prohibited by law, though the Negroes recognize that, like all magic, it may be good or bad, depending on the circumstances and motivations of its use.[164]

Joseph Williams regarded Voodoo, Obeah, and Myalism as distinct religions, having in common only their African origin. While Voodoo was primarily inspired by the Dahomeans, Obeah and Myalism, according to Williams, came from the Ashanti, "obayifo" being the Ashanti word for witch.[165]

It was Williams's feeling that in the beginning Obeah and Myalism were two distinct and antagonistic forms.

Obeah, no less than Myalism . . . derive their [*sic*] origin from the Ashanti. The latter was the old religious dance modified somewhat by circumstances and surroundings in Jamaica, but substantially the same as practiced in West Africa. The former, on the other hand was Ashanti witchcraft, essentially antagonistic to Myalism which made one of its chief objects the "digging up" of Obeah.[166]

He continued:

In any case, the fact remains that actually the forces of Myalism and Obeah today have degenerated into a common form of witchcraft not unfrequently associated with devil worship, and even those of the blacks who belittle its general influence, in practice show a wholesome fear of the powers of the Obeah man.[167]

In another work Williams wrote:

Obeah, as the continuation of Ashanti witchcraft, is professionally a projection of spiritual power with the harm of an individual as an objective. Practically, its end is attained through fear, supplemented if needs be by secret poisoning. The agent is the servant of the Sasabonsam or Devil who is invoked and relied upon to produce the desired effect. Consequently real obeah must be regarded as a form of Devil-worship.[168]

Obeah, then, was entirely concerned with witchcraft, and as such had little room for dance. Not so, however, Myalism, which came into being through the Myal dance. In spite of the prohibition of large gatherings of Negro slaves and their use of drums, there was little interference with purely local gatherings of the slaves of only one plantation. According to Williams, the Ashanti priests, or Obiamen

> . . . as a precaution against complete proscription . . . began to further disguise what was left of the old religious rites under cover of one of the dances that were permissible in the local amusements, until it was gradually appropriated to his own purposes. This dance in its adapted form became known to the Whites as the myal-dance.
>
> This subtle appropriation of an alien dance completely disguised the true purposes of the *okomfo* (Obiaman) as far as the Planters were concerned, but as a consequence the *okomfo* himself gradually lost his own identity until he became known to the Whites as myal-man, or leader in the myal-dance.[169]

In his book on West Indian dances, Earl Leaf mentioned a ritual dance which was "much favored by the Obeah believers."[170] This dance was the Pocomania, meaning "just a little crazy" and while Leaf attributed the dance to Obeah believers, it was more than likely one of the dances of Myalism, a term defined by Williams as

> . . . the old tribal religion of the Ashanti . . . with some modifications due to conditions and circumstances. It drew its name from the Myal dance that featured it, particularly in the veneration of the minor deities who were subordinate to Accompong, and in the commemoration or intercession of ancestors.[171]

As late as 1924 the Myal dance was observed by Beckwith, who described its function and procedures as follows:

> The myal dance is somewhat out of date in Jamaica, the religious dances of the so-called "Revivalists" having taken its place; but in such backward sections as the Cockpits of St. Elizabeth it is still employed in cases of baffling illness. In such cases the Myal-man is generally summoned to the sick person's yard, the drum played, a company of dancers formed and songs sung invoking the spirit of the dance, in order to "bring the

spirit to tend the sickness." When the company is worked up to the proper pitch of excitement, the Myal-man or an associate claims possession by the spirit, in which condition it is revealed to him what herbs to use for a cure or what sorcery to employ to overcome the obeah which has been "laid" for the patient. If the patient eventually dies it can be claimed that he has not followed the prescription exactly or that his enemy's obeah has too strong a power over him for the remedies to prove effectual.[172]

An interesting aside to the discussion of Myalism occurred in one of Jamaican author Claude McKay's books. Upon his arrival in the African city of Casablanca, he had the opportunity to see a magic rite performed by some Guinea sorcerers. McKay was shocked at seeing this ritual, in which the sorcerers "looked and acted exactly like certain peasants of Jamaica who give themselves up to the celebrating of a religious sing-dance orgy known as Myalism."[173] The fact that McKay recognized these rituals of exorcising the devils indicates the few changes which had occurred in transplanting them from Africa to the New World.

Obeah, then, was a form of witchcraft of the Ashanti in which there was little or no need for dance, since the Obiamen were primarily concerned with charms, curses, and poisons. Myalism, on the other hand, received its name from the Myal dance and, as the Ashanti religion, was concerned with curing or destroying the curse of Obeah. The healing or curing occurred through dance ceremonies much as in Voodoo and Shango, with possession supposedly leading to the cure. Both Beckwith and Williams felt that Myalism had been renewed in the Methodist revivalism or Shouters' cults. As an extension of Myalism, then, the Shouters should be investigated.

Shouters

In their discussion of the retention and reinterpretation of Africanisms in Trinidad, the Herskovitses noted that the "motor behavior while singing, such as swaying of the body, and the manner in which handclapping is done with cupped hands rather than with flattened palms . . . is African."[174] This swaying and clapping was the basis for a cult in Trinidad called the "Shouters." Frequently the singing, clapping, and moving around the room led to possession, perhaps by the "Holy Ghost," just as in Voodoo or Shango, with their respective loa, or gods. The Shouters' cult, however, was more acceptable since it existed under the auspices of the Protestant Church and the songs were hymns, usually from the hymnal of the Methodist Church.

Williams expressed the opinion that the Shouters' cult was just a revival of Myalism in a more acceptable form and stated that "under the guise of Methodist Revivalism, the long persecuted and seemingly forgotten Myalism was taking a new lease on life. . . ."[175] He continued:

> . . . one easily distinguishes from all other religious groups in Jamaica these high-strung, emotional fanatics who are recognized by the peculiar tempo of their songs no less than by the grotesque hip movement that characterizes their sliding gait, as clothed in white and in single file, they parade the streets before they have aroused their spirits to the proper pitch of excitement in preparation for the "sarvice" which is to follow.[176]

In his monograph, Coleman discussed the folk music of Trinidad and wrote that "the religious music, chants, wails, trumpets and other melodious expressions of religious enthusiasm common among the Spiritual Baptist cult or Shouters is most noteworthy."[177]

In describing a service of the Shouters or "Spiritual Baptists," as he called them, Coleman wrote that they

> . . . enjoy singing hymns from the Sankey and Moody collection and the manner of rendering them shows a measure of lugubrious quality by reason of drawn notes and slurs from one tone to another, accompanied by a full voice and an element of paradoxical enthusiasm. The volume of sound increases from verse to verse and it is not long before the singers change their rhythm, introducing handclapping as the tempo becomes faster until the hymn is transmuted at length into a swing idiom.[178]
>
> There are occasions I am told when the benches are moved back and a circle is formed wherein the congregation shuffle around fairly quickly and grunt rhythmically for the major part of an hour, at the end of which time they seem completely in a trance-like condition. Then they start babbling some gibberish which is denominated for obvious reasons as "Speaking in Tongues after Pentecost." Sweat frequently pours from the

worshippers most profusely and I am told they assume what might be described as an auto-hypnotic appearance.[179]

The Herskovitses wrote extensively about the Shouters in their book, *Trinidad Village*. While each congregation was autonomous, the church retained unity in a basic core of ritual which included "baptism, proving, mournin', and the phenomenon of possession by the 'Spirit'. . . ."[180] "Proving" appeared to be similar to the confession of the Catholic faith: confessing sins and then "proving" oneself to be a believer by testifying.

The possession which occurred in the services was brought on by the singing of hymns. The worshipper became possessed by the "Spirit" which

> . . . touches [him] . . . with an unseen hand, and a shiver electrifies his body, causing him to stiffen and then to begin to shake. The "Spirit" fills him with joy, causing him to dance, to speak in tongues, to prophesy, to "see."[181]

In a description of a service of the Shouters, the Herskovitses reported that:

> The men on the side bench were dancing; one of them, like the teacher herself, went shaking clear around the central altar, hopping on one foot, until he settled into his dance step. The singer shook and danced alternately; two women in white danced and shook in place; while a church assistant in training, her head bound with a kerchief, who watched the door, also shook in place—hands clenched, arms half-raised, her angular frame shaken by a continuous quivering of the arms that extended itself to the entire body. What happened to the hymn that "bring a strong spirit to rejoice everybody" was as interesting musically as the dancing was dramatically, for it almost disappeared in the "ram-bam-i-bam-bam" of the full-throated song leader.[182]

The woman who was posted at the door undoubtedly was used as a lookout, since

> . . . as a sect, the Shouters were banned in Trinidad in 1917 on the grounds that they were "an unmitigated nuisance." Despite the ban, the groups continued to flourish in secret and recently the prohibition was repealed.[183]

The Shouters, then, like Voodoo and Shango believers and

to some extent like the Myalists, used singing and clapping to bring on possession. While this possession was not by an African deity or loa, the devotee was possessed by the "Spirit" or the "Holy Ghost." As in Myalism and the other religions, this possession took place in the form of dance while prophesying. Speaking in tongues, as in Voodoo and Shango, could also occur.

Shouting (as, for example, in the ring shouts which were held in the praise-houses soon after Christianity was introduced to the slaves) was a common occurrence on the plantations of the United States. These shouts are further discussed in a later chapter.

The last major religion which was similar to Voodoo and Shango, in which possession occurred through song and dance, was Nañigo. Its practice centered in Cuba.

Nañigo

The Cuban dance cult, Nañigo, was similar to both Voodoo and Shango in that deities of African origin (mainly Yoruban) were personified through the dance. Its ceremony to the sun, however, was unique to Nañigo. In this dance "termed *diablito* (little devil) [they] salute the sun at its zenith. With nude torsos painted yellow and bells on dungarees and skirts, they chant and dance joyfully to the sun."[184]

Harry Johnston, when attempting to describe what he termed the "secret Masonic societies," mentioned "Nyanego," which he thought may have been "associated with immoral purposes. They [the believers in Nañigo] originated in a league of defense against the tyranny of the masters in the old slavery days."[185] The Nañigo cult did originate in the form of a secret society which had, among other functions, the purpose of conserving the "ancient song, dance and animal sacrifice" of the Carabali or inhabitants of the Calabar River region of Africa.[186] While the Carabali were originally shark-worshippers, because of many influences they eventually transformed their rites "into cock and goat sacrifice."[187]

An article of questionable validity appeared in a 1937 issue of the *Literary Digest*. The title was "Voodooism" but the subject covered was actually Nañigo. The article purported the use of human sacrifice during the Nañigo rites, and described the main god of Nañigo to be Chango.[188] Chango was probably Shango, the same god of the cult in Trinidad.

The main ceremonies of Nañigo were similar to those of Shango. According to the *Literary Digest* article, these ceremonies "fall on the Day of Santa Barbara (December 4), the Day of Saint Lazarus (December 17), and the Day of Kings (January 6)."[189]

Also discussed in the article was the existence of many Nañigo cultists in the United States and Cuba. It was stated that out of the estimated 500,000 believers in Nañigo in Cuba, approximately 100,000 where white persons, many in high positions.[190]

Of the sacred dances of the Cuban Nañiga cult, Leaf wrote:

> The religious rhythm-dances of the several African tribes represented among the slaves were eventually blended into a single form, which became known in the new land as *Nañiga*, and which is still practiced by the descendants of these slaves throughout the island of Cuba to this day [1948]. In Camaguey and in Oriente provinces, *Nañiga* remains little changed from the day of the slave to the present. The dances of the Congo and the rhythms of the Gold Coast are the principle ingredients of every *Nañiga* ceremony.[191]

Leaf included in his description the same Nañigo dance previously mentioned, the Diablito, stating that it was an "exotic dance ceremony not encountered elsewhere."[192] He continued:

> Shining black bodies stripped to the waist, decorated in cabalistic designs with yellow paint, rippling and swaying in unison with the percussion beater, tiny bells attached to dungaree trousers and cotton print skirts tinkling "like shattered glass echoing down marble halls," deep-throated, sonorous voices raised in adulation to the sun, the whole ceremony an impressive and exciting manifestation of the Negro's primordial joy.[193]

Ortiz, an expert of Afro-Cuban music, dance, and religion, said that this Diablito was performed "to the beat of four drums and other percussion instruments."[194] He then named some of the African deities which could possess a person during the religious rites. These gods were the same as those of Shango, and included Ogun, Ochun, Shango, and many others. In his discussion of a dancer possessed by Ogun, Ortiz reported that "a possessed dancer, charmed by the warlike Ogun will execute an impressionistic Pyrrhic dance brandishing a machete just as the African god did."[195]

Lekis added:

> . . . his [Ogun's] dances dramatize two functions. One is Ogun in his war character brandishing a machete. The other features his role as a worker, using his machete to cut grasses in the field or as a blacksmith at his forge.[196]

The first god honored in a ceremony was usually Eleggua, who was considered the " 'opener and closer of the door.' He summoned the gods."[197] Eleggua appeared to be the same as the Haitian Voodoo loa Legba, the guardian of the crossroads and the loa who allowed the gods to enter into the Voodoo temple.

Lekis continued that Chango (Shango) was the "god of virility, of force, of lightning and thunder . . . [and] is also the god of savage untamed sexuality. No other . . . dances with . . . more uninhibited eroticism."[198]

Ortiz noted that the dances to Shango, among other gods, "in which phallic pride is exalted and movements of onanism and sexual copulation are imitated, are nothing more than survivors of ancient magic dances to bring rain and fertility to the land."[199]

Pointing out that many of the African or primitive dances were considered licentious and obscene, Ortiz said "we are prejudiced by our background when we observe their customs. There isn't vice or sin in sex for the primitive."[200]

During a trance or possession dance, Ortiz wrote that

> . . . the possessed dancer never surrenders himself to expressions that may be scandalous or out of place in the social atmosphere in which his mystic grotesque dance is performed. Even the most shocking ones always correspond to patterns or modulations pre-established and attributed to a particular god or deity, according to tradition.[201]

Neither would this dancer sing an inappropriate song nor would he drink anything except water and the specific drink of the god possessing him:

. . . none of them is apt to drink beer, nor cider, nor soda, nor cocoa water, nor fruit juice, nor coffee. The "saints" did not . . . drink them in Africa, according to the legends; neither can they do them in Cuba.[202]

Ortiz concluded by saying that the dancer will not dance any but the dance of the "saint" who has mounted him. The dances,

. . . even the most convulsive, as well as their most extravagant episodic expressions, always have patterns which are predetermined in the traditional culture and correspond to symbolic types which are programatic and collectively preaccepted.[203]

Nañigo, in all its aspects, except the ceremony to the sun, seems to be quite closely related to both Voodoo and Shango. Since so many of the Africans imported to the United States were from exactly the same areas as those imported to the West Indies, and since many of the mainland slaves were seasoned in the West Indies, it is highly probable that the dances reached the mainland.

And so, as the drums beat for the Calenda and Chica seen by Père Labat and Moreau de St.-Méry, and continued pulsing for the John Canoe and Gombay, so they pounded and throbbed for Voodoo, Shango, and Nañigo. Just how these drum rhythms and dances influenced later dance among the blacks in the United States will be explained.

⧉⧉⧉ NOTES FOR CHAPTER 2

1. Harold Courlander, *The Drum and the Hoe; Life and Lore of the Haitian People* (Berkeley: University of California Press, 1960), p. 6.

2. John Hope Franklin, *From Slavery to Freedom. A History of Negro Americans*, Vintage Books (3d ed.; New York: Random House, 1969), pp. 68-69.

3. Sir Hans Sloane, *A Voyage to the Islands Madera, Barbados, Nieves, S. Christophers and Jamaica with the Natural History of the Herbs and Trees, Four-footed Beasts, Fishes, Birds, Insects, Reptiles, Etc. of the Last of Those Islands; to which is prefix'd An Introduction, wherein is an Account of the Inhabitants, Air, Waters, Diseases, Trade, etc. of that Place, with Some Relations concerning the Neighbouring Continent, and Islands of America* (2 vols.; London: B. M., 1707), I, xlviii.

4. *Ibid.*, I, xlviii-xlix.

5. William Beckford, *A Descriptive Account of the Island of Jamaica; With Remarks upon the Cultivation of the Sugar-Cane, throughout the different Seasons of the Year, and chiefly considered in a Picturesque Point of View; Also Observations and Reflections upon what would probably be the Consequences of an Abolition of the Slave-Trade, and of the Emancipation of the Slaves* (2 vols.; London: T. and J. Egerton, 1790), II, 387.

6. De M. L. E. Moreau de St.-Méry, *Danse*, trans. by Anthony Bliss (Philadelphia, 1796), p. 45.

7. Bryan Edwards, *The History, Civil and Commercial, of the British West Indies; With a Continuation to the Present Time* (4 vols.; 5th ed.; London: T. Miller, 1819), II, 102.

8. Moreau de St.-Méry, *Danse*, pp. 44-45.

9. Matthew Gregory Lewis, *Journal of a West India Proprietor, 1815-1817*, ed. by Mona Wilson (New York: Houghton Mifflin Company, 1929), p. 74.

10. Sloane, *A Voyage to the Islands*, I, lii.

11. Père Labat, *Nouveau Voyage Aux Isles de l'Amerique*, trans by Anthony Bliss (2 vols.; The Hague, 1724), II, 52.

12. Beckford, *Descriptive Account of the Island of Jamaica*, II, 387.

13. Edwards, *History, Civil and Commercial, of the British West Indies*, II, 102-03.

14. Lewis, *Journal*, p. 74.

15. *Ibid.*

16. Sloane, *Voyage to the Islands*, I, xlix.

17. Beckford, *Descriptive Account of the Island of Jamaica*, II, 388.

18. George Pinckard, *Notes on the West Indies* (2 vols.; 2d ed.; London: Baldwin, Cradock, Joy, and L. B. Seeley, 1816), I, 126.

19. Moreau de St.-Méry, *Danse*, p. 43.

20. *Ibid.*

21. *Ibid.*

22. Labat, *Nouveau Voyage*, II, 52.

23. *Ibid.*

24. *Ibid.*

25. *Ibid.*, II, 52-53.

26. Moreau de St.-Méry, *Danse*, pp. 45-46.

27. Michel-Etienne Descourtilz, *Voyages d'un Naturaliste en Haiti, 1799-1803*, trans. by Anthony Bliss (3d ed.; Paris: Librairie Plon, Les Petits-Fils de Plon & Nourrit, 1935), p. 125.

28. Pinckard, *Notes*, I, 127.

29. Charles W. Day, *Five Years Residence the West Indies* (2 vols.; London: Colburn & Co., 1852), I, 47-48.

30. James Edward Alexander, *Transatlantic Sketches, Comprising Visits to the Most Interesting Scenes in North and South America, and the West Indies,*

with *Notes on Negro Slavery and Canadian Emigration* (Philadelphia: Key & Biddle, 1833), p. 94.

31. Katherine Dunham, "Form and Function of Primitive Dance," *Educational Dance*, IV (October, 1941), 4.

32. Lafcadio Hearn, *Two Years in the French West Indies* (New York: Harper & Brothers, 1890), p. 146.

33. Martha Warren Beckwith, *Black Roadways. A Study of Jamaican Folk Life* (Chapel Hill: University of North Carolina Press, 1929), p. 214.

34. Moreau de St.-Méry, *Danse*, pp. 51-52.

35. *Ibid.,* pp. 54-55.

36. Edward Long, *The History of Jamaica or, General Survey of the Ancient and Modern State of that Island: With Reflections on Its Situation, Settlements, Inhabitants, Climate, Products, Commerce, Laws, and Government* (3 vols.; London: T. Lowndes, 1774), II, 424.

37. Fredrika Bremer, *The Homes of the New World; Impressions of America,* trans. by Mary Howitt (2 vols.; New York: Harper and Brothers, 1853), II, 274.

38. *Ibid.,* II, 419.

39. Spenser St. John, *Hayti, or the Black Republic* (New York: Scribner & Welford, 1889), p. 160.

40. *Ibid.*

41. J. Stewart, *A View of the Past and Present State of the Island of Jamaica; with Remarks on the Moral and Physical Condition of the Slaves, and on The Abolition of Slavery in the Colonies* (Edinburgh: Oliver & Boyd, 1823), p. 270.

42. Henry H. Breen, *St. Lucia: Historical, Statistical, and Descriptive* (London: Longman, Brown, Green & Longmans, 1844), p. 196.

43. Katherine Dunham, "The Negro Dance," in Sterling A. Brown, Arthur P. Davis, and Ulysses Lee, *The Negro Caravan* (New York: Dryden Press, 1941), p. 997.

44. F. W. Wurdemann, *Notes on Cuba, Containing An Account of Its Discovery and Early History; a Description of the Face of the Country, Its Institutions, and the Manners and Customs of Its Inhabitants. With Directions to Travelers Visiting the Island* (Boston: James Munroe and Company, 1844), p. 113.

45. Charles L. Edwards, *Bahama Songs and Stories. A Contribution to Folk-Lore* (Boston: Houghton, Mifflin and Company, 1895), p. 17.

46. *Ibid.*

47. L. D. Powles, *The Land of the Pink Pearl; or, Recollections of Life in the Bahamas* (London: Sampson, Low, Marston, Searle, and Rivington, 1888), pp. 148-49.

48. Labat, *Nouveau Voyage*, II, 53.

49. Carole Engram, personal interview, Pasadena, California, May 8, 1970.

Miss Engram taught in Louisiana and witnessed several Mardi Gras parades in New Orleans.

50. "John Canoe," as spelled by Martha Warren Beckwith in her several writings on the subject, is the form here accepted. The term has been spelled in other ways, however: John Connu, Joncanoe, Jonkanoo, John Kanoo, John-coonas, and John Kuners.

51. Long, *History of Jamaica*, II, 424.

52. *Ibid.*

53. *Ibid.*

54. William Young, *A Tour through the Several Islands of Barbadoes, St. Vincent, Antigua, Tobago, and Grenada in the Years 1791 and 1792*, in Bryan Edwards, *An Historical Survey of the Island of Saint Domingo, together with an account of the Maroon Negroes in the Island of Jamaica; & a History of the War in the West Indies, in 1793 and 1794* (London: John Stockdale, 1801), p. 275.

55. Lewis, *Journal*, p. 54.

56. Beckwith, *Black Roadways*, p. 149.

57. Alexander Barclay, *A Practical View of the Present State of Slavery in the West Indies; or, an Examination of Mr. Stephen's "Slavery of the British West India Colonies." Containing more Particularly an Account of the Actual Condition of the Negroes in Jamaica: with Observations on the Decrease of Slaves since the Abolition of the Slave Trade, and on the Probable Effects of Legislative Emancipation: also, Strictures on the Edinburgh Review, and on the Pamphlets of Mr. Cooper and Mr. Bickell* (2d ed.; London: Smith, Elder and Co., 1827), p. 11.

58. For example, see: Beckford, *A Descriptive Account of the Island of Jamaica*, I, 389-90; Stewart, *A View of the Past and Present State of the Island of Jamaica*, pp. 273-74; Rev. R. Bickell, *The West Indies As They Are; or, A Real Picture of Slavery: but More Particularly As It Exists in the Island of Jamaica* (London: J. Hatchard and Son, and Lupton Reefe, 1825), p. 214; James M. Phillippo, *Jamaica: Its Past and Present State* (Philadelphia: James M. Campbell and Co., 1843), pp. 93-94; and Margaret Shedd, "Carib Dance Patterns," *Theatre Arts Monthly*, XVII (January, 1933), 65-77.

59. Lewis, *Journal*, p. 52.

60. Martha Warren Beckwith, "Christmas Mummings in Jamaica" in *Jamaica Folk-Lore* (New York: American Folk-Lore Society, 1928), p. 8.

61. Beckwith, *Black Roadways*, p. 151.

62. Cyrnic R. Williams, *A Tour Through the Island of Jamaica, from the Western to the Eastern End in the Year 1823* (London: Hunt and Clark, 1826), pp. 25-26.

63. Helen Roberts, "Some Drums and Drum Rhythms of Jamaica," *Natural History*, XXIV, No. 2 (March-April, 1924), 247.

64. H. Carrington Bolton, "Gombay, A Festal Rite of Bermudian Negroes," *Journal of American Folklore*, III, No. 10 (July-September, 1890), 223.

65. M. M. Hansford, "The Gombey Dance," *Dancing Times* (London), December, 1938, p. 276.

66. Bolton, "Gombay, A Festal Rite of Bermudian Negroes," p. 223.

67. Hansford, "The Gombey Dance," p. 275.

68. Lythe Orme DeJon, "The Gombeys of Bermuda," *Dance Magazine,* XXX, No. 5 (May, 1956), 33.

69. *Ibid.,* 54.

70. *Ibid.*

71. Wurdemann, *Notes on Cuba,* pp. 83-84.

72. Fernando Ortiz, *Los Bailes y el Teatro de los Negros en el Folklore de Cuba,* trans. by Dorothy Latasa Kiefer (Havana: Cardenas y cia, 1951), p. 195.

73. *Ibid.,* p. 192.

74. Mrs. Carmichael, *Domestic Manners and Social Condition of the White, Coloured, and Negro Population of the West Indies* (2 vols.; London: Whittaker, Treacher, and Co., 1833), II, 296.

75. Williams, *A Tour Through the Island of Jamaica,* pp. 21-23.

76. W. J. Gardner, *A History of Jamaica from its Discovery by Christopher Columbus to the Year 1872. Including an Account of its Trade and Agriculture; Sketches of the Manners, Habits and Customs of All Classes of its Inhabitants; and a Narrative of the Progress of Religion and Education in the Island* (2d ed.; New York: D. Appleton and Company, 1909), pp. 99-100.

77. *Ibid.,* p. 192.

78. Esteban Montejo, *The Autobiography of a Runaway Slave,* ed. by Miguel Barnet, trans. by Jocasta Innes, Meridian Books (New York: World Publishing Company, 1969), p. 76.

79. *Ibid.,* p. 78.

80. Beckwith, "Folk Games of Jamaica," in *Jamaica Folk-Lore,* p. 7.

81. Beckwith, *Black Roadways,* p. 195.

82. Katherine Dunham, *Katherine Dunham's Journey to Accompong* (New York: Henry Holt and Company, 1946), p. 25.

83. Pinckard, *Notes on the West Indies,* II, 325-26.

84. Joseph H. Howard, *Drums in the Americas* (New York: Oak Publications, 1967), p. 107.

85. Katherine Dunham, "The Dances of Haiti," *Acta Anthropologica,* II, No. 4 (November, 1947), 53.

86. Melville J. Herskovits and Frances S. Herskovits, *Trinidad Village* (New York: Alfred A. Knopf, 1947), p. 158.

87. Dunham, "The Dances of Haiti," 53.

88. Katherine Dunham, "Ethnic Dancing," *Dance Magazine,* XX (September, 1946), 34.

89. Montejo, *Autobiography of a Runaway Slave.* p. 131. This quotation differs from the original text in that the third and fourth sentences have been transposed.

90. Beckford, *Descriptive Account of the Island of Jamaica,* II, 388-89.

91. Pinckard, *Notes on the West Indies,* II, 47-50.

92. Joseph J. Williams, *Psychic Phenomena of Jamaica* (New York: Dial Press, 1934), pp. 183-85.

93. Edwards, *History, Civil and Commercial, of the British West Indies,* II, 103-04. Other authors discussing funeral customs include: Barclay, *Practical View of the Present State of Slavery in the West Indies,* pp. 134-36; Phillippo, *Jamaica,* pp. 94-95; and Stewart, *View of the Past and Present State of the Island of Jamaica,* pp. 274-76.

94. Gardner, *History of Jamaica,* p. 386.

95. Beckwith, "Folk Games of Jamaica," p. 8.

96. Zora Neale Hurston, *Tell My Horse* (Philadelphia: J. B. Lippincott Company, 1938), pp. 71-73.

97. Harold Courlander, "Dance and Dance-Drama in Haiti," in *The Function of Dance in Human Society,* by Franziska Boas (New York: Boas School, 1944), pp. 38-39.

98. Herskovits and Herskovits, *Trinidad Village,* p. 159.

99. *Ibid.,* p. 284.

100. *Ibid.,* p. 149.

101. Dunham, "Dances of Haiti," 53.

102. Barclay, *Practical View of the Present State of Slavery in the West Indies,* p. 10.

103. Carmichael, *Domestic Manners and Social Condition,* I, 175-76.

104. Richardson Wright, *Revels in Jamaica, 1682-1838* (New York: Dodd, Mead and Company, 1937), p. 235; Gardner, *History of Jamaica,* p. 385.

105. Beckwith, "Christmas Mummings in Jamaica," p. 48.

106. For more extensive treatment of this subject, see Stewart, *View of the Past and Present State of the Island of Jamaica,* Chapter XX.

107. *Ibid.,* p. 325.

108. Carmichael, *Domestic Manners and Social Condition,* I, 229-30.

109. *Ibid.,* II, 245.

110. The information dealing with African religion is primarily based on the work of Melville J. Herskovits, "The Contemporary Science: Africanisms in Religious Life," Chapter VII in his *The Myth of the Negro Past* (Boston: Beacon Press. 1958), pp. 207-60.

111. Maria Leach, ed.; *Funk and Wagnalls Standard Dictionary of Folklore, Mythology, and Legend* (2 vols.; New York: Funk and Wagnalls Company, 1949), II, 1161. Voodoo, vodun, vaudous, voudoo, and vodu are a few of the ways to spell the word "Voodoo"; except within a direct quotation, the Anglicized spelling "Voodoo" is used here.

112. *Ibid.,* II, 1161-62.

113. Erika Bourguignon, "Trance Dance," in *Dance Perspectives 35* (Autumn, 1968), 28.

114. George E. Simpson, "The Belief Systems of Haitian Vodun," *American Anthropologist,* XLVII (1945), 35-38.

115. Moreau de St.-Méry, *Danse*, pp. 47-48.

116. Médéric L. E. Moreau de Saint-Méry, *Description Topographique et Politique de la Partie Espagnole de l'isle Saint-Domingue; avec des Observations Generales sur le Climat, la Population, les Productions, le Caractère, & les Moeurs des Habitans de Cette Colonie, & un Tableau Raissoné des Différentes Parties de son Administration; accompagnée d'un Nouvelle Carte de la Totalité de l'isle,* trans. by Anthony Bliss (2 vols.; Philadelphia, 1797-98), I, 46.

117. Dunham, "Dances of Haiti," 13.

118. Herskovits, "Rada," in Leach, ed.; *Funk and Wagnalls Standard Dictionary of Folklore,* II, 919.

119. Alfred Metraux, *Voodoo in Haiti,* trans. by Hugo Charteris (London: Andre Deutsch Ltd., 1959), p. 365.

120. Several excellent books exist dealing with Voodoo, including: Harold Courlander, *Haiti Singing* (Chapel Hill: University of North Carolina Press, 1939); Courlander, *The Drum and the Hoe* (Berkeley: University of California Press, 1960); Maya Deren, *Divine Horsemen, The Living Gods of Haiti* (London: Thomas and Hudson, 1953); Katherine Dunham, *Island Possessed* (Garden City, New York: Doubleday and Company, 1969); Melville J. Herskovits, *Life in a Haitian Valley* (New York: Alfred A. Knopf, 1937); Zora Neale Hurston, *Tell My Horse* (Philadelphia: J. B. Lippincott Company, 1938); Alfred Metraux, *Haiti: Black Peasants and Voodoo,* trans. by Peter Lengyel (New York: Universe Books, 1960); and Metraux, *Voodoo in Haiti,* trans. by Hugo Charteris (London: Andre Deutsch Ltd., 1959).

121. Moreau de St.-Méry, *Danse*, pp. 49-50.

122. St. John, *Hayti, or the Black Republic.*

123. "Cannibalism in Hayti," *New York World,* Sunday, December 5, 1886, p. 9.

124. W. B. Seabrook, *The Magic Island* (New York: Harcourt, Brace and Company, 1929).

125. Richard A. Loederer, *Voodoo Fire in Haiti,* trans. by Desmond Ivo Vesey (New York: Literary Guild, 1935), pp. 9-20.

126. Dunham, "Dances of Haiti," 19.

127. *Ibid.,* 21.

128. Deren, *Divine Horsemen,* p. 235.

129. Herskovits, *Life in a Haitian Valley,* p. 177.

130. Dunham, "Dances of Haiti," 48-50.

131. Herskovits, *Life in a Haitian Valley,* pp. 263-64.

132. Metraux, *Voodoo in Haiti,* p. 190.

133. Dunham, *Island Possessed,* pp. 98-99.

134. *Ibid.,* pp. 135-36.

135. Courlander, *Drum and the Hoe,* p. 129.

136. Courlander, *Haiti Singing,* p. 103.

137. Metraux, *Voodoo in Haiti,* pp. 190-91.

138. Courlander, *Haiti Singing*, p. 114.

139. Metraux, *Voodoo in Haiti*, p. 191.

140. Courlander, "Dance and Dance Drama in Haiti," p. 42.

141. Deren, *Divine Horsemen*, p. 252.

142. Dunham, *Island Possessed*, pp. 101-02.

143. Dunham, "Dances of Haiti," 50.

144. Deren, *Divine Horsemen*, p. 234.

145. Courlander, *Haiti Singing*, pp. 160-61.

146. Metraux, *Voodoo in Haiti*, p. 191.

147. Dunham, *Island Possessed*, p. 109.

148. Courlander, "Dance and Dance-Drama in Haiti," p. 41.

149. Joseph J. Williams, *Voodoos and Obeahs. Phases of West Indian Witchcraft* (New York: Dial Press, 1932), p. 210.

150. Moreau de St.-Méry, *Description Topographique*, I, 46-47.

151. Deren, *Divine Horsemen*, pp. 240-41.

152. Dunham, "Dances of Haiti," 54.

153. Melville J. Herskovits, "Shango," in Leach, ed., *Funk and Wagnalls Standard Dictionary of Folklore*, II, 1004.

154. *Ibid.* Herskovits has written a clear explanation of syncresis in "African Gods and Catholic Saints in New World Negro Belief," *American Anthropologist*, XXXIX, No. 4, Part I (1937), 635-643.

155. Herskovits and Herskovits, *Trinidad Village*, pp. 323-25.

156. *Ibid.*, p. 331.

157. "Omele Drums," in Leach, ed.; *Funk and Wagnalls Standard Dictionary of Folklore*, II, 821.

158. Herskovits and Herskovits, *Trinidad Village*, p. 334.

159. *Ibid.*, p. 336.

160. *Ibid.*, p. 337.

161. Stewart, *View of the Past and Present State of the Island of Jamaica*, p. 276.

162. *Ibid.*, p. 277.

163. Hesketh J. Bell, *Obeah. Witchcraft in the West Indies* (2d ed.; revised; London: Sampson, Low, Marston and Company, 1893), p. 28.

164. Herskovits, "Obia or Obeah," in Leach, ed.; *Funk and Wagnalls Standard Dictionary of Folklore*, II, 808.

165. J. Williams, *Voodoos and Obeahs*, p. 128.

166. *Ibid.*, p. 213.

167. *Ibid.*, p. 236.

168. J. Williams, *Psychic Phenomena of Jamaica*, p. 109.

169. *Ibid.*, pp. 72-73.

170. Earl Leaf, *Isles of Rhythm* (New York: A. S. Barnes and Company, 1948), p. 59.

171. Williams, *Voodoos and Obeahs,* p. 145.

172. Beckwith, "Christmas Mummings in Jamaica," p. 50.

173. Claude McKay, *A Long Way From Home* (New York: Lee Furman, Inc., 1937), pp. 296-97.

174. Herskovits and Herskovits, *Trinidad Village,* p. 316.

175. Williams, *Voodoos and Obeahs,* p. 171.

176. Williams, *Psychic Phenomena,* p. 196.

177. Stanley Jackson Coleman, ed., *Myth and Mystery in Curious Caribbean Cults* (Douglas, Isle of Man: Folklore Academy, 1960), no pagination.

178. *Ibid.*

179. *Ibid.*

180. Herskovits and Herskovits, *Trinidad Village,* p. 192.

181. *Ibid.*

182. *Ibid.,* p. 222.

183. Lisa Lekis, *Dancing Gods* (New York: Scarecrow Press, Inc., 1960), p. 132.

184. Leach, ed.; *Funk and Wagnalls Standard Dictionary of Folklore,* II, 784.

185. Harry H. Johnston, *The Negro in the New World* (London: Methuen and Co. Ltd., 1910), p. 65.

186. Carleton Beals, *America South* (Philadelphia: J. B. Lippincott Company, 1937), pp. 147-48.

187. *Ibid.,* p. 148.

188. "Voodooism: Cuban Authorities Battle Cult Practising Kidnaping and Human Sacrifice," *Literary Digest,* January 2, 1937, p. 29.

189. *Ibid.*

190. *Ibid.*

191. Leaf, *Isles of Rhythm,* p. 30.

192. *Ibid.,* p. 52.

193. *Ibid.*

194. Ortiz, *Los Bailes y el Teatro,* p. 109.

195. *Ibid.,* p. 152.

196. Lekis, *Dancing Gods,* p. 69.

197. *Ibid.,* p. 68.

198. *Ibid.,* p. 69.

199. Ortiz, *Los Bailes y el Teatro,* p. 161.

200. *Ibid.,* p. 162.

201. *Ibid.,* pp. 151-52.

202. *Ibid.,* p. 152.

203. *Ibid.,* p. 153.

3

DANCE ON THE PLANTATIONS

With the blacks, the drums and the calabash left Africa. Still the drumming sounded, but now with the metallic clank of overturned buckets and tubs on the ship deck. The drums, and those who played them, arrived in the New World, and the dances they accompanied reached the West Indies, where they continued much as they had in Africa.

It was only as the drums and people reached the United States that the sound of Africa diminished. The drums were prohibited, and yet the rhythms of Africa lived on in new forms among the slaves as bare feet stomped on the hard earth, hands clapped, and songs were sung.

The continued arrival of slave ships from Africa kept the rhythms and traditions alive, also. When the slave trade was abolished the only remaining link with tradition was provided through the arrival of West Indian blacks. Many black people from the Caribbean came or were brought to the mainland, and the African rhythms and dances did not entirely die.

▣▣▣ THE BEGINNING

In "A Relation from Master John Rolfe," quoted by John Smith, it was said that "about the last of August [1619] came in a dutch man of warre that sold us twenty Negars."[1] No mention was made by either Rolfe or Smith of the name of the ship, its point of origin, or its destination.

The ship, and the quotation regarding the ship have caused a great deal of controversy. Authors who have quoted Smith as having said that the Negroes were landed in 1619 by a Dutch ship have given as their source Smith's book, *The Generall Histoire of Virginia*, published in 1624. However, the quotation regarding the landing of the Negroes did not appear until the fourth edition, published in 1627. Why did Smith wait through three editions before he included his often-quoted statement?

Was it, as suggested by Alexander Brown, not a Dutch ship which brought the first slaves but rather a ship named the *Treasurer,* owned by the notorious Robert Rich, later to become the Earl of Warwick?[2] Was the *Treasurer* sent out of Jamestown by John Smith and Rich for the express purpose of procuring Negro slaves for the Virginia Colony, since it proved impossible to enslave the Indians?

Brown cited, among other pieces of well documented evidence, a quotation from a biographical sketch of John Rolfe, the husband of Pocahontas and the man who wrote the original statement for Smith's history:

> In January, 1625, Rolfe's father-in-law [the father of Rolfe's first wife], Captain William Pierce, owned Angelo, a negro woman, one of the first negroes brought to Virginia in the Earl of Warwick's ship, the *Treasurer*, in August, 1619.[3]

Elizabeth Donnan, however, discounted the idea of the *Treasurer* being the first ship to bring slaves to the United States. She reported that a plan to procure slaves was made but "the change in the Virginia government *probably* [italics mine] made it impossible of accomplishment."[4] However, the records of the Virginia Colony for that period of time mysteriously disappeared, so that it can never be known exactly what did happen.[5]

No matter who brought them, the fact remains that Africans

were found on the American mainland in 1619.[6] At first the blacks were treated the same as the white indentured servants: after their period of servitude, they were released. As in the West Indies, one rationale for enslaving "heathens" was that they could be brought to Christianity, and in the beginning they were freed after conversion. Freeing the Negroes upon their acceptance of the Christian faith or after a period of indentured servitude, however, proved so uneconomical that by the time Robert Beverley's *History and Present State of Virginia* was published in 1705, a sharp distinction had been made between servants and slaves.

> Slaves are the Negroes, and their Posterity, following the condition of the Mother, . . . They are called Slaves, in respect of the time of their Servitude, because it is for a Life. . . .
>
> Servants, are those which serve only for a few years, according to the time of their Indenture, of the Custom of the Country.[7]

A distinction was also made by Beverley between women servants and women slaves.

> Sufficient Distinction is also made between the Female-Servants, and Slaves; for a White Woman is rarely or never put to work in the Ground, if she be good for anything else: And to Discourage all Planters from using any Women so, Their Law imposes the heaviest Taxes upon Female-Servants working in the Ground . . . Whereas on the other hand, it is a common thing to work a Woman Slave out of Doors; nor does the Law make any Distinction in her Taxes, whether her Work be Abroad, or at Home.[8]

Thus the condition of the Negro in the United States was clarified at this early stage: he was to remain in official bondage for 160 years.

With the increase of slave population, the passage of more stringent laws regulating them was necessary to maintain order. There were increasing rebellions and insurrections among these "happy, contented slaves," and plots were discovered to burn both Boston and New York in the early 1700's. Nearly every area had its rebellions. The Cato conspiracy, or Stono insurrection, in South Carolina in 1739 had great indirect influence on the dance of the Negro in the United States. John Hope Franklin wrote that the

> . . . so-called Cato conspiracy . . . began about twenty miles
> west of Charleston on a plantation at Stono. The slaves killed
> two guards in a warehouse and secured arms and ammunition
> and proceeded to escape toward Florida and freedom. Joined
> by other Negroes, they marched to the beating of two drums and
> killed all whites that interfered.[9]

The Stono insurrection led to the passage of strict regulations in South Carolina which were soon copied by other states. Among the prohibitions were the assembly of groups of Negroes and the use of drums of any kind. The whites already felt that Negroes could send messages by drum and when the Stono revolutionaries marched to the sound of drums, they were banned entirely.

> The slave-owners found to their cost that drums which beat for
> dances could also call to revolt, and thus it came about that in
> many parts of the New World the African types of hollow-log
> drums were suppressed, being supplanted by other percussion
> devices less susceptible of carrying messages and could thus
> be restricted to beating dance rhythms.[10]

▯▮▯▮ MUSICAL INSTRUMENTS

Though drums were prohibited in most places, still some survived. Two ex-slave residents of Harris Neck, Georgia, remembered drums well. In an interview, Rosa Sallins of Harris Neck remembered when messages were "beat out" on a drum in the Georgia Sea Islands:

> Dat wuz tuh let us know wen deah wuz tuh be a dance aw a
> frolic. Wen dey hab a dance obuh on St. Catherines, dey beat
> duh drum tuh tell us about it. Duh soun would carry obuh duh
> watuh an we would heah it plain as anything. Den duh folks
> heah beat duh drum tuh let em know about it in udduh
> settlements.[11]

Another resident of Harris Neck, Issac Basden, stated that "I use tuh dance tuh duh drum."[12] He said that the drum beat would call people to dances or funerals, but the beat was distinctive for each. Two kinds of drums existed, according to Basden: a kettle drum and a bass drum. The bass drum stood "bout two an a half foot high."[13]

F. J. Jackson of Grimball's Point, Georgia, explained that drums were made from a hollow beehive log. They were constructed by stretching a hide over the hole and then cutting a hoop that would lock around the log. "Den yuh cut strips uh deah hide and make bans tuh hole duh head cuvuh tight."[14]

Several other Georgia coastal residents verified the making of drums as well as their uses.[15] However, the use of drums by the slaves did not appear to be widespread; there are few references to them in the literature except in two geographical areas: the Georgia coastal islands and Louisiana. The use of drums in the Georgia Sea Islands was understandable since the people were isolated, not only from each other but also from the whites. Many studies have been done on the retention of Africanisms in this area, including the study of the language, called Gullah.

The type of drum used in Louisiana was undoubtedly influenced by the customs of the West Indians who migrated there. A. C. Pruitt, an ex-slave from St. Martinville, Louisiana, described in an interview how these drums were made: "Dey take de big sugar hogshead and stretch rawhide over de top. Den de man straddle de barrel and beat on de top for de drum."[16]

There were other improvised instruments also. John Cole, of the Oglethorp plantation in Georgia, reported several methods of constructing instruments:

> Stretch cow-hides over cheese-boxes and you had tambourines. Saw bones from off a cow, knock them together, and call it a drum. Or use broom-straws on fiddle-strings, and you had your entire orchestra.[17]

Another ex-slave, Thomas Goodwater stated that "some time there was a tambourine beater, some time dey use ole wash tubs an' beat it wid sticks, an' some time dey just clap their han's."[18] As will be seen in a later chapter, both the tambourine and the bones were incorporated into the minstrel shows, and the popular endmen were frequently called Mr. Tambo and Brother Bones.

James Bolton described another popular instrument of the slaves: the quills, frequently called reeds. He related that:

> . . . somebody allus blowed on quills. Quills was a row of whistles made outen reeds, or sometimes they made 'em outen bark. Every whistle in the row was a different tone and you could play any kind of tune.[19]

The most primitive of all instruments, the human body, was described by Eliza Overton. "We wud all sing an' pat our hans an' feet to keep time for the dance."[20]

One of the earliest references to any type of musical instrument used by the Afro-Americans was that of Thomas Jefferson. In his discussion on the differences between black and white, including the reasons for colonizing the freed slaves rather than "keeping them in the society," the Negroes were described in an unfavorable light. The only complimentary thing Jefferson said was that, "In music they are more generally gifted than the whites with accurate ears for tune and time."[21] He negated this statement, however, by noting that, of course, the Negroes had not yet proven themselves in composition. In a footnote, Jefferson made the following statement:

> The instrument proper to them is the Banjar, which they brought hither from Africa, and which is the original of the guitar, its chords being precisely the four lower chords of the guitar.[22]

Jefferson was but one of many to mention the banjar or banjo. Others included A. G. Bradley, who had a slave named Reuben who would entertain Bradley's visitors. "Reuben was reckoned the best hand to 'pick a banjer' in the whole neighbourhood."[23]

An ex-slave, George Dillard, in answer to a question concerning his dancing ability stated that, "I was right spry; but I was at my best in de job of picking' de banjer. I shorely did love to pick dat box while de other niggers danced away."[24]

John Davis recounted a story told him by Dick, a Negro. According to Davis, Dick said:

> "My young master was a mighty one for music, and he made me learn to play the Banger. I could soon tune it sweetly, and of a moonlight night he would set me to play, and the wenches

to dance. My young master himself could shake a desperate foot at the fiddle; there was nobody that could face him at a *Congo Minuet.* . . ."[25]

By far the most popular instrument played appeared to be the fiddle. This was probably due to the influence of the slave owners who frequently used Negro musicians for their own "white folks' " dances. Many owners purchased fiddles for their slaves, and one who was able to play well brought a much higher price on the market. If the masters did not purchase the instrument, slaves either manufactured or bought their own.

One ex-slave said:

> I fust learned how to play on a long gourd with horsehair on it. . . . That was the fust of my learning to play. After a while I bought me a fiddle for $1.80, and after so long a time I bought me a fiddle sure enough.[26]

Sally Ashton told of the unusual kind of life led by a good fiddler:

> Ole fiddler was a man named Louis Cane. Chile, he sho' could strung dat fiddle. Never did do much work, but Marsa use to keep him, 'cause he use to have him play fo' de balls in de big house. Marse use to pay him, too. We never did pay him, 'cause we ain't never had nothin'.[27]

His Highness, Bernhard, Duke of Saxe-Weimar Eisenach, attended a ball on a plantation near Charleston, South Carolina. Much amused, he described the slave orchestra:

> . . . the whole music consisted of two violins and a tamborine. This tamborine was struck with a terrible energy. The two others scraped the violin, the truest signification of the word; one of them cried out the figures, imitating with his body all the motions of the dance. The whole of it amuse me much. . . .[28]

Many others, too numerous to mention here, also reported the use of the fiddle at both owner and slave dances.[29]

The slave orchestras that played for the white owners were usually composed of fiddlers and frequently a tambourine player. Slave dances were accompanied by the banjo, fiddle, quills, tambourine, bones, or, infrequently, a drum or pots and pans beaten like drums—or just the human voice with clapping and stamping. Rarely were all these instruments used together; most slave dances were accompanied by a single instrument. The variety of dances performed to such accompaniment was infinite.

▣▣▣ TYPES OF DANCES

Depending upon the affability of the master, slaves could hold dances and frolics on their own plantation or they could obtain a pass to visit another plantation. A written pass was necessary, since groups of white men called patrollers roamed the area, beating any Negro caught away from his plantation without this pass.

Some masters encouraged dancing, and, according to an entry in the diary of Bennett Barrow, even forced the Negroes to dance. "January 1, 1846: . . . finding no Cotton to thrash sent for the Fiddle and made them Dance from 12 till dark. . . ."[30] This forced dancing was probably at least partly in the interest of health, like that done on the slave ships. In addition, slaves were frequently asked, or forced, to entertain the whites at the "Big House" with their singing, dancing, and general antics. William Russell, on a tour of the South mentioned one of these occasions:

> . . . after dinner, as we sat on the steps, the children were sent
> for to sing for us. They came very shyly, and by degrees. . . .
> With much difficulty the elder children were dressed into line;
> then they began to shuffle their flat feet, to clap their hands,
> and drawl out in a monotonous sort of chant something about
> the "River Jawdam," after which Mrs. Crafts rewarded them
> with lumps of sugar which were as fruitful of disputes as the
> apple of discord. A few fathers and mothers gazed at the scene
> from a distance.[31]

Robert Moton, later president of Tuskegee Institute, commented on a houseboy named Sam and his trips to the "Big House":

> Sam was a favourite on the plantation . . . a remarkable
> acrobat . . . and could perform what were to me many very

"In the Store" by E. W. Kemble, in *Century Magazine* (1887)

wonderful acrobatic feats, in addition to being a wonderfully good reel and jig dancer and a remarkably fine singer. . . . Under Sam's direction I practised many of his accomplishments, and with his careful tutelage became a close second. As a result, he and I were frequently called into the "big house" to perform.[32]

Buck, Buck and Wing

Discussing the summons to appear at the "Big House" to sing and dance the Buck and Wing for the guests, ex-slave Dan Barton reported that:

Them smart-alec niggers 'd make the white folks yell wit' laughin' at their crazy antics. You know a nigger is jest a born show-offer. They'd dance the buck and wing and another step nobody does any more. It went two steps to the right, two steps to the left. The womens shake their skirts and the mens dance 'round them.[33]

While the above description of the step "nobody does anymore" is not detailed enough to identify, the dance sounds much like the description of the Chica given by St.-Méry.

James Wiggins, who lived on the Revell plantation in Maryland, remembered that when he was about nine or ten years old,

. . . I was taken to Annapolis, how I used to dance in the stores for men and women, they would give me pennies and three cent pieces, all of which was given to the Revells. They bought me shoes and clothes with the money collected. . . . As a child I was very fond of dancing the jig and buck.[34]

The Buck dance, according to one ex-slave, was danced only by the men.[35] However, her statement is unique among descriptions of the dance.

Wesley Jones recollected that big barbecues used to be given at a store and were attended by white and black alike. "Dey had a platform built not fer from de barbecue table to dance on. Any darky dat could cut de buck and de pigeon wing was called up to de platform to perform fer ev'ybody."[36]

Pigeon Wing

The Pigeon Wing appears to have been performed over a large geographical area. References were made to the Pigeon Wing from South Carolina to Texas, and from Indiana to Mississippi. Horace Overstreet, of Beaumont, Texas, remembered the dance by another name. Overstreet stated that on Christmas and July 4, a big dance would be held on their plantation. ". . . jus' a reg'lar old breakdown dance. Some was dancin' Swing de Corner, and some in de middle de floor cuttin' de chicken wing."[37]

Fannie Berry described the Pigeon Wing as follows: "Dere was cuttin' de pigeons wings—dat was flippin' yo' arms an' legs roun' an' holdin' ya' neck stiff like a bird do."[38]

The Pigeon Wing and the Buck dance appear as authentic dances of the Negro on the plantation, much before they were picked up for the minstrel shows and billed as the Buck and Wing.

Jig

Slaves were not always summoned to the Big House to perform; frequently the whites came to the quarters to view the dances. This happened particularly at Christmas time, but also during dance contests. These contests were often arranged by the slave-owners and were of two types.

In one kind of contest the slaves of one owner were pitted against those of another. Liza Jones, an old ex-slave who belonged to the Bryants said that:

Old Massa Day and Massa Bryant, dey used to put dey niggers together and have de prize dances. Massa Day allus lose, 'cause us allus beat de niggers at dancin'.[39]

According to James W. Smith, who lived on a plantation in Palestine, Texas, his master owned a slave named Tom, whom he would pit against all comers in jigging contests. The master built a platform for the contests and the slaves came from a wide area to see who would jig the best. Mr. Smith described one of the most exciting contests he had ever seen:

I must tell you 'bout de best contest we ever had. One nigger
on our place was de jigginest fellow ever was. Everyone round
tries to git some body to best him. He could put de glass of
water on his head and make his feet go like triphammers and
sound like de snaredrum. He could whirl round and sich, all de
movement from his hips down. Now it gits noised round a
fellow been found to beat Tom and a contest am 'ranged for
Saturday evenin'. There was a big crowd and money am bet,
but master bets on Tom, of course.

So dey starts jiggin'. Tom starts easy and a little faster
and faster. The other fellow doin' de same. Dey gits faster and
faster and dat crowd am a-yellin'. Gosh! There am 'citement.
Dey jus' keep a gwine. It look like Tom done found his match,
but there am one thing yet he ain't done—he ain't made de
whirl. Now he does it. Everyone holds he breath, and de other
fellow starts to make de whirl and he makes it, but jus' a
spoonful of water sloughs out his cup, so Tom am de winner.[40]

The other type of contest arranged by the white owners was
devised only for their own slaves. Usually the competition was
to determine the best Cake-Walk couple.

Cake-Walk

Cake walkin' wuz a lot of fun durin' slavery time. Dey swept
de yards real clean and set benches 'round for de party.
Banjoes wuz used for music making'. . . . De couple dat
danced best got a prize. Sometimes de slave owners come to
dese parties 'cause dey enjoyed watchin' de dance, and dey
'cided who danced de best.[41]

In Virginia, the common festival dance was the Cake-Walk.
Festivals were held on many occasions, but particularly at
harvest time or crop-over.

The slaves would assemble en masse—dressed in their Sunday
best—with glowing tallow dips or pine knots forming a ring of
light. Master and mistress would be there, one of whom would
award the prize for the best "cuttin' of figgers." Sometimes the
mistress of the big house would donate the prize cake; when
provided by slave row, it would be made often of cornmeal
decorated with cabbage leaves, the whole baked in ashes. . . .[42]

Entertainer Tom Fletcher heard stories about the Cake-Walk from his grandfather, who had won many prizes in cake-walking on the plantation. Fletcher quoted his grandfather as saying, "Your grandmother and I, we won all the prizes and were taken from plantation to plantation."[43]

Fletcher related that his grandfather had told him that when the Cake-Walk began it was known as the "chalk line walk."

> Sometimes on pleasant evenings, boards would be laid down for an impromptu stage before the verandah so the guests could have a good view of the proceedings and a real shindig would take place with singing and dancing. The cake-walk, in that section and at that time, was known as the chalk line walk. There was no prancing, just a straight walk on a path made by turns and so forth, along which the dancers made their way with a pail of water on their heads. The couple that was the most erect and spilled the least or no water at all was the winner.[44]

When left to themselves, without white interference, the slaves performed a variety of other dances. Most of the dances were held on Saturday nights and such a wide variety of dances was done that only the most common of them can be mentioned.

Ring Dance

One of the more primitive dances was done in a ring and called simply the Ring Dance. It appeared comparable to the dance done in the West Indies by the Congo Negroes. Hettie Campbell of St. Mary's Island, Georgia, described the dance:

> We does plenty uh dances in those days. Dance roun' in a ring. We has a big time long bout wen crops come in an everybody bring sumpm tuh eat wut they makes an we all gives praise fuh the good crop an then we shouts an sings all night. An wen the sun rise, we stahts tuh dance. It ain' so long since they stop that back in the woods but these young people they does new kines uh dances.[45]

Guion Johnson described another type of dance, very similar to the Ring Dance, which was done on St. Helena's Island in the Sea Islands.

One South Carolina planter who had been having trouble in disciplining his slaves supplied his people with fiddles and drums and "promoted dancing." To his gratification the ill temper of the slaves disappeared and peace was once more established on the plantation. Their dancing was a sort of shuffle which animated the whole body, and was performed individually rather than by couples. The dance was usually held at night in the open or in one of the cabins and the entire group participated in the merrymaking.[46]

Buzzard Lope

Survivals of African dance were found in the so-called animal dances seen in America. These dances took many forms, but the one mentioned most frequently by ex-slaves was a dance called the Buzzard Lope. Many of the ex-slaves in the Sea Island region remembered doing the Buzzard Lope, but very few described it. Anna Johnson of Harris Neck, Georgia, said "One uh duh dances call duh Buzzard Lope. We still dance dat tuhday."[47]

Edward Adams, in his *Congoree Sketches*, described the exploits of Big Charleston as narrated by a Negro named Tad:

'De first time I see Big Charleston been at a dance. . . . You could hear 'em laughin' and talkin' a mile. Dey come to de road jumpin' to de drum and steppin' as high as a man's head. And as de night wored on you ought er seen some of dem niggers cut de buck and de buzzard lope, and sidin' 'round dem sisters like er rooster 'round er hen.[48]

The Buzzard Lope had been known to song-collector Lydia Parrish since 1915. M. J. Herskovits told her that he had seen a similar dance done in Dahomey. She described the Buzzard Lope seen in the Georgia Sea Islands as follows:

On Sapelo Island, I found in the Johnson family a combination of the old dance form with rather more modern steps than the original African pantomime warranted. Of the twins, Naomi did the patting while Isaac did the dancing; an older brother rhythmically called out the cues in a sharp staccato, and another one lay on the floor of the wide veranda representing a dead cow. Anyone who has seen turkey buzzards disposing of "carr'on" will recognize the aptness of the following directions . . .

March aroun'!	(the cow)
Jump across!	(see if she's daid)
Get the eye!	(always go for that first)
So glad!	(cow daid)
Get the guts!	(they like 'em next best)
Go to eatin'!	(on the meat)
All right! — cow mos' gone!	
Dog comin'!	
Scare the dog!	
Look aroun' for mo' meat!	
All right! — Belly full!	
— "Goin' to tell the res' "[49]	

The parenthetical asides were given to Miss Parrish by the Negroes who were performing the dance.

Other animal dances mentioned with the Buzzard Lope were the Turkey Trot, Snake Hip, and those mentioned by Emma and Mary Stevens of Sunbury, Georgia.

> We do git tuh gedduh an hab dance an pahties an big suppuhs, we does duh Snake Hip and duh Buzzard Lope. An addalas dance we did duh Fish Tail an duh Fish Bone an duh Camel Walk.[50]

Water Dances

Among the most interesting dances performed on the plantations were those in which water was carried on the head as a part of the dance. A bucket or glass of water balanced on the head was particularly used as a method of determining the winner in the contest or challenge dances. As mentioned previously, water glasses were sometimes used during Jig and Cake-Walk contests. Fannie Berry described a dance she called "Set the Floor," which could be done with a glass of water on the dancer's head.

> Dey come up an' bend over toward each other at de waist, an' de woman put her hands on her hips an' de man roll his eyes all roun' an' grin an' dey pat de flo' wid dey feet jus' like dey was puttin' it in place. Used to do dat bes' on dirt flo' so de feet could slap down hard against it. Sometimes dey would set

de flo' alone—either a man or a woman. Den dey would set a glass of water on dey haid an' see how many kinds of steps dey could make widout spillin' de water.[51]

Set the Floor sounds much like St.-Méry's description of the Calenda, by virtue of the fact that it contained foot tapping or patting and could be done either in couples or alone. Perhaps it was the Calenda with an Anglicized name and the addition of water.

An ex-slave from Virginia, Betty Jones, recalled performing a dance with water:

Anyhow we'd go to dese dances. Ev'y gal wid her beau, an' sech music! Had two fiddles, two tangerines [tambourines], two banjos, an' two sets of bones. Was a boy named Joe dat used to whistle too. Dem devilish boys would git out in de middle of de flo' an' me . . . and de devil right wid 'em. Set a glass of water on my haid, an' de boys would bet on it. I had a great big wreaf roun' my haid an' a big ribbon bow on each side, an' didn't waste a drop of water on none of 'em.[52]

This particular water dance may have been of African origin. Africans carried nearly everything on their heads, a custom which persisted when they left the mother country. There are numerous references to carrying things on the head in the West Indies, in New Orleans, and in many other parts of the South. Hannah Crasson, an ex-slave living near Raleigh, North Carolina, told the following of her aunt: "One of the slaves, my aint, she wuz a royal slave. She could dance all over de place wid a tumbler of water on her head, widout spilling it. She sho could tote herself."[53]

Two ex-slaves, Fred Brown, from Louisiana, and Lewis Jones, of Texas, mentioned putting a glass of water on the head during a jigging contest,[54] much in the manner previously described by Smith. Water was also mentioned in conjunction with the Buck dance. "A prize was given to the person who could 'buck dance' the steadiest with a tumbler of water balanced on the head. A cake or a quilt was often given as the prize."[55]

Apparently even the Juba dance was done in some areas with water balanced on the head, since the word for water bucket in the Georgia Sea Islands was "Juba haltuh."[56]

Juba

Another dance of African origin was the Juba, which has been mentioned in conjunction with the West Indies as a sacred dance. Apparently in Africa this dance was called the Djouba. As it moved to the United States, it became a secular dance distinguished by the "patting" which accompanied it. This patting, which was called "patting Juba" was the stamping, clapping, and slapping of arms, chest and thighs, which appeared extensively when drums were prohibited.

According to Dunham:

> In its original African form, the Juba or Jumba or Majumba, as it is called in the West Indies, is primarily a competitive dance of skill. One person steps forward in the circle of dancers and begins exhibiting his skill, whereupon he is joined by a member of the opposite sex who joins him in this exhibition. The people in the circle may rotate for a certain number of measures, or may remain stationary, all the while clapping rhythmically and encouraging the competitors with song and verse.[57]

As William Smith described the Juba, the main figure was the banjor-man:

> Tumming his banjor, grinning with ludicrous gesticulations and playing off his wild notes to the company [*sic*]. Before him stood two athletic blacks, with open mouth and pearl white teeth, clapping "Juber" to the notes of the banjor. . . . I had never seen Juber clapped to the banjor before, and you may suppose I looked upon such a novel scene, with some degree of surprise . . . ! The clappers rested the right foot on the heel, and its clap on the floor was in perfect unison with the notes of the banjor, and palms of the hands on the corresponding extremities; while the dancers were all jigging it away in the merriest possible gaiety of heart, having the most ludicrous twists, wry jerks, and flexible contortions of the body and limbs, that human imagination can devine.[58]

Dr. John Wyeth, in describing the life of the slaves on his plantation near Huntsville, Alabama, gave a vivid description of the method used for patting Juba:

> . . . there were accompanists who "patted" with the hands, keeping accurate time with the music. In patting, the position

was usually a half-stoop or forward bend, with a slap of one hand on the left knee followed by the same stroke and noise on the right, and then a loud slap of the two palms together. I should add that the left hand made two strokes in half-time to one for the right, something after the double stroke of the left drumstick in beating the kettledrum.[59]

Wyeth was tutored by an old slave named Billy in the proper method of playing the banjo. During these lessons, Wyeth learned many of the old slave songs, including the words to "Juba."

And so for an hour or more my instructor would continue with the exploits of his hero, Jimmie Rose, while the others in twos or fours danced away, "cutting the pigeon-wing," "the backstep," "the double shuffle," and other steps which required not only a keen sense of keeping time with the music, but agility and muscular power of a high order.

The real negro music as I knew it was, as one would expect, simple and crude, and quite unlike that which modern negro minstrelsy has made popular. One of the best-known "jig," or short-step, [sic] banjo and dance tunes was called "Juba."

> Juba dis and juba dat;
> Juba kill a yaller cat.
> Juba up and juba down;
> Juba runnin' all aroun'.[60]

Several ex-slaves gave the same words as Wyeth had reported. John Davenport of South Carolina said that Juba was "a 'Juber' game," while William Pratt stated, "We used to dance jigs by ourself, and we danced the 'hack-back,' skipping backwards and forwards facing each other. When one danced a jig he would sing, 'Juber this, Juber that, Juber kills a yellow cat.' "[61]

A different set of words was given by W. C. Handy, who reported the song went:

> Juba jump and Juba sing,
> Juba cut dat pigeon's wing;
> Juba kick off Juba's shoe,
> Juba dance dat Jubal Jew.[62]

Probably many verses accompanied the Juba. Thomas Talley added more verses to those already given by Wyeth and Handy:

Juba, whirl dat foot about.
Juba, blow dat candle out. Juba! Juba!

Juba circle, Raise de Latch.
Juba do dat Long Dog Scratch. Juba! Juba![63]

Talley also had underlined word sequences and said that the underlined expressions were dance steps. Included in the dance steps were the following: "Juba skin dat Yaller Cat" ('skin' is used in this verse rather than 'kill'), "cut dat Pigeon's Wing," "Jubal Jew," "Raise de Latch," and "Long Dog Scratch."[64]

Juba, according to *The Dictionary of Folklore*, has survived today in the form of a song and dance called "Hambone," which is a Negro hand-patting rhythm. The rhythm is made by "clapping the hands and slapping shoulder, chest, thighs, and buttocks."[65]

Quadrilles, Cotillions, and Reels

The white influence in the later days of slavery can certainly be seen in the types of dance done by the slaves. As in the West Indies, this influence reached the field hands via the house servants. A caste system developed in which the house slaves felt themselves on a higher level than the field hands and wielded considerable influence on the others.

Austin Steward, a slave for twenty-two years, described a slave dance on Colonel A.'s plantation and said the following regarding house slaves:

> House servants were of course, "the stars" of the party: all eyes were turned to them to see how they conducted [themselves].
> . . . The field hands . . . look to the house servant as a pattern of politeness and gentility. And indeed, it is often the only method of obtaining any knowledge of the manners of what is called "genteel society"; hence, they are ever regarded as a privileged class; and are sometimes greatly envied . . . .[66]

Dunham stated that the plantation dances were mostly of the circle and hand-clapping type, but were strongly influenced by the English Square Dance and the French Quadrille.[67] This influence may be apparent in the following description given

Slave sale, in Bibb, *Narrative of the Life and Adventures of Henry Bibb, an American Slave* (1850)

Henry E. Huntington Library, San Marino, California

by ex-slave Christopher Columbus Franklin, who was a slave in Bossier Parrish, Louisiana.

> De white folks 'low dem to have de frolic with de fiddle or banjo or windjammer. Dey dances out on de grass, forty or fifty niggers. . . . Sometimes dey call de jig dance and some of dem sho' dance it, too. De prompter call, "All git ready." Den he holler, "All balance," and den he sing out, "Swing your pardner," and dey does it. Den he say, "First man head off to de right," and dere dey goes. Or he say, "All promenade," and dey goes in de circle. One thing dey calls, "Bird in de Cage." Three joins hands round de gal in de middle, and dance round her, and den she git out and her pardner git in de center and dey dance dat way awhile.[68]

Liza Mention, an ex-slave who worked on a plantation in McDuffie County, Georgia, remembered that:

> Dances in dem days warn't dese here huggin' kind of dances lak dey has now. Dere warn't no Big Apple nor no Little Apple neither. . . . Dey had a string band wid a fiddle, a trumpet, and a banjo, but dere warn't no guitars lak dey has dis day. One man called de sets and us danced de cardrille (quadrille), de virginia reel, and de 16-hand cortillion.[69]

Other popular dances showing the white influence were the Figure Dance, which must have been similar to current Square Dances, and the Sixteen Figure Round Dances, like that described by Mrs. Mention above. Isaac Stier described the dances done on his plantation in Mississippi.

> Us danced plenty, too. Some o' de men clogged an' pigeoned, but when us had dances dey was real cotillions, lak de white folks had. . . . I use to call out de figgers: "Ladies, sasshay, Gents to de lef', now all swing." Ever'body lak my calls an' de dancers sho' moved smooth an' pretty. Long after de war was over de white folks would 'gage me to come 'roun' wid de band an' call de figgers at all de big dances. Dey always paid me well.[70]

Courlander listed the following dances, which were done along the east coast of the United States, as old secular dances of Afro-American origin: "Buzzard Lope, Juba, Mobile Buck, Mosquito Dance, Ball the Jack, Snake Hip, Fish Tail, Fish Bone, Camel Walk, and Come Down to the Mire."[71] This last dance,

"Come Down to the Mire," will be discussed as one of the religious dances of the slaves.

The strains of "Juba dis, and Juba dat," and "Raise yo' right foot, kick it up high/Knock dat Mobile Buck in de eye"[72] echoed throughout the plantations of the South, accompanied by patting, stamping, clapping, and slapping.

Life on the plantation was not so leisurely that dances were an everyday occurrence. In all probability the relative infrequency of the dances caused many ex-slaves to remember the occasions with special pleasure.

▣⋮▣⋮▣ SPECIAL OCCASION DANCES

When the further importation of slaves was prohibited by the United States in 1808, many of the older states turned to breeding slaves for interstate sale. Great coffles of slaves, chained together, would travel by foot, usually from Virginia to the Deep South. Jennie Kendricks related that her grandmother, one of those who walked from Virginia to Georgia,

> . . . used to tell me how the slave dealers brought her and a
> group of other children along much the same as they would
> a herd of cattle, when they reached a town all of them had to
> dance through the streets and act lively so that the chances
> for selling them would be greater.[73]

The buying and selling of human beings was an occasion — not festive, of course — at least for those being bought and sold — but an occasion nevertheless. Many slaves never had to undergo this ordeal, but many did, and as often as four or five times during their lives. The slaves were paraded about, dressed in their best. Their teeth were checked, the women were pinched, and decisions were made on the working capabilities of the men and the child-bearing abilities of the women. Bare backs were checked, for scarred backs meant that a slave was a bad actor, or so they said. With the propensity of many white overseers and owners to whip, it was amazing that anyone underwent the ordeal of slavery without some scars.

And sometimes, in the dark, dank slave pens, or on the banjo-table—another name for auction block—the slaves were forced, again, to dance.

In Memphis, as in nearly all Southern cities, there was a slave-pen or trading yard.

> We stayed in there three or four weeks. They would fix us all up and carry us in a great big old room and circle us all around every morning and every evening. They would have us up in the show room to show us to the people. They would hit us in the breast to see if we was strong and sound. Monkeys would play with us and see if any boogies [lice] was in our heads. They would do pretty well if they found any, but if they didn't they would slap us. They had the monkeys there to keep our heads clean. They made us dance and made us take exercise all the time we was there.[74]

Jolly Old Uncle Buck, as described by interviewer Orland Armstrong, was sold when his master died and the estate was broken up. He was chained to four other boys in a warehouse awaiting his sale. He recalled the following incident of the banjo-table:

> "Git on de table, Fred," de bossman say.
>   Fred he climb on, an' stan' waitin'. De white man auctioneer was bustlin' round. He had ter have some writin' folks make out some papers, an' wasn' quite ready fer de sale to start. So Fred he jus' stan' on de table.
>   By-'m-by—Plunk, plunk, plunkety plunk! Dat nigger wid de banjo settin' on de bench waitin' to be sold, he plunk his banjo. Den he rattle inter a real chune. Hi-yo! Fred 'gin ter shuffle roun' on his big feet, an' fine'ly he can't stan' it no longer. He gotta dance. He slap his big feet on de banjo table, an' we all pat wid de banjo music. White man laugh an' clap dey han's. Make him dance some mo'. Wouldn't let de auctioneer start till Fred dance de buck-an'-wing. Yo-ho! It sho'ly was funny!
>   De white man what bought Fred say he done paid hundert dollars mo' fo' dat nigger cause he could dance like dat![75]

Solomon Northup, born a freeman, was kidnapped and taken to the Deep South where he was sold in New Orleans. After remaining in slavery for twelve years he was freed because of influential friends and returned home, only to find his wife and children stolen. Northup described his stay in Freeman's slave pen:

> After being fed, in the afternoon, we were again paraded and made to dance. Bob, a colored boy, who had some time belonged to Freeman, played on the violin. Standing near him, I made bold to inquire if he could play the "Virginia Reel." He answered he could not, and asked me if I could play. Replying in the affirmative, he handed me the violin. I struck up a tune, and finished it. Freeman ordered me to continue playing, and seemed well pleased, telling Bob that I far excelled him.[76]

Ability to play an instrument or to dance added to the value of a slave. However, this ability did not stop the slave from being sold or even raffled off to a winning ticket holder. In 1738 Mary Stagg, a dancing teacher in Williamsburg, Virginia, advertised a grand assemblage with "several grotesque dances never yet performed in Virginia and a likely young Negro fellow to be raffled."[77] The *Virginia Gazette* ran an advertisement in 1753 for the sale of "an orderly Negro or mulatto who can play well the violin." Another offering for sale in the same paper was "a young healthy Negro fellow . . . who (plays) extremely well on the French horn. A third person begged for the return of a slave who took his fiddle with him."[78]

The slaves had to dance aboard ship, had to dance on the auction block, and had to dance and play upon command to entertain the white folks. Dance could be considered a curse of the black people, and yet it was not. Through dance, a link was maintained with the past, and an escape made temporarily from the present. Dance had always been a part of the black culture, the black experience. There was dancing at Christmas, corn-shucking, and quiltings. There were dances at weddings and funerals; but the most common of all occasions were the Saturday night dances.

Saturday Night Dances

Saturday night was the big night of the week, since most slaves worked a five-and-a-half or six-day week. This left only one night for them to enjoy themselves — depending, of course, on the humor of the master. Frequently dances or frolics were held on the plantation, celebrating no special occasion other than the fact that it was Saturday night.

Georgia Baker, who was a slave in Crawfordville, Georgia, said:

> When dey got behind wid de field wuk, sometimes slaves wuked atter dinner Saddays, but dat warn't often. But, oh, dem Sadday nights! Dat was when slaves got together and danced. George, he blowed de quills, and he sho could blow grand dance music on 'em. Dem Niggers would jus' dance down. Dere warn't no foolishment 'lowed atter 10:00 o'clock no night.[79]

Isabella Dorroh's master was slightly more liberal with his slaves than Mrs. Baker's master:

> Marse Fair let his niggers have dances and frolics on his plantation, and on Saturdays dey danced til 12 o'clock mid-night. Sometimes dey danced jigs, too, in a circle, jumping up and down.[80]

Aunt Hattie Clayton claimed that she

> . . . kin heah de banjers yit. Law me, us had a good time in dem days. Us danced most eb'ry Sattidy night an' us made de rafters shake wid us foots. Lots o' times Ole Missus would come to de dances an' look on. An' whin er brash nigger boy cut a cute bunch uv steps, de menfolks would give 'im a dime or so.[81]

Toby Jones, another ex-slave, said that on Saturday nights the pleasure of talking about Africa, where they had "done what they wanted," was interspersed with dancing.[82]

Frequently the anticipation of the evening's dance would begin early on Saturday, as described by Georgianna Gibbs of Portsmouth, Virginia:

> Sadday only worked half-day, an' dem slaves would sho' carry on 'cause dey was gonna celebrate dat night. Ole Charlie Snipes was de lead man, an' he was de bigges' cut-up in de quarters. We'd all be hoein' pertaters 'long behindst Charlie, an' he would be prancin' an' singin' chunes for us to chop by. Dis de song Charlie used to sing on Saddays:
>
> > "Gwine to de ball
> > Feet de de diddle

Whose gwine to de ball?
Feet de de diddle
Gwine wear a raid gown
Feet de de diddle. . . ."

An' keep it up, puttin' in words an' kickin' de clods in step.
An sometimes dey take it up all over de fiel', jus' a feet de de
diddlin' an' steppin' high an' choppin' right in chune. Ole
overseer was name Barnes, an' he would yell an' cuss an' lash
de slaves near him wid his cowhide, but he couldn't stop all
dem slaves from feelin' good, 'cause dey gonna "set de flo'"
dat night.[83]

Sometimes a slaver owner would not allow frolics on his
own plantation but did permit traveling to the next plantation
where a dance was in progress. Albert Hill, an ex-slave from
Walton County, Georgia, explained how this worked.

Massa . . . don't 'low de parties. But we kin go to Massa
Dillion's place next to us and dey has lots of parties and de
dances. We dances near all night Saturday night, but we has
to stay way in de back where de white folks can't hear us.
Sometimes we has de fiddle and de banjo and does we cut dat
chicken wing and de shuffle![84]

Ellen Campbell, of Augusta, Georgia, told how it was when
slaves from other plantations came to hers for a frolic.

Den sometimes on Sadday night we have a big frolic. De nigger
frum Hammond's place and Phinizy place, Eve place, Clayton
place, D'Laigle place all git togedder fer big dance and frolic.
A lot o' de young white sports used to come dere and push de
nigger bucks aside and dance wid de wenches.[85]

Many amusing things occurred during these sojourns to
nearby plantations. For example, Uncle Hilliard Johnson, who
was seventy-nine years old at the time he was interviewed by
the Alabama Writers' Project in 1937, stated that:

See, I wa'n't so ole, jes' a young boy in slavery time, but I
recall.young Massa told Tom, a young nigger dere, one time
not to go to de frolic.
    "Clean up dem dishes and go ter bed," he say. And Tom
said "Yassuh" but Marse Nep watch Tom th'oo de do' and atter
while Tom slip out and away he went, wid young Massa right
'hin' him. He got dere and foun' Tom cuttin' groun' shuffle big

as anybody. Young Massa called him, "Tom," he say, "Tom, didn't I tell you you couldn't come to dis frolic?" "Yassuh," says Tom, "You sho' did, and I jes' come to tell 'em I couldn't come!"[86]

Neal Upson, another ex-slave, remembered a frolic on his plantation in Oglethorpe County, Georgia, which was attended by slaves from other plantations.

> One time a houseboy from another plantation wanted to come to one of our Saddy night dances, so his marster told him to shine his boots for Sunday and fix his hoss for de night and den he could git off for de frolic. Abraham shined his marster's boots 'til he could see hisself in 'em, and dey looked so grand he was tempted to try 'em on. Dey was a little tight but he thought he could wear 'em, and he wanted to show hisself off in 'em at de dance. Dey warn't so easy to walk in and he was 'fraid he might git 'em scratched up walkin' through de fields, so he snuck his Marster's hoss out and rode to de dance. When Abraham rid up dar in dem shiny boots, he got all de gals' 'tention. None of 'em wanted to dance wid de other Niggers. Dat Abraham was sho struttin' 'til somebody run in and told him his hoss had done broke its neck. He had tied it to a limb and sho 'nough, some way, dat hoss had done got tangled up and hung its own self. Abraham begged de other Nigger boys to help him take de daid hoss home, but he had done tuk deir gals and he didn't git no help. He had to walk 12 long miles home in dem tight shoes. De sun had done riz up when he got dar and it warn't long 'fore his Marster was callin': "Abraham, bring me my boots." Dat Nigger would holler out: "Yas suh! I'se a-comin'." But dem boots wouldn't come off 'cause his foots had done swelled up in 'em. His marster kept on calling and when Abraham seed he couldn't put it off no longer, he jus' cut dem boots off his foots and went in and told what he had done. His marster was awful mad and said he was a good mind to take de hide off Abraham's back. "Go git my hoss quick, Nigger, 'fore I kills you," he yelled. Den Abraham told him: "Marster I knows you is gwine to kill me now, but your hoss is done daid." Den pore Abraham had to out and tell de whole story and his marster got to laughin' so 'bout how he tuk all de gals away from de other boys and how dem boots hurt him dat it looked lak he never would stop. When he finally did stop laughin' and shakin' his sides he said "Dat's all right

"A Negro Ball, Charleston" by Eyre Crowe, in his *With Thackeray in America* (1893)

Abraham. Don't never let nobody beat your time wid de gals."
And dat's all he ever said to Abraham 'bout it.[87]

Most of the dances done at these frolics were the white-influenced dances such as Set Dances, Quadrilles and Cotillions. Some times there were Jigs, cutting "de Pigeon's Wing," and Cake-Walks, but for the most part, the dances appeared to be Set or Figure (Square) Dances. Ring games were also played. Once the white influence took hold, it spread rapidly, as evidenced by the types of dances done in the late 1840's and 1850's. Although the ages of the ex-slaves interviewed by the Works Progress Administration's Federal Writers' Project in 1936-1937 ranged between 70 and 120, very few could remember the dances done in the early 1840's. Most of the ex-slaves talked about the immediate pre-Civil War years, and it is upon this information the conclusion about white influence on the Negro dance is drawn.

Christmas Dances

Christmas preparations, festivities, and customs appear to have varied from one plantation to another. In most cases, the slaves participated to some degree in Christmas festivities. Accounts vary as to the actual preparations the slaves made for the holidays. Christmas was usually a three-day holiday beginning on December 25. Louis Cain, a slave in North Carolina described his part in the festivities as follows:

> On Christmas I'd stand by the gate, to open it for the company, and they'd throw nuts and candy to me. That night all the slaves what could brung they banjoes and fiddles and played for the white folks to dance all night.[88]

A different view was presented by Fanny Smith Hodges. "De white folks had big dances in de Big House and de niggers played de fiddle. Christmas time de slaves had dances."[89]

Christmas morning there was a widespread custom in the South called "Christmas gift." As Charlie Barbour said, "De fust one what said Christmas gift ter anybody else got a gif', so of cou'se we all try ter ketch de marster."[90]

James Bolton described Christmas in Georgia similarly:

Christmas we allus had plenty good sumpin' to eat and we all got togedder and had lots of fun. We runned up to the big house early Christmas mornin' and hollered out: "Mornin', Christmas Gif'!"[91]

Mrs. Nicholas Eppes, a Southern matron, remembered that:

On Christmas morning the white folks were wakened at day-dawn by shouts of "Crismus Gif', Crismus Gif', Marster! Crismus Gif', Mistis." And the cry was repeated until each name in the family had been called; then they betook themselves to the open field, where presently a huge bonfire would blaze while the dark figures circled merrily around it.[92]

According to the Rev. Irving Lowery, this Christmas gift came in the form of a dram of whiskey.[93] On most plantations, however, the adults received a dram plus their one pair of shoes for the year and/or their two sets of work clothes.

Cindy Kinsey, like Mrs. Eppes, remembered dancing around a large bonfire, and continued with a description of the gifts:

When Crismus come, . . . hit be so cole, and Old Marse, he let us make a big fiah, a big, big fiah in de yahd rou' which us live, an us all dance round de fiah, and Ole Missy she brang us Crismus Giff. What war de giff? . . . de mostly red woolen stockings and some times a pair of shoeses, an my wus we proud. An Ole Marse Louis, he giv de real old niggahs, both de mens and de womans, a hot toddy, . . .[94]

Many of the white owners would gather in the quarters to watch the slaves dance. James Lucas, who at one time belonged to Jefferson Davis, stated, "Den on Chris'mus Eve dey was a big dance an' de white folks would come an' see de one what dance de bes'. Marster an' Mistis laugh fit to kill at de capers us cut."[95] Easter Jackson, of Georgia, recalled that at Christmas they had such a good time that "even de 'white folks' turned out for de dances which went 'way into de night."[96]

The Christmas dances were of many types, but in general like those done at the Saturday night frolics. There were Set and Figure Dances, the Virginia Reel, Cotillions, and others of a similar nature. James Avirett described them as follows:

The Christmas festivities were very far from being confined to the white people, as the servants had their full share of it in their own way. This was clearly shown by the notes of music, snatches of songs and the peculiar noise, all their own, of "double shuffle," "the break down," "chi'kin in de bred tray," and the graceful "pigeon wing," followed by their genuine "cake walk."[97]

One interesting description of the slaves' Christmas is found in the diary of Rev. John Pierpont, who wrote of the dance he saw performed on a South Carolina plantation on December 25, 1805.

> Some of them who were native Africans did not join the dance with the others but, by themselves gave us a specimen of the sports and amusements with which the benighted & uncivilized children of nature, divest themselves, before they become acquainted with the more refined & civilized amusements of life. Clapping their hands was their music and distorting their frames into the most unnatural figures and emiting the most hideous noises in their dancing. Jumping, running, and climbing trees was last recourse in the interval and the whole exhibited a scene which might more than compare with the bachannal feasts and amusements of antiquity.[98]

Writing of his life in the South, Jacob Stroyer witnessed the Christmas customs of the slaves:

> . . . they would spend half a day in dancing in some large cotton house or on a scaffold, the master providing fiddlers who came from other plantations if there were none on the place, and who received from $15-20 on these occasions.
> A great many of the strict members of the church who did not dance would be forced to do it to please their masters; the favorite tunes were "The Fisher's Hornpipe," "The Devil's Dream," and "Black-Eyed Susan." No one can describe the intense emotion in the negro's soul on those occasions when they were trying to please their masters and mistresses.[99]

In an article entitled "Recollections of Southern Plantation Life," Henry Ravenel described a Jig which he saw performed by the slaves at Christmas. The excellent picture given by Ravenel makes one wonder if he was seeing St.-Méry's Calenda under another name.

> The jig was an African dance and a famous one in old times, before more refined notions began to prevail. However it was

always called for by some of the older ones who had learned the steps, and never failed to raise shouts of laughter, with applause of the performers. . . .

It was strictly a dance for two, one man and one woman on the floor at a time. It was opened by a gentleman leading out the lady of his choice and presenting her to the musicians. She always carried a handkerchief held at arm's length over her head, which was waved in a graceful motion to and fro as she moved. The step, if it may be so called, was simply a slow shuffling gait in front of the fiddler, edging along by some unseen exertion of the feet, from one side to the other—sometimes courtesying down and remaining in that posture while the edging motion from one side to the other continued.

Whilst this was going on, the man danced behind her, shuffling his arms and legs in artistic style, and his whole soul and body thrown into the dance. The feet moved about in most grotesque manner stamping, slamming, and banging the floor, not unlike the pattering of hail on the housetop. The conflict between brogans and the sanded floor was terrific. It was hard work, and at intervals of five or ten minutes, he was relieved by another jumping into the ring with a shout, and shuffling him out. Whenever any striking attitude was assumed, or unusual antics performed, there would be shouts of applause from the spectators.[100]

The dances of the plantation slaves at Christmas were the same as those performed throughout the year. Other than the custom of "Christmas Gift," very few distinctive traditions existed in the South as they had in the Caribbean. With the exceptions of Wilmington and Hillsborough, North Carolina, where the presence of John Canoe men was noted,[101] neither John Canoe nor Gombay dancers appear to have existed in this country. There must have been some relief from daily work at Christmas time, however, since the stories of dances attended abound.

Corn-Shucking and Quilting Dances

Corn shuckings were exciting times in the lives of most of the plantation slaves: nearly any difference in the dull routine of daily living could be said to be exciting.

'Bout the most fun we had was at corn shuckin's whar they put
the corn in long piles and called in the folkses from the
plantations nigh round to shuck it. Sometimes four or five hunnert
head of niggers 'ud be shuckin' corn at one time. . . . We started
shuckin' corn 'bout dinnertime and tried to finish by sundown
so we could have the whole night for frolic. Some years we 'ud
go to ten or twelve corn shuckin's in one year.[102]

The practice and conduct of the corn shucking appears to
have been fairly standard throughout the South. Accounts from
ex-slaves in a wide region described the corn shuckings almost
identically. Jake McLeod of Timmonsville, South Carolina, remembered:

When corn haulin time come, every plantation haul corn en put
it in circles in front of de barn. Have two piles en point two
captains. Dey take sides en give corn shuckin like dat. Shuck
corn en throw in front of door en sometimes shuck corn all
night.[103]

The purpose of the "corn captain" or "general" was twofold.
First, the two generals agreed that the sizes of the two corn piles
were exactly equal, to the ear; and more important, these generals were to set the tempo of the shucking by their singing.[104]
Singing was carried on in the typical call-response fashion, and
the generals were usually elected on the basis of their ability
to improvise words to songs.

When the piles were equally divided, the two generals
would choose up sides and then would take their places atop
the corn pile. On a signal the shucking began: " . . . de faster
dey sung, de faster dey shucked de corn. Evvy now and den dey
passed de corn liquor 'round, and dat holped 'em to wuk faster.
. . . "[105] When a red ear of corn was found, the custom varied:
Lina Hunter said that "evvy Nigger dat found a red ear got a
extra swig of liquor."[106] In North Carolina, according to Tanner
Spikes, "Dey kisses when dey fin' a red year. . . . "[107] In some
areas both kissing and drinking was awarded the red ear finder.

Atter de sun went down dey wuked right on by de light of pine
torches and bonfires. Dem old pine knots would burn for a long
time and throw a fine bright light. Honey, it was one grand
sight out dar at night wid dat old harvest moon a-shinin', fires
a-burnin', and dem old torches lit up. I kin jus' see it all now,
and hear dem songs us sung.[108]

"The Shucking" by W. L. Shepard, in *Century Magazine* (1882)

"The Dance" immediately following the corn shucking,
by W. L. Shepard, in *Century Magazine* (1882)

Dance on the Plantations 113

As the piles of corn grew smaller and smaller, the generals would begin a song similar to this one:

> Lookin' fur de las' year, [ear]
> Bang-a-ma-lango!
> Lookin' fur de las' year,
> Bang-a-ma-lango!
> Roun' up de co'n, boys,
> Bang-a-ma-lango!
> Roun' up de co'n, boys.
> Ban-a-ma-lango![109]

When the last ear was shucked:

Three or four strapping bucks would lift the young marster to their shoulders and the crowd would fall in line behind. Then they would march three times around the "big house," as the marster's house was always called, singing as they marched, coming to a halt at the tables under the trees, . . . [110]

The food varied from area to area, but sometimes included "hopping-John" (a mixture of black-eyed peas and rice), pumpkin custards, roast pig, hominy, corn bread, and barbecued meat.

Atter supper dey started up playin' dem fiddles and banjoes, and de dancin' begun. White folkses danced de twistification up at de big house but us had reg'lar old breakdowns in a house what Marster let us have to dance in. Wid all dat toddy helpin' em 'long, sometimes dey danced all night, . . . [111]

Some of the tunes mentioned as accompanying the dancing included "Billy in de Low Grounds" or "Turkey in the Straw," so the dances were probably of the Square Dance type.

William Cullen Bryant witnessed a corn-shucking dance in South Carolina and wrote:

One of them took his place as musician, whistling, and beating time with two sticks upon the floor. Several of the men came forward and executed various dances, capering, prancing, and drumming with heel and toe upon the floor, with astonishing agility and perseverance, though all of them had performed their daily tasks and had worked all the evening, and some had walked from four to seven miles to attend the corn-shucking. From the dances a transition was made to a mock military parade, a sort of burlesque of our militia trainings, in which the words of command and the evolutions were extremely ludicrous.[112]

A long-time resident of Georgia described in 1882 the change, through the years, in the types of dances performed.

The dance of late years is a modification of the cotillon, the old-time jig having given place to this, . . . There is a great deal of jig-dancing in these cotillons, and the man who cannot "cut the pigeon-wing" is considered a sorry dancer indeed; but still it purports to be a cotillon. Endurance is a strong point in the list of accomplishments of the dancer, and, other things being equal, that dancer who can hold out the longest is considered the best. The music is commonly made by a fiddler and a straw-beater, the fiddle being far more common than the banjo, in spite of tradition to the contrary.

With the cotillon a new and very important office, that of "caller-out," has become a necessity. The "caller-out," though of less importance than the fiddler, is second to no other. He not only calls out the figures, but explains them through the performance. He is never at a loss, "Genmen to de right!" being a sufficient refuge in case of embarrassment, since this always calls forth a full display of the dancers' agility, and gives much time.[113]

The corn shucking was a plantation institution which was nearly always accompanied by dancing. Quiltings (putting on the backing and tying the quilts or blankets) varied in importance from area to area, and were frequently accompanied by dancing, too. According to ex-slave Mary Wright, on Kentucky plantations these quiltings were all-day affairs.

I remember wen we uster hev big time quilting on dem days we sho had a big time fore we start in de morning wid a water melon feast, den weums quilt erwhile den a big dinner war spread out den after dinner we'd quilt in the evening den supper and a big dance dat night, wid de banjo a humming en us niggers a dancing, . . .[114]

Millie Simpkins, aged 109, recalled quiltings with pleasure.

De only fun de young folks had wuz w'en de ole folks had a quiltin'. W'ile de ole folks wuz wukin' on de quilt de young ones would git in 'nuther room, dance en hab a good time. Dey hab a pot turned down at de do'er ter keep de white folks fum 'yearin' dem.[115]

The "turned down pot" mentioned by this old ex-slave was a common object at slave parties and prayer meetings. The belief was that all the sound would go into the pot and be absorbed, thus keeping the noise from the white owners.

Wedding and Funeral Dances

The common procedure for getting married among the Southern slaves was first to obtain permission from the master to marry, and then to "jump the broom." There was no church ceremony. Jumping the broom as a manner of getting married was of obscure origin. Most frequently the master would hold the broomstick while the couples jumped over it. Some say that the couple had to jump over singly and then jump backward over it, too. If the feet touched the broom during the jump, the marriage would fail.

> At one time a man wanted a wife and all he had to do was to ask old Master for the gal, and then if he said "Yes," all they had to do was to go on and go to bed. . . . It was considered a big wedding to jump over the broomstick but when you just asked for them and go on to bed after getting the permission, then that was a little wedding.[116]

When the slave getting married was either a house slave or a particular pet of the family, a larger wedding might be held.

> When I was quite a girl I went to a colored person's wedding. She was as black as that thing there (card table top) but she was her young master's woman and he let her marry because he could get her anyhow if he wanted her. He dressed her up all in red. . . . After the ceremony there was a dance. She and her husband belonged to the church and they didn't dance, but the rest of them did, and the white men and women were standing 'round looking at them dance all night.[117]

Fannie Berry, recalling her own ceremony, said that she was married in the parlor of the big house. The white folks organized the wedding and reception and during the reception a dance was held. "We could sing in dar, an' dance ol' squar' dance all us choosed, ha! ha! ha! Lord! Lord! I can see dem gals now on dat flo'; jes skippin' an' a trottin'. . . ."[118]

At her wedding, Lina Hunter remembered having two dances:

> Us had a big fine supper and had two dances. Sho' . . . dat
> ain't no mistake. Us did have two dances, one was at home,
> and den us went over to my brother's house whar he give us
> another one and served cake and wine to de weddin' party.
> Atter us drunk dat wine, it warn't no trouble to dance for de
> rest of de night.[119]

Tom Mills remembered attending a wedding where the
dancing continued for three days and three nights.

> We danced these old square dances, what you call the Virginia
> Reel, and the round dances like the Schottische, Polka, waltzes,
> and all them. I was a dancin' fool, I wanted to dance all the
> time. I inherited that from my mother. She was a terrible
> dancer.[120]

Funerals and burials were separate social occasions in
Southern plantation life. When a slave died he was usually
buried immediately or at least within a day. On some plantations all the slaves were relieved from work to attend the burial,
while on others only the bereaved family attended. Because of
the difficulty in obtaining a minister, however, frequently the
official funeral would be held a month or even several months
later. When the preacher finally arrived on the plantation, he
might officiate at several funerals during his stay.

In the early plantation life in this country, the burial was
conducted in much the same manner as in the West Indies,
where the African influence was strongest. According to May
Waring:

> In former times the burial took place at night, and a long
> procession of friends and relatives, bearing lighted torches,
> escorted the corpse to the graveyard. After the interment a
> funeral feast was held, and every one was expected to bring
> from the graveyard and lay before the door a clod of earth, as
> proofs that he had really been to the burial, on pain of being
> haunted by the "sperrit" of the deceased.[121]

There were many burial customs involving dance among
primitive peoples. W. O. E. Oesterley, in discussing some of
these, pointed out that perambulation or dancing around the

corpse or grave served a specific purpose. "The magic circle thus formed keeps away unwelcome spirit-visitors. . . ." or possibly it may have been a "means of 'keeping in' the spirit of the deceased, and thus preventing him from getting abroad and doing mischief."[122]

In the Georgia Sea Islands, one of the areas least influenced by the whites, there was evidence of just this circular sort of dancing about the grave. James Collier, an ex-slave living in Brownville, Georgia, recalled that in the old days "the mourners beat the drum on the way to the cemetery; after arriving they marched around the grave in a ring and beat the drum and shouted. They call it the dead march."[123] Tonie Houston, also of the Sea Islands, remembered:

> Den at duh time fuh buryin, duh drum would beat an all would lay flat on duh groun on dey faces befo duh body wuz placed in duh grave. Den all would rise and dance roun duh grave. Wen duh body wuz buried, duh drum would give signal wen all wuz tuh rise aw fall aw tuh dance aw sing.[124]

Ben Sullivan, of St. Simon's Island, watched a forbidden burial ceremony in his youth.

> Now, ole man Dembo he use tuh beat duh drum tuh duh fewnul, but Mr. Cooper he stop dat. He say he dohn wahn drums beatin roun duh dead. But I watch em had a fewnul. I gits behine duh bush an hide an watch an see wut dey does. Dey go in a long pruhcession tuh duh buryin groun an dey beat duh drums long duh way an dey submit duh body tuh duh groun. Den dey dance roun in a ring an dey motion wid duh hans. Dey sing duh body tuh duh grabe and den dey let it down an den dey succle roun in duh dance.[125]

Most of the references indicating dance among the slave burial traditions have come from the Georgia Sea Islands. Because of their relative seclusion, the Sea Islanders were not influenced by the whites and the church to the same degree that other slaves were. Therefore many unusual customs persisted in the Sea Islands which were not in evidence in other parts of the South. Perhaps these surviving Sea Island traditions retained more of the African influence than can be found elsewhere.

One reference was given, however, by an ex-slave who had

not lived in the Sea Islands. Hamp Kennedy lived in Mississippi during slavery and remembered a wake which he had attended.

> When a nigger died, we had a wake an' dat was diffrunt too
> from what 'tis today.
> At de wake we clapped our han's an' kep' time wid our feet
> — *Walking Egypt*, dey calls hit — an' we chant an' hum all night
> till de nigger was *funeralized*.[126]

There was also one reference to dance being performed around the bed of a dying woman. Remembering the early life as a plantation owner's daughter, Letitia Burwell recalled with horror the death of a favorite slave, Aunt Fanny.

> Several days before her death we were sitting with her mistress
> and master in a room overlooking her house. Her room was
> crowded with negroes who had come to perform their religious
> rites around the death-bed. Joining hands, they performed a
> savage dance, shouting wildly around her bed. This was horrible
> to hear and see, especially as in this family every effort had
> been made to instruct their negro dependents in the truths of
> religion; and one member of the family, who spent the greater
> part of her life in prayer, had for years prayed for Aunt Fanny
> and tried to instruct her in the true faith. But although an
> intelligent woman, she seemed to cling to the superstitions
> of her race.[127]

Slave auctions, Saturday night dances, Christmas, corn shuckings and quiltings, weddings and funerals: these were the special occasions on which black people danced. Some of the most interesting of the slave dances, however, occurred not on such occasions but rather as a part of black religious ceremonies.

▊▌▊▌▊ SACRED DANCE

Shuffling, shuffling, faster and faster; clapping and singing, the room alive with the movement of the ring as it circled round and round. Singing, shouting, getting the spirit; these were the elements basic to the sacred dances of the plantation. Gone were the drums, the gourds, and the clanking iron of the West Indian sacred dance; only the human body provided the sound in singing, shuffling, and clapping. Under the guise of Protestantism, the Ring-Shout retained the characteristics of African sacred dance. The purpose of the Shout was possession, as it was in Voodoo, Shango, and Nañigo. Possession in the Shout, however, was by the spirit of the Lord, not Damballa or Shango.

Dance was frowned upon by many Protestant churches in the South, yet the need to worship in this way had not been eradicated from the plantation slave. The Afro-American was forced to improvise and substitute to fulfill needs acceptably in the eyes of the church.

> . . . in west Africa religious dancing . . . takes place until the devotee is possessed by the deity. There is clapping of hands and beating of drums while spectators gather to see one after another in the circle submitting to the powerful force of the seizure. The drummers do not stop until all who are under the spell have recovered.[128]

Black religious dance in this country was improvised to fit within the structure of the Protestant church. Rhythmic movement was inspired by the beat of well-known hymns. The drums, so important to African and West Indian religious ceremonies, were gone, but the human voice and the sound of shuffling feet were substituted. The clapping remained, the circle was retained, and the seizures of religious possession or ecstasy survived. While not actually dances, the Shout and Ring-Shout were certainly substitutes for the dancing common to African and West Indian religious ceremonies.

The Ring-Shout

The Shout in the United States was a most interesting survival of Africa. The origin of the name "Shout" for this particular ceremony puzzled many scholars. Lydia Parrish, however, gave a plausible explanation. She stated:

> Dr. L. D. Turner has discovered that the Arabic word "Saut" (pronounced like our word "shout"), in use among the Mohammedans of West Africa, meant to run and walk around the Kaaba [Islamic shrine].[129]

Parrish reported that she had seen "Negroes do the holy dance around the pulpit in their churches in such a manner."[130]

The Shout took two forms, depending upon the locale in which it was seen. The first type was the Ring-Shout, found in Georgia and South Carolina. In North Carolina and Virginia, however, a second type was found: a Shout performed as a solo.[131] A book written by Allen, Ware, and Garrison contended that the Ring-Shout was known only in South Carolina and states south. However in their discussion of the Shout the authors reported "an interesting fact that the term 'shouting' is used in Virginia in reference to a peculiar motion of the body not wholly unlike the Carolina shouting."[132]

Allen *et al.* also contended that the Shout was confined to the Baptists,[133] yet Charles Lyell, in a discussion of the effect of Methodism on Negro music and dance said in 1849:

> Of dancing and music the negroes are passionately fond. On the Hopeton plantation above twenty violins have been silenced by the Methodist missionaries, yet it is notorious that the slaves were not given to drink or intemperance in their merry-makings. At the Methodist prayer-meetings, they are permitted to move round rapidly in a ring, joining hands in token of brotherly love, presenting first the right hand and then the left, in which manoeuvre, I am told, they sometimes contrive to take enough exercise to serve as a substitute for the dance, it being in fact, a kind of spiritual *boulanger*, while the singing of psalms, in and out of chapel, compensates in no small degree for the songs they have been required to renounce.[134]

Since the Protestant church branded both the fiddle and the dance as sinful, and the drum had previously been banned due to its inflammatory nature, something had to be substituted "for the rhythm and excitement of the dance that would satisfy and still be 'in the Lord.' "[135] Howard Odum and Guy Johnson reported that marching services were instituted by the church.

> Sometimes they marched two by two, a "sister and brother in the Lord," sometimes they marched singly, and at other times they marched in a general "mix-up." At first they followed a leader to a simple melody, keeping step and working into a rhythmic swing. Then as they became more excited they became more expressive. . . .[136]

Very early in the history of the Shout certain rules were developed. One of the most interesting was that the feet or legs must not cross.

> In the ballroom dance the feet are crossed, while in the "shout," a religious exercise, they are apart. The distinction between religious dancing (the shout) and crossing the feet was early made by the Port Royal Negroes. The shout was apparently used as a sort of safety valve for releasing the rhythmic energies of the plantation Negroes. This they could do in all good conscience and under religious auspices, but to "cross the feet" was sin.[137]

Parrish added that a further restriction had been placed on the Shout.

> The feet are not supposed to leave the floor or to cross each other, such an act being sinful. The shouting proceeds with a curious shuffling, but controlled step which taps out with the heel a resonant syncopation fascinating in its intricacy and precision.[138]

Similarly, Wash Wilson, a slave in Louisiana, explained that: "Us 'longed to de church, all right, but dancin' ain't sinful iffen de foots ain't crossed. Us danced at de arbor meetin's but us sho' didn't have us foots crossed!"[139]

If the feet had to remain in contact with the floor and the legs had to stay uncrossed, it would seem that the movement would be greatly limited. The descriptions of the Ring-Shout, however, prove that much movement occurred despite the peculiar restrictions.

One of the earliest was written by a Northern teacher sent by the Freedman's Bureau to teach the Negroes in the Sea Islands. Miss Laura Towne, in a letter to her family dated April 27, 1862, appeared aghast at the whole proceeding.

> Tonight I have been to a "shout," which seems to me certainly the remains of some old idol worship. The negroes sing a kind of chorus, — three standing apart to lead and clap, — and then all the others go shuffling round in a circle following one another with not much regularity, turning round occasionally and bending the knees, and stamping so that the whole floor swings. I never saw anything so savage. They call it a religious ceremony, but it seems more like a regular frolic to me. . . .[140]

H. G. Spaulding, writing in 1863, looked upon the Shout with more tolerance than did Miss Towne. Spaulding felt that it was "both a natural and a rational expression of devotional feeling."[141] Because Spaulding's description of the Shout was explicit and also one of the first to be published, it has been quoted in length. Spaulding reported that after the praise meeting,

> . . . there usually follows the very singular and impressive performance of the *"Shout,"* or religious dance of the negroes. Three or four, standing still, clapping their hands and beating time with their feet, commence singing in unison one of the peculiar shout melodies, while the others walk round in a ring, in single file, joining also in the song. Soon those in the ring leave off their singing, the others keeping it up the while with increased vigor, and strike into the shout step, observing most accurate time with the music. This step is something halfway between a shuffle and a dance, as difficult for an uninitiated person to describe as to imitate. At the end of each stanza of the song the dancers stop short with a slight stamp on the last note, and then, putting the other foot forward, proceed through the next verse. They will often dance to the same song for twenty or thirty minutes, once or twice, perhaps, varying the monotony of their movement by walking for a little while and joining in the singing. The physical exertion, which is really very great, as the dance calls into play nearly every muscle of the body, seems never to weary them in the least, and they frequently keep up a shout for hours, resting only for brief intervals between the different songs.[142]

Viewing a Shout in the same area as the one seen by Towne, W. C. Gannett observed the steadily growing excitation produced by the continuous movement.

> The "shout" is a peculiar service in which a dozen or twenty jog slowly round a circle behind each other with a peculiar shuffle of the feet and shake of the arms, keeping time to a droning chant and hand-clapping maintained by the by-standers. As the exercise continues, the excitement increases, and occasionally becomes hysterical.[143]

The editors of *The Nation* gave a more detailed picture of the actual type of movement done in the Ring-Shout. They re-

ported in 1867 that when the formal religious meeting had concluded, the benches were pushed back to the wall and

> . . . all stand up in the middle of the floor, and when the
> "sperichil" is struck up, begin first walking and by-and-by
> shuffling round, one after the other, in a ring. The foot is hardly
> taken from the floor, and the progression is mainly due to a
> jerking, hitching motion, which agitates the entire shouter, and
> soon brings out streams of perspiration. Sometimes he dances
> silently, sometimes as he shuffles he sings the chorus of the
> spiritual, and sometimes the song itself is also sung by the
> dancers. But more frequently a band, composed of some of the
> best singers and of tired shouters, stand at the side of the room
> to "base" the others, singing the body of the song and clapping
> their hands together or on the knees. Song and dance are alike
> extremely energetic, and often, when the shout lasts into the
> middle of the night, the monotonous thud, thud of the feet
> prevents sleep within half a mile of the praise-house.[144]

Frances Leigh had a Shout presented in honor of her birth-
day, which she spent on a Georgia plantation. Her impression
was similar to Towne's, and she reported that the only difference
between a Frolic and a Shout was that the participants did not
lift the heel in the religious dance. Leigh described the Shout
she saw:

> First they lit two huge fires of blazing pine logs, around which
> they began to move with a slow shuffling step, singing a hymn
> beginning "I wants to climb up Jacob's ladder." Getting warmed
> up by degrees, they went faster and faster, shouting louder and
> louder, until they looked like a parcel of mad fiends.
>   When, after nearly an hour's performance, I went down to
> thank them, and to stop them—for it was getting dreadful, and I
> thought some of them would have fits—I found it no easy matter
> to do so, they were so excited.[145]

A participant in a Shout, Silvia King stated:

> De black folks gits off down in de bottom and shouts and sings
> and prays. Dey gits in de ring dance. It am jes' a kind of shuffle,
> den it git faster and faster and dey gits warmed up and moans
> and shouts and sings and dances. Some gits 'xhausted and drops
> out and de ring gits closer. Sometimes dey sings and shouts all
> night, but come break of day, de nigger got to git to he cabin.[146]

Other Forms of the Shout

The Shout existed in other forms, although Ring-Shouts were the most common. Benjamin Botkin described other types of Shout:

> One might shout acceptably while standing in one place, the feet either shuffling, or rocking backward and forward, tapping alternately with heel and toe, the knees bending, the body swaying, and the hands clapping. Or the singer could alternately advance and retreat. Not infrequently two singers would shout facing one another in a sort of competition of skill or endurance. Sometimes this was done with great dignity and grace, but not infrequently one of the singers, in an attempt to outdo the other, would introduce body motions that seemed to have very little to do with religion.[147]

Parrish described the form used by a black named Margaret, whom she had observed in the early 1900's during a Shout:

> Margaret . . . could outdo the Ouled Nail Dancers, of Biskra — if she wished. As it was, she wiggled her hips shamelessly, held her shoulders stiff—at the same time thrusting them forward— kept her feet flat on the floor, and, with the usual rhythmic heel-tapping progressed with a real style around the circle. . . . Few young Negroes will do it, and the Big Apple, with the stamp of the white man's approval, has recently been more popular.[148]

Other women Shouters were also observed by Parrish. She stated that:

> Edith . . . every now and then . . . gives a stylized, angular performance as though copying the poses of the figures in Egyptian decorations. The way she holds her arms and hands is perfect . . . statuesque, rhythmic pauses . . . or the pause Gertrude makes with head and shoulders bowed slightly forward, arms held close to her body, elbows bent in a supplicating gesture.[149]

Most of the Shouters with a unique movement style appeared to be women. Botkin said that sometimes one of the women Shouters "would throw her hands high above her head and pivot slowly, or would indulge in steps that seemed to carry with them a reminiscence of more formal dancing seen at one of the balls at the big house."[150]

Finally, there was a type of Shout described by both Botkin and Parrish as "Down to de Mire." Because of the minor differences in the procedure, both descriptions are given.

> In the center of the ring, one member gets down on his knees and, with head touching the floor, rotates with the group as it moves around the circle. The different shouters as they pass, push the head "down to the mire." The several arms reaching out to give a push make an unusually picturesque pattern. The refrain — repeated relentlessly — corresponds in its character and rhythmic beat to that of the drums in a song which accompanied an ominous ceremonial dance seen.[151]

Botkin, on the other hand, described the Shout and conjectured upon its origin as follows:

> . . . one sister . . . lowers herself inch by inch to her knees and then still "lowerer and lowerer" till her head touches the ground while the group sings . . . and then rises slowly to her feet again as they bid her "rise from de mire, higherer." Then another tries, and another. The one who succeeds in performing the feat most slowly and steadily takes great pride, apparently, not only in outdoing her companions but in having definitely established her status as a good church member. I have been told that this is very ancient. If so, it is not impossible that it may be a relic of a primitive test based on the sound psychological principle that fear or a guilty conscience affects the perfect correlation of nerve and muscle.[152]

Other Forms of Sacred Dance

The church tried desperately to break people of the great "sin" of dancing. From the pulpit, dance was regularly denounced. The horror of transgression of the dance was even versified by the Reverend Anthony Binga, a Baptist minister:

> The careless soul who goes to balls,
> And seeks for pleasures there,
> With sinful conduct, says to all,
> In Heav'n I have no share.

Remember those, and those alone,
  Who spurn the dancing floor,
Shall dwell with God upon his throne,
  And live forevermore.
Come then, each one, and make the vow,
  Before the God of all,
And say to saints who hear you now:
  "I'll ne'er attend a ball." [153]

It was little wonder that many ex-slaves succumbed to the pressure of the church. One remembered her days of sin with horror:

> I was a wild thing when I was young. Why I was more on dancing than my Ole Missy, and she taught me to dance, too. Well, after I joined the church, I didn't have no desire to dance no more. You know, I really object to Christians dancing. . . . I see sin in dancing. I prayed to the Lord to take that off of me, and he sho' did. For a long time, you know, I could not git religion 'cause I wanted to dance, yessirree, I know what my religion done for me; it cleared my soul for all eternity. Dancing was an injury to me, I see it now. . . .
> The only real sin I committed, I was a dancer, that's all. [154]

Alice Alexander, an ex-slave in Louisiana, recalled:

> I was a sinner and loved to dance. I remembuh I was on the floor one night dancing and I had four daughters on the floor with me and my son was playing de music—that got me! I jest stopped and said I wouldn't cut another step and I haven't. I'm a member of the Baptist Church and been for 25 or 30 years. I jined 'cause I wanted to be good 'cause I was an awful sinner. [155]

In spite of such strong sentiments, dancing persisted and grew. It was impossible to rid a people totally of such a basic element in their culture. To Bishop Daniel Payne's disgust, he found the Shouts continuing even as he preached against them. Payne found it nearly impossible to reason with a young man who was leading a Shout. This young man insisted that "'Sinners won't get converted unless there is a ring. . . . At camp meeting there must be a ring here, a ring there, a ring over yonder, or sinners will not get converted.'" [156]

At camp meetings, revivals and "experience" meetings some semblance of dance continued in spite of the preaching against it. Frederika Bremer, in her 1853 book, notes that she saw just a glimpse of a dance in progress at a camp meeting. She looked into a tent and saw that

> women were dancing "the hold dance" for one of the newly-converted. This dancing, however, having been forbidden . . . ceased immediately. . . . I saw merely a rocking movement of women, who held each other by the hand in a circle. . . .[157]

Bremer, in her wide travels, also attended an "African" church service in New Orleans. There were obvious cases of possession, according to her description of the service.

> The words were heard, "Yes, come Lord Jesus!" . . . and they who thus cried aloud began to leap—leaped aloft with a motion as of a cork flying out of a bottle, while they waved their arms and their handkerchiefs in the air, as if they were endeavoring to bring something down, and all the while crying aloud, "Come, oh come!" And as they leaped, they twisted their bodies round in a sort of cork-screw fashion, and were evidently in a state of convulsion; sometimes they fell down and rolled in the aisle, amid loud, lamenting cries and groans.[158]

Some of these sacred dances were given rather curious names. There apparently existed a "Flower Dance." Frederick Davenport said:

> A correspondent writes me that there is a church near Appomattox in which great preparations are made for the revival every September. Certain of the membership are specially trained for the "flower dance," which takes place in the church and is not very unlike the red-Indian variety in its form and in its effect.[159]

Both Davenport and B. Z. Goldberg commented on a dance known as the "Roper Dance." Goldberg reported:

> In Alabama, the faithful find even greater exhaltation in the Roper dance. Here, too, they march about a central figure that claps his hands and shouts vociferously until he falls into a trance of ecstasy. This is a signal for the entire congregation to join in embraces between the opposite sexes, with all the force of maddened passion. The dance is commenced at the close of the services and continues indefinitely.[160]

Several authors mention a dance called "Rocking Daniel." Newbell Puckett was told about the Rocking Daniel by Matthew

"The Sabbath among Slaves," from Bibb, *Narrative of the Life and Adventures of Henry Bibb, an American Slave* (1850)

Butler, of Columbia, Mississippi. Butler said that it "'Take a little bit of man to rock Dan' . . . and one of my informants tells me that this type of dance is sometimes of a sensual nature where men and women dance together." [161]

Davenport described the Rocking Daniel in greater detail, saying:

> The Primitive Orthodox Zion Baptist Church at Yamassee, Florida, holds a "Rocking Daniel" dance at the close of the communion service. The membership forms a circle in front of the pulpit, in the centre of which the leader stands. They move around the leader in single file, singing "Rock Daniel, rock Daniel, rock Daniel till I die." Then they fall into regular step and gesticulate and shout till exhaustion intervenes. [162]

Pearl Primus, with her extensive knowledge of the dance of Africa, summarized the sacred dance of the Afro-American. She first wrote of "ecstatic possession" as she herself had seen it:

> This seems to be the general pattern. First the shaking of the head, slowly, side to side. Then faster, emphasizing like the mutterings of a volcano — growing, growing — tossing back and forth till suddenly passion bursts like a bomb — tearing the voice with its heat, stamping the feet madly to the earth, beating the arms convulsively upward. [163]

Primus then concluded with the following statement:

> In emotional impact, group reaction, rhythms, tempos, actual steps and the exact precision with which they were done, dance in the Southern Baptist Churches so closely resembles the dance in Africa as to leave no doubt in the mind that the American form emerged from the African. [164]

▢:▢:▢ NOTES FOR CHAPTER 3

1. John Smith, *The Generall Historie of Virginia, New England, and the Summer Isles: with the Names of the Adventurers, Planters, and Governours from their first beginning an: 1584 to this present 1626. With the Proceedings of those Severall Colonies and the Accidents that Befell them in all their Journyes and Discoveries. Also the Maps and Descriptions of all those Countryes,*

their Commodities, people, Government, Customs, and Religion yet knowne, Divided into Sixe Bookes (London: I. D. and I. H. for Michael Sparkes, 1627), p. 126.

2. Alexander Brown, *The First Republic in America. An Account of the Origin of this Nation, Written from the Records then (1624) Concealed by the Council, rather than from the Histories then liscensed by the Crown* (Boston: Houghton, Mifflin and Company, 1898).

3. *Ibid., The Genesis of the United States. A Narrative of the Movement in England, 1605–1616, which Resulted in the Plantation of North America by Englishmen, Disclosing the Contest Between England and Spain for the Possession of the Soil Now Occupied By the United States of America; Set Forth Through a Series of Historical Manuscripts now first printed together with a reissue of rare contemporaneous tracts, accompanied by bibliographical memoranda, notes, and Brief Biographies collected, arranged, and edited by Alexander Brown. With 100 Portraits, Maps and Plans* (2 vols.; London: William Heinemann, 1890), II, 987.

4. Elizabeth Donnan, *Documents Illustrative of the History of the Slave Trade to America* (4 vols.; Washington, D.C.: Carnegie Institution of Washington, 1931), IV, 3.

5. For other viewpoints on the earliest importation of slaves to the United States, see: Wesley Frank Craven, *Dissolution of the Virginia Company. The Failure of a Colonial Experiment* (New York: Oxford University Press, 1932), pp. 130-31; Susan M. Kingsbury, ed., *The Records of the Virginia Company of London. The Court Book from the Manuscript in the Library of Congress* (4 vols.; Washington, D.C.: Government Printing Office, 1906), I, 115; Edward D. Neill, *Virginia Vetusta, During the Reign of James the First. Containing Letters and Documents Never Before Printed. A Supplement to the History of the Virginia Company* (Albany, N.Y.: Joel Munsell's Sons, 1885), pp. 112-15; and John R. Spears, *The American Slave Trade. An Account of Its Origin, Growth and Suppression* (New York: Charles Scribner's Sons, 1900), pp. 1-7.

6. The year 1619 was, of course, not the first time that Africans landed on the mainland of the United States, since one of Columbus's captains was a man of African descent. Other blacks had been in various exploring parties in the United States. However, 1619 marks the beginning of the transportation of large numbers of blacks to this country.

7. Robert Beverley, *The History and Present State of Virginia, in Four Parts* (London: R. Parker, 1705), p. 35.

8. *Ibid.*, p. 36.

9. John Hope Franklin, *From Slavery to Freedom, A History of Negro Americans*, Vintage Books (3d ed.; New York: Random House, 1969), pp. 80-81.

10. Melville J. Herskovits, *The Myth of the Negro Past* (Boston: Beacon Press, 1958), p. 138.

11. Georgia Writers' Project, *Drums and Shadows; Survival Studies Among the Georgia Coastal Negroes* (Athens: University of Georgia Press, 1940), p. 130. Because the interviews in this and other Federal Writers' Project works were

written in dialect, the original statement has been quoted exactly as written, no matter how poor the attempt at capturing the dialect.

12. *Ibid.*, p. 122.

13. *Ibid.*

14. *Ibid.*, p. 100.

15. See also interviews with James Collier, Tonie Houston, and James Lewis in the Georgia Writers' Project, *Drums and Shadows*, pp. 62, 66-67, 148.

16. Federal Writers' Project, *Slave Narratives. A Folk History of Slavery in the United States From Interviews with Former Slaves* (17 vols.; Washington, D.C.: Typewritten Records Prepared by the Federal Writers' Project, 1936-1938), XVI, Part 3, p. 219.

17. *Ibid.*, IV, Part 1, p. 227.

18. *Ibid.*, XIV, Part 2, p. 169.

19. *Ibid.*, IV, Part 1, p. 99.

20. *Ibid.*, X, 267.

21. Thomas Jefferson, *Notes on the State of Virginia; Written in the Year 1781, some what corrected and enlarged in the Winter of 1782* (Paris: 1782), p. 257.

22. *Ibid.*

23. A(rthur) G(ranville) Bradley, *Sketches from Old Virginia* (London: Macmillan Co., Ltd., 1897), p. 255.

24. Federal Writers' Project, *Slave Narratives*, I, 111.

25. John Davis, *Travels of Four Years and a Half in the United States of America; During 1798, 1799, 1800, 1801, and 1802.* (Bristol: R. Edwards, 1803), pp. 379-80.

26. Fisk University, Social Science Institute, *Unwritten History of Slavery, Autobiographical Accounts of Negro Ex-Slaves*, Social Science Source Document No. 1 (Washington, D.C.: NCR Microcard Editions, 1968), p. 64.

27. Virginia Writers' Project, *The Negro in Virginia* (New York: Hastings House, 1940), p. 91.

28. Duke of Saxe-Weimar Eisenach Bernhard, *Travels Through North America During the Years 1825 and 1826* (2 vols.; Philadelphia: Carey, Lea and Carey, 1828), I, 212.

29. For a few of the other examples see, for example, John Frederick H. Claiborne, "A Trip Through the Piney Woods," *Publications of the Mississippi Historical Society*, IX,ed. Franklin L. Riley (Oxford, Miss.: Mississippi Historical Society, 1906), pp. 535-38, for a delightful account of Old John and the wolves; G. W. Featherstonhaugh, *Excursion Through the Slave States from Washington on the Potomac to the Frontier of Mexico; with Sketches of Popular Manners and Geological Notices* (New York: Negro Universities Press, 1968 [originally published by Harper and Brothers, 1844]), p. 127; and Caroline Gilman, *Recollections of a New England Bride and of a Southern Matron* (Rev. ed.; New York: G. P. Putnam and Co., 1852), p. 116.

30. Edwin A. Davis, *Plantation Life in the Florida Parishes of Louisiana, 1836-1846 as Reflected in the Diary of Bennett H. Barrow* (New York: Columbia University Press, 1943), p. 381.

31. William Howard Russell, *My Diary North and South* (Boston: T. O. H. P. Burnham, 1863), p. 126.

32. Robert Russa Moton, *Finding a Way Out. An Autobiography* (College Park, Md.: McGrath Publishing Co., 1969 [orig. pub. by Doubleday, Page, and Co., 1920]), pp. 18-19.

33. Lyle Saxon, Edward Dreyer, and Robert Tallant, comp.; Works Progress Administration Louisiana Writers' Project, *Gumbo Ya-Ya* (Boston: Houghton, Mifflin Company, 1945), p. 240.

34. Federal Writers' Project, *Slave Narratives*, VIII, 66-67.

35. *Ibid.*, XVI, Part 1, p. 38.

36. *Ibid.*, XIV, Part 3, p. 73.

37. *Ibid.*, XVI, Part 3, p. 160.

38. Virginia Writers' Project, *Negro in Virginia*, p. 92.

39. Federal Writers' Project, *Slave Narratives*, XVI, Part 1, p. 243.

40. *Ibid.*, XVI, Part 4, p. 34.

41. *Ibid.*, IV, Part 2, p. 348.

42. Virginia Writers' Project, *Negro in Virginia*, p. 89.

43. Tom Fletcher, *The Tom Fletcher Story — 100 Years of the Negro in Show Business* (New York: Burdge and Company, Ltd., 1954), p. 19.

44. *Ibid.*

45. Georgia Writers' Project, *Drums and Shadows*, pp. 186-87.

46. Guion Griffis Johnson, *A Social History of the Sea Islands: With Special Reference to St. Helena Island, S.C.* (Chapel Hill, N.C.: University of North Carolina Press, 1930), p. 143.

47. Georgia Writers' Project, *Drums and Shadows*, p. 131. See also interviews with Emma and Mary Stevens, Alec Anderson, and Jane Lewis in Georgia Writers' Project, *Drums and Shadows*, pp. 115, 141, and 148.

48. Edward C. L. Adams, *Congoree Sketches, Scenes from Negro Life in the Swamps of the Congoree and Tales by Tad and Scip of Heaven and Hell with Other Miscellany* (Chapel Hill, N.C.: University of North Carolina Press, 1927), p. 52.

49. Lydia Parrish, *Slave Songs of the Georgia Sea Islands* (New York: Creative Age Press, Inc., 1942), p. 111.

50. Georgia Writers' Project, *Drums and Shadows*, p. 115. A note in parentheses by the interviewer of these two women says that "all efforts failed to persuade the women to describe these dances. Evidently thinking of the antics of their neighbors at the recent dance they laughed repeatedly, shaking their heads and nudging one another but refusing to be cajoled into a demonstration."

51. Virginia Writers' Project, *Negro in Virginia*, pp. 92-93.

52. *Ibid.*, p. 93.

53. Federal Writers' Project, *Slave Narratives,* XI, Part 1, p. 191.

54. *Ibid.,* XVI, Part 1, p. 158; and Part 2, p. 238.

55. *Ibid.,* IV, Part 2, p. 151.

56. Georgia Writers' Project, *Drums and Shadows,* p. 251.

57. Katherine Dunham, "The Negro Dance," in Sterling A. Brown, Arthur P. Davis, and Ulysses Lee, eds., *The Negro Caravan* (New York: Dryden Press, 1941), pp. 997-98.

58. William B. Smith, "The Persimmon Tree and the Beer Dance," *Farmer's Register,* VI (April, 1838), cited in Bruce Jackson, ed., *The Negro and his Folklore in Nineteenth-Century Periodicals,* Vol. XVIII, Publications of the American Folklore Society, Bibliographical and Special Series, Kenneth S. Goldstein, ed. (Austin: University of Texas Press, 1967), p. 7.

59. John Allan Wyeth, *With Sabre and Scalpel* (New York: Harper Bros., 1914), p. 59.

60. *Ibid.,* p. 62.

61. Federal Writers' Project, *Slave Narratives,* XIV, Part 1, p. 242; and Part 3, p. 278.

62. W. C. Handy, ed., *Blues: An Anthology* (New York: Albert and Charles Boni, 1926), p. 34.

63. Thomas W. Talley, *Negro Folk Rhymes* (New York: Macmillan Company, 1922), p. 9.

64. *Ibid.*

65. Maria Leach, ed., *Funk and Wagnalls Standard Dictionary of Folklore, Mythology and Legend* (New York: Funk and Wagnalls Company, 1949), I, 477.

66. Austin Steward, *Twenty-Two Years a Slave, and Forty Years a Freeman: Embracing a Correspondence of Several Years While President of Wilberforce Colony, London, Canada West* (Rochester, N.Y.: William Alling, 1857), pp. 20-21.

67. Dunham, "The Negro Dance," in Brown, Davis, and Lee, *Negro Caravan,* p. 998.

68. Federal Writers' Project, *Slave Narratives,* XVI, Part 2, p. 58.

69. *Ibid.,* IV, Part 3, p. 124.

70. *Ibid.,* IX, 145.

71. Harold Courlander, *Negro Folk Music, U.S.A.* (New York: Columbia University Press, 1963), p. 200.

72. Talley, *Negro Folk Rhymes,* p. 1.

73. Federal Writers' Project, *Slave Narratives,* IV, Part 3, p. 1.

74. Mr. Chapman, interviewed by Mrs. Ophelia Settle Egypt, for Fisk University, Social Science Institute, *Unwritten History of Slavery,* p. 33.

75. Orland Kay Armstrong, *Ole Massa's People: The Old Slaves Tell Their Story* (Indianapolis: Bobbs-Merrill Company, 1931), p. 261.

76. Solomon Northup, *Twelve Years a Slave* (London: Sampson Low Son and Company., 1853), p. 79.

77. Virginia Writers' Project, *Negro in Virginia*, p. 36.

78. *Ibid.*, p. 35.

79. Federal Writers' Project, *Slave Narratives*, IV, Part 1, p. 46.

80. *Ibid.*, XIV, Part I, p. 327.

81. *Ibid.*, I, 76.

82. *Ibid.*, XVI, Part 2, p. 249.

83. Virginia Writers' Project, *Negro in Virginia*, pp. 65-66.

84. Federal Writers' Project, *Slave Narratives*, XVI, Part 2, p. 137.

85. *Ibid.*, IV, Part 4, p. 224.

86. *Ibid.*, I, 229.

87. *Ibid.*, IV, Part 4, pp. 64-66.

88. *Ibid.*, XVI, Part 1, p. 186.

89. *Ibid.*, IX, 69.

90. *Ibid.*, XI, Part 1, p. 74.

91. *Ibid.*, IV, Part 1, p. 100.

92. Mrs. Nicholas Ware Eppes, *The Negro of the Old South. A Bit of Period History* (Chicago: Joseph G Branch Publishing Company, 1925), p. 9.

93. Irving E. Lowery, *Life on the Old Plantation in Ante-Bellum Days* (Columbia, So. Carolina: State Company, 1911), p. 65.

94. Federal Writers' Project, *Slave Narratives*, III, 193.

95. *Ibid.*, IX, 92.

96. *Ibid.*, IV, Part 2, p. 300.

97. James Battle Avirett, *The Old Plantation; How We Lived in Great House and Cabin Before the War* (New York: F. Tennyson Neely Company, 1901), p. 193.

98. A. C. Ravitz, "John Pierpont and the Slaves' Christmas," *Phylon*, XXI, No. 4 (Winter, 1960), 384.

99. Jacob Stroyer, *My Life in the South* (3d ed.; Salem: Salem Observer Book and Job Print, 1885), pp. 47-48.

100. Henry William Ravenel, "Recollections of Southern Plantation Life," *Yale Review*, XXV, No. 4 (June, 1936), 768.

101. Dougald MacMillan, "John Kuners," *Journal of American Folklore*, XXXIX, No. 151 (1926), 53-57.

102. Federal Writers' Project, *Slave Narratives*, IV, Part 1, pp. 99-100.

103. *Ibid.*, XIV, Part 3, p. 160.

104. Some excellent examples of corn-shucking songs appear in an article entitled "Folk-Lore and Ethnology. American Folk-Lore Society," *Southern Workman*, XXIV, No. 2 (February, 1895), 30-32.

105. Federal Writers' Project, *Slave Narratives*, IV, Part 2, pp. 266-67.

106. *Ibid.*, p. 267.

107. *Ibid.*, XI, Part 2, p. 310.

108. *Ibid.*, IV, Part 2, p. 267.

109. "Cornshuckin' Down South," *New York Sun*, Monday, November 11, 1895, p. 4.

110. *Ibid.*

111. Federal Writers' Project, *Slave Narratives*, IV, Part 2, p. 284.

112. William Cullen Bryant, *Letters of a Traveller; or, Notes of Things Seen in Europe and America* (New York: George P. Putnam, 1850), pp. 86-87.

113. David C. Barrow, "A Georgia Corn Shucking," *Century Magazine*, XXIV, No. 6 (October, 1882), 878.

114. Federal Writers' Project, *Slave Narratives*, VII, 62.

115. *Ibid.*, XV, 67.

116. Fisk University, Social Science Institute, *Unwritten History of Slavery*, p. 99.

117. *Ibid.*, pp. 3-4.

118. Federal Writer's Project, *Slave Narratives*, XVII, 2.

119. *Ibid.*, IV, Part 2, pp. 270-71

120. *Ibid.*, XVI, Part 3, p. 91.

121. May A. Waring, "Mortuary Customs and Beliefs of South Carolina Negroes," *Journal of American Folklore*, VII, No. 27 (October-December, 1894), 318.

122. W. O. E. Oesterley, *The Sacred Dance* (2d ed.; Brooklyn, N.Y.: Dance Horizons, Inc., n.d.), p. 222.

123. Georgia Writers' Project, *Drums and Shadows*, p. 62.

124. *Ibid.*, p. 67.

125. *Ibid.*, p. 180.

126. Federal Writers' Project, *Slave Narratives*, IX, 86.

127. Letitia M. Burwell, *A Girl's Life in Virginia Before the War* (New York: Frederick A. Stokes Company, 1895), p. 163.

128. R. A. Schermerhorn, *These Our People. Minorities in American Culture* (Boston: D. C. Heath and Company, 1949), p. 90.

129. Parrish, *Slave Songs of the Georgia Sea Islands*, p. 54.

130. *Ibid.*

131. *Ibid.*

132. William Francis Allen, Charles Pickard Ware, and Lucy McKim Garrison, *Slave Songs of the United States* (New York: A. Simpson and Co., 1867), p. xiv.

133. *Ibid.*, p. xv.

134. Charles Lyell, *A Second Visit to the United States of North America* (2 vols.; New York: Harper and Brothers, 1849), I, 269-70.

135. Howard W. Odum and Guy B. Johnson, *The Negro and His Songs* (Hatboro, Pa.: Folklore Associates, Inc., 1964), p. 34.

136. *Ibid.*

137. Mason Crum, *Gullah; Negro Life in the Carolina Sea Islands* (Durham, N.C.: Duke University Press, 1940), p. 140.

138. Parrish, *Slave Songs of the Georgia Sea Islands*, p. 85.

139. Federal Writers' Project, *Slave Narratives*, XVI, Part 4, p. 198.

140. Rupert Sargent Holland, ed., *Letters and Diary of Laura M. Towne, Written from the Sea Islands of South Carolina, 1862-1884* (Cambridge: Riverside Press, 1912), p. 20.

141. H. G. Spaulding, "Under the Palmetto," *Continental Monthly*, IV (July-December, 1863), 197.

142. *Ibid.*

143. W. C. Gannett, "The Freedmen at Port Royal," *North American Review*, CI (July, 1865), 10.

144. "The Magazines for June," *The Nation*, May 30, 1867, p. 433.

145. Frances Butler Leigh, *Ten Years on a Georgia Plantation Since the War* (London: Richard Bentley and Son, 1883), p. 59.

146. Federal Writers' Project, *Slave Narratives*, XVI, Part 2, p. 294.

147. Benjamin A. Botkin, *A Treasury of Southern Folklore* (New York: Crown Publishers, 1949), p. 658.

148. Parrish, *Slave Songs of the Georgia Sea Islands*, p. 55.

149. *Ibid.*, pp. 55-56.

150. Botkin, *Treasury of Southern Folklore*, p. 658.

151. Parrish, *Slave Songs of the Georgia Sea Island*, p. 71.

152. Botkin, *Treasury of Southern Folklore*, p. 659.

153. Anthony Binga, *Binga's Addresses on Several Occasions.* (2d ed.; Printed by Vote of the General Association of Virginia, 190?), pp. 11-12.

154. Fisk University, Social Science Institute, *Unwritten History of Slavery*, p. 10.

155. Federal Writers' Project, *Slave Narratives*, XIII, 6.

156. Daniel Alexander Payne, *Recollections of Seventy Years* (2d ed.; New York: Arno Press and the New York Times, 1968 [Originally published in Nashville, Tenn.: A.M.E. Sunday School Union, 1888]), p. 254.

157. Fredrika Bremer, *The Homes of the New World; Impressions of America*, trans. by Mary Howitt (2 vols.; New York: Harper and Brothers, 1853), I, 311.

158. *Ibid.*, II, 236.

159. Frederick Morgan Davenport, *Primitive Traits in Religious Revivals* (New York: Macmillan Company, 1917), pp. 54-55.

160. B. Z. Goldberg, *The Sacred Fire: The Story of Sex in Religion* (New York: Horace Liveright, 1930), p. 306.

161. Newbell Niles Puckett, *Folk Beliefs of the Southern Negro* (New York: Negro Universities Press, [originally published by the University of North Carolina Press, 1926] 1968), pp. 543-44.

162. Davenport, *Primitive Traits*, p. 55. An excellent description of religious services for Father Divine, held in Old Fort, Georgia, is given in the Georgia Writers' Project, *Drums and Shadows*, p. 11. In the same source is another, quite detailed piece on a service held for Bishop Grace, p. 48.

163. Pearl Primus, "Primitive African Dance (and Its Influence on the Churches of the South)," in Anatole Chujoy, ed., *The Dance Encyclopedia* (New York: A. S. Barnes, 1949), p. 389.

164. *Ibid.*

4

DANCE
IN THE NORTH,
ON THE LEVEE,
& IN NEW ORLEANS

▣:▣:▣ While the Breakdowns, the Cake-Walk, fiddle playing, and patting Juba were taking place on the plantations there were Afro-American dances in other places as well.

Those who lived in many of the towns of the South were giving dances. One of these slaves dances, performed to the sound of banjo and singing, was witnessed by Nicholas Cresswell in Maryland in 1774. According to Cresswell, the songs were as droll as the sound of the music and the words sung generally dealt with the treatment of slaves by masters and mistresses "in a very satirical stile and manner. . . . Their Dancing is most violent exercise, but so irregular and grotesque I am not able to describe it."[1]

Cresswell may have seen a hip-shaking dance, since what he saw defied description in conventional terms. However, the more closely the Negroes imitated the dances of the whites, the more acceptable their dances were to white observers, and the easier for them to describe.

Two visitors to Montgomery, Alabama, happened upon a Christmas ball given by slaves who had been granted a week's holiday. The Turnbulls were quite impressed and surprised with what they saw, reporting:

> . . . who do you think we saw? About sixty negroes, all dancing except four or six, to the music of two violins and a banjo, as hard as they could dance! The men seemed to shuffle on their heels in a wonderful manner, and a negro was standing on a chair, calling out what figures were to be performed in the Virginia Reel, which they were dancing.[2]

◼◼◼◼ DANCE IN THE NORTH

In Northern cities with Negro populations there was frequent mention of dance. In New York the Dutch burghers and farmers sometimes traveled forty or more miles to the city, "where they witnessed African dances performed by Negroes."[3]

In New York's early days, a makeshift drum, made of an eel pot covered with sheepskin, was played with the bare hands. According to one report:

> A Negro named Charley, who was said to be 125 years old, "did most of the beating," to the strains of strange African songs. He also led the dance, when young and old, black and white, "would put in the double-shuffle heel-and-toe break-down."[4]

One of the popular congregation spots for Manhattan Negroes in the early 1700's was the Catherine Market. After selling the products of their masters, many slaves would gather to dance and the bystanders would frequently pay to see the Negroes do a Jig or Breakdown.

> The dancers brought along boards, called shingles, upon which they performed. These wooden planks were usually about five or six feet long and equally wide, and were kept in place during the dancing by four of their companions. Rarely in their deft "turning and shying off" did they step from the boards. Music was usually provided by one of their party, who beat a

rhythm with his hands on the sides of his legs. Tom-toms were also used in their music making.[5]

Contests evolved from these gatherings and the "city slaves" (those residing in Manhattan) were usually considered much better than the "country slaves" (those who lived on Long Island or New Jersey).

> The most famous dancers were Ned (Francis), "a little wiry Negro slave"; Bob Rawley, who called himself "Bobolink Bob"; and a chap named Jack, who was referred to as "smart and faithful." The talent displayed by these dancers made one awed observer exclaim that the blacks danced as though they "scarcely knew they were in bondage."[6]

Washington Irving referred to the dancing of the Long Island Negroes in his book *Salmagundi*. In his description of Tucky Squash, Irving said, "and as to dancing, no Long Island negro could shuffle you 'double-trouble,' or 'hoe corn and dig potatoes' more scientifically. . . ."[7]

One of the most interesting holidays on which Negro dance occurred was that called Pinkster Day. It was held on Pentecost or Whitsunday and, according to Alice Earle, the name was derived from the Dutch word for Pentecost.[8] This holiday was most popular in upstate New York, although Pinkster Day celebrations were seen in New York City as well.

James Fenimore Cooper, describing Pinkster Day in New York City in 1757, said that it was "the great Saturnalia of New York blacks."[9] The Pinkster fields, according to Cooper, were, at that time "up near the head of Broadway, on the common."[10] He continued his description:

> . . . nine-tenths of the blacks in the city, and of the whole country within thirty or forty miles, indeed, were collected in thousands in those fields, beating banjoes, singing African songs, drinking, and worst of all, laughing in a way that seemed to set their very hearts rattling within their ribs. . . . The features that distinguish a Pinkster frolic from the usual scenes at fairs, and other merry-makings, however, were of African origin. . . . Among other things, some were making music, by beating on skins drawn over the ends of hollow logs, while others were dancing to it, in a manner to show that they felt infinite delight. This, in particular, was said to be a usage of their African progenitors.[11]

Joel Munsell, a noted historian of Albany, New York, said that one of the most glorious festivals of his boyhood was Pinkster Day, held on the site now known as Capitol Hill. He described Pinkster Day, or Week, as a Negro festival in which:

> The dances were the original Congo dances, as danced in their native Africa. They had a chief, Old King Charley. The old settlers said Charley was a prince in his own country, and was supposed to have been one hundred and twenty-five years old at the time of his death![12]

Munsell continued:

> As a general thing the music consisted of a sort of drum, or instrument constructed out of a box with sheep skin heads, upon which old Charley did most of the beating, accompanied by singing some queer African air. Charley generally led off the dance, when the Sambos and Philises, juvenile and antiquated, would put in the double-shuffle heel-and-toe breakdown, in a manner that would have thrown Master Diamond and other modern *cork*-onions somewhat in the *shade*.[13]

Munsell quoted at length from Dr. James Eights, who had observed the Pinkster Day festivities in his youth, when slavery had existed in New York State. Eights recalled that:

> The dance had its peculiarities, as well as everything else connected with this august celebration. It consisted chiefly of couples joining in the performances at varying times, and continuing it with their utmost energy until extreme fatigue or weariness compelled them to retire and give space to a less exhausted set; and in this successive manner was the excitement kept up with unabated vigor, until the shades of night began to fall slowly over the land, and at length deepen into the silent gloom of midnight.
>
> The music made use of on this occasion, was likewise singular in the extreme. The principal instrument selected to furnish this important portion of the ceremony was a symmetrically formed wooden article usually denominated [by] an *eel*-pot, with a cleanly dressed sheep skin drawn tightly over its wide and open extremity. . . . Astride this rude utensil sat Jackey Quackenboss, then in his prime of life and well known energy, beating lustily with his naked hands upon its loudly sounding head, successively repeating the ever wild, though euphonic cry of *Hi-a-bomba, bomba, bomba*, in full harmony

with the thumping sounds. These vocal sounds were readily taken up and as oft repeated by the female portion of the spectators not otherwise engaged in the exercises of the scene, accompanied by the beating of time with their ungloved hands, in strict accordance with the eel-pot melody.

Merrily now the dance moved on, and briskly twirled the lads and lasses over the well trampled green sward; loud and more quickly swelled the sounds of music to the ear, as the excited movements increased in energy and action; rapid and furious became their motions, as the manifold stimulating potions, they from time to time imbibed, vibrated along their brains, and gave a strengthening influence to all their nerves and muscular powers; copiously flowed the perspiration, in frequent streams from brow to heel, and still the dance went on with all its accustomed energy and might; . . .[14]

King Charley, according to Eights, was born in Angola, Guinea, and was brought early to the United States and sold. Eights remembered him as "tall, thin, and athletic; and although the frost of nearly seventy winters had settled on his brow, its chilling influence had not yet extended to his bosom. . . ."[15] King Charley was of stately form and could easily be found in the midst of the dancing throng. He was characterized as

. . . moving along with all the simple grace and elastic action of his youthful days, now with a partner here, and then with another there, and sometimes displaying some of his many amusing antics, to the delight and wonderment of the surrounding crowd, and which, as frequently, kept the faces of this joyous multitude broadly expanded in boisterous mirth and jollity.[16]

According to William Walsh, the dance done at these Pinkster Day festivities in Albany was called the Toto Dance, and it "partook so largely of savage license that it gradually came to be shunned by respectable whites."[17] At some time between 1811 and 1813, the Albany Common Council prohibited any further celebration of Pinkster Day because of its licentious nature. Munsell speculated the prohibition came about because of the death of King Charley, since, after his death, "it was observed with less enthusiam, and finally sank into . . . a low nuisance. . . ."[18]

Could it be that this dance was the Calenda? The accompa-

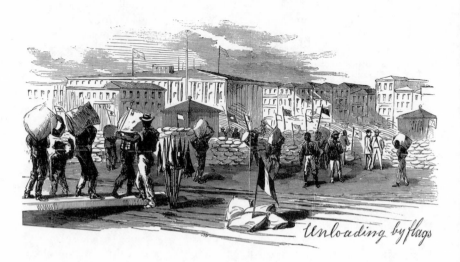

"Unloading by flags" on the levee in New Orleans, in *Harper's Weekly* (1867)

niment of drums sounds much like those of the Calenda, as does the cry which goes with the drums: "Hi-a-bomba, bomba, bomba!" As described, the dance movements themselves sound much like those of the Calenda danced in New Orleans, about which more will be said in a later section.

While dances or balls were held among the free Negroes living in the towns and cities, they were patterned so closely after the dance of the whites that they will not be discussed here. However, there was one geographical area where both plantation dances and new dances were performed. This was the immense region along the Ohio and Mississippi Rivers down to New Orleans.

▩▩▩ DANCE ON THE LEVEE

Many slaves not immediately needed for work on plantations were hired out by their owners to the highest bidders. The term of service was generally one year and wages earned went to the master. Many slaves were hired out as carpenters, blacksmiths, or cobblers, and some as roustabouts or stevedores on the Mississippi River. Immediately following the Civil War nearly all of the river jobs were handled by former slaves directly from the plantations of the South. It was no wonder that the customs of the plantation followed them.

Life on the river was rough, as were the towns where the giant paddlewheelers put in to port. Most of these ports had specific sections for the steamboating Negroes, and dance halls soon sprang up in many of these areas.

One of the major ports was at the head of the river: Cincinnati—a rough-and-tumble town from which the flatboats started down the Ohio to the Mississippi. Lafcadio Hearn wrote one of the most vivid descriptions of levee life and the Bucktowns and Sausage Rows which sprang up wherever the Negroes settled.

Writing about a Cincinnati dance hall, Hearn described the best of the dancers as "a stumpy little roustabout named Jem Scott who is a marvelous jig-dancer and can waltz with a tumbler full of water on his head without spilling a drop."[19]

Hearn wrote that "you may see the old slave dances nightly performed to the air of some ancient Virginia-reel in the dance houses of Sausage Row, or the 'ball-rooms' of Bucktown."[20] As the musicians struck up a lively tune:

> Sometimes the men advancing leaped and crossed legs with a double shuffle, and with almost sightless rapidity. Then the music changed to an old Virginia reel, and the dancing changing likewise, presented the most grotesque spectacle imaginable. The dancing became wild; men patted juba and shouted, the negro women danced with the most fantastic grace, their bodies describing almost incredible curves forward and backward; limbs intertwined rapidly in a wrestle with each other and with the music; the room presented a tide of swaying bodies and tossing arms, and flying hair.[21]

The Coonjine, another of the river dances, was still "re-membered in scattered areas through the Antilles"[22] as late as 1963. In the Caribbean, however, the dance was performed during carnival time and called the "Counjaille," while in the United States the Coonjine was performed on the waterfront by the black roustabouts and "was a rhythmic shuffle affected to expedite loading and unloading. . . ."[23] Harold Courlander reported:

> The term Counjaille, or Coonjine, is still used in southern United States waterfront areas to mean moving or loading cotton, an activity that once, in all probability, was accompanied by Counjaille-type songs and rhythms. Negro children on the docks and levies sang such songs as:
>
> > Throw me a nickel, throw me a dime
> > If you want to see me do the Coonjine.[24]

According to Mary Wheeler, the Coonjine was a combination of song and dance connected with freight handling on the steamboats.

> The "plank walk" springs under a heavy weight or even under the lighter step of the rouster when he trots back again empty handed for more freight. To avoid jarring, the feet are dragged along the stage plank accompanied by a song that takes its rhythm from the shuffling feet and swaying shoulders.[25]

Allen, Ware, and Garrison mentioned the Coonjai and described it as a sort of Minuet.[26] Unfortunately, although the authors apparently saw the dance, they described the musical accompaniment rather than the movements.

To the sound of "Throw me a nickel, throw me a dime,/ If you want to see me do the coonjine," the big river boats moved on down the teeming, twisting Mississippi to the city of New Orleans, the capital of Voodoo in the United States, the home of Congo Square, and later the birthplace of ragtime and jazz.

▣▣▣ DANCE IN NEW ORLEANS

Dansé Calinda, boudoum, boudoum!
Dansé Calinda, boudoum, boudoum![27]

Congo Square! The Calenda, Bamboula and Congo. Bras de Coupé. Marie Laveau. Voodoo. St. John's Eve. Bayou St. John. Cordon Bleu. Gens de couleur. Quadroon balls. Early morning duelling and bullfights. Bienville and Andrew Jackson. The Spanish, French, and Americans. Creoles and Cajuns. The Mississippi River and Lake Pontchartrain. Ragtime and jazz. Cotton and sugar cane, and the drum.

All of these were associated with what has been called America's most interesting city: a city with a long and varied past—the Crescent City—New Orleans. Most Americans know something of the Mardi Gras and have an inkling that gumbo is something to eat. They have heard of Rampart and Canal Streets, the French Quarter, Storyville, Louis Armstrong, and Jelly Roll Morton. Young people may be familiar with Dr. John and Night-trippers and have heard "When the Saints Go Marchin' In." Yet how many people are aware of the Code Noir or the Kaintucks, gris-gris or root healers, the Salle d'Orléans, or the system termed placee? These, too, were a part of New Orleans.

New Orleans. Founded by a French Canadian in 1718, the city was settled by both French Canadians and immigrants from France. The city passed from French to Spanish rule in 1762, an occupation which was to last until 1800. During this period there "were occasional migrations of Spanish-speaking people from the West Indies . . . ."[28] The language, customs, and allegiance, however, remained French.

The presence of both the French and the Spanish in New Orleans created two circumstances which greatly influenced the Negro dance there. First, the Roman Catholic church was the major religious influence in the city, and second, there was a close relationship between Louisiana and the West Indies.

> During the Spanish occupation the government was administered from Madrid by way of Havana; under French rule, ships stopping at New Orleans called also at other colonial ports in the West Indies, and planters from Martinique, Guadeloupe, Haiti, and Santo Domingo frequently exchanged visits with the Louisiana settlers, comparing notes on agricultural and other problems.[29]

The Catholic church, it will be remembered from the discussion of dance in the West Indies, had a more tolerant attitude toward the Negro as a human being than did most Protestant sects. Of all the southern states, Louisiana was the only one to be primarily Catholic. The climate was right, then, for the syncretism of Catholic and African beliefs, resulting in Voodoo, upon the arrival of the Haitians and Santo Domingans. The wealthy West Indian planters and their slaves immigrated to New Orleans in the midst of the slave uprisings on the islands. These insurrections — outgrowths of the French Revolution — had an interesting effect on New Orleans. In 1800, France regained control of New Orleans in the midst of the Haitian war for independence. When the French army was defeated by Toussaint l'Ouverture's successor, Haitian Jean-Jacques Dessalines, in 1803, Napoleon decided to sell the whole of the Louisiana Territory to the United States.

When Haiti declared her independence in 1804, all white inhabitants were either killed or forced to flee, many taking their slaves with them. More than 8,000 immigrants arrived from Santo Domingo. "In the late spring of 1809, thirty-four vessels from Cuba set ashore in New Orleans more than 5,500 immigrants; about one-third of whom were white."[30] It was no wonder, then, that so many of the black West Indian dances also became known in New Orleans.

Negro slaves had been present in the city of New Orleans from its first settlement, and the influx of West Indians added greatly to the Negro population. Even prior to this immigration, New Orleans distinguished between three classes of people: blacks, whites, and gens de couleur. Although the Code Noir issued at Versailles in 1724 forbade intermarriage or concubinage between whites and slaves, the law was obviously not enforced. The class distinction arose from the fact that the offspring of these unions rarely became slaves, "since it was customary when a white man had a child by a Negro slave for him to free the mother, whereby the child was freed automatically."[31] Elsewhere in the South the white masters frequently sold their own mulatto offspring.

Under the Code Noir, however, these free mulattos could marry neither slaves nor whites but were restricted to their own class. There was one alternative open to a woman: to become the mistress of a white man. Since one drop of white blood was sufficient to allow freedom from slavery and to open the doors to an education, the holding of property and all privileges *except* marriage, many such women chose the course of concubinage. This choice contributed to one of the most unusual social phenomena in the South — the Quadroon Ball.

Quadroon Balls

A quadroon, according to one of the more illustrious visitors to New Orleans, His Highness Bernhard, Duke of Saxe-Weimar Eisenach, was "the child of a mestize mother and a white father, as a mestize is the child of a mulatto mother and a white father."[32] (His Highness has, however, described an octoroon, since a quadroon is one-quarter Negro and the offspring of a mulatto mother and white father.) During his visit to New Orleans, Bernhard gained an insight into the condition of the quadroon women. He reported:

> The quadroons are almost entirely white: from their skin no one
> would detect their origin; nay many of them have as fair a
> complexion as many of the haughty creole females. . . .
> Formerly they were known by their black hair and eyes, but at
> present there are completely fair quadroon males and females.
> Still, however, the strongest prejudice reigns against them on
> account of their black blood, and the white ladies maintain, or

affect to maintain, the most violent aversion towards them. Marriage between the white and coloured population is forbidden by the law of the state. As the quadroons on their part regard the negroes and mulattoes with contempt, and will not mix with them, so nothing remains for them but to be the friends, as it is termed, of the white men.[33]

The origin of the quadroon balls is obscure, but one author reported that in 1790, when New Orleans had a population of eight thousand, there were fifteen hundred unmarried women of color. "The fairest of these were trained and educated by their mothers and presented each year at the quadroon balls."[34]

It is unfortunate that Lyle Saxon did not state the source of his population figures, since Oliver Evans (also undocumented) wrote that "in 1769 there were only 31 *gens de couleur* in New Orleans; twenty years later, there were 1,700."[35] It seems highly improbable that out of a total of 1,700 people, 1,500 would be women. In any event, a considerable number of unmarried women of color probably did exist, and undoubtedly many were introduced to white male society at the quadroon balls.

There is a wealth of material written by observers of these dances, since the balls were considered one of the sights of New Orleans. It was a rare male visitor who did not attend at least one quadroon ball during his stay in the city. The balls, for the most part, were sponsored by the quadroon women in order to provide a setting for proper introductions and selection. Eventually promoters took over the sponsorship of the balls and a higher admission price was charged.

The only women present were free women of color, and none but upper-class white men were allowed to attend. Mulatto men and lower-class whites were excluded. Because of the constant brainwashing by the white supremecists, many quadroon women agreed that an extra-marital affair with a white man was preferable to marriage with a mulatto. This fact, of course, caused a problem for the quadroon males because of the dearth of mulatto women, yet few of the observers of the balls appeared concerned with this difficulty.

Thomas Ashe, an Englishman visiting New Orleans in November, 1806, pointed out distinctions and biases based on color, and was one of the first to remark on the great beauty of the quadroon women.

Notwithstanding the beauty and wealth of these women, they
are not admitted . . . to the white assemblies. They have
therefore a ball-room of their own, which is well attended,
and where as beautiful persons and as graceful dancing is
witnessed, as in any other assemblies of the sort whatever.
A distinction subsists between ladies of colour of a very
singular sort; those who are but one remove from the African
cast, are subordinate to those who are from two to three, or
more. . . .[36]

Another early tourist, Major Amos Stoddard, was also impressed by the great beauty of these mulatto women and found
them ladies in behavior as well. "Gentlemen of distinction
resort to their ball-rooms, and other places of amusement, where
decency and decorum maintain their empire."[37]

As early as 1807, the following announcement appeared in
the French language newspaper, the *New Orleans Moniteur:*

Grand Bal Paré
Dans la Salle Chinoise
Mardi prochain, 25 Aout 1807
Pour les Blancs & Femmes de Couleur libres.[38]

From the Pontchartrain Ballroom comes the following announcement directed to the women of the community regarding
the plan to be open on Sunday:

The DRESS AND MASKED BALLS will be given in the
following order.
For White persons—SUNDAYS, Tuesdays, Thursdays and
Fridays.
For Quadroons—Mondays, Wednesdays, and Saturdays.[39]

The quadroon balls were frequently held in the Condé
Street Ballroom until they were moved to the newly completed
St. Phillip Theatre in 1810. Some time in the 1830's, they were
again moved, this time to the Orleans Ballroom or the *Salle
d'Orleans.*[40] When the balls declined in popularity, the ballroom
was purchased by the Catholic Church and used as a convent.

An English actor visiting New Orleans described the setting of a ball he attended:

On entering the *salle,* which was a large, handsome, well-
lighted room, I found a company, consisting of about a hundred,

or a hundred and twenty—male and female; the dancing was at its height; but as orderly, decent, and well-conducted as in the *salons* of Paris or New York.

Around the room, ranged on divans, in solemn state, watchful as owls, and wrinkled as Hecate, sat the mothers of these Odalisques; vigilant she-dragons, with Argus-eyes, keeping sentinel-watch over their daughters' charms.[41]

Arrangement for obtaining one of the quadroons as a mistress were not made with the woman herself but rather with her mother. A rather unsympathetic observer, G. Featherstonhaugh, described the process as follows:

When one of them attracts the attention of an admirer, and he is desirous of forming a liaison with her, he makes a bargain with the mother, agrees to pay her a sum of money. . . . She is now called "une placee"; those of her caste who are her intimate friends give her fetes, and the lover prepares "un jolie appartement meuble." With the sole exception of "going to church," matters are conducted very much as if a marriage had been celebrated. . . . [She] brings up sons to be rejected by the society where the father finds his equals, with daughters to be educated for the Quadroon balls, and destined to pursue the same career which the mother has done. Of course it frequently happens that the men get tired of them and form new liaisons; when this happens they return to their mother. . . .[42]

Duels were apparently rather commonplace at these balls, and many times were brought about by some visitor paying too much attention to the favorite of a native or Creole. Edward Sullivan remarked that upon entering the salon

. . . you are requested to leave your IMPLEMENTS; by which is meant your bowie knives and revolvers, and you leave them as you would your overcoat on going into the opera, and get a ticket with their number, and on your way out they are returned to you.[43]

Notwithstanding the checking of weapons, the duels continued. Warner stated that "duels were common incidents . . . of the *cordon bleu* balls . . . the affairs of honor being settled by a midnight thrust in a vacant square behind the cathedral, or adjourned to a more French daylight encounter at 'The Oaks,' or 'Les Trois Capalins.' "[44]

Because of the great emphasis on the "refinements" of the white race, it was only natural that the dances performed at the balls would be those of white society. Since anything Negroid or African was frowned upon by the gens de couleur, and since many of the quadroons had been educated in Paris, the dances were the same as those of a salon in France. Sullivan, having heard of the beauty and graceful dancing of the quadroons, made a specific point of attending some of the balls.

> I certainly was not disappointed. Their movements are the most
> easy and graceful that I have ever seen. They danced one
> figure, somewhat resembling the Spanish fandango, without
> castanets, and I never saw more perfect dancing on any stage.[45]

If a quadroon ball and a white masked ball happened to be held on the same evening, many of the white gentlemen, after making their appearance at the masked ball

> . . . hasted away to the quadroon ball . . . where they amused
> themselves more, and were more at their ease. This was the
> reason why there were more ladies than gentlemen present
> at the [white] ball, and that many were obliged to form
> "tapestry."[46]

His Highness, Karl Bernhard, felt it his duty to attend a quadroon ball in order to gain an understanding of the customs and habits of the people of New Orleans. Yet, at the same time, he was fearful of incurring the wrath of the white women at the masked ball. In a state of indecision, he finally accepted the offer to attend the quadroon ball where:

> I must avow I found it much more decent than the masked ball.
> . . . Cotillions and waltzes were danced, and several of the
> ladies performed elegantly. I did not remain long there that I
> might not utterly destroy my standing in New Orleans, but
> returned to the masked ball and took great care not to disclose
> to the white ladies where I had been. I could not however
> refrain from making comparisons, which in no wise redounded
> to the advantage of the white assembly. As soon as I entered
> I found a state of formality.
>   If it be known that a stranger, who has pretensions to mix
> with good society, frequents such balls as these, he may rely
> upon a cold reception from the white ladies.[47]

The quadroon ball has been discussed at length not because of its contribution to the understanding of the Negro dance but rather as a social phenomenon. Its interest lies in the complete rejection of any African heritage whatsoever, and the total acceptance of white habits and values.

Assumption of the habits and values of the white masters certainly occurred on the plantations, particularly among the house-slaves, but never had this acceptance been as complete nor as widespread as it was among the quadroons. The whites who patronized the quadroon balls seem not to have considered the position of the quadroons an unjust one; had their condition been thought shameful or disreputable, certainly the distinguished visitors to New Orleans would not have been taken to the dances.

Evans summed up the future and the fate of these proud gens de couleur with the advent of Jim Crowism after the Civil War:

> Before the Jim Crow legislation, a single drop of white blood had been considered sufficient to guarantee special privileges for its possessor; from then on, a single drop of Negro blood was considered sufficient to deprive him of them.[48]

Congo Square

Boudoum, boudoum! The giant hollow drums reverberated through the Sunday stillness, played by men who sat astride them and pounded with hands and feet. The sound of sticks hitting smaller drums, the clanging of triangles, and the thudding, pounding echo of hundreds of bare feet slapping the hard earth; these sounds, intermixed with the roar of a wounded bull, the screech of circus baboons; the panting dissonance of the Indians playing a wild game of racquette; these were the sounds of Congo Square.

In the early days of New Orleans, northwest of the city limits, stood an open field known as Congo Plains. Here the Indians and Creoles would play racquette, a ball game. Here also, in the summer months, the circus and menagerie of M. Gaëtano of Havana[49] would set up its tents. At various points in time, bullfights, cockfights, and dogfights were also held here.

"The Love Song" drawn in Congo Square, New Orleans,
by E. W. Kemble, in *Century Magazine* (1886)

The most famous event here, however, was the Sunday dance of the Negro slaves.

No one seems to know when the black dances on Congo Plains, or, as it eventually was called, Congo Square, began; but they continued well into the 1880's. Herbert Asbury, a New Orleans historian, speculated that the dances began in 1805, after the takeover of New Orleans by the Americans. He reported that the Americans relaxed the strict laws of the French and Spanish which prohibited the assemblage of Negroes for any reason.[50]

Asbury's thesis appears highly unlikely since the Americans were not noted for their leniency toward either dance or Negro slaves. A further statement by Asbury that "dances were held in many places, including an abandoned brickyard in Dumaine Street,"[51] a well-known Voodoo meeting place, makes one wonder if there was Voodoo connected with the dances of Congo Square. While Asbury does not state that the Congo Square dances were Voodoo rites, his reference to the "abandoned brickyard" in a chapter dealing with Congo Square might lead one to believe that the dances were associated with Voodoo. While some of the dancers in Congo Square were undoubtedly believers in Voodoo, the dances were not Voodoo dances. Unlike Congo Square dances, Voodoo rites were never open to the public.

More than likely Asbury was correct in his assumption that the Congo Square dances began after the Louisiana Purchase. However, this was not because the Americans relaxed the laws but because they passed even more prohibitive legislation. From 1800 to 1810 a great number of West Indians emigrated to New Orleans, bringing with them Voodoo, with all its secret ceremonies and dances. The whites naturally feared secret Negro meetings and frowned upon the clandestine meetings of the Voodoo believers. As the belief in Voodoo spread among the Negro slaves, however, the number of secret meetings and dances increased. The fear of the whites developed to the point that in 1817, the New Orleans City Council felt it necessary to pass the following legislation:

> Article 6. The assemblies of slaves for the purpose of dancing or other merriment, shall take place only on Sundays, and solely in such open or public places as shall be appointed by the Mayor, and no such assembly shall continue later than sunset, and all

slaves who shall be found assembled together on any other day than Sunday, or who, even on that day, shall continue their dances after sunset, shall be taken up by the officers of police, constables, watchmen or other white persons, and shall be lodged in the public jail, where they shall receive from 10 to 25 lashes, on a warrant from the mayor or a justice of the peace; the clauses specified in the preceding article against all owners or occupants of houses or lots, forming or tolerating such assemblies on their premises, being in full force against them.[52]

The site designated by the Mayor was Congo Square, where the slaves could be kept under careful surveillance for any signs of plotting against the whites. This certainly did not reflect the relaxation of laws assumed by Asbury, but was in fact a stringent protective device for the whites. By what means Congo Square came to be used for these dances is of little consequence, however. The fact remained that Sunday dances were held in Congo Square before 1817 and they developed to such a point after the legislation that they were second only to the quadroon balls as a tourist attraction.

The parallels existing in the Congo Square dances seen by Christian Schultz in 1807 and the dances of the Jamaican Negroes observed by Sir Hans Sloane one hundred years earlier[53] are striking. Both authors described the primary instrument of accompaniment as a long, narrow drum, and the dancers as being ornamented with animal tails. Schultz, in his description of a Sunday afternoon in New Orleans, found the whole affair rather unpleasant.

In the afternoon, a walk in the rear of the town will still more astonish their bewildered imaginations with the sight of twenty different dancing groups of the wretched Africans, collected together to perform their *worship* after the manner of their country. They have their own national music, consisting for the most part of a long kind of narrow drum of various sizes, from two to eight feet in length, three or four of which make a band. The principal dancers or leaders are dressed in a variety of wild and savage fashions, always ornamented with a number of tails of the smaller wild beasts, and those who appeared most horrible always attracted the largest circle of company.[54]

The African drum, transported to the West Indies but prohibited in most parts of the United States, seems to have re-emerged in Congo Square. Nearly every observer of the Congo Square dances mentioned the instruments used for accompaniment, the prime sound being provided by a variety of drums. Benjamin Latrobe described four different types of drums he saw used on a Sunday afternoon:

> An old man sat astride of a cylindrical drum about a foot in diameter, & beat it with incredible quickness with the edge of his hand & fingers. The other drum was an open staved thing held between the knees and beaten in the same manner. They made an incredible noise.[55]

At a short distance from this first group of musicians was a second with differently constructed drums:

> One . . . consisted of a block cut into something of the form of a cricket bat with a long & deep mortice down the center. This thing made a considerable noise, being beaten lustily on the side by a short stick. In the same orchestra was a square drum, looking like a stool, which made an abominably loud noise; . . .[56]

The square, stool-like drum must have been a type of gombay or gumbé drum, already mentioned as accompanying the Jamaican John Canoes.

George Washington Cable gave the most complete description of the construction and method of playing the Congo Square drums.

> The drums were very long, hollowed, often from a single piece of wood, open at one end and having a sheep or goat skin stretched across the other. One was large, the other much smaller. The tight skin heads were not held up to be struck; the drums were laid along on the turf and the drummers bestrode them, and beat them on the head madly with fingers, fists, and feet,—with slow vehemence on the great drum, and fiercely and rapidly on the small one. Sometimes an extra performer sat on the ground behind the larger drum, at its open end, and "beat upon the wooden sides of it with two sticks." The smaller drum was often made from a joint or two of very large bamboo, in the West Indies where such could be got, and this is said to be the origin of its name; for it was called the *Bamboula.*[57]

According to Joseph Howard, "the musician who played the Bambula in Louisiana was called the 'Bel Tambouye.' The instrument was a keg with a cowhide head . . . ."[58]

Other instruments mentioned were the calabash or gourd rattle, the triangle, an animal jawbone scraped by a stick or metal object, a banjo or set of quills, and a curious instrument described by Latrobe as

> . . . a stringed instrument which no doubt was imported from Africa. On the top of the finger board was the rude figure of a man in a sitting posture, & two pegs behind him to which the strings were fastened. The body was a calabash. It was played upon by a very little old man, apparently eighty or ninety years old.[59]

As for the dances performed in Congo Square, Latrobe found little pleasing to the eye, and remarked that "I have never seen anything more brutally savage, and at the same time dull & stupid, than this whole exhibition."[60] What Latrobe saw in 1819 to cause his repulsion was a group of five or six hundred Negroes

> . . . formed into circular groupes [sic] in the midst of four of which, which I examined (but there were more of them), was a ring, the largest not ten feet in diameter. In the first were two women dancing. They held each a coarse handkerchief extended by the corners in their hands, & set to each other in a miserably dull & slow figure, hardly moving their feet or bodies.
> Most of the circles contained the same sort of dancers. One was larger, in which a ring of a dozen women walked, by way of dancing, round the music in the center.[61]

The dance of the two women had many of the same characteristics as the Chica dance of the West Indies described by St.-Méry.[62]

Another early spectator of the Congo Square dances was cited by Lyle Saxon as having recorded the following entry in his diary on April 11, 1817:

> I witnessed a negro dance. Their postures and movements somewhat resembled those of monkeys. One might, with a little imagination, take them for a group of baboons. Yet as these poor wretches are entirely ignorant of anything like civilization (for their masters with-hold everything from them that in the least might add to the cultivation of their minds), one must not be surprised at their actions. The recreation is at least natural and they are free in comparison with those poor wretches, the slaves of their passions.[63]

Many appeared disturbed by the types of dances occurring in Congo Square, yet the attraction these held for tourists was steadily increasing; so much so that in *Paxton's Directory of 1822*, a guide to the City of New Orleans, a condemnation of Circus Square was felt necessary. (Circus Square was the proper name for the area, while Congo Square was the popular designation.)

> The Circus PUBLIC SQUARE, is planted with trees, and enclosed, and is very noted on account of its being the place where the Congo and other negroes DANCE, CAROUSE AND DEBAUCH ON THE SABBATH, to the great injury of the morals of the rising generation; it is a foolish custom, that elicits the ridicule of most respectable persons who visit the city; but if it is not considered good policy to abolish the practice entirely, surely they could be ordered to assemble at some place more distant from the houses, by which means the evil would be measurably remedied.[64]

As time passed, attitudes seemed to change toward the "carousing and debauching" of Congo Square. An article in the *New Orleans Daily Picayune*, dated 1846, called the activities "novel, interesting, and highly amusing,"[65] a far cry from the "brutally savage" of Latrobe. The *Daily Picayune* account continued:

> In various parts of the square a number of male and female negroes assemble, dressed in their holiday clothes, with the very gayest bandana handkerchiefs upon the heads of the females, and, accompanied by the thumping of a banjo or drum . . . perform the most grotesque African dances. . . . At one time there will be five or six upon the ground dancing and breaking down for dear life, and occasionally laughing and screaming with delight, while the companions who surround them find it difficult to sit or stand still, so infectious is the desire to dance among the blacks.[66]

Describing the sights and sounds of Congo Square which inspired Louis Gottschalk to compose some of his early works, his biographer, Henry Didimus, stated:

> Upon entering the square the visitor finds the multitude packed in groups of close, narrow circles, of a central area of only a few feet; and there in the center of each circle, sits the musician, astride a barrel. . . . there, too, labor the dancers male and

"The Bamboula" drawn in Congo Square, New Orleans,
by E. W. Kemble, in *Century Magazine* (1886)

female. . . . The head rests upon the breast, or is thrown back upon the shoulders, the eyes closed, or glaring, while the arms, amid cries, and shouts, and sharp ejaculations, float upon the air, or keep time, with the hands patting upon the thighs, to a music which is seemingly eternal.

The feet scarce tread wider space than their own length; but rise and fall, turn in and out, touch first the heel and then the toe, rapidly and more rapidly, till they twinkle to the eye, which finds its sight too slow a follower of their movements.[67]

The dance being done, according to Didimus, was the Bamboula, although his description was unlike any other and sounded more nearly like a Don Pétro dance. Marshall and Jean Stearns stated that the heel and toe step described above was one of the basic steps of Afro-American dance, the "flat-footed Shuffle."[68]

The most widely quoted description of the activities of Congo Square is that of George Washington Cable. While of a romanticized nature, Cable's writings do suggest the environment surrounding Congo Square. His descriptions of the dances themselves, however, are so sketchy and general as to make one wonder whether he had personally observed them. His bias and condescending attitude toward the Negro is obvious, and he frequently appears to include things because they fit a stereotyped view of the Negro.

The first dance Cable attempted to describe was the one described above by Didimus: the Bamboula. There seems to have been no record of a dance by this name in Africa or the West Indies until quite recent times (and then only in the Virgin Islands). The smaller of the two drums used for the dance, however, was called the bamboula or baboula, perhaps giving the dance its name.

To the two drums were added the clapping of the surrounding circle and a type of call and response singing. Cable stated that

A sudden frenzy seizes the musicians. The measure quickens, the swaying, attitudinizing crowd starts into extra activity, the female voices grow sharp and staccato, and suddenly the dance is the furious Bamboula.

Now for the frantic leaps! Now for frenzy! Another pair are in the ring! The man wears a belt of little bells. . . . And still another couple enter the circle. What wild—what terrible delight! The ecstasy rises to madness; one—two—three of the dancers fall—*bloucoutoum! boum!*—with foam on their lips and are dragged out by arms and legs from under the tumultuous feet of crowding newcomers. The musicians know no fatigue; still the dance rages on. . . .[69]

The preceding passage strengthened the common impression of the savagery and wildness of the Negro. Cable's choice of words—"frenzy," "furious," "frantic," "wild," "madness"—reinforced the commonly held beliefs of many whites. He went beyond credibility, however, with his statement of the dancers falling "with foam on their lips." In a social gathering of this type, it was an extreme rarity for one person, much less three people, to become possessed. Apparently Cable was trying to make a connection between Congo Square and Voodoo rituals. This attempt casts further doubt on Cable's credibility.

The Bamboula was characterized by greater group movement than usual: Cable characterized it as "attitudinizing and swaying" and Henry Castellanos said that "one might have imagined a group of serpents interlacing one another. . . ."[70] Castellanos stated:

What made these dances so odd and peculiar was the vibratory motions of the by-standers, who in different styles contributed to the lascivious effect of the scene, while the principal characters were going through the figures. The performances were usually greeted by the vociferous acclamations and clapping of hands of all the assistants, and toward the close there followed such a whirling of the whole mass that one might have imagined a group of serpents interlacing one another, and casting a charm upon the throng of dancers and spectators.[71]

Castellanos described the Congo Square scene almost as if he were writing a guidebook for white tourists.

Attired in their picturesque and holiday dresses, they would gather by thousands in the afternoon under the shade of old sycamores, and romp in African revelries to the accompaniment of the tam-tam and jaw-bones. Nothing could be more interesting than to see their wild and grotesque antics, their mimicry of courtly dances in the act of making an obeisance, and the dances peculiar to their country. In the midst of the ludicrous contortions and gyrations of the Bamboula, not unlike those performed in the equally famous Voudou dance, they would sing with a pleasing though somewhat monotonous rhythm strange Creole songs, the burden of one of which, I remember, was:

DANSE CALINDA, bou doum, bou doum.[72]

It is strange that in the midst of dancing the Bamboula, the song would be "Danse Calinda." Perhaps what was being viewed was not the Bamboula at all, but the well-known Calenda.

The Calenda was undoubtedly danced in Congo Square, since it was a favorite dance of all the West Indies. Cable stated that the Calenda "was the favorite dance all the way from there [Louisiana] to Trinidad."[73] However, he also continued that, due to the lascivious nature of the Calenda, it was banned from Congo Square sometime around 1843.

From his description, it is doubtful if Cable actually saw the Calenda being danced. He described it as "a dance of multitude, a sort of vehement cotillion. The contortions of the encircling crowd were strange and terrible, the din was hideous."[74]

Other dances mentioned by Cable in connection with Congo Square were the Babouille, the Cata (or Chacta), the Counjaille, the Voudou, and the Congo. Of the latter two, Cable said, "to describe [them] would not be pleasant."[75]

The Congo dance, described by St.-Méry as the Chica, was also performed in Congo Square. The name "Congo" was probably given to the dance in this country because it was performed particularly by the Congolese. Even though the observers described the dance under a variety of names, the movement descriptions leave no doubt that the dance being done was the Chica-Congo.[76]

Asbury, in an attempt to distinguish between the Bamboula and the Calenda, actually described neither of them, but rather the Chica-Congo. It is interesting that Asbury changed the words of the old chant from "Dansé Calinda" to "Dansez Bamboula" to prove his point.

> The movements of the Calinda and the Dance of the Bamboula were very similar, but for the evolutions of the latter the male dancers attached bits of tin or other metal to ribbons tied about their ankles. Thus accoutered, they pranced back and forth, leaping into the air and stamping in unison, occasionally shouting "Dansez Bamboula! Badoum! Badoum!" while the

women, scarcely lifting their feet from the ground, swayed their bodies from side to side and chanted an ancient song as monotonous as a dirge.[77]

Later, Asbury quoted a *New York World* correspondent's account of the dancing in Congo Square. When the reporter asked some women to recite the words of a chant they were singing, he was told that he would not understand them since, *"C'est le Congo!"* The dance described resembles the Chica-Congo even more closely than that described by Asbury:

> . . . women did not move their feet from the ground. They only writhed their bodies and swayed in undulatory motions from ankles to waist. . . . The men leaped and performed feats of gymnastic dancing. . . .[78]

A final account of the Chica-Congo identified the dance by its proper name. Lafcadio Hearn lived in New Orleans for approximately ten years, and in a letter written in 1885 to his friend Henry Krehbiel, the famous music critic, he stated:

> Yes, I have seen them dance, but they danced the Congo, and sang a purely African song. . . . As for the dance — in which the women do not take their feet off the ground — it is as lascivious as is possible. The men dance very differently, like savages leaping in the air.[79]

To get the full impact of a Sunday afternoon in Congo Square, it is necessary only to read Grace King's description of the activities. The commercialism of the square is obvious, and although King said the dancers returned home to another week of slavery, her words probably describe the square after the Civil War.

> A bazaar of refreshments filled the sidewalks around; lemonade, ginger beer, pies, and the ginger cakes called "estomac mulattre," set out on deal tables, screened with cotton awnings, whose variegated streamers danced also in the breeze. White people would promenade by to look at the scene, and the young gentlemen from the College of Orleans, on their way to the theatre, always stopped a moment to see the negroes dance "Congo." At nightfall the frolic ceased, the dispersed revellers singing on their way home to another week of slavery and labour: "Bonsoir, dansé, Soleil, couché."[80]

The dances of Congo Square, one of the most exciting places in New Orleans, came to an end sometime in the 1880's. Robert Goffin said the end came when "the city administrators divided the place into lots."[81] This was doubtful, however, since Congo Square still exists, although after the Civil War the name was changed to Beauregard Square. Congo Square probably fell into disuse when the need for it ended. In the 1880's the Negro migration to the North began. Storyville came into existence; Negro dance halls were built; and the throbbing excitement of the drums of Congo Square became an echo of the past.

Throughout its existence, Congo Square dancing was confused with the dances of Voodoo. That Voodoo existed in New Orleans there is no doubt. But nearly as many misconceptions surround New Orlean's Voodoo ceremonies as those of Haiti. Voodoo, however, did play a part in New Orleans' past.

Voodoo in New Orleans

A Living Cat Eaten by the Voodoo King. Unparalleled
Scenes of Savagery in the Pontchartrain Swamps. Negro Crones
Beat Time Upon Ox Skulls. Becoming Impassioned, the Fetich
[sic] Worshipers Tear Off Their Clothes and Dance Naked.[82]

These statements are all subheadlines for an article published in 1896 in the *New Orleans Times-Democrat*; and they typify the sensationalist approach used by many writers on Voodoo in New Orleans. Many false statements surrounded it, making it appear savage, bloodthirsty, and terrifying. Some authors, interestingly enough, gave St.-Méry's description of a Voodoo ceremony in Santo Domingo, and, attaching their own name to his description, wrote as if this same ceremony had been witnessed in New Orleans.

The study of Voodoo in New Orleans is incomplete when compared to the work done in Haiti. Except for the work of one or two researchers, no actual study has been done; there are only accounts of people who claim to have witnessed Voodoo rites.

It was practically impossible for non-initiates to see a real ceremony. They could, however, see a social dance under the impression that they were seeing Voodoo rites. Luke Turner, who was supposedly the nephew of Marie Laveau, the great Voodoo priestess, said:

> "Now, some white people say she hold hoodoo dance on Congo Square every week. But Marie Laveau never hold no hoodoo dance. That was a pleasure dance. They beat the drum with the shin bone of a donkey and everybody dance like they do in Hayti. Hoodoo is private. She give the dance the first Friday night in each month and they have crab gumbo and rice to eat and the people dance. The white people come look on, and think they see all, when they only see a dance."[83]

One of the few people to conduct research in Louisiana on Voodoo, or "Hoodoo," as it was frequently called, was Zora Neale Hurston. She studied with several well-known Hoodoo doctors, including Luke Turner, quoted above. As a student of Kitty Brown, she participated in a Hoodoo dance, which she said was always done for a specific purpose.

> It is always a case of death-to-the-enemy that calls forth a dance. They are very rare even in New Orleans now, even with the most inner circle, and no layman ever participates, nor has ever been allowed to witness such a ceremony.[84]

Joe Goodness, an observer of the Congo Square dances said:

> I can remember the Congo Square dances on Sunday afternoons, too. . . . People thought they was Voodoo dances and it's true that a lot of the people who danced there was Voodoos, but they really wasn't the real thing. The regular dances wasn't the real thing. The regular dances wasn't ever held in public.[85]

Most of the incomplete sketches of Voodoo rites in New Orleans dealt with the worship of a snake, lewd and obscene dances usually performed in a state of undress, the eating of something cooked in a cauldron, or drunkenness and debauchery. Very little was said about the attainment of a state of possession, except through the use of alcohol. These accounts probably do not deal with real Voodoo ceremonies, since so few people observed them. There are, however, a few writings on the dance of the Voodoos which appear more truthful. Many speak of the Calenda as being a Voodoo dance, but most of the dances described remain unnamed.

Tallant interviewed a woman named Lala, who called herself the living successor to the Voodoo throne. He described a dance she performed for him as follows:

> She put her hands on her hips and did a shuffling dance which consisted mostly of stepping forward twice, then backward once, some shaking of her bony hips and shoulders, and much rolling of her prominent eyes.[86]

Lala then described a dance, performed by Marie Laveau, which sounds similar to the Calenda described by Labat:

> "When Marie Laveau danced she held a big fish up high and she shaked all over . . . like this!" She lifted her arms and held an imaginary fish, and her body moved faster with shoulders, hips and eyes rolling in unison. "That is real hoodoo dance," she said. "Nobody but me knows how to do it now."[87]

Voodoo in Louisiana, according to Cable, "bore as a title of greater solemnity the additional name of Maignan,"[88] and the words "Voodoo Maignan" frequently appear in connection with the "Dansé Calinda" chant.

J. W. Buel, in a widely copied description of a Voodoo dance, stated that in the midst of the snake worshipping ceremony, a woman sprang up

> . . . with a body waving and undulating like [a] . . . snake. . . . Confining herself to a spot not more than two feet in space, she began to sway on one and the other side. Gradually the undulating motion was imparted to her body from the ankles to the hips. Then she tore the white handkerchief from her forehead. This was a signal, for the whole assembly sprang forward and entered the dance.
>
> The beat of the drum, the thrum of the banjo, swelled louder and louder. . . . Above all the noise rose . . .:
>
> > Houm! dance Calinda,
> > Voudou! Magnian,
> > Aie! Aie!
> > Dance Calinda![89]

A slightly different version of the Calenda was given by G. W. Nott in a newspaper article:

> . . . and then the famous "Calinda" would begin. At first a single dancer, then another and another, until finally the whole

"A Voodoo Dance" drawn by John Durkin to illustrate an article of the same title by Charles Dudley Warner, in *Harper's Weekly* (1887)

assembly took part. The spasmodic jerks and contortions of the dancers keeping time to the primitive tam-tams would increase intensity with each new addition, until with eyes rolling and mouths foaming, gasping for breath, the frenzied contestants would sink to the floor unconscious.[90]

One of the more interesting and rational accounts of a Voodoo ceremony was given by C. D. Warner, who witnessed the rites at noon in a private home. Admission was procured through continued efforts of a friend, a believer in Voodoo. Warner said that "it was an incantation rather than a dance—a curious mingling of African Voodoo rites with modern 'spiritualism' and faithcure."[91] After describing the people present and the preparations for the ceremony, Warner stated that the Apostles' Creed and two prayers to the Virgin Mary were recited in French. Then:

> The colored woman at the side of the altar began a chant in a low, melodious voice. It was the weird and strange "Dansé Calinda". . . . The chant grew, the single line was enunciated in stronger pulsations, and other voices joined in the wild refrain,
> Dansé Calinda, boudoum, boudoum!
> Dansé Calinda, boudoum, boudoum!
> bodies swayed, the hands kept time in soft patpatting, and the feet in muffled accentuation. The Voudou arose, removed his slippers . . . and then began in the open space a slow measured dance, a rhythmical shuffle, with more movement of the hips than of the feet, backward and forward, round and round, but accelerating his movement as the time of the song quickened and the excitement rose in the room.[92]

Warner found it difficult to believe what he had seen and commented that:

> While the wild chanting, the rhythmic movement of hands and feet, the barbarous dance, and the fiery incantations were at their height, it was difficult to believe that we were in a civilized city of an enlightened republic. Nothing indecent occurred in word or gesture, but it was so wild and bizarre that one might easily imagine he was in Africa or in hell.[93]

The Voodoo ceremony which has been described most frequently occurred on St. John's Eve, June 23. This Midsummer's Day has a long and interesting history dating back to pagan times but is best known now as the nativity of St. John the

Baptist. Since he and Shango are considered as one and the same by the followers of the religious Shango group, and since Shango and Damballa, the serpent god, are sometimes equated, it was no wonder that this day was chosen by the Voodoos as a holy day. During ancient times, Midsummer's Day was connected with sun worship and certain beliefs existed regarding fires and bathing on this particular day.[94]

Most of the accounts of the St. John's Eve festivities indicate that they took place somewhere on the shores of Lake Pontchartrain, near the Bayou St. John. Hundreds of fires dotted the landscape, and besides the dancing and eating, nude bathing was a part of the ritual. Most of these accounts are of little value here since they are but examples of sensationalist newspaper writing and only repeat the stereotype of "naked savages," dancing with "grotesque and obscene gestures";[95] "twistings and contortions," "frothing at the mouth";[96] and, "dancing around the pot."[97]

Marie Laveau, the most famous Voodoo priestess or queen of New Orleans, supposedly initiated this St. Johns Eve celebration. Her nephew, who also was a Voodoo doctor, remembered a celebration he had seen as a boy:

"Out on Lake Pontchartrain at Bayou St. John she hold a great feast every year on the Eve of St. John's, June 24th. It is Midsummer Eve, and the Sun give special benefits then and need great honor. The special drum be played then. It is a cowhide stretched over a half-barrel. Beat with a jaw-bone. Some say a man but I think they do not know. I think the jawbone of an ass or a cow. She hold the feast of St. John's partly because she is a Catholic and partly because of hoodoo.

The ones around her altar fix everything for the feast. Nobody see Marie Laveau for nine days before the feast. But when the great crowd of people at the feast call upon her, she would rise out of the waters of the lake with a great communion candle burning upon her head and another in each one of her hands. She walked upon the waters to the shore. As a little boy I saw her myself. When the feast was over, she went back into the lake, and nobody saw her for nine days again."[98]

Many legends have grown concerning the powers Marie Laveau possessed. She was considered the last of the great Voodoo queens. Although the date of her death is obscure (she

was still living in the mid-1880's), when she died much of Voodoo died with her. Legend says that Laveau was "supposed to
have been attended by a huge rattlesnake. The morning after
her death he was seen crawling away to the woods above Lake
Pontchartrain and was never seen again."[99] Voodoo, too, except
in a mild form, became a thing of New Orleans past.

Other Negro Dances in New Orleans

Cable offered insight into Afro-American dance with his
comment that true African dance is "a dance not so much of legs
and feet as of the upper half of the body, a sensual, devilish thing
tolerated only by Latin-American masters. . . ."[100] And tolerated by Latin-American masters it was. Besides the quadroon
balls, Congo Square, and the Voodoo dances, there were references to many other aspects of Negro dance in New Orleans.

One of these accounts, by Rev. Timothy Flint, is exception-
ally interesting because of the similarities between the "King of
the Wake" which he mentions and the West Indian John Canoe.
Although Flint did not state the time of year during which the
following event occurred, he did remark that the great Congo
dance was performed.

> Some hundreds of negroes, male and female, follow the king
> of the wake, who is conspicuous for his youth, size, the
> whiteness of his eyes, and the blackness of his visage. For
> a crown he has a series of oblong, gilt-paper boxes on his head,
> tapering upwards, like a pyramid. From the ends of these boxes
> hang two huge tassels, like those on epaulets. He wags his head
> and makes grimaces. By his thousand mountebank tricks, and
> contortions of countenance and form, he produces an irresistible
> effect upon the multitude. All the characters that follow him, of
> leading estimation, have their own peculiar dress, and their own
> contortions. They dance, and their streamers fly, and the bells
> that they have hung about them tinkle.[101]

With the many West Indians living in New Orleans, it would be
surprising if the John Canoe-men had not put in an appearance.

Or perhaps this king was the forerunner of the King of the
Zulus—the Negro Mardi Gras leader. Because the Mardi Gras
was a segregated carnival, the Negroes had to develop their own

festivities, and the leader of this parade was King Zulu in honor of the group beginning the black Mardi Gras, the Zulu Social Aid and Pleasure Club. Groups of women maskers accompanied the parade. These women were organized into clubs or societies with names such as the Baby Dolls, the Gold Diggers, and the Zigaboos. Also accompanying the parade were the societies of male Negroes, the best-known societies being those which masqueraded as various American Indian tribes. These highly organized groups or tribes gave themselves names such as the Golden Blades, the Creole Wild Wests, and the Yellow Pocahontas. Festivities of this black Mardi Gras were climaxed with a Zulu ball.[102]

There is some evidence that the dances of Congo Square either spread throughout the plantations of the area or existed there simultaneously. An excellent example of the Chica-Congo was given in the description of a New Year's Day celebration on a plantation. The dance described was called the Pilé Chactas by Alceé Fortier:

> The woman had to dance almost without moving her feet.
> It was the man who did all the work: turning around her,
> kneeling down, making the most grotesque and extraordinary
> faces, writhing like a serpent, while the woman was almost
> immovable. After a little while, however, she began to get
> excited, and untying her neckerchief, she waved it around
> gracefully, . . .[103]

How far the dances of Congo Square and the West Indian immigrants spread cannot be ascertained. Perhaps they existed only in that area at that period of time, and when the drums of Congo Square were stilled, the dances were forgotten. Yet with so many of the visitors to the city viewing these dances, perhaps some remained. The *rhythms* of Congo Square have been linked definitely to the development of ragtime and jazz, but it is difficult to make a definitive statement about such an ephemeral aspect as movement.

It is certain that the true African dance was not so much of the feet and legs, but rather of the body and particularly the hips. Perhaps something of the Congo Square dances does live on in the no-contact, body-wriggling dances of today. If these dances live, they do so in spite of the next period in the history of Negro dance.

The next period was that of the stereotyped "darky": the Jim Crow and Zip Coon era—the era of burnt-cork and black-face, of the shuffling, comic simpleton and the Negro dandy. It is one of the saddest and most degrading eras in the history of American entertainment: the era of the minstrel.

▣▣▣ NOTES FOR CHAPTER 4

1. Nicholas Cresswell, *The Journal of Nicholas Cresswell, 1774-1777* (New York: Dial Press, 1924), p. 18.

2. Jane M. G. Turnbull and Marion Turnbull, *American Photographs* (2 vols.; 2d ed.; London: T. C. Newby, 1860), II, 70.

3. Roi Ottley and William J. Weatherby, eds., *The Negro in New York, An Informal Social History* (New York: New York Public Library, 1967), p. 10.

4. *Ibid.*

5. *Ibid.*, pp. 25-26.

6. *Ibid.*, p. 26.

7. Washington Irving, *Salmagundi; or, The Whim-Whams and Opinions of Launcelot Langstaff, Esq. and Others* (2 vols.; New York: D. Longworth, 1807), I, 98.

8. Alice Morse Earle, "Pinkster Day," *Outlook*, April 28, 1894, p. 743.

9. James Fenimore Cooper, *Satanstoe; or, The Littlepage Manuscripts. A Tale of the Colony* (2 vols.; New York: Burgess, Stringer and Co., 1845), 1, 65. Cooper gained much material for this novel from Ann Grant, *Memoirs of an American Lady*, published in 1808.

10. *Ibid.*, I, 66.

11. *Ibid.*, I, 70.

12. Joel Munsell, *Collections on the History of Albany, from its Discovery to the Present Time, with Notices of its Public Institutions, and Biographical Sketches of Citizens Deceased* (2 vols.; Albany, N.Y.: J. Munsell, 1867), II, 56.

13. *Ibid.*

14. *Ibid.*, II, 326.

15. *Ibid.*, II, 325.

16. *Ibid.*, II, 326.

17. William S. Walsh, *Curiosities of Popular Customs and of Ceremonies, Observances, and Miscellaneous Antiquities* (Philadelphia: J. B. Lippincott Company, 1898), p. 813.

18. Munsell, *Collections on the History of Albany*, II, 323.

19. Lafcadio Hearn, "Levee Life," *Cincinnati Commercial*, March 17, 1876, p. 2.

20. *Ibid.*

21. *Ibid.*

22. Harold Courlander, *Negro Folk Music, U.S.A.* (New York: Columbia University Press, 1963), p. 191.

23. Lyle Saxon, Edward Dreyer, and Robert Tallant, comps., Works Progress Administration Louisiana Writers' Project, *Gumbo Ya-Ya* (Boston: Houghton, Mifflin Company, 1945), p. 382.

24. Courlander, *Negro Folk Music,* p. 191.

25. Mary Wheeler, *Steamboatin' Days* (Baton Rouge: Louisiana State University Press, 1944), p. 92.

26. William Francis Allen, Charles Pickard Ware, and Lucy McKim Garrison, *Slave Songs of the United States* (New York: A. Simpson and Company, 1867), p. 113.

27. Charles Dudley Warner, *Studies in the South and West with Comments on Canada* (New York: Harper and Brothers, 1889), p. 69.

28. Oliver Evans, "Melting Pot in the Bayous," *American Heritage,* XV (December, 1963), 31.

29. *Ibid.,* 49.

30. W. Adolphe Roberts, *Lake Pontchartrain,* (Indianapolis: Bobbs-Merrill Company, 1946), p. 113.

31. Evans, "Melting Pot," 50.

32. Duke of Saxe-Weimar Eisenach, Bernhard, *Travels Through North America during the Years 1825 and 1826* (2 vols.; Philadelphia: Carey, Lea and Carey, 1828), II, 61.

33. *Ibid.*

34. Saxon, Dreyer, and Tallant, *Gumbo Ya-Ya,* p. 159.

35. Evans, "Melting Pot," 50.

36. Thomas Ashe, *Travels in America, Performed in the Year 1806, For the Purpose of Exploring the Rivers Alleghany, Monongahela, Ohio, and Mississippi, Ascertaining the Produce and Condition of Their Banks and Vicinity* (London: B. McMillan, 1809), p. 314.

37. Amos Stoddard, *Sketches, Historical and Descriptive, of Louisiana* (Philadelphia: Mathew Carey, 1812), pp. 321-22.

38. "Grand Bal Paré." *New Orleans Moniteur,* August 22, 1807, p. 3, col. 2.

39. *New Orleans As It Is: Its Manners and Customs—Morals—Fashionable Life—Profanation of the Sabbath—Prostitution—Liscentiousness [sic]—Slave Markets and Slavery, etc., etc., etc.* (Utica, N.Y.: DeWitt C. Grove, 1849), p. 46.

40. Herbert Asbury, *The French Quarter* (Garden City, N.Y.: Garden City Publishing Co., 1938), p. 133.

41. George Vandenhoff, *Leaves from an Actor's Notebook; with Reminiscenses and Chit-Chat of the Green Room and the Stage in England and America* (New York: D. Appleton and Company, 1860), pp. 208-09.

42. G. W. Featherstonhaugh, *Excursion Through the Slave States, from Washington on the Potomac to the Frontier of Mexico; with Sketches of Popular Manners and Geological Notices* (New York: Negro Universities Press, 1968 [originally published by Harper and Brothers, 1844]), pp. 141-42.

43. Edward Sullivan, *Rambles and Scrambles in North and South America* (2d ed.; London: Richard Bentley, 1853), p. 211.

44. Charles Dudley Warner, *Studies in the South and West with Comments on Canada* (New York: Harper and Brothers, 1889), p. 50.

45. Sullivan, *Rambles and Scrambles*, p. 210.

46. Bernhard, *Travels Through North America*, II, 58.

47. *Ibid.*, II, 62-63.

48. Evans, "Melting Pot," p. 50.

49. Roberts, *Lake Pontchartrain*, p. 157. While Roberts says the circus was known as the Gaëtano's Circus from Havana, George Washington Cable ("The Dance in Place Congo," *Century Magazine*, XXXI [February, 1886] 518) says the circus was that of "Havana M. Cayetano." Undoubtedly Gaëtano and Cayetano are variations of the same name.

50. Asbury, *French Quarter*, pp. 237-39.

51. *Ibid.*

52. Henry Bradshaw Fearon, *Sketches of America, A Narrative of a Journey of Five Thousand Miles through the Eastern and Western States of America; Contained in Eight Reports Addressed to the Thirty-Nine English Families by Whom the Author was Deputed, in June, 1817, to Ascertain Whether Any, and What Part of the United States would be Suitable for their Residence. With Remarks on Mr. Birkbeck's "Notes" and "Letters"* (London: Printed for Longman, Hurst, Rees, Orme, and Brown, 1818), pp. 279-80.

53. See Chapter II.

54. Christian Schultz, *Travels on an Inland Voyage through the States of New-York, Pennsylvania, Virginia, Ohio, Kentucky and Tennessee, and through the Territories of Indiana, Louisiana, Mississippi and New Orleans; Performed in the Years 1807 and 1808; Including a Tour of Nearly Six Thousand Miles. With Maps and Plates* (2 vols.; New York: Isaac Riley, 1810), II, 197.

55. Benjamin Henry Boneval Latrobe, *Impressions Respecting New Orleans, Diary and Sketches, 1818-1820*, ed. by Samuel Wilson, Jr. (New York: Columbia University Press, 1951), pp. 49-50.

56. *Ibid.*, pp. 50-51.

57. George Washington Cable, "The Dance in Place Congo," *Century Magazine*, XXXI (February, 1886), 519. Although not acknowledged in this particular article, it is known that one of Cable's chief references was the writing of Moreau de St.-Méry, previously quoted in Chapter II. It appears that Cable kept St.-Méry's description of the drums nearly intact in this article, without giving due credit, and so casting a shadow of doubt on his own integrity.

58. Joseph Howard, *Drums in the Americas* (New York: Oak Publications, 1967), p. 202.

59. Latrobe, *Impressions,* p. 50.

60. *Ibid.,* p. 51.

61. *Ibid.,* pp. 49-50.

62. See Chapter II.

63. Mr. Flugel, cited by Lyle Saxon, *Fabulous New Orleans* (New York: D. Appleton-Century Company, 1941 [originally published in 1928]), pp. 233-34.

64. *Paxton's Directory of 1882,* quoted in Wm. Head Coleman, comp., *Historical Sketch Book and Guide to New Orleans and Environs* (New York: Will H. Coleman, 1885), p. 22. It is interesting to note that by the time *Paxton's Directory* was published, New Orleans had overflowed its city limits, and the open-field known as Congo Plains had now been totally surrounded by houses.

65. "Congo Square," *New Orleans Daily Picayune,* March 22, 1846, p. 2.

66. *Ibid.*

67. Henry Didimus [Henry Edward Durell], quoted in Rudi Blesh and Harriet Janis, *They All Played Ragtime. The True Story of American Music* (New York: Alfred A. Knopf, 1950), p. 83.

68. Marshall and Jean Stearns, *Jazz Dance. The Story of American Vernacular Dance* (New York: Macmillan Company, 1968), p. 19.

69. Cable, "Dance in Place Congo," 523. For an account of one of the most famous Bamboula dancers, Bras-Coupé, see Cable's "The Story of Bras-Coupé," in Arlin Turner, ed., *Creoles and Cajuns. Stories of Old Louisiana* (Gloucester, Mass.: Peter Smith, 1965).

70. Henry C. Castellanos, *New Orleans As It Was* (2d ed. New Orleans: L. Graham Co., Ltd., 1905), p. 298.

71. *Ibid.*

72. *Ibid.,* p. 158.

73. Cable, "Dance in Place Congo," 527.

74. *Ibid.*

75. *Ibid.*

76. Refer to Chapter II for St.-Méry's description of the movement pattern. For clarity, the dance will be referred to here as the Chica-Congo.

77. Asbury, *French Quarter,* p. 243.

78. *New York World* correspondent's account of Congo Square dancing, quoted in Asbury, *French Quarter,* p. 252.

79. Henry Edward Krehbiel, *Afro-American Folksongs. A Study in Racial and National Music* (4th ed.; New York: G. Schirmer, Inc., 1914), p. 125.

80. Grace Elizabeth King, *New Orleans. The Place and the People* (New York: Macmillan Company, 1937 [originally printed 1895]), p. 340.

81. Robert Goffin, *Jazz from Congo to Swing* (England: Musicians Press Ltd., 114 Charing Cross Rd., W.C. 2, 1946), p. 16.

82. "Dance of the Voodoos," *New Orleans Times-Democrat,* June 24, 1896.

83. Zora Neale Hurston, *Mules and Men,* (Philadelphia: J. B. Lippincott Company, 1935), pp. 240-41.

84. *Ibid.*, p. 297-

85. Robert Tallant, *Voodoo in New Orleans* (New York: Macmillan Company, 1946), p. 18.

86. *Ibid.*, pp. 175-76.

87. *Ibid.*, p. 176.

88. George Washington Cable, "Creole Slave Songs," *Century Magazine,* XXXI (April, 1886), 815, 817.

89. J. W. Buel, *Metropolitan Life Unveiled, or the Mysteries and Miseries of America's Great Cities* (St. Louis, Mo.: Historical Publishing Co., 1882), p. 528. For an exact copy of Buel's words with no credit given Buel, see W. H. Seymour's "A Voudou Story," *New Orleans Daily Picayune,* July 3, 1892, p. 14.

90. G. William Nott, "Marie Laveau, Long High Priestess of Voodooism in New Orleans," *New Orleans Times-Picayune,* November 19, 1922, Magazine Section, p. 2. Nott's description of Voodoo dancing is an example of plagiarism from the writings of Moreau de St.-Méry. That Nott's description would agree with G. W. Cable's is not surprising, since Cable took his description nearly verbatim from St.-Méry. Nott, on the other hand, took a more circuitous route than did Cable. Nott credited his information to a Creole lady, a Madam X and her book *Souvenirs d'Amerique.* Madam X used verbatim with no credit the Voodoo Don Pedro ceremony passage from St.-Méry and stated that the ceremony was seen in New Orleans. It is unfortunate that some writers feel no guilt at lifting the words of others without due credit being given.

91. Warner, *Studies in the South and West,* p. 64.

92. *Ibid.*, pp. 69-70.

93. *Ibid.*, p. 73.

94. For a full account of these customs, see James George Frazer, *The Golden Bough. A Study in Magic and Religion* (2 vols.; 3d ed.; New York: Macmillan Company, 1935), I, 246-52.

95. "Dance of the Voodoos," *New Orleans Times-Democrat,* June 24, 1896.

96. Coleman, *Historical Sketch Book and Guide to New Orleans,* p. 231.

97. "The Vous Dous Incantation," *New Orleans Times,* June 28, 1872, p. 1.

98. Hurston, *Mules and Men,* p. 241.

99. Zora Neale Hurston, "Hoodoo in America," *Journal of American Folk-Lore,* XLIV, No. 174 (October-December, 1931), 326.

100. Cable, "Dance in Place Congo," 520.

101. Timothy Flint, *Recollections of the Last Ten Years in the Valley of the Mississippi,* ed. by George R. Brooks (Carbondale: Southern Illinois University Press, 1968 [originally published 1826]), p. 103.

102. Robert Tallant, *Mardi Gras* (Garden City, N.Y.: Doubleday and Company, Inc., 1948), pp. 230-49.

103. Alceé Fortier, "Customs and Superstitions in Louisiana," *Journal of American Folk-Lore,* I, No. 2 (July-September, 1888), 137.

5

JIM CROW & JUBA

My old misses long time ago,
She took me down de hill side to jump Jim Crow;
Fus 'pon de heel tap, den 'pon de toe,
Eb'ry Monday morning I jump Jim Crow.

Oh lord, ladies, don't you know
You nebber get to Heben till you jump Jim Crow.[1]

By the time Thomas Dartmouth Rice made his appearance as Jim Crow in 1828, the American public had been well prepared to accept him. In some cases his forerunners had been authentic Negroes, but in general they had been whites in blackface. The stereotypes which were to be fully developed by minstrelsy were begun long before, at the time when this nation was born.

In 1767 an announcement appeared in the *New-York Journal* for a performance by Mr. Bayly, a "sleight of hand artist," to be held on April 14, 1767. At the end of each of the three parts of the program there was an interlude of dancing by Bayly and a Mr. Tea. Ending the third part, Tea presented a *Negro*

Dance, In Character.[2] Even before the Revolutionary War, Americans were being entertained by impersonations of Negroes, and particularly of Negro dancing.

Before 1800 several plays were presented with Negro characters (usually played by whites), but the performance by Tea is the first found which specifies dance. The second extant reference to Negro dance does not appear until 1796, but the addition of one word, "comic," seems to indicate the beginning of one important and typical aspect. On November 25, 1796, a Madame Gardie appeared on the Boston stage in *A Comic Dance, In Character of a Female Negro.*[3] Again the performer was white impersonating a Negro.

The legitimate theatre was also aiding the development of Negro stereotypes before 1800. According to Loften Mitchell, a play presented in 1795 entitled *The Triumph of Love* introduced

> . . . a shuffling, cackling, allegedly comic Negro servant. *The Politicians* in 1797 continued this stereotype. The course was therefore established—the course that was to lead the black man to be represented on the American stage as something to be ridiculed and a creature to be denied human status.[4]

The first reference to a Negro performing a dance did not come until 1808, and then he was billed as an "exotic." Included in the Pepin and Breschard Circus, which played in New York City, a performer was billed as the "Young African," who, among other things, "will exhibit many steps of Hornpipe, on Horseback, in full speed, without losing the measure of the music."[5]

From 1821 to 1823, a company composed of Negro actors and actresses called The African Company performed at a theatre in New York City. Not a great deal seems to be known about The African Company other than the fact that it provided the inspiration for the career of the great Negro tragedian, Ira Aldridge. A member of the company, Mr. Bates, performed a hornpipe.[6] The theatre was apparently harrassed continuously by the police and groups of white rowdies, who finally destroyed the building. The African Company appears to have been dissolved in 1823 following this incident.

It is obvious that there was an interest in Negro dancing even at this early period. However, since most of the dancers and actors were whites impersonating Negroes, what was seen by the public was not the authentic Negro but rather "the Negro as a stage character . . . as a caricature rather than as a human being."[7]

❏❙❏❙❏ JIM CROW

In the plays mentioned, Negro roles had been incidental, and the dances had been performed as entr'acte stunts.

> The first performer of a song and dance, that is, of a sketch in which the darky performer was sufficient unto himself and was deprived of any support from persons of another complexion, seems to have been "Jim Crow" Rice.[8]

The story of Rice, a white actor, seeing a lame Negro groom singing and dancing, has been told and retold in many different versions. Supposedly copying the exact posture, movements, and song of the old Negro, T. D. Rice performed Jim Crow in blackface in the late 1820's with resounding success.

Rice performed his dance to a slightly modified version of "Jump Jim Crow":

> Wheel about, turn about,
>   Do jus' so:
> An' ebery time I turn about,
> I jump Jim Crow.[9]

Hans Nathan imagined the scene as follows:

> How strained, sprawling, and distorted his posture was, and yet how nonchalant — how unusually grotesque with its numerous sharp angles, and yet how natural! . . . Rice, according to his own words, wheeled, turned, and jumped. In windmill fashion, he rolled his body lazily from one side to the other, throwing his weight alternately on the heel of one foot and on the toes of the other. Gradually, he must have turned away from his audience, and, on the words "jis so," jumped high up and back into his initial position. While doing all this, he rolled his left hand in a half-seductive, half-waggishly admonishing manner. Imaginative though he was, he was undoubtedly inspired by the real Negro.[10]

Marshall and Jean Stearns, however, felt that Nathan's description was slightly inaccurate. The jump accompanied the words "I jump Jim Crow."

> The earliest phrase "jis so" simply calls attention to the all-important style—the cramped yet rhythmic circling *before* the jump, which is a syncopated hop in the flat-footed Shuffle manner rather than a jump 'high up' as Nathan suggests.[11]

The Stearns wrote that the dance performed by Rice was perhaps "a blend of Jig and Shuffle, with the jump coming from a jig, and the arm and shoulder movements from a shuffle."[12]

Was this dance of "Daddy" Rice indeed a Negro dance? Was the Jim Crow seen by so many millions of people authentically Afro-American? The Stearns seemed to think that Rice copied the dance of the old Negro exactly; that here, in fact, was one of the earliest examples of a professional white dancer borrowing from the Negro. "The first of many Afro-American dances to become a world wide success, Jump Jim Crow's appeal was universal. . . ."[13]

Nearly as much controversy raged over the authenticity of the performance of Jim Crow as it did over the actual beginnings of this dance on the stage. Fanny Kemble, the English actress who lived on a Georgia plantation in 1838-1839, said:

> I have seen Jim Crow—the veritable James: all the contortions, and springs, and flings, and kicks, and capers you have been beguiled into accepting as indicative of him are spurious, faint, feeble, impotent—in a word, pale Northern reproductions of that ineffable black conception. It is impossible for words to describe the things these people did with their bodies, and, above all, with their faces, the whites of their eyes, and the whites of their teeth, and certain outlines which either naturally and by the grace of heaven, or by the practice of some peculiar artistic dexterity, they bring into prominent and most ludicrous display.[14]

Charles Haywood considered all minstrel characters nothing more than variations of the original "rigid stereotype" created by Rice.

> What Rice did . . . was to highlight, exaggerate, and distort the Negro's movements. . . . This white showman, inspired

In Dahomey, from *Theatre Arts Monthly* (August, 1942).
From left are Hattie McIntosh, George Walker, Ada Overton
Walker, Bert Williams and Lottie Williams.

by a *unique* Negro, transformed him, through his dramatic skill into a theatrical comic personality.[15]

Constance Rourke, on the other hand, felt that Rice's portrait was of the authentic Negro. A rounded picture of the plantation Negro was developed on the American stage, wrote Rourke,

> . . . in a series of sketches which attempted a close portraiture. These were boldly continued in the early thirties by Jim Crow Rice, who was white. His songs, dances, and lingo followed those of Negroes on the plantations and rivers of the Southwest.[16]

While Rice may have faithfully reproduced the postures and dance of one old lame Negro named Jim Crow, two things make us question whether the dance was representatively Negro. First, the old man observed by Rice was crippled, resulting in a distortion of the dance movements; and second, Rice (who was, above all, a showman) may have exaggerated the funnier movements to retain audience appeal through his hundreds of performances.

About the first performance of the Jim Crow dance there is a touching, if perhaps apocryphal, story. Rice decided to premier the dance in Pittsburgh and, being without a costume, borrowed the clothes of a handyman named Cuff. Since Cuff had but one set of clothes, he was forced to wait backstage in a state of undress while Rice performed Jim Crow. In the midst of the performance, the steamboat which Cuff always helped to unload approached, and a small voice was suddenly heard on stage saying, "Massa Rice, Massa Rice, gi' me nigga's hat,—nigga's coat,—nigga's shoes,—gi' me nigga's t'ings! . . ."[17]

The "small voice" has recently been compared to that of the modern Negro critic, Sterling Brown.

> To a culture with a chronic itch to impersonate the Negro, he [Brown] has been saying for nearly forty years: Give us back our clothes. Restore to us the meaning of our own experience! For our lives have been robbed of their significance by malicious portrayals and slanderous misrepresentations, called stereotypes. And not only on the minstrel stage, but in fiction, poetry, and drama; in cinema, radio, and advertising; wherever false images of us have been projected by a hostile white society.[18]

Rice, then, rather than giving audiences a true picture of Negro dance, may have created the first clear-cut, long-lasting caricature of that dance: that grotesque, shuffling, peculiar, eccentric, jumping, loose-limbed, awkward, funny and, of course, rhythmic dance. The effect of Rice's stereotype was so strong that Isaac Goldberg later wrote, "Rice's 'Jim Crow' gave to our stage a type and to our language a striking phrase that ever after was to stigmatize our physical and psychic segregation of the Negro."[19]

Only one other dancer had anywhere near the effect of Rice on minstrelsy. That dancer, a Negro, was known as Master Juba.

⊟⫶⊟⫶⊟ JUBA

Master Juba, the stage name adopted by William Henry Lane, was born a free man and came to the fore on the American stage in the 1840's. The dance named Juba, it will be remembered, came from Africa to the West Indies and eventually to the United States, where it evolved into a rhythmic, stamping, clapping, patting type of dance.

Master Juba was noted for his Jig dancing; Marian Winter reported that by 1845, "it was flatly stated by members of the profession that Juba was 'beyond question the very greatest of all dancers.'"[20] Living at that same time was Master John Diamond, a white dancer (considerably older than Juba) who "prided himself on his skill at negro dancing."[21] This was the same Master Diamond of whom Thomas Nichols wrote:

> In New York, some years ago, Mr. P. T. Barnum had a clever boy who brought him lots of money as a dancer of negro break-downs; made up, of course, as a negro minstrel, with his face well blackened, and a woolly wig. One day Master Diamond, thinking he might better himself, danced away into the infinite distance.[22]

To determine once and for all the best dancer — the white Diamond or the black Juba — a series of challenge dances was initiated in 1844. The first match was held at John Tryon's Amphitheatre.[23] The outcome was uncertain. However, two more matches were held at the Chatham and Bowery Theatres, with Master Juba finally winning the distinctive title, "King of All Dancers."[24] Soon after the contests Juba joined a minstrel troupe and in 1845, touring with three white minstrels, received what Winter called the "unprecedented distinction of *top billing*"[25] on the program.

In 1846 Juba joined the recently organized minstrels, White's Serenaders,[26] and in 1848 traveled to London to join Pell's Ethiopian Serenaders, another minstrel group. In an announcement appearing in the *Illustrated London News*, the reengagement of Pell's group was reported and further, "Boz's description of Juba fully confirmed by Public Opinion and the Press."[27] On July 1, 1848, the *News* stated that, "The most brilliant assemblage of rank and fashion have honoured the Gardens to witness the unparalleled PERFORMANCES of JUBA, immortalised by Boz in his *American Notes*. . . ."[28]

"Boz's description" was, of course, that of Charles Dickens in his book, *American Notes*, written shortly after his visit to the United States in 1842. While Dickens did not name the young Negro dancer he saw at Five Points in New York City, his description closely resembles later observations of Juba's dancing and is therefore included here. Dickens advised his readers that the dance he saw was a regular Breakdown, which began with five or six couples moving onto the floor and

> . . . marshalled by a lively young negro, who is the wit of the assembly, and the greatest dancer known.
>
> But the dance commences. Every gentleman sets as long as he likes to the opposite lady, and the opposite lady to him, and all are so long about it that the sport begins to languish, when suddenly the lively hero dashes in to the rescue. Instantly the fiddler grins, and goes at it tooth and nail; there is new energy in the tambourine. . . . Single shuffle, double shuffle, cut and crosscut: snapping his fingers, rolling his eyes, turning in his knees, presenting the backs of his legs in front, spinning about on his toes and heels like nothing but the man's fingers on the tambourine; dancing with two left legs, two right legs, two wooden legs, two wire legs, two spring legs — all sorts of legs and no legs — what is this to him? And in what walk of life, or dance of life, does man ever get such stimulating applause as thunders about him, when, having danced his partner off her feet, and himself too, he finishes by leaping gloriously on the

Juba at Vauxhall Gardens, London, from *Illustrated London News*
(August 5, 1848)

barcounter, and calling for something to drink, with the chuckle of a million of counterfeit Jim Crows, in one inimitable sound?[29]

A critic who viewed Master Juba's London performance wrote a similar description. Never, wrote the critic, had there been such

. . . mobility of muscles, such flexibility of joints, such boundings, such slidings, such gyrations, such toes and heelings, such backwardings and forwardings, such posturings, such firmness of foot, such elasticity of tendon, such mutation of movement, such vigor, such variety, such natural grace, such powers of endurance, such potency of pattern.[30]

Another critic appeared amazed that such dancing could exist.

But the Nigger Dance is a reality. The "Virginny Breakdown," or the "Alabama kick-up," the "Tennessee Double-shuffle," or the "Louisiana Toe-and-Heel," we know to exist. If they did not, how could Juba enter into their wonderful complications so naturally? How could he tie his legs into such knots, and fling them about so recklessly, or make his feet twinkle until you lose sight of them altogether in his energy. The great Boz immortalised him; and he deserved the glory thus conferred.[31]

Unfortunately Master Juba did not live long enough to return to the United States and dance again upon the stages of this country. He died in 1852, aged about twenty-seven, while still in London. Had he lived, his influence on American dance might have been more profound. According to Winter:

In America it was Juba's influence primarily which kept the minstrel show dance, in contrast to the body of the minstrel show music, in touch with the integrity of Negro source material. There was almost a "school after Juba."[32]

Winter asserted it was due to the influence of Master Juba that "the minstrel show dance retained more integrity as a Negro art form than any other threatrical derivative of Negro culture."[33]

Did the minstrel show dance, in fact, remain closer to the original Negro art form than any other theatrical derivative? It probably did; but this was not to say that authentic Negro dances were presented on the minstrel stage. The music, appearance and speech of the blackfaced minstrel had veered so sharply from the original that in no way could these elements be considered representative of the real Negro. It was only when dance was compared with the other elements of minstrelsy that it appeared to be authentic.

This may have been due, in part, to the dancing of Master Juba, but other factors were also involved. First, there were innumerable opportunities for viewing the dance of the Negroes, and many visitors to the South commented publicly on the slave dances they had seen. Sometimes the slaves were called to the "Big House" to perform for guests, as in the case of Robert Moton. Frequently guests were entertained by a trip to the slave quarters to watch a dance in progress. Of course, there was always Congo Square with its authentic dances and innumerable observers. There were also opportunities to see Negro dancing in the North. Opportunities for observing and copying Negro dances were abundant.

Second, many of the Negro dances seemed both grotesque and amusing to whites, so that few changes were needed before presenting them on the stage. Describing a slave ball in honor of her arrival on the plantation, Fanny Kemble wrote:

> The languishing elegance of some – the painstaking laboriousness
> of others – . . . at last so utterly overcame any attempt at
> decorous gravity on my part that I was obliged to secede. . . .
> it is only wonderful to me that we were not made ill by the
> . . . effort not to laugh. . . .[34]

In the case of Jim Crow, however, Rice was copying a dance already distorted by the fact that the Negro model was crippled.

One question remains regarding the supposedly genuine Negro dances of minstrelsy. Since Juba reputedly exerted a profound influence on the retention of authentic Negro dance on the stage, how authentic were the dances of Juba himself? The Jig is certainly not attributed to any Afro-American influence but rather is considered of Irish and English derivation. Did the fact that Juba happened to be black lead people to assume that he was performing real Negro dances – or was he, in truth, a Negro dancer performing an Irish dance?

Jig and Clog dancing have a common element: the sound produced by the shoes tapping on the floor. On the other hand,

. . . because it is danced on the naked earth with bare feet, African dance tends to modify or eliminate such European styles as the Jig and the Clog. . . . the African style is often flat-footed and favors gliding, dragging, or shuffling steps.[35]

One of the characteristics of American tap dancing is that the dancer acts somewhat as a musical instrument. The dancing of Juba was compared, by one critic, to the bones and banjo,[36] indicating that sound must have been an important factor. No writer discussing Juba's dancing mentioned any movement of the upper body (the Jig and Clog both call for a stiff, erect upper body). Yet, there is still mention of typically Afro-American steps in the dance of Juba: the single shuffle, the double shuffle, "such slidings," and "such gyrations."

It appears that while Juba's dancing was not what is commonly thought of as Afro-American dance, it did contain many of the characteristics of the dance. Apparently Master Juba had produced something new: a blending of Irish and Afro-American dance tied together by rhythm. The Stearnses believed that the unique element in Juba's dance was rhythm, and that "he was apparently *swinging*—relatively speaking—naturally and effortlessly."[37]

Influenced by both Rice and Juba (Rice creating the character of the stereotyped "darky" and Juba fusing two styles of dance into a new form), the dances of the minstrel stage were, to say the least, eclectic.

⬛⬛⬛ DANCES OF THE MINSTREL STAGE

Rice, who has been called the father of blackface minstrelsy, first performed Jim Crow in 1828, yet it was not until sometime in the 1840's that the first formal minstrel troupe was organized. The first group were the Virginia Minstrels, composed of Dan Emmett (who later composed the song "Dixie"), Frank Brower, Billy Whitlock, and Dick Pelham.[38] All four were white, as were nearly all minstrels until after the Civil War.

As more companies were organized, a standard program

format developed. This pattern was fairly universal by the 1850's and consisted of three parts. The regulation "first part" was designed to show off the entire company as they sat in a semi-circle, flanked by endmen Mr. Tambo and Mr. Bones. The dignified interlocutor sat in the center and carried on a question-answer session with the comic endmen. The first part began with an overture, continued with the comic question-answer period, included some comic and sentimental songs, and ended with the final Walk-Around.

The second part was the Olio, in which a variety of singing, dancing, and speaking acts were performed. The final part, known as the Afterpiece, had, at the beginning of minstrelsy, "attempted to reproduce dramatically the mingled simplicity and cunning of the Negro. . . ."[39] Eventually, the Afterpiece became an extravaganza performed by the entire cast and was usually a burlesque of a serious drama popular at the time.

In a discussion of blackface minstrelsy, Arthur Todd felt the shows were based to a large extent on elements of Negro dance coming directly from Africa.

> These shows were basically a development of the primitive tradition of circle and hand clapping dances. For theatrical purposes, the entertainers were seated in a semi-circular line of chairs on the stage. Here the ringleader of the dance became, in transition, the "interlocutor" or master of ceremonies. Those who sang the melody for the dance were transposed into the Chorus, some becoming "end" men, one at either "end" or side of the circle. The rest of the chorus performed the same functions as did the line in Africa—they clapped their hands or shook tambourines. Every man in the chorus had the opportunity for a solo bit of some sort, just as had the Negro in many of his primitive African ceremonies.[40]

Tom Fletcher, on the other hand, attributed the format of Part One of the minstrel show to a Negro family of entertainers named Luca. John Luca, his wife and four sons appeared during the 1840's, and according to Fletcher:

> Their act was something like this. After singing their opening song, all six would sit down in chairs which had been set in a semi-circle on the stage. The father would sit near the center, and he was the one who gave the word when to sit down.
> The presentation of the John Luca family, according to all

the information I have ever been able to dig up, was the
original appearance of the "minstrel, first part" format.
I am happy to believe that this information is authentic.[41]

Part One in the traditional minstrel show always ended with
a dance, called the Walk-Around, done by the entire cast. Sometimes this was repeated as the finale of Part Three also. Discussing the Walk-Around, Nathan said in 1943 that this dance
was still well remembered. "Its square, heavy, nonchalant,
droll movements — borrowed from and modelled after the dance
of the Southern Negroes . . . anticipated the popular dances
of the present day."[42]

The Walk-Around was mentioned usually in connection
with the Breakdown or old fashioned Hoe-Down. The Walk-
Around was derived from the Ring-Shout and the Breakdown
from the old challenge dances such as the Juba.

Douglas Gilbert described the Walk-Around:

> At a chord from the orchestra, the company rose to their feet.
> As the orchestra began a lively tune in 2/4 time, one of the
> company would step down stage from the semi-circle, walk
> around for sixteen bars of the music and do one step of a reel,
> finish with a break, then resume his place in the semicircle as
> another stepped out and repeated the performance, varying,
> though, with a different step. This would continue until six
> or more dancers had appeared. Then all the dancers came down
> stage and danced together while the rest of the company
> patted time and shuffled.[43]

While Gilbert suggested that only the dancers participated
in the Walk-Around, eventually it grew to include the entire
cast. Probably the first Walk-Around to be presented was one
written by Dan Emmett for the Virginia Minstrels. The song
was "Lucy Long" and others followed in rapid succession including "Old Dan Tucker" and "Dixie."

Charles Sherlock described the format of the Walk-Around
and continued with a description of a Breakdown which sounds
similar to that of the Juba.

> The walk-around was always made the finale of the first part,
> and was usually repeated at the end of the show as a spectacle
> on which to drop the curtain. It was intended to be written in
> march-time, and to its spirited strains the whole company would

circumnavigate the stage, in a dance-step that was little more than a jerky elevation of the legs below the knees, much like the "buck and wing" dances of the present day. It was as long ago as this—the walk-around being in highest estate with Bryant's Minstrels in the sixties—that the spatting of dance-time with the outspread palms on the knees was invented. To this manual accompaniment the breakdowns were often done. Cleverly executed, this tattoo will set the saltatorial nerves in motion as quickly as the catchiest music.[44]

Constance Rourke compared the Walk-Around to the New Orleans holiday dances described by Flint. She added that the dances were accompanied by cries and shouts from the dancers after the manner of the plantation slave.

The climax of the minstrel performance, the walkaround, with its competitive dancing in the mazes of a circle, was clearly patterned on Negro dances in the compounds of the great plantations, which in turn went back to the communal dancing of the African. The ancestry was hardly remote. . . . Often the walkarounds of minstrelsy were composed only of bold pantomime and matched dancing, accompanied by strident cries and the simplest binding of words, the words gaining their color from slave life. . . .[45]

It appears that the early minstrel Walk-Around could have had its basis in genuine Negro dance. The challenge dances accompanied by patting and clapping were probably of Afro-American origin, as was the Ring-Shout. However, the only similarity which has been pointed out between the Walk-Around and the Ring-Shout was the fact that both forms traveled in a circle.

Another famous minstrel dance was the Essence Dance. Sherlock said this "most resembled the dancing of the real negro."[46] The Stearnses believed that "the Essence was the first popular dance—for professionals—from the Afro-American vernacular."[47] The Stearnses continued by saying that, "minstrelsy's most famous dance, The Essence of Old Virginia, came from the Shuffle and led to the early Soft Shoe."[48] The leading exponent of the dance was Dan Bryant, a blackface minstrel who perfected it in the 1850's.

Originally performed by Billy Newcomb, the Essence was done in fast time, but as Bryant perfected the dance, it was performed quite slowly. The main feature of the Essence dance appeared to be the movement of the heels and toes without changing the position of the legs so that the performer appeared to glide across the floor. Sherlock called this the "rocking heel, which is an element of pedal motion in every negro dance."[49] Along with this foot motion was an intricate series of shuffles.

While parts of the Walk-Around may be authentically Afro-American, it seems that the Essence was wholly authentic. Negro dance, as previously stated, makes great use of shuffling, gliding, and dragging movements and so did the Essence. The toe-heel motion was certainly an element in Afro-American dance, as shown by Ravenel, who observed it at a slave dance held at Christmas. Ravenel described the same step as "a slow shuffling gait . . . edging along by some unseen exertion of the feet. . . ."[50]

Many other dances have been described as popular in blackface minstrelsy. Some are of doubtful Afro-American origin, while others are unrelated to Negro dance. The Jig and Clog, two of the most popular minstrel dances, were probably not of Negro origin. However, Ralph Keeler, who was instituted as a "troupe's jig-dancer" auditioned for the position by dancing Juba "to the time which the comedian himself gave me by means of his two hands and one foot, and which is technically called 'patting.'"[51] Perhaps some dances called Jigs were in reality the Juba dance. Matthews said that as minstrelsy progressed the "clog-dances became more intricate and more mechanical — and thereby still more remote from the buck-and-wing dancing of the real Negro."[52]

Other dances mentioned in connection with minstrelsy included the Chicken Flutter and the following, all in the repertoire of the Bryant minstrels: the "Sugar Cane Reel, Congo Coconut Dance, Burlesque African Polka, Corn Shucking Jig, Miss Issippi Fling, Zouave Clog Reel, Smoke House Reel, Union Breakdown . . . and Fling D'Ethiope."[53] These dances were developed for minstrelsy and had probably little relation to real Negro dance. Rourke stated that the minstrels also performed the Walking Jaw-Bone, Dubble Trubble, and Grapevine Twist,[54] all definitely of Negro origin. However, she did not document her statement.

Of all dances performed by the blackface minstrels, the ones which appear most definitely related to the Afro-American heritage are the challenge or competitive section of the Walk-Around and the Essence Dance. All others seem to have been choreographed for minstrel performance, and have little relation to the actual Negro dance. It seems unfortunate that with all the opportunities for seeing the real thing that so little authentic Negro dance was actually used. Perhaps these burnt-cork performers got caught up in the very stereotypes they were creating and began believing them.

According to Winter it was Juba's influence which kept minstrel show dance closer to the original Negro art form than other theatrical derivatives of Negro culture. Yet the similarity was only relative. By the period of the decline of minstrelsy, any resemblance between the blackface stereotype and the real Negro was quite remote. Yet in the minds of many of the minstrel audience, the real Negro was exactly that caricature, that stereotype, which minstrelsy so carefully created and cultivated.

Blackface minstrels danced and sang; therefore all Negroes danced and sang. Blackface performers were funny; therefore all Negroes were comedians. Blackface minstrels wore very dark make-up with grotesquely painted lips and fright wigs; therefore all Negroes must resemble this image. This latter stereotype was so strongly held that when genuine Negroes formed minstrel troupes after the Civil War, they also blackened their already black faces, painted on grotesque lips and wore fright wigs. The effects of minstrelsy have lasted even to the present day.

▣:▣:▣ BLACFACE MINSTRELSY AND ITS EFFECTS

By the time real black minstrels began performing, in the 1860's, the stereotypes previously developed by the blackface performers were so set they could not be broken. The first company formed was Lew Johnson's Plantation Minstrel Company, begun in the early 1860's. Langston Hughes and Milton Meltzer said of this group that "although many of this troup's members were quite dark—being Negro—they nevertheless followed the custom of the white minstrel troupes and blackened their faces and circled their lips with red or white to make their mouths twice normal size."[55] Many other all-black companies were organized, among them the Georgia Minstrels, the Great Non-pareil Coloured Troupe, the Colored Hamtown Singers, and Haverly's Mastodon Genuine Coloured Minstrels. A highly successful integrated group called Primrose and West's Forty Whites and Thirty Blacks was formed in 1893. During this period many great Negro artists became prominent. They will be mentioned in a later chapter.

To the traditional minstrel routines performed primarily for white audiences the Negro brought a certain vitality, a freshness and originality. James Weldon Johnson stated that "they brought a great deal that was new in dancing, by exhibiting in their perfection the jig, the buck and wing, and the tantalizing stop-time dances."[56] Hughes and Meltzer believed that

> . . . as a large group of Negroes performing for the first time on the American stage, they brought with them their indigenous qualities and the genuine basic beat. They revealed new dances, songs and comedy routines that the whites had not yet appropriated. The stop-time taps, the sand [dance] and the Virginia essence were introduced.[57]

One of the effects of blackface minstrelsy, then, was to pave the way for the appearance on the stage of genuine Negroes. Johnson stated that the minstrel companies

> . . . did provide stage training and theatrical experience for a large number of coloured men. They provided an essential training and theatrical experience which, at the time, could not have been acquired from any other source. Many of these men, as the vogue of minstrelsy waned, passed on into the second phase, or middle period, of the Negro on the threatrical stage in America; and it was mainly upon the training they had gained that this second phase rested.[58]

Even though minstrelsy paved the way, in how many instances has the genuine Negro appeared on the popular stage? Hasn't the Negro comedian, singer, musician or dancer been infinitely more successful than the serious black actor on our stages and screens? Has Hollywood yet produced the life story of a black hero: Toussaint l'Ouverture, Frederick Douglass, Malcolm X, or Muhammad Ali?

As Margaret Butcher stated:

> Negro expression, when flattering and obsequiously entertaining to the majority ego, is readily accepted, and becomes extremely popular in a vulgarized, stereotyped form. When more deeply and fully representative, with undiluted idioms, it has invariably been confronted with apathy and indifference and has been faced with a long struggle for acceptance and appreciative recognition. In the minstrel role, for instance, where at best the Negro was only half himself, at the worst a rough caricature, he was instantly popular and acceptable.[59]

Harry Overstreet has said that the image is more powerful than the reality. According to Overstreet:

> The image of the Negro as a kind of clown, with comic turns of speech and ludicrous behavior, has robbed him of dignity. The images of him as lazy, childishly dependent, and dishonest have excused us from having confidence in him; while the images of him as vicious and sexually irresponsible have put him outside the pale.[60]

Overstreet continued with one of the other images created by minstrelsy, the myth of the contented slave:

> Great harm has been done by the "contented slave" stereotype. It has fixed in the minds of the whites the image of a docile creature, happiest when taken care of; and it has made them unable to think of the Negro as having the same urge as a white man to make something of himself.[61]

Blackface minstrelsy was probably responsible for creating the image of the happy, contented slave. In its early days when the Afterpiece still purported to portray plantation life realistically, minstrelsy was obviously pro-slavery. There was little reference to dog-pack hunts for runaway slaves or to whippings; instead the Frolics, the Breakdowns, and the singing were depicted. A glance at any of the old minstrel programs will show at once the distortion which occurred. For example, for one grand finale, billed as Mr. William Welch's original afterpiece and entitled *The Old Plantation, Or, Away Down South in Dixie*, the following description was given:

Field hands, cotton pickers, the neighbors and their children, and the colored folks in general will unite and endeavor to present the most realistic sketch of Negro life in the South before the war, ever produced in minstrelsy, introducing solos, duets, choruses, moonlight pastimes, cotton field frolics, and terminate the scene with the exciting VIRGINIA REEL.[62]

Minstrel songs also reflected this contented slave stereotype. Verses of a typical minstrel song, "We'll All Make a Laugh," from *Christy and Wood's New Song Book,* illustrate this:

Now darkies, sing and play, and make a little fun;
We'll dance upon de green, and beat de Congo drum
We'ere a happy set ob darkies, and we're 'sembled here to play,
So strike de bones and tambourine, and drive dull care away.

Some masses [masters] love dar darkies well, and gib 'em what dey want—
Except it is dar freedom—and *dat* I know, dey won't:
Howeber, *we* am happy, and contented whar we am,
As a serenading party, and a scientific band.

Old massa feeds us bery well, and makes us work all day;
But after sun is set at night he lets us hab our way.
He often comes to see our sports—a fine segar he quaffs—
'Case de merriment ob niggers often make him laugh.[63]

Minstrelsy created many stereotypes, not all of which depict the Negro as inferior. Some of these are quite favorable and actually admit Negro superiority in certain areas. For example: the Negro is more gifted in certain types of music, dancing, and acting than white people; he has greater emotional warmth; he is more religious; he can take sorrows and disappointments more easily; and he can handle animals better. However, according to Gunnar Myrdal:

All such favorable beliefs seem to have this in common, that they do not raise the question concerning the advisability or righteousness of keeping the Negro in his place in the caste order. They do not react against the major need for justification. They rather make it natural that he shall remain subordinate.[64]

Robert Moton had a vivid impression of a minstrel show seen when he was a boy. His words seem to summarize the effects of blackface minstrelsy on both white and black Americans:

Some twenty or thirty men with faces blackened appeared in a semicircle with banjos, tambourines, and the like. The stories they told and the performances they gave were indeed most interesting to me, but I remember how shocked I was when they sang, "Wear dem Golden Slippers to Walk dem Golden Streets," two men dancing to the tune exactly as it was sung by the people in the Negro churches of my community. . . . I felt that these white men were making fun, not only of our colour and of our songs, but also of our religion. . . . White minstrels with black faces have done more than any other single agency to lower the tone of Negro music and cause the Negro to despise his own songs. Indeed, the feeling of the average Negro to-day [1920] is that the average white man expects him to "jump jim-crow" or do the buffoon act, whether in music or in other things.[65]

▣▣▣ NOTES FOR CHAPTER 5

1. *Sketches and Eccentricities of Col. David Crockett, of West Tennessee* (New York: J. and J. Harper, 1833), p. 41.

2. "Sleight of Hand Artist," *New-York Journal or the General Advertiser,* No. 1266, Thursday, April 9, 1767, n.p.

3. L. A. Hall, "Some Early Black-Face Performers and the First Minstrel Troop," *Harvard Library Notes*, I, No. 2 (October, 1920), 41.

4. Loften Mitchell, *Black Drama; the Story of the American Negro in the Theatre* (New York: Hawthorn Books, Inc., 1967), p. 18.

5. George C. D. Odell, *Annals of the New York Stage* (15 vols.; New York: Columbia University Press, 1927), II, 305-06.

6. *Ibid.,* III, 71.

7. Arthur Todd, "Four Centuries of American Dance: Dance Before the American Revolution—1734-1775," *Dance Magazine*, XXIV (March, 1950), 21.

8. Brander Matthews, "The Rise and Fall of Negro Minstrelsy," *Scribner's Magazine*, LVII (June, 1915), 755.

9. *Ibid.*

10. Hans Nathan, *Dan Emmett and the Rise of Early Negro Minstrelsy* (Norman, Okla.: University of Oklahoma Press, 1962), p. 52.

11. Marshall and Jean Stearns, *Jazz Dance. The Story of American Vernacular Dance* (New York: Macmillan Company, 1968), p. 41.

12. *Ibid.,* p. 40.

13. *Ibid.,* p. 42.

14. Francis Anne Kemble, *Journal of a Residence on a Georgian Plantation in 1838-1839* (New York: Harper and Brothers, 1863), pp. 96-97.

15. Charles Haywood, *Negro Minstrelsy and Shakespearean Burlesque, A Reprint from Folklore and Society, Essays in Honor of B. A. Botkin* (Hatboro, Pa.: Folklore Associates, 1966), p. 77.

16. Constance Rourke, *The Roots of American Culture and Other Essays,* ed. by Van Wyck Brooks, Harvest Books (New York: Harcourt, Brace and World, Inc., 1942), p. 263.

17. Robert Nevin, "Stephen Foster and Negro Minstrelsy," *Atlantic Monthly,* XX (November, 1867), 610.

18. Robert Bone, "Preface to the Atheneum Edition," in Sterling Brown, *Negro Poetry and Drama and The Negro in American Fiction* (New York: Atheneum, 1969 [originally published 1937]), n.p.

19. Isaac Goldberg, "How Minstrelsy Really Began: Part II," *The Afro-American* (Baltimore), January 13, 1934, n.p.

20. Marian Hannah Winter, "Juba and American Minstrelsy," *Dance Index,* VI, No. 2 (February, 1947), 31.

21. Nathan, *Dan Emmett,* p. 61.

22. Thomas Low Nichols, *Forty Years of American Life* (2d ed.; London: Longmans, Green, and Co., 1874), pp. 369-70.

23. Winter, "Juba," 33.

24. *Ibid.,* 34.

25. *Ibid.,* 32.

26. T. Allston Brown, "The Origin of Negro Minstrelsy," in Charles H. Day, *Fun in Black; or, Sketches of Minstrel Life, with the Origin of Minstrelsy, by Col. T. Allston Brown, Giving a History of Ethiopian Minstrelsy from 1799* (New York: Robert M. DeWitt, 1874), p. 9.

27. "Vauxhall Gardens – Boz's Description of Juba," *Illustrated London News,* June 24, 1848, p. 404.

28. "Vauxhall Gardens – Unprecedented Success," *Illustrated London News,* July 1, 1848, p. 420.

29. Charles Dickens, *American Notes and Pictures from Italy,* (London: Chapman and Hall, Ltd., 1892), p. 43.

30. Winter, "Juba," 35.

31. "Juba at Vauxhall," *Illustrated London News,* August 5, 1848, p. 77.

32. Winter, "Juba," 38.

33. *Ibid.,* 31.

34. Kemble, *Journal,* p. 97.

35. Stearns and Stearns, *Jazz Dance,* pp. 14-15.

36. Winter, "Juba," 36.

37. Stearns and Stearns, *Jazz Dance,* p. 47.

38. There are several studies tracing the development of minstrelsy, including the previously mentioned works by Brander Matthews, Hans Nathan,

and Robert Nevins and the following works: Laurence Hutton, "The Negro on the Stage," *Harper's New Monthly Magazine,* June, 1889, pp. 131-45; Laurence Hutton, *Curiosities of the American Stage* (New York: Harper and Brothers, 1891); Hans Nathan, "The First Negro Minstrel Band and Its Origin," *Southern Folklore Quarterly,* XVI, No. 2 (1952), 132-44; Dailey Parkman and Sigmund Spaeth, *"Gentlemen, Be Seated!" A Parade of Old-Time Minstrels* (Garden City, N.Y.: Doubleday, Doran and Company, Inc., 1928); and Carl Wittke, *Tambo and Bones. A History of the American Minstrel Stage* (Durham, N.C.: Duke University Press, 1930).

39. Brander Matthews, "Banjo and Bones," *Saturday Review of Politics, Literature, Science and Art* (London), June 7, 1884, pp. 739-740.

40. Arthur Todd, "Four Centuries of American Dance: Negro American Theatre Dance, 1840-1900," *Dance Magazine,* XXIV (November, 1950), 21.

41. Tom Fletcher, *The Tom Fletcher Story — 100 Years of the Negro in Show Business* (New York: Burdge and Company, Ltd., 1954), pp. 37, 39.

42. Hans Nathan, "Two Inflation Songs of the Civil War," *Musical Quarterly,* April, 1943, p. 248.

43. Douglas Gilbert, *Lost Chords* (Garden City, N.Y.: Doubleday, Doran and Company, Inc., 1942), pp. 13-14.

44. Charles Sherlock, "From Breakdown to Ragtime," *Cosmopolitan,* October, 1901, p. 635.

45. Constance Rourke, *American Humor* (New York: Harcourt, Brace and Company, 1931), pp. 88-89.

46. Sherlock, "From Breakdown to Ragtime," p. 633.

47. Stearns and Stearns, *Jazz Dance,* p. 50.

48. *Ibid.*

49. Sherlock, "From Breakdown to Ragtime," p. 634.

50. Henry William Ravenel, "Recollections of Southern Plantation Life," *Yale Review,* XXV, No. 4 (June, 1936), 768.

51. Ralph Keeler, "Three Years a Negro Minstrel," *Atlantic Monthly,* XXIV (July, 1869), 74.

52. Matthews, "Rise and Fall of Negro Minstrelsy," p. 758.

53. Nathan, "Two Inflation Songs," pp. 248-49.

54. Rourke, *Roots of American Culture,* p. 270.

55. Langston Hughes and Milton Meltzer, *Black Magic. A Pictorial History of the Negro in American Entertainment* (Englewood Cliffs, N.J.: Prentice-Hall, Inc., 1967), p. 26.

56. James Weldon Johnson, *Black Manhattan* (New York: Alfred A. Knopf, 1930), p. 89.

57. Hughes and Meltzer, *Black Magic,* p. 26.

58. Johnson, *Black Manhattan,* p. 93.

59. Margaret Just Butcher, *The Negro in American Culture* (New York: Alfred A. Knopf, 1967), p. 27.

60. Harry A. Overstreet, "Images and the Negro," *Saturday Review*, August 26, 1944, p. 5.

61. *Ibid.*

62. Playbill, "The Great Callender Colossal Consolidated Colored Minstrel Festival," Theatre Collection, Lincoln Center of the Performing Arts, New York.

63. *Christy's and White's Ethiopian Melodies. Containing Two Hundred and Ninety-One of the Best and Most Popular and Approved Ethiopian Melodies Ever Written. Being the Largest and Most Complete Collection Ever Published. Comprising The Melodeon Song Book; Plantation Melodies; Ethiopian Song Book; Serenader's Song Book, and Christy and Wood's New Song Book. Published under the Authority of George Christy and Charles White, the Original Delineators of the Popular Ludicrous Negro Character* (Philadelphia: T. B. Peterson, 185?), p. 43.

64. Gunnar Myrdal, *An American Dilemma. The Negro Problem and Modern Democracy*, Harper Torchbooks (2 vols.; New York: Harper and Row, 1962 [originally published 1944]), I, 108.

65. Robert Russa Moton, *Finding a Way Out. An Autobiography* (College Park, Md.: McGrath Publishing Co., 1969 [originally published by Doubleday, Page and Co., 1920]), p. 59.

6

FROM MINSTRELSY TO "DARKTOWN FOLLIES"

❖❖❖❖ From its beginnings in 1843, blackface minstrelsy was to have an effect lasting well over one hundred years. It reached the height of popularity in the late 1850's and 1860's and remained the most popular form of entertainment in America for a fifty-year period. Even in decline the minstrel show lasted well into the present century.

The stereotypes developed by minstrelsy were many: the happy, funny, shuffling, lazy Jim Crow character; the childish and irresponsible but loyal and contented singing and dancing slave; and the freed Negro whose prototype was a character by the name of Zip Coon. This third character was the town Negro: the gaudily dressed, shifty, smart-talking dandy of the streets, with ruffled shirt, gold watch chain, and patent leather shoes. Minstrelsy left us, then, with two main Negro caricatures: the clown and the dandy.

▊▊▊ NEGRO MINSTREL DANCERS

Minstrelsy also left us with the remembrance of a few old plantation dances and with the names of a few authentic Negro performers. In the old Georgia Minstrel troupe, which was eventually renamed for its white manager, Charles Callender, were three famous Negro stars. James Bland, the composer of "In the Evening by the Moonlight" and "Carry Me Back to Old Virginny," was one. Another was Sam Lucas, of whom more will be said shortly. The third was Billy Kersands, a dancer and comedian.

Kersands was a leading exponent of the Essence Dance. Marshall and Jean Stearns quoted Negro minstrel and ragtime composer Arthur Marshall as saying "'Kersands did the Virginia Essence perfectly . . . so much so that when he did it in front of Queen Victoria he had her laughing heartily over it!'"[1] Tom Fletcher, who knew Kersands, described him as

> . . . a natural born comic. Large of stature and with an extra large mouth—which he used to advantage in his comical antics—he was also a good acrobat and tumbler and an excellent dancer. His original dance creations were the soft shoe and buck-and-wing, the dances that were very popular in the early days of show business; the type which are still used today in all musical shows, . . . Now taught by dancing teachers and known as the "soft shoe," this dance was called the "Virginia Essence" by Kersands. He danced it to a slow, four-four rhythm, and for all of his two hundred pounds, was as light on his feet as a person half his size.[2]

Another famous minstrel dancing act was that of the Bohee Brothers. These two were exponents of the Soft Shoe and, according to Edward Marks, "They were, so far as I know, the first team to play banjos while dancing."[3] Traveling to England with one of the minstrel companies, they were well received there both as performers and teachers. One of the brothers, James Bohee, instructed the Prince of Wales on the banjo and did not return to the United States.[4]

Many specialty or "eccentric" dances developed during the decline of minstrelsy were carried on into burlesque and vaudeville. For example, according to a letter written by a Negro minstrel troupe leader in 1879, one of his performers, a Mr. Benjamin Franklin, "waltzes with a pail of water on his head and plays the french horn at the same time."[5] The same letter indicated the versatility of such performers: a man named W. H. Terrell could do the "Iron Jaw" performance [an acrobatic stunt] and "a Jig Dance and a Clog and Double Song and Dance and other tricks."[6]

A Negro artist remembered from the days of minstrelsy was Ernest Hogan, who later became prominent in Will Marion Cook's Negro musical, *Clorindy—The Origin of the Cakewalk.* During his days with a minstrel troupe called the Georgia Graduates, Hogan "scored a success introducing a dance step, the Pasmala—a walk forward plus three backward hops with incidental gestures."[7] James Weldon Johnson wrote that he

> . . . was a notable exception among black-face comedians; his comic effects did not depend upon the caricature created by the use of cork and a mouth exaggerated by paint. His mobile face was capable of laughter-provoking expressions that were irresistible, notwithstanding the fact that he was a very good-looking man.[8]

With few exceptions, most of the Negro minstrel dancers were noted for a variety of talents other than their dancing abilities. Of necessity they were comedians, singers, actors, or instrumentalists and sometimes were all these things. Even Master Juba, with all his dancing expertise, was also an expert on the tambourine. As minstrelsy declined and the Negro performers found work in medicine shows and carnivals, the circus,[9] vaudeville, and the theatre, the dancers maintained their many talents, and also, for a long period of time, their blackface stereotypes.

▯▮▯▮ "UNCLE TOM'S CABIN"

Uncle Tom's Cabin provided one of the first opportunities for Negroes to appear on the stage. Sam Lucas, who began his career with the Georgia Minstrels, appeared in it and eventually became known as "the Grand Old Man of the Negro theatre."[10] He was primarily an actor and comedian rather than a dancer and his career was so long that he lived to play the role of Uncle Tom in the first screen version of Miss Stowe's book in 1915.

As a play *Uncle Tom's Cabin* had an interesting history. It was first produced on the stage in 1852 and came to be the most popular abolitionist drama of the period. For the most part, how-ever, the black characters were played by white actors in black-face. Eventually Negroes were allowed to play their own roles in the play and little by little the drama became more melodra-matic and sentimental. Groups of dancers were added and, ac-cording to a note appearing in the *New York Dramatic Mirror* in 1890 *"Uncle Tom's Cabin* is playing in the English provinces with a ballet of negro girls. They dress entirely in black and send the audience home feeling as though they attended a funeral."[11]

By 1892 Topsy, played by Jennie Chapman, was introducing "several clever breakdowns";[12] and by 1899 the drama was graced by a Cake-Walk. According to the *Dramatic Mirror*:

> Historical accuracy has been put so far aside that a modern swell cake walk was introduced without the least hesitation, and the various specialties brought in—some of them dragged in—had more the flavor of last week's vaudeville than of the South before the war.[13]

Sterling Brown was led to comment that

> . . . plays derived from Harriet Beecher Stowe's novels performed at least two disservices: they glorified the Negro's submissiveness and they fostered the error that the mixed blood characters, merely because they were nearer white, were more intelligent and militant, and therefore more tragic in their enslavement.[14]

About minstrelsy itself M. B. Leavitt was forced in 1912 to state:

> This depiction of the colored race as it was in the South then and is now, with very rare exceptions, so far as representation and talent are concerned, is quite a lost art. Very many of the younger generations are players "at" the negro and not "of" him.[15]

▣▣▣ IN THE MINSTREL MODE

During the early 1890's as the blackface minstrel show was declining in popularity, another avenue for the Negro dancer opened which was to lead to some of the most exciting dance ever seen. Negro dancers, singers, comedians, composers, and directors were finally knocking on the door of the American stage.

Unfortunately, only those Afro-Americans who could play the minstrel roles were welcome. Productions of this era generally used stereotyped minstrel images, make-up, and plot complications. Speaking of this period (and for future decades) Ralph Matthews said:

> The work of the pioneer sepia showman was pretty well circumscribed. America accepted him only in the form that exploited his inherent abilities. Thus the musical comedy field, that gave him opportunity for singing and dancing, talents that are attributed to the black man as a racial heritage, flourished. . . .[16]

One of the first of these theatre pieces was closely related to minstrelsy. In 1891 a production called *The South Before the War* was brought from Louisville to New York City. "This was an entertainment made up of plantation scenes, songs and dances, with some specialties"[17] and featured the Virginia Essence done by dancer Eddie Leonard. In the chorus was a twelve-year-old dancer who was to become world-famous: Bill Robinson.[18]

In 1889 *The Creole Show*, an all-Negro production organized by white Sam T. Jack, opened in New York. According to the Stearns it was one of the first productions to omit blackface make-up,[19] but the biggest change was in the introduction of women into the all-Negro cast. Featured in *The Creole Show* was a line of sixteen singing and dancing chorus girls. Aside from this however, the show maintained the standard minstrel format. There was mention of the girls creating the semi-circle with a woman interlocutor and male end men. The finale consisted of a dance called the Cake-Walk, starring Miss Dora Dean and Charles Johnson.

Tom Fletcher commented:

> The old "chalk-line walk" was revived with fancy steps by Charlie Johnson a clever eccentric dancer, who later married Miss Dora Dean also a dancer, and formed the world-famous team of Johnson and Dean, one of America's foremost vaudeville acts. The "chalk-line walk" then became known as the "Cake Walk."[20]

Johnson and Dean became a lasting vaudeville act, still performing in the late 1930's. Miss Dean, a beautiful woman, was the first Negro to wear thousand dollar costumes, and, "Johnson and Dean sold themselves to audiences through their well-dressed elegance and impressive personalities."[21]

In an interview, Charles Johnson said that he first heard of the Cake-Walk from his mother, ex-slave Eliza Diggs Johnson, who "told of the cakewalks held on the Missouri plantation where she was born."[22] The Cake-Walk, as discussed in a previous chapter, was originally a kind of shuffling movement which evolved into a smooth walking step with the body held erect. The backward sway was added, and as the dance became more of a satire on the dance of the white plantation owners, the movement became a prancing strut. Fletcher reported that the inclusion of women in shows such as *The Creole Show* "made possible all sorts of improvisations in the Walk, and the original was soon changed into a grotesque dance."[23]

The Cake-Walk was a great exhibition dance, wrote Marian Winter, "with such superb theatrical potentialities that it served as a Negro re-entry permit to the stage."[24] Cake-Walking seemed there to stay and it appeared in many productions following *The Creole Show*; particularly noted for their Cake-Walking were Bert Williams and George Walker. An interesting comment on this satirical dance was given by Mark Sullivan, who said that the Cake-Walk was done in the gay nineties by white society

> . . . as a solo performance, at first by men only who imitated a
> colored man strutting in a prize contest . . . [with] head held
> high, chin up, elbows out, shoulders thrown back, and,
> especially prominent, an exaggerated frontal protuberance. . . .
> The cakewalk was the first appearance of a negro movement in
> ball-room dancing, harbinger of more to follow. . . .[25]

In 1895, John Isham, the Negro advance agent for *The Creole Show*, organized another production, *The Octoroons*. The minstrel format was still retained, with the show divided into three distinct parts, the Afterpiece consisting of "a cakewalk jubilee, a military drill, and a 'chorus-march-finale.'"[26]

In 1896 Isham produced *Oriental America*. This was the first all-Negro show to open on Broadway. While *Oriental Amer-*

ica retained the minstrel three-part program, it did offer one break from tradition. Rather than the cake-walking afterpiece, the finale consisted of a selection of operatic arias, "which may help to explain why the show soon closed."[27]

Negro drama historian Frederick Bond suggested that the 1890's marked a shift from one minstrel stereotype to another. Whereas in blackface minstrelsy the main image had been that of the plantation Negro, the image now became that of a "bunglesome imitator, trying to take over . . . modern culture."[28] The Negro was no longer the docile "darky," but rather was now portrayed as the "ridiculous 'coon.'"[29]

In 1898 a musical was produced called *A Trip to Coontown.* Written by Negro Bob Cole, with Sam Lucas of minstrel fame as the star, *A Trip to Coontown* was a production including several firsts. According to Johnson, this was

> . . . the first Negro show to make a complete break from the minstrel pattern, the first that was not a mere potpourri, the first to be written with continuity and to have a cast of characters working out the story of a plot from beginning to end; and, therefore, the first Negro musical comedy. It was, furthermore, the first coloured show to be organized, produced, and managed by Negroes.[30]

While Sam Lucas was starring in *A Trip to Coontown,* his fellow minstrel, Ernest Hogan, was opening in another Negro musical, *Clorindy—The Origin of the Cakewalk.* Written by Will Marion Cook with lyrics by Paul Laurence Dunbar, it was originally designed to star Williams and Walker, the great dancing and comedy team. Cook said his initial idea was to create a story of "how the cakewalk came about in Louisiana in the early Eighteen Eighties."[31] After months of unsuccessful attempts, the show was finally booked at the Casino Roof Garden, but Williams and Walker were out of town, so Ernest Hogan assumed the lead. Having retained his many talents from minstrel days, Hogan took charge and

> . . . hurriedly gathered three or four sensational dancers. He seemed to know everybody. In short, it was just as well that we didn't go on that night [because of rain], for Hogan really needed the extra time to whip the dancers into shape, especially

the cakewalk. After all, our subtitle was "The Origin of the Cakewalk" and we mustn't fall down on that part of the performance.[32]

Clorindy was apparently an instantaneous success. As writer-producer-conductor, Cook remembered opening night:

When I entered the orchestra pit, there were only about fifty people on the Roof. When we finished the opening chorus, the house was packed to suffocation. . . . At the finish of the opening chorus the applause and cheering were so tumultuous that I simply stood there transfixed, my hand in the air, unable to move until Hogan rushed down to the footlights and shouted: "What's the matter, son? Let's go!"[33]

Cook also recalled the superb effort put forth by his performers; his enthusiasm knew no bounds.

My chorus sang like Russians, dancing meanwhile like Negroes, and cakewalking like angels, black angels!
Negroes were at last on Broadway, and there to stay! Gone was the uff-dah of the minstrel! Gone the Massa Linkum stuff! We were artists and we were going a long, long way. . . . Nothing could stop us, and nothing did for a decade.[34]

Clorindy appears to have accomplished two things: first, the potential of the syncopated Negro music was demonstrated because Cook was "the first competent composer to take . . . rag-time and work it out in a musicianly way."[35] Secondly, it introduced the Cake-Walk, with its real charm and high-stepping grace, to the legitimate stage. Langston Hughes, commenting on *Clorindy*, said that, "performed by handsome couples, the women gorgeously gowned, and nobody in blackface, the dance was a joy."[36] For Cook, however, the following season was not to be as successful as the summer of 1898. His next attempt, *Jes Lak White Folks*, closed shortly after opening but not before it introduced Abbie Mitchell to theatregoers. Later Miss Mitchell became famous in the theatre world. The comedian featured in *Jes Lak White Folks* was Irving Jones, who developed a dance known as the Palmer House Walk, which was "the comedy exaggeration of a bowlegged waiter's stride as he carries a tray high above his head."[37]

Oh, have you ever seen Miss Dora Dean,
She is the sweetest gal you ever seen.
Some day I'm going to make this Gal my Queen.
On next Sunday morning, I'm going to marry
Miss Dora Dean.[38]

Inspired by the beautiful Dora Dean of the Johnson and Dean cake-walking act, Bert Williams wrote the song "Miss Dora Dean," which introduced Williams and George Walker to the New York stage. Williams and Walker, the cake-walking comedy team from the West Coast, became one of the most highly paid teams in the theatre.

When quite young, George Walker traveled from his home-town of Lawrence, Kansas, to California by working with medicine shows. Used as an attention-getter, Walker would sing, dance, and play the tambourine and bones until enough people gathered so that the quack doctor could profitably make his sales pitch. Walker remembered "that white people are always interested in what they call 'darky' singing and dancing; and the fact that I could entertain in that way as no white boy could made me valuable. . . ."[39]

At this period little was known of the "love, the humor, and the pathos"[40] of the Afro-American. The minstrel image was so strongly established that the field was open for the study and development of a picture of the real Negro. Arthur Todd believed that "it is thanks to two men, in particular, Bert A. Williams and George W. Walker, that Negro dancing began to flourish into full flower."[41]

Before leaving California for New York, Williams and Walker had the opportunity to meet some native Dahomeans who had been imported for the San Francisco Midwinter Fair. Both were impressed with these Africans and decided that they would try to "delineate and feature native African characters as far as we could, and still remain American, and make our acting interesting and entertaining to American audiences."[42] This they later attempted to do with shows such as *A Senegambian Carnival,* *In Dahomey,* and *Abyssinia,* but the American stereotype of the Negro was so strong that they had to prostitute the original material in order to appear. This stereotype was to continuously haunt Bert Williams, who was forever confined to his role of a clown even though he aspired to serious drama.

The ingredients in the comedies of Williams and Walker usually consisted of "one dishonest, overbearing, flashily dressed character (Walker) and one kindly, rather simple, hard-luck personage (Williams):"[43] the dandy and the clown—exactly the images developed by minstrelsy, yet with a difference. That deviation from the standard was the slight element of sadness, of pathos, of humanity, injected into the character Williams chose to portray.

George Walker has been described as the

. . . spick and span Negro, the last word in tailoring, the highest stepper in the smart coon world. How the fellow did prance in the cakewalk, throwing his chest and his buttocks out in opposite directions, until he resembled a pouter pigeon more than a human being![44]

Bert Williams, on the other hand,

. . . shuffled along in his hopeless way; always penniless, always the butt of fortune, and always human. He reblackened his face, enlarged his mouth, wore shoes which extended beyond the limits of even extraordinary feet, but he never transcended the precise lines of characterization.[45]

As might be expected, the dancing of the pair followed their stage characterizations. "Walker did a neat cakewalk . . . and Williams would follow behind him doing a slow loose-jointed mooch dance."[46] White dancer-actor James Barton reported that Williams performed "a lazy grind, or Mooche. It was popular among Negroes in the South, with rotary hip-slinging and maybe a hop or shuffle."[47] Mary Jane Hungerford credited Williams with originating "swaying, shuffling variations in the soft-shoe style."[48]

Walker, on the other hand, was described by dancer Walter Crumbley as "the greatest of the strutters, and the way he promenaded and pranced was something to see."[49] He has also been credited as the man who "turned the Strut into the Cakewalk and made it famous."[50]

Williams and Walker also danced the Buck and Wing but

the Cake-Walk was their trademark. Johnson said that Williams and Walker "made the cake-walk not only popular, but fashionable."[51] By making the Cake-Walk both popular and fashionable, Williams and Walker paved the way for many dances to come; they also paved the way for the Negro in the legitimate theatre.

Williams and Walker did more than bring popularity to Negro dance, however. Booker T. Washington felt that the comedy of Williams helped everyone understand and appreciate "something of the inner life and peculiar genius . . . of the Negro."[52] Yet there was an aura of sadness surrounding Bert Williams, a feeling of thwarted ambition, of hopeless frustration — perhaps because of the minstrel stereotype, which insisted that the only thing a black man could be was a comedian or a clown. Bert Williams on the stage was a clown, yet W. C. Fields called him "the funniest man I ever saw and the saddest man I ever knew."[53]

Also with the Williams and Walker company was one of the brightest women stars of the period, Ada Overton (Mrs. George Walker). Her great abilities on the stage and her eccentric dancing added much to the Williams and Walker productions. James Weldon Johnson questioned whether Ada Overton Walker had yet been surpassed in her specialties on the American stage.

Walker retired from the stage in ill health in 1907. Shortly after his retirement, Bob Cole, who wrote *A Trip to Coontown* and many other musicals, died, and Williams defected to the white stage, joining the *Ziegfeld Follies*. With the removal of three of the brightest lights in Negro threatre history, there was a lull in activities. It seemed that the Negro had been banished from Broadway to appear only on the stages of Harlem.

"Darktown Follies"

It was the *Darktown Follies*, produced in Harlem's Lafayette Theatre in 1913, which began the nightly procession of whites to Harlem for entertainment. It was also the *Darktown Follies* which introduced the second Negro dance to sweep the country. The dance was Ballin' the Jack, which appeared in the finale of the first act. Johnson said this finale was

. . . one of those miracles of originality which occasionally
come to pass in the world of musical comedy. . . . The whole
company formed an endless chain that passed before the
footlights and behind the scenes, round and round, singing and
executing a movement from a dance called "ballin' the jack," one
of those Negro dances which periodically come along and
sweep the country.[54]

This serpentine, circular, shuffling dance could certainly
have been related to the plantation Ring-Shout; undoubtedly it
was of Negro origin. Parrish saw "Ball the Jack" in the Georgia
Sea Islands and stated that "Snake Hip" would be a more appropriate name for the dance which kept the "head and shoulders
stationary . . . but there [was] a flow of undulating rhythm from
chest to heels, with a few rotations in the hip region. . . ."[55]
The *Dictionary of Folklore* described "Ball the Jack" as "a dance
accompanied by handclapping . . . the head and feet remaining
still and the rest of the body undulating, with a rotation of the
hips called 'snake hips.' "[56]

Van Vechten was impressed with this circular dance of
Darktown Follies and wrote that it was "done with spontaneity
and joy in the doing. A ballet in ebony and ivory and rose.
. . . They stepped about and clapped their hands and 'grew mad
with their bodies.' . . ."[57]

Besides Ballin' the Jack, *Darktown Follies* had a wide
variety of dancing. There was some tap dance done by Toots
Davis and Eddie Rector,[58] a Cake-Walk finale, and a dance called
the Texas Tommy. Ethel Williams, one of the stars of *Darktown*,
told Marshall Stearns that the Texas Tommy

. . . was like the Lindy but there were two basic steps — a kick
and hop three times on each foot, and then add whatever you
want, turning, pulling, sliding. Your partner had to keep you
from falling — I've slid into the orchestra pit more than once.[59]

Darktown Follies was the only bright spot in Negro musical
comedy for nearly ten years, until 1921. It broke away from the
minstrel tradition since it introduced a romantic interest on the
stage, something which could not be done before. Each of the
shows between 1890 and World War I seemed to widen the gap
from strict minstrelsy, although in many productions the break
seemed almost imperceptible. Blackface makeup was dropped

early in the progression away from minstrelsy, yet Bert Williams continued to make up throughout his career. The all-male minstrel shows ended almost immediately with the introduction of women in *The Creole Show* (1891). With the introduction of a continuous story line in *A Trip to Coontown* (1898), the three distinct sections of the minstrel program also disappeared. Elegance and sophistication were certainly introduced into the threatre by Johnson and Dean, Williams and Walker, James Weldon Johnson and his brother J. Rosamond Johnson, Bob Cole, Will Marion Cook, Paul Laurence Dunbar, and many others. Humanity and pathos were definitely a part of the character played by the great Bert Williams.

Yet the minstrel stereotype remained. The cliché of the happy, singing, dancing, funny black man continued; persistent also was the Negro as smart-talking dandy. But there *was* a break with minstrel tradition between 1895 and 1913. As Sterling Brown has written:

> These plays were fresher and less artificial than the minstrel
> shows. . . . But the blackface tradition was too fixed in the
> American threatre, and blackface meant chicken stealing and
> the rest of the clowning and such dialect as this from no less
> a writer than Dunbar: "Don't you know dere's no sich word in
> the dictionnumgary as perskivered. . . . I's got de best
> edjumingation."[60]

A complete break with minstrelsy was a long time coming, but it was hastened by one of the best musical comedies presented in the American theatre. Despite its name, *Shuffle Along* (1921) helped create the standards by which musicals are judged. It introduced some Negro dances which are remembered even now, and some people who were among the greatest stars of Broadway: Florence Mills, Josephine Baker, and the teams of Miller and Lyles and Sissle and Blake.

▣▣▣ NOTES FOR CHAPTER 6

1. Marshall and Jean Stearns, *Jazz Dance. The Story of American Vernacular Dance* (New York: Macmillan Company, 1968), p. 51.

2. Tom Fletcher, *The Tom Fletcher Story — 100 Years of the Negro in Show Business* (New York: Burdge and Company, Ltd., 1954), p. 61.

3. Edward B. Marks, *They All Sang. From Tony Pastor to Rudy Vallée* (New York: Viking Press, 1935), p. 92.

4. James Weldon Johnson, *Black Manhattan* (New York: Alfred A. Knopf, 1930), p. 93.

5. John J. Jennings, *Theatrical and Circus Life* (San Francisco, Calif.: A. L. Bancroft and Company, 1882), p. 225.

6. *Ibid.*

7. Stearns and Stearns, *Jazz Dance*, p. 119.

8. Johnson, *Black Manhattan*, pp. 102-03.

9. Chapters 9 and 10 in Stearns and Stearns, *Jazz Dance*, provide detailed information on dance in the small Negro minstrel shows, medicine shows, and carnivals. These shows persisted in the South until well into the 1940's. (Stearns and Stearns, *Jazz Dance*, p. 59.)

10. Langston Hughes and Milton Meltzer, *Black Magic. A Pictorial History of the Negro in American Entertainment* (Englewood Cliffs, N.J.: Prentice-Hall, Inc., 1967), p. 27.

11. "The Handglass—'Uncle Tom's Cabin,'" *New York Dramatic Mirror*, December 6, 1890, p. 5.

12. "At the Theatres: Grand—'Uncle Tom's Cabin,'" *New York Dramatic Mirror*, June 11, 1892, p. 2.

13. "At the Theatres: Third Avenue—'Uncle Tom's Cabin,'" *New York Dramatic Mirror*, April 29, 1899, p. 16.

14. Sterling A. Brown, *Negro Poetry and Drama and The Negro in American Fiction* (New York: Atheneum, 1969), p. 109.

15. Michael Bennett Leavitt, *Fifty Years in Theatrical Management* (New York: Broadway Publishing Co., 1912), p. 38.

16. Ralph Matthews, "The Negro Theatre—A Dodo Bird," in Nancy Cunard, *Negro Anthology* (London: Wishart and Co., 1934), p. 312.

17. Johnson, *Black Manhattan*, p. 96.

18. Stearns and Stearns, *Jazz Dance*, p. 180.

19. *Ibid.*, p. 118.

20. Fletcher, *Tom Fletcher Story*, p. 41. For a discussion of the origin of the Cake-Walk as performed on the plantations by Negro slaves, see Chapter III.

21. Stearns and Stearns, *Jazz Dance*, p. 286.

22. "Cakewalk King; 81 Year Old Charles E. Johnson Still Dreams of New Comeback with Dance Step of Gay 90's," *Ebony*, February, 1953, p. 100.

23. Fletcher, *Tom Fletcher Story*, p. 103.

24. Marian Hannah Winter, "Juba and American Minstrelsy," *Dance Index*, VI, No. 2 (February, 1947), 45.

25. Mark Sullivan, *Our Times. The United States 1900-1925* (6 vols.; New York: Charles Scribner's Sons, 1932), IV, 242. The Cake-Walk was truly a dance of imitation, with the whites now imitating the blacks, who were already satirizing the whites.

26. Johnson, *Black Manhattan*, p. 96.

27. Stearns and Stearns, *Jazz Dance*, p. 119.

28. Frederick W. Bond, *The Negro and the Drama* (Washington, D.C.: Associated Publishers, Inc., 1940), p. 35.

29. *Ibid.*, p. 36.

30. Johnson, *Black Manhattan*, p. 102.

31. Will Marion Cook, "Clorindy, the Origin of the Cakewalk," *Theatre Arts*, XXXI (September, 1947), 61.

32. *Ibid.*, p. 64.

33. *Ibid.*

34. *Ibid.*, p. 65.

35. Johnson, *Black Manhattan*, p. 103.

36. Langston Hughes, "The Negro and American Entertainment," in John P. Davis, ed., *The American Negro Reference Book* (2d ed.; Englewood Cliffs, N.J.: Prentice-Hall, Inc., 1966), p. 831.

37. Marks, *They All Sang*, p. 87.

38. Chorus to the song "Miss Dora Dean," written by Bert Williams. Quoted from a Christmas card sent by Chas. E. and Dora Dean Johnson, n.d., Schomburg Collection of Negro Literature and History, New York, N.Y.

39. George W. Walker, "The Real 'Coon' on the American Stage," *Theatre Magazine* (New York), August 1906, p. 224.

40. *Ibid.*, p. ii.

41. Arthur Todd, "Four Centuries of American Dance. Negro American Theatre Dance, 1840-1900," *Dance Magazine*. XXIV (November, 1950), 33.

42. Walker, "Real 'Coon,' " p. i.

43. Jessie Fauset, "The Gift of Laughter," in Lindsay Patterson, comp. and ed., *Anthology of the American Negro in the Threatre. A Critical Approach* (New York: Publishers Company, Inc., 1967), p. 32.

44. Carl Van Vechten, *In the Garrett* (New York: Alfred A. Knopf, 1920), pp. 313-14.

45. *Ibid.*, pp. 312-13.

46. Jack Donahue, "Hoofing," *Saturday Evening Post*, September 14, 1929, p. 29.

47. Stearns and Stearns, *Jazz Dance*, p. 117.

48. Mary Jane Hungerford, *Creative Tap Dancing* (New York: Prentice-Hall, Inc., 1939), p. 11.

49. Stearns and Stearns, *Jazz Dance*, p. 122.

50. *Ibid.*

51. Johnson, *Black Manhattan*, p. 104.

52. Booker T. Washington, "Interesting People — Bert Williams," *American Magazine,* September, 1910, p. 600.

53. W. C. Fields, quoted in Fauset, "Gift of Laughter," p. 33.

54. Johnson, *Black Manhattan,* p. 174. This same Circle Dance finale was purchased by Florenz Ziegfeld and became one of the greatest hits of the *Ziegfeld Follies.*

55. Lydia Parrish, *Slave Songs of the Georgia Sea Islands* (New York: Creative Age Press, Inc., 1942), p. 117.

56. "Ball the Jack," in Maria Leach, ed., *Funk and Wagnalls Standard Dictionary of Folklore, Mythology, and Legend* (2 vols.; New York: Funk and Wagnalls Company, 1950), I, 112.

57. Van Vechten, *In the Garrett,* pp. 316-17.

58. Stearns and Stearns, *Jazz Dance,* p. 127.

59. Ethel Williams, quoted by Stearns and Stearns, *Jazz Dance,* p. 129.

60. Brown, *Negro Poetry and Drama,* p. 112.

7

FROM DANCE HALL
TO THEATRE

▣▐▣▐▣ After the Civil War there was a gradual
migration of Negroes northward: at first not
many left, but the trend was established.
Many of those remaining in the South became
tenant farmers and their days were not too
different from those of slavery. For the majority of Negroes in the South, the church served
as the social center: the church — with its ban
on dancing.

During the reign of Ernest Hogan and
Williams and Walker in the North, what did
the Southern Negro do for entertainment? Of
course there were the traveling carnivals and
circuses. There were the small all-Negro minstrel troupes touring the South. Eventually
there developed a Negro vaudeville circuit
called T.O.B.A., the Theatre Owners' Booking
Association (frequently nicknamed "Tough
On Black Actors"). Many well-known Negroes
began their careers with T.O.B.A.; such entertainers as Bessie Smith, the Whitman Sisters,
and Tom Fletcher were headliners on this

circuit. There was, naturally, a white vaudeville circuit also, but only the Negro superstars were accepted for its tours. Bill Robinson, Johnson and Dean, and Bert Williams all traveled the white circuit.[1]

▒▒▒ DANCE HALLS

For the most part the Southern Negro had to create his own entertainment. Despite the church ban on dance, black people in the South continued to dance. In a study conducted by Atlanta University in the early 1900's concerning "Morals and Manners Among Negro Americans," some interesting comments were made on the wholesome amusements available to young people. One of the Negro civic leaders in Alabama responded that in his area "many are making the effort to eliminate the dance by the skating rink and such other amusements as will take up their time at times when they usually go to the dance halls."[2] A respondent from Florida stated that "The greatest amusement here for young people is dancing and I do not consider this wholesome."[3] From Maryland an answer stated that there was practically no provision made for the amusement of young people and the "tendency to theatrical and house and ball dances [is] harmful."[4] A respondent in Oklahoma answered that "our greatest struggle in this direction is to counteract the influence of the dive Negro as seen in the music and dancing."[5] "The dance halls are the curse of the day,"[6] came an answer from West Virginia.

The Jook House

Despite the ban of the church and the chagrin of the civic leaders, the Negro continued to dance. Segregated public dance halls developed throughout the South. There also developed a peculiar institution called the jook, or jook house. Jook is the anglicized pronunciation of "dzugu," a word from the Gullah dialect of the African Bambara tribe meaning "wicked." Jook came to mean a Negro pleasure house: either "a bawdy house or house for dancing, drinking and gambling."[7] It was in these jooks that "the Negro dances circulated over the world"[8] were created. Before being seen on the stage by the outside world, these dances made the rounds of the Southern jooks.

According to Hurston, one of the dances originating in a jook was the Black Bottom. This dance "really originated in the Jook section of Nashville, Tennessee, around Fourth Avenue. This is a tough neighbourhood known as Black Bottom—hence the name."[9] Another dance was the Big Apple which originated in an abandoned church converted into a Negro dance-hall near Columbia, South Carolina.[10] The Big Apple contained many vestiges of its Afro-American origin, including (at the beginning of the dance) moving with a shuffling step around in a circle with arms waving and hips undulating. Even after being rearranged by Arthur Murray into a popular ballroom favorite, some of the original Ring-Shout influence was still observable, as evidenced by Bosley Crowther's comment that, "it would seem to bear striking resemblance to some sort of mass convulsion, embracing as it does all the weird and assorted shakings of shoulders and shanks."[11]

During the same time period that Ballin' the Jack was being introduced to white audiences in the *Darktown Follies*, a huge Negro migration to the North was beginning. The combination of World War I, with its plentiful jobs in the defense industry, and years of poor crops and a rise of lynchings in the South drew thousands of Negroes to the North. In 1916 "an official investigation by the Department of Labor set the total migration of Negroes from the South over a period of 18 months at 350,000."[12] Many of these Southern Negroes came to New York City; the growth of Harlem was phenomenal. The biggest influx occurred in the 1920's. Harlem grew from a community of 50,000 blacks in 1914 to 80,000 by 1920 to 200,000 by 1930.[13]

When the Southern Negroes moved North they took with them their dance. They brought the Big Apple and the Black Bottom, the Charleston and Ballin' the Jack, the Shimmy and the Mooche. New dances were invented at the big Harlem ball-rooms: the Savoy, the Renaissance, the Alhambra. The dances included the Lindy Hop, Jitterbug, Shag, Suzi-Q, Camel Walk and Truckin'.[14]

Harlem Night Clubs

Dances, frequently developed at one of the ballrooms, were picked up by Negro entertainers and used in their acts at the Cotton Club, Leroy's, or Smalls' Paradise. The entertainers rarely became well known, but many were excellent dancers and did much to popularize the dances. Dancers included the Cotton Club's Cora La Redd (who did much to popularize Truckin') "Rubber Legs" Williams, and Chuck Robinson and J. Alexander of Smalls' Paradise.[15]

The 1920's saw the Black Renaissance, the literary awakening of the Negro writer. As Langston Hughes said, this was the time when "the Negro was in vogue."[16] Naturally some of the new dances were described by the literary figures residing in Harlem. In *Home to Harlem*, Claude McKay wrote the following description of an act at the Congo Club:

> They danced, Rose and the boy. Oh, they danced! An exercise of rhythmical exactness for two. There was no motion she made that he did not imitate. They reared and pranced together, smacking palm against palm, working knee between knee, grinning with real joy. They shimmied, breast to breast, bent themselves far back and shimmied again. Lifting high her short skirt and showing her green bloomers, Rose kicked . . . , the boy kicked even with her. They were right there together neither going beyond the other.[17]

White people from downtown began coming to Harlem to sit in the bars and cabarets, to watch the black dancers, to stare at black people. Langston Hughes wrote:

> The lindy-hoppers at the Savoy even began to practice acrobatic routines, and to do absurd things for the entertainment of the whites, that probably never would have entered their heads to attempt merely for their own effortless amusement. Some of the lindy-hoppers had cards printed with their names on them and became dance professors teaching the tourists. Then Harlem nights became show nights for the Nordics.[18]

These dances, originated by the Negro in the South or in Harlem, became popular with the white watchers and thus spread out from Harlem to the white world. In 1926 Lester Walton wrote:

These Negro dances invariably become the rage with white people months and sometimes years, after colored people have waxed enthusiastic over them. When the Charleston became a fad with the white public, colored folk were hoofing the Black Bottom. Now, when the Gay White Way, Fifth Avenue, Riverside Drive and Long Island are turning to the Black Bottom, Negroes from coast to coast are going wild over the latest dance known as Messin' Around.[19]

⊟⊟⊟ DANCE IN THE THEATRE

The trend toward the adoption of anything black—and particularly of Afro-American dance—all began with *"Shuffle Along, Running Wild,* and the Charleston," as Langston Hughes wrote.[20] *Shuffle Along* (1921) marked the beginning of the Black Renaissance, which was not to end until the economic crash of 1929.

Written by two teams (Flournoy Miller and Aubrey Lyles, and Noble Sissle and Eubie Blake), *Shuffle Along* "did anything but shuffle. It exploded onto the stage."[21] The star of the production was Florence Mills, and an unknown girl, Josephine Baker, was in the chorus line; Hall Johnson and William Grant Still played in the orchestra. Hughes called it "a honey of a show. Swift, bright, funny, rollicking, and gay, with a dozen danceable, singable tunes,"[22] among them "I'm Just Wild About Harry" and "Love Will Find a Way."

Florence Mills

Florence Mills began her career early in life, joining her sisters in a singing-dancing act billed as The Mills Trio. Known as Baby Florence, she won medals in amateur Cake-Walk and Buck dancing contests.[23] Not until *Shuffle Along*, however, did she become a star. She has been described as follows:

> . . . an attractive-looking, bright-eyed and sweet-voiced singer, a graceful, magnetic and vivacious dancer, she had a delicate grace, daintiness and refinement, a femininity, which made her a real terpsichorean artist.[24]

Leaving *Shuffle Along*, Miss Mills starred in Lew Leslie's *Plantation Revue* (which also played in London), *Dixie to Broadway*, and *Blackbirds* (1926). She was to star in *Blackbirds of 1928*, but she died in November, 1927. Receiving her nickname "Little Blackbird" from a song she sang in *Dixie to Broadway*, she was once asked about her fame. According to a newspaper account, she was said to have replied: "But I'm not famous . . . I have my own way of dancing—and singing—and it happens to be popular."[25] The newspaper article continued: "Happens to be popular! Her eccentric dancing, with its comedy streak and jocose tricks, will remain the outstanding contribution to terpsichore for many a long day."[26]

It was *Shuffle Along* that brought her fame and fortune. Claude McKay saw her and wrote:

> Florence Mills ran away with the show, mimicking and kicking her marvelous way right over the heads of all the cast and sheer up to the dizzying heights until she was transformed into a glorious star.[27]

McKay also had insight into the effect of *Shuffle Along*:

> I thought I'd feature *Shuffle Along* in *The Liberator*. I wanted especially to do this because the Negro radicals of those days were always hard on Negro comedy. They were against the trifling, ridiculous and common side of Negro life presented in artistic form. Radical Negroes take this attitude because Negroes have traditionally been represented on the stage as a clowning race. But I felt that if Negroes can lift clowning to artistry, they can thumb their noses at superior people who rate them as a clowning race.[28]

"Shuffle Along" and "Runnin' Wild"

Shuffle Along had some long-lasting effects on the American theatre, particularly in the area of dance. Doris Abramson thought that *Shuffle Along*, "originally written and produced by Negroes for a Negro audience, was to become, along with jazz and the blues, what white audiences expected of Negroes."[29] Mary Jane Hungerford stated that it was *Shuffle Along* which was "responsible for the beginning of popularity for real tap dancing."[30] Richard Watts reported that "the influence of the Negro revue was felt in other ways, in addition to its lesson in semi-barbaric movement."[31] According to Watts, *Shuffle Along* started the search for dances of apparent Negroid origin which resulted in the popularity of the Black Bottom, the Charleston and the Staircase Dance.[32] The Stearnses, reflecting on the success of *Shuffle Along*, stated:

> Attention was focused on the talents of the Negro in
> vernacular comedy, song, and dance, and jobs opened up for
> Negro performers. Above all, musical comedy took on a new and
> rhythmic life, and chorus girls began learning to dance to jazz.[33]

Shuffle Along also began a rash of Negro musical comedies: such productions as *Put and Take*, the *Plantation Revue, Strut Miss Lizzie, Liza* (with dancer Eddie Rector), and *Runnin' Wild* (1923). "A dance, rather than any dancer, was the hit of *Runnin' Wild*,"[34] and this dance was the Charleston.

Frederick Bond made the following remarks concerning *Runnin' Wild* and the Charleston:

> Before the interest in *Shuffle Along* had hardly cooled, Miller
> and Lyles, who were by now the two best known Negro
> dramatists of the race, carried to Broadway another brisk, and
> thrilling production, *Runnin' Wild*. While this latter ambitious
> attempt was not to be classed with the former, perhaps its
> greatest feature was its introduction of the Charleston dance.
> Like most American dances, it was a distinct Negro creation,
> heretofore little known except in Harlem and its native South
> Carolina. But following its association with *Runnin' Wild*, it
> suddenly became not only nationally but internationally
> accepted.[35]

The Charleston actually was first introduced in Irving C. Miller's production *Liza*, but did not really become popular until James P. Johnson composed his hit song "Charleston" for *Runnin' Wild*. James Weldon Johnson noted that when the dance began "the major part of the chorus [supplemented] the band by beating out the time with hand clapping and foot-patting. . . . the effect was electrical. Such a demonstration of beating out complex rhythms had never before been seen on a stage in New York."[36]

One of the better descriptions of the Charleston was written by Gilbert Seldes not long after he first saw it performed in *Runnin' Wild*.

The first impression made by the Charleston was extraordinary. . . . [I felt] pleasure in seeing a dance which uses the whole body far more than the now conventional steps of the fox-trot and one-step. The Charleston as an exhibition dance employed to advantage what the extravagant shimmy had brought in—the quiver of the body otherwise motionless, the use of the torso in dance; it added the movements of the hips, thighs, buttocks, made familiar since *Shuffle Along*—the characteristic negro freedom of movement, frank and engaging; the patting which accompanies the blues was varied to slapping and the hand fell on any portion of the body, in a frenzy. As if excited by the dance to the point where they did not care whether they were graceful or not, the chorus assumed the most awkward postures—knock-knees, legs "akimbo," toes turned in until they met, squattings, comic little leaps sidewise. And then the visual high point of the dance, these seemingly grotesque elements were actually woven, in the rhythm of the dance, into a pattern which was full of grace and significance, which was gay and orgiastic and wild.[37]

There was some question about the creation of the Charleston, George White having taken credit for originating it in a *Scandals* production. In a pointed letter to the *New York Times*, Will Marion Cook refuted White's claim to both the Charleston and Black Bottom, saying that frequently dances were seen and then "discovered by white theatrical producers and sold to the public as an original creation."[38] Cook continued, "It is doubtful if Mr. White even saw a 'Charleston' until he attended the final rehearsals of *Runnin' Wild*."[39]

White's claim to the dance was not the first time credit for the Charleston had been taken from the Negro. Roark Bradford, who wrote the original story upon which Marc Connelly based *Green Pastures*, also wrote a newspaper article entitled "New Orleans Negro Declared Not Guilty of the Charleston." Bradford said that the original Negro step was known as the Jay-Bird, "which seems to have been a vague basis of distortion for the Charleston . . . ." However, he continued that "racially speaking, no Negro ever originated anything that required as much physical exertion as the present brand of Charleston."[40] Bradford, like so many Southerners, thought he knew all about the Negro and considered himself a student of Negro dance, yet he had obviously never seen authentic Afro-American or African dance, nor even the dances of Congo Square. Bradford made another comment which revealed not only his ignorance, but his personal bias: "The fact is that his Yankee brother has libeled the Negro race again [by crediting the Negro with the Charleston], just as he did in tracing the alleged origin of jazz music to him."[41]

Bradford could well have been correct, though, in his statement that the Charleston was a distortion of a step known as the Jay-Bird. An old Negro dance song was discovered which, when repeated over and over, certainly has the feeling of a Charleston rhythm.

> Jay Bird settin' on a hickory limb
> Down in de harvest gahdens;
> Picked up a brickbat, hit 'em on de jaw,
> Down in de harvest gahdens.[42]

A more objective observer, Harold Courlander, said that while the Charleston had some characteristics of traditional Negro dance, the dance itself "was a synthetic creation, a newly-devised conglomerate tailored for wide spread popular appeal."[43] Courlander was probably correct in his assumption, since no record of the Charleston being performed on the plantation has been discovered. However, there is widespread evidence that the Jay-Bird was done, and other specific movement sequences have been discovered in dances of Afro-American origin which relate directly to the Charleston, leading one to believe that the dance was, at least, strongly influenced by Negro dance.

The Charleston probably came from the "star" or challenge dances which were all a part of the dance called Juba. Some authors consider the Charleston the direct descendant of the Juba dance,[44] while Katherine Dunham found Charleston steps being done in Haiti and called by the name of La Martinique.[45] Melville Herskovits found "a perfect example of the Charleston" in the ancestral rites for the chief of an Ashanti tribe,[46] while Frederick Kaigh, after extensive study of African witchcraft, stated that "the children of Africa were doing the Charleston before Julius Caesar had so much as heard of Britain—and they are doing it still."[47] The particular sequence of steps for the Charleston appearing in *Runnin' Wild* probably was, as Courlander suggested, newly devised for popular appeal. That the Charleston changed from its original version was stated by Wilbur Young quite clearly.

At first, the step started off with the simple twisting of the feet, to rhythm in a lazy sort of way. [This could well be the Jay-Bird.] When the dance hit Harlem, a new version was added. It became a fast kicking step, kicking the feet, both forward and backward and later done with a tap.[48]

Undoubtedly before the dance was put on the stage even further changes were made, so Courlander's thesis seems plausible.

An outgrowth of the Charleston, the Black Bottom was introduced on the stage in Irving C. Miller's 1924 production of *Dinah*. "The Black Bottom gained a popularity which was only little less than that of the Charleston."[49] The Black Bottom, too, changed from the original dance. Stearns and Stearns stated that, "the chief gesture that survived on the ballroom floor was a genteel slapping of the backside, along with a few hops forward and back."[50]

Hurston commented that "when the Negroes who knew the Black Bottom in its cradle [Nashville] saw the Broadway version they asked each other, 'Is you learnt dat NEW Black Bottom yet?'"[51] As Hurston suggests, this was proof that the Black Bottom had undergone such modification that it was no longer *their* dance.

Following the Charleston of *Runnin' Wild* and the Black Bottom of *Dinah*, there were still more Negro musicals. Sissle and Blake collaborated on *Chocolate Dandies* (1924) in which Josephine Baker became a featured star through her clowning in the chorus line. Also in the production was a new eccentric dancer, Johnny Hudgins, "who was a comic pantomimist in blackface."[52]

Josephine Baker

Miss Baker began her career traveling the vaudeville circuit with Bessie Smith. When she was fifteen, she attempted to join the *Shuffle Along* show but when her age was discovered she was dismissed, to return again at sixteen. According to Noble Sissle, Miss Baker became a protégée of Eubie Blake and him. She "had difficulty remembering her dance routines but usually she replaced the steps we had taught her with something entirely

Josephine Baker in the Folies Bergères, taken from a French postcard

new and more spectacular."[53] Following her chorus line experiences in *Shuffle Along* and *Chocolate Dandies*, she traveled to Paris with *La Revue Nègre* in 1925. Baker, who was hailed in Paris as the personification of *le jazz hot*, was credited with "creating the continued vogue for jazz music in France."[54]

The *New York Times* stated that Baker's "real stardom dated from 1926, when she romped onstage at the Folies Bergères in Paris wearing a girdle of bananas and nothing else."[55] In a review of her dancing, Andre Levinson described her as

> . . . a sinuous idol that enslaves and incites mankind. Thanks to her carnal magnificence, her exhibition comes close to pathos. It was she who led the spellbound drummer and the fascinated saxophonist in the harsh rhythm of the Blues. It was as though the jazz, catching on the wing the vibrations of this mad body, were interpreting, word by word, its fantastic monologue. The music is born from the dance and what a dance! Certain of Miss Baker's poses . . . had the compelling potency of the finest examples of Negro sculpture. It was no longer a grotesque dancing girl that stood before the audience, but the Black venus that haunted Baudelaire.[56]

While Miss Baker was a star of great magnitude in Europe from 1926 on, she did not achieve stardom in the United States, despite repeated attempts, until her appearance here in 1951. While in later years she was known primarily for her singing and beautiful costumes, Miss Baker continued to dance and in her 1951 appearance included the Black Bottom.[57] In the field of dance, Josephine Baker will probably be most remembered for her introduction of the Charleston and Black Bottom to European audiences.

Florence Mills and Josephine Baker, two of the greatest Negro stars of the 1920's, both began their Broadway careers as dancers in a chorus line. The chorus lines in these Negro productions were to have a lasting effect on Broadway musicals. "The precision work by the chorus line was a new departure. For the first time the chorus danced closely together with a swinging rhythm."[58]

In addition, there certainly was a new interest in dance. These black dances moved from being spectator dances to being participant dances. The dancing craze spread throughout the country as everyone tried the Big Apple, the Charleston, and the Black Bottom. There even was a premium placed on the hiring of Negro domestics who could Charleston well enough to teach it to the lady of the house.[59] During this period, however, the dances became greater attractions than the black dancers performing them. It was not until *Blackbirds of 1928* that a Negro dancer achieved stardom, and that dancer was the inimitable Bill "Bojangles" Robinson.

Bill Robinson

Produced by Lew Leslie, *Blackbirds of 1928* was to have starred Florence Mills. After her death the role was taken by Adelaide Hall, but the performer who stood out above all others was Bill Robinson. Stearns and Stearns felt that Robinson "achieved his lone success in spite of *Blackbirds*, for the sets were a series of stereotypes with Negro children eating watermelons and so forth."[60] Robinson, when he was "discovered" was already fifty years old and had been dancing since the 1890's, when he had appeared in *The South Before the War*.

During the past few years a cloud has hung over Robinson's image; he has been called an "Uncle Tom" and accused of doing disservice to the race. This reputation was due mainly to his unfortunate movie role as a shuffling, acquiescent, funny servant (the minstrel stereotype of the contented slave) of Shirley Temple. Robinson took over and continued Step 'n' Fetchit's role on the movie screen. Robinson's real contributions, however, were made not on the screen but rather in the dance.

> It is not a condemnation of Bill Robinson that he was rarely seen in a part which reflected beneficially on the Negro race. Rather has it been the fault of the producers themselves, who never allow sympathetic coloured characters to find their way into pictures.[61]

Bill Robinson, who died in 1949 at the age of 71, was a legend in his time. Many things have been written about his accomplishments, from his youthful dancing for pennies on the streets of Richmond, to his acquisition of the name "Bojangles," his ability to run backwards, his diet of four quarts of ice cream

Bill "Bojangles" Robinson

Carl Van Vechten (Permission granted through the courtesy ⊔₁ Saul Mauriber, photographic executor of the estate of Carl Van Vechten)

daily, his affinity for the police, his charitable contributions, and his dream of creating the famous Stair Dance. Above all Bill Robinson was a great tap dancer and an unparalleled entertainer.

That Robinson never wore the standard tap shoes but chose, instead, wooden-soled shoes is a matter of record. Also a matter of record was his ability in dancing to create sound — nearly any rhythmic sound produced by a drum. Langston Hughes described his dancing as

> . . . *human percussion.* No dancer ever developed the art of tap
> dancing to a more delicate perfection, creating little running
> trills of rippling softness or terrific syncopated rolls of mounting
> sound, rollicking little nuances of tap-tap-toe, or staccato runs
> like a series of gun-shots. Bojangles, dancing alone on a stage
> with the orchestra quiet, could make tantalizing, teasing
> offbeats, sometimes merging into a series of restful continuous
> bars of sound that would build up in tempo and volume to a
> climax like a burst of firecrackers. Some writers on American
> Negro jazz have classified the percussion rhythms of Bill
> Robinson's feet as among the finest of sounds in jazz music.[62]

Alain Locke said much the same thing but related the sound to an African heritage.

> A Bojangles performance is excellent vaudeville, but listen
> with closed eyes, and it becomes an almost symphonic
> composition of sounds. What the eye sees is the tawdry American
> convention; what the ear hears is the priceless African
> heritage. . . .[63]

In a most interesting and unusual chapter on Robinson, the Stearnses pointed out that his contribution to tap dance was that "he brought it up on the toes, dancing upright and swinging . . . with a hitherto unknown lightness and presence."[64] Robinson made an outstanding contribution to American dance in his style of tap dancing.

Earl Tucker

Making his Broadway debut also in *Blackbirds of 1928* was another dancer whose style of dance was far from that of Robinson. This was Earl "Snake Hips" Tucker, who had first danced in New York at a Harlem night club called Connie's Inn. The dance performed by Tucker was the old Southern Negro dance known as the Snake Hip, a relic of the even older Congo dance previously discussed. A calmer version of the Snake Hip has been seen recently in the movements of Elvis Presley,[65] so the dance continues even yet.

The Stearnses included an excellent description of Tucker's dance, only a part of which is quoted here. According to their account,

> . . . the fact that the pelvis and the whole torso were becoming increasingly involved in the movement was unavoidably clear. As he progressed, Tucker's footwork became flatter, rooted more firmly to the floor, while his hips described wider and wider circles, until he seemed to be throwing his hips alternately out of joint to the melodic accents of the music.[66]

Critics often shied away from attempting to describe Tucker's dance because of the apparent sexual implications. One article in *American Dancer* praised him but described his as "a dance that has never been shown before. It is his [Tucker's] conception of the low down dance":[67] not a very clear description, but a provocative one. Hurston felt that Tucker was one of the very few performers of the real Negro school it had ever been her pleasure to see in New York.[68]

Authentic as Tucker undoubtedly was, his style of dance was too shocking to most observers to really affect the dance of the period. The Stearnses believed that even in 1968 Tucker, "the king of eccentric dancers, pantomiming the facts of life, would still be far ahead of the times."[69]

One other dance came out of the 1920's, and this was the Lindy Hop, popularized at Harlem's Savoy Ballroom. As described previously by Hughes, the Lindy became an acrobatic dance mainly for the entertainment of white spectators. The Lindy dancers separated eventually into two distinct schools, each with its own devotees: the floor school, or those who preferred steps done on the floor; and those who preferred steps done in the air, naturally much more spectacular. The air steps led directly to the development of the Jitterbug seen during the 1940's.

Two leading exponents of the Lindy were Leon James, who was considered king of the Savoy, and Al Minns. Minns and

James formed a team and performed a program on the history of jazz dance with Marshall Stearns as narrator. After Stearns' death in 1966, they still performed, narrating and demonstrating many of the old dances from the Turkey Trot through the Lindy to the current fad dances.

The Lindy Hop, like the Charleston and Black Bottom, was probably devised for popular appeal. However, traces of Afro-American origin may be seen in the hip movement or shimmy, the shuffling steps, and the time allowed for improvisation during the breakaway phase of the dance. Perhaps there is even a trace of the old challenge dance in the Lindy. In a description of the Lindy seen at the Savoy, Arnold Haskell stated that "there was a strong feeling of rivalry amongst the couples. . . . They improvised and separated, men and women performing intricate steps in front of one another, and then coming together again."[70]

In his article, "Dances of Harlem," John Banting described the Lindy Hop as a synthesis of all the other popular dances of Afro-American origin. One of these improvisations was "the Geetchie Walk consisting of strutting proudly alone and slightly wriggling from head to feet, the head shaking rather like a musical timer."[71] This is certainly a description of the Shimmy, called by some the Shake Dance. Since the Lindy contained a step known as the Geetchie Walk, and since many of the hip-shaking dances in the United States are of Afro-American origin,[72] the origin of the Lindy Hop could be credited to the black American.

During the 1920's from the production of *Shuffle Along* to that of *Blackbirds of 1928*, the minstrel stereotype was somewhat altered, but white audiences still wanted the Negro to entertain them with comedy, singing, and dancing. The black musical comedies of the period were much more successful than the black dramatic fare, even though the plays (*Emperor Jones, All God's Chillun Got Wings, In Abraham's Bosom,* and *Porgy*) were in the main written by white playwrights, with their biases. The Negro was certainly portrayed in a more favorable light, in most cases, and yet it was difficult to overcome the strongly implanted images.

James Weldon Johnson summed up the years between 1855 and 1930:

> The past seventy-five years have seen vast changes in the
> position of the Negro in the theatre. Beginning as a mere butt

of laughter, he has worked on up through minstrelsy and the musical-comedy shows to become a creator of laughter; to become a maker of songs and dances for the people. This alone is an achievement not to be despised.[73]

However, there were some restrictions placed upon the singing and dancing of the Negro. White audiences obviously enjoyed the Negro's song and dance, but only in the proper setting, which was usually burlesque, vaudeville, or musical comedy. It was to be many years before a Negro was allowed to join a ballet company or sing at the Metropolitan Opera. Margaret Butcher summed up the plight of the Negro dancer:

> The realization that for many years the Negro dancer could not aspire above the vaudeville level is a sorry one. His accomplishments within such a narrow medium of footwork and eccentricity were possible only through sheer genius. What Stella Wiley, Ada Overton, Florence Mills, "Peg Leg" Bates, Pete, Peaches, and Duke, the Berry Brothers, and Bill Robinson could have done in a freer medium with more artistic background can only be imagined.[74]

In 1937 Sterling Brown succinctly clarified the position of the Negro then in the American theatre, "Broadway, for all of its growing liberal attitude, is still entranced with the stereotypes of the exotic primitive, the comic stooge and the tragic mulatto."[75]

Certainly in the dance, as well as the theatre, Brown's "comic stooge" had been present and accepted by audiences. While the "tragic mulatto" was a more suitable theme for drama, it was by means of the "exotic primitive" that black dancers gained success on the concert stage. Following unsuccessful attempts by many dancers, it was Asadata Dafora (Horton)'s production, *Kykunkor,* which showed the potential available in "primitive" dance.

░░░ NOTES FOR CHAPTER 7

1. The T.O.B.A. has been so well covered in two other books that it is not discussed further here. These sources are: Langston Hughes and Milton Meltzer, *Black Magic. A Pictorial History of the Negro in American Entertainment* (Englewood Cliffs, N.J.: Prentice-Hall, Inc., 1967); and Marshall and Jean

Stearns, *Jazz Dance. The Story of American Vernacular Dance* (New York: Macmillan Company, 1968).

2. "Morals and Manners Among Negro Americans," *Atlanta University Publications No. 18* (1914), p. 91.

3. *Ibid.*, p. 93.

4. *Ibid.*, p. 94.

5. *Ibid.*, p. 95.

6. *Ibid.*, p. 97.

7. Zora Neale Hurston, "Mimicry," in Nancy Cunard, *Negro Anthology* (London: Wishart and Co., 1934), p. 44. Music in the jook houses was frequently provided by a large, gaudily decorated, coin-operated phonograph; hence the origin of the term "juke-box."

8. *Ibid.*

9. *Ibid.*

10. Kyle Crichton, "Peel That Apple—the Story of the 'Big Apple,'" *Collier's*, December 4, 1937, p. 22.

11. Bosley Crowther, "From the 'Turkey Trot' to the 'Big Apple,'" *New York Times Magazine*, November 7, 1937, p. 14.

12. Peter M. Bergman, *The Chronological History of the Negro in America* (New York: Harper and Row, 1969), p. 378.

13. Gilbert Osofsky, "Harlem: The Making of a Ghetto," in John Henrik Clarke, ed., *Harlem. A Community in Transition* (New York: Citadel Press, 1969), p. 25.

14. Writers' Program, New York (City), "Dance," in *The Dance*, Research Studies Compiled by Workers of the Writers' Program of the Works Progress Administration in New York City, for "Negroes of New York," Article No. 1, unpublished manuscript in Schomburg Collection of Negro Literature and History, 1938, p. 3.

15. Wilbur Young, "Dances Originating in Harlem," in *The Dance* (unpublished), Article No. 4, p. 3.

16. Langston Hughes, *The Big Sea* (New York: Hill and Wang, 1940), p. 223.

17. Claude McKay, *Home to Harlem* (New York: Harper and Brothers, 1928), p. 93.

18. Hughes, *Big Sea*, p. 226.

19. Lester A. Walton, "Lucky Roberts Autographs Songs for the Prince" (no publication given), Dance Clipping File, Dance Collection, Lincoln Center of the Performing Arts, New York, October 17, 1926. n.p.

20. Hughes, *Big Sea*, p. 223.

21. Loften Mitchell, *Black Drama. The Story of the American Negro in the Theatre* (New York City: Hawthorn Books, Inc., 1967), p. 76.

22. Hughes, *Big Sea*, p. 223.

23. James Weldon Johnson, *Black Manhattan* (New York: Alfred Knopf, 1930), p. 197.

24. W. H. Ferris, "Writer Reviews Negro Stage For Past Forty Years; Cites Notables," *Pittsburgh Courier*, November 19, 1927, n.p.

25. Robert Campbell, "Florence Mills' Life Story," *Philadelphia Tribune*, December 22, 1927, n.p.

26. *Ibid.*

27. Claude McKay, *A Long Way from Home* (New York: Lee Furman, Inc., 1937). p. 142.

28. *Ibid.*, p. 141.

29. Doris E. Abramson, *Negro Playwrights in the American Theatre 1925-1959* (New York: Columbia University Press, 1969), p. 26.

30. Mary Jane Hungerford, *Creative Tap Dancing* (New York: Prentice-Hall, Inc., 1939), p. 14.

31. Richard J. Watts, "Musical Comedy and Revue Dancing—How Did It Develop?" *Dance Magazine*, II (January, 1929), 17.

32. *Ibid.*, 60.

33. Stearns and Stearns, *Jazz Dance*, p. 139.

34. *Ibid.*, p. 145.

35. Frederick W. Bond, *The Negro and the Drama* (Washington, D.C.: Associated Publishers, Inc., 1940), p. 121.

36. Johnson, *Black Manhattan*, p. 190.

37. Gilbert Seldes, "Shake your Feet," *New Republic*, November 4, 1925, p. 283.

38. Will Marion Cook, "Letter to the Editor of the *New York Times*," *New York Times*, December 26, 1926, Sec. 7, p. 8.

39. *Ibid.*

40. Roark Bradford, "New Orleans Negro Declared Not Guilty of the Charleston" (no publication given), January 3, 1926, Dance Clipping File, Dance Collection, Lincoln Library of the Performing Arts, Lincoln Center, New York, n.p.

41. *Ibid.*

42. Mary Virginia Bales, "Some Negro Folk Songs of Texas," in J. Frank Dobie, ed., *Follow de Drinkin' Gou'd*, Publications of the Texas Folk-Lore Society, VII (Austin, Texas: Texas Folk-Lore Society, 1927), p. 106. That the Jay-Bird was a popular dance song on the plantations is evidenced by the fact that it is also found in other sources besides Bales. The first to publish the song was Talley in 1922. (Thomas W. Talley, *Negro Folk Rhymes* [New York: Macmillan Company, 1922], pp. 14-15.) Talley gave four verses, none of which were exactly like those given by Bales. The first two verses are quoted here.

De Jaybird jump from lim' to lim',
An' he tell Br'er Rabbit to do lak him.
Br'er Rabbit say to de cunnin' elf:
'You jes want me to fall an' kill myself.'

Dat Jaybird a-settin' on a swingin' lim'.
He wink at me an' I wink at him.

He laugh at me w'en my gun 'crack,'
It kick me down on de flat o' my back.

Another version was given by Dorothy Scarborough, *On the Trail of Negro Folksongs* (Cambridge: Harvard University Press, 1925), pp. 110-11, who quoted the song as follows:

Jay-bird sittin' on a hickory limb;
He winked at me and I winked at him,
And I picked up a rock an' hit him on the chin.
And he said, 'Now, look here, Mr. Wilson,
　　Don't you do dat agin.'

Scarborough gave yet another version of Jay-Bird, sent her by a friend, Mrs. Tom Bartlett:

"Jay-bird settin' on a hickory limb;
I picked up a rock an' hit him on the chin.
'Good God, Nigger! Don't you do that again!'
　　Whoo-jamboree, a-whoo-whoo!"

While each of the versions is slightly different, all versions retain the same rhythm and could well be the forerunner of the Charleston step.

43. Harold Courlander, *Negro Folk Music U.S.A.* (New York: Columbia University Press, 1963), p. 189.

44. Among the authors describing the Charleston as coming from Juba are the following: Bales, "Some Negro Folk Songs," in Dobie, ed., *Follow de Drinkin' Gou'd*, pp. 105-06; Alain Locke, *The New Negro* (New York: Albert and Charles Boni, 1925), p. 218; and Stearns and Stearns, *Jazz Dance*, p. 29.

45. Katherine Dunham, "The Negro Dance," in Sterling A. Brown, Arthur P. Davis, and Ulysses Lee, *The Negro Caravan* (2d ed.; New York: Dryden Press, 1941), p. 999. In the West Indies, the terms Juba and Martinique were used synonymously.

46. Melville J. Herskovits, *The Myth of the Negro Past* (Boston: Beacon Press, 1958 [originally published 1941]), p. 146.

47. Frederick Kaigh, *Witchcraft and Magic of Africa* (London: Richard Lesley and Co. Ltd., 1947), p. 21.

48. Young, "Dances Originating in Harlem," in *The Dance* (unpublished), Article No. 4, p. 5.

49. Johnson, *Black Manhattan*, p. 190.

50. Stearns and Stearns, *Jazz Dance*, p. 111.

51. Hurston, "Mimicry," in Cunard, *Negro Anthology*, p. 46.

52. Stearns and Stearns, *Jazz Dance*, p. 146.

53. Noble Sissle, "How Jo Baker Got Started," *Negro Digest*, August, 1951, p. 17.

54. Hughes and Meltzer, *Black Magic*, p. 340.

55. "Josephine Baker Is Beset by More Woes," *New York Times*, March 13, 1969, Sec. L, p. 50.

56. Andre Levinson, "The Negro Dance Under European Eyes," quoted

in Edith J. R. Isaacs, *The Negro in the American Theatre* (New York: Theatre Arts, Inc., 1947), p. 73.

57. "Music. Josephine's Return," *Newsweek*, March 12, 1951, p. 82.

58. Stearns and Stearns, *Jazz Dance*, p. 147.

59. Allon Schoener, ed., *Harlem On My Mind. Cultural Capital of Black America 1900-1968* (New York: Random House, 1968), p. 66.

60. Stearns and Stearns, *Jazz Dance*, p. 151.

61. Peter Noble, *The Negro in Films* (London: British Yearbooks Ltd., 1948), pp. 63-64. Comments such as those of Mark Hellinger ("Broadway Loves Bill Robinson," *Pittsburgh Courier*, November 15, 1930, n.p.) did not help Robinson's image in later years either, although they demonstrate primarily the bias of the author. Hellinger wrote "Bill Robinson—the world's finest tap dancer. A colored chap who is one of the whitest men I ever knew. . . ." "A great character, this Bill Robinson. A colored man who is white."

62. Langston Hughes, *Famous Negro Music Makers* (New York: Dodd, Mead and Company, 1957), p. 49.

63. Alain Locke, *The Negro and His Music* (Washington, D.C.: Associates in Negro Folk Education, 1936), p. 135.

64. Stearns and Stearns, *Jazz Dance*, pp. 186-87. Chapter 23 of this book shows a totally different egotistical and unpleasant view of Robinson than anything previously published. It is also extremely well documented.

65. *Ibid.*, p. 3.

66. *Ibid.*, p. 236.

67. "Broadway Whispers," *American Dancer*, II (September, 1928), 30.

68. Hurston, "Mimicry," in Cunard, *Negro Anthology*, p. 46.

69. Stearns and Stearns, *Jazz Dance*, p. 238.

70. Arnold L. Haskell, *Balletomania. The Story of an Obsession* (New York: Simon and Schuster, 1934), p. 281.

71. John Banting, "The Dances of Harlem," in Cunard, *Negro Anthology*, p. 323. The "Geetchie" which Banting mentioned is probably a misspelling of the word "Geechee," meaning a Negro from the tidewater section of Georgia and South Carolina. That the particular step described by Banting was called the "Geetchie Walk" leads one to suspect an even stronger Negro influence on the Lindy Hop, since the Geechee Negroes are the Sea Island people. The Sea Islanders, it will be remembered, were nearly totally isolated from the whites, so that there was an extremely strong retention of Africanisms.

72. Chadwick Hansen, "Jenny's Toe: Negro Shaking Dances in America," *American Quarterly*, XIX (Fall, 1967), 554-63.

73. Johnson, *Black Manhattan*, p. 224.

74. Margaret Just Butcher, *The Negro in American Culture* (New York: Alfred A. Knopf, 1967), pp. 94-95.

75. Sterling A. Brown, *Negro Poetry and Drama and The Negro in American Fiction* (New York: Atheneum, 1969 [originally published 1937]), p. 139.

8

BLACK CONCERT DANCE

⠿⠿⠿ The comic, the dandy, and the exotic primitive: these three images were well established in the black theatre of the late 1920's. The all-Negro musical comedies could do little to alter the stooge and city-slicker roles, since these were the only ones acceptable to white audiences, and to be successful financially, the productions had to be viewed by audiences at least partly white. By the 1920's these stereotypes were so pervasive that many black people also believed that they were accurate.

The Emperor Jones, as well as other plays of the period, furthered the image of the Negro as an exotic primitive — partially savage, heathen, and uncivilized, and yet interesting in a brutal sort of way. Differences between black and white were highlighted and dramatized in the attempt to avoid portraying the Negro as a human being with the same feelings, emotions, and sensitivities of the white.

Black people like Frederick Douglass,

James Weldon Johnson, and Booker T. Washington achieved success through perseverance, intelligence, and ambition but most whites seemed to consider them odd rather than exemplary. Blacks were supposed to be clowns and comedians, not human beings.

▣▣▣▣ THE EARLIEST PIONEERS

Through the 1920's black dancers had appeared on the American stage in tap, soft shoe, and jazz routines. These types of dance were considered "natural" and black performers had been well accepted in them. Yet there were many Afro-Americans who aspired to other types of dance. These people paved the way for the eventual success of Asadata Dafora (Horton) and Katherine Dunham, and were in fact the earliest black American pioneers in the area of concert dance.

Hemsley Winfield

Hemsley Winfield is a name unknown to most, but he was one of the real forces in opening concert dance to the Negro. He was born in Yonkers, New York, in 1906. Winfield's mother was a playwright and it was in one of his mother's plays, *Wade in the Water* (1927), that he and a company of actors and dancers made their debut in the Cherry Lane Theatre in Greenwich Village.

While not primarily a dancer, Winfield later filled in for an actress in Oscar Wilde's play *Salome*, performing Salome's dance. Encouraged by this success, he turned to dance as a means of expression. When he was twenty-five, Winfield organized the Negro Art Theatre in Harlem, which later became the Negro Art Theatre Dance Group. This group of eighteen dancers was sometimes known as the New Negro Art Dancers and included Edna Guy, Ollie Burgoyne, and Randolph Sawyer.

The first concert given by this group was in a small theatre on top of Manhattan's Chanin Building on April 29, 1931, "before an audience that overtaxed the capacity of the midget house."[1] The concert was billed as the "First Negro Concert in America."[2] Included in the performance were two solos danced by Edna

Guy, "Figure From Angkor-Vat" and "Temple Offering," both influenced by the Denishawn school of dance. Also included were two suites, one based on African themes and the other on Negro spirituals.[3] In his review, John Martin wrote that this was the "outstanding novelty of the dance season."[4] That Martin would term this beginning effort of the Negro in concert dance a "novelty" is indicative of the prevailing feeling of white people toward the attempts made by the Negro to achieve seriousness, depth, and dignity. Martin's review was not overly favorable toward Winfield's solo, "Bronze Study," which the review continued, "proved to be merely the exhibition of an exemplary physique."[5]

Winfield and his company continued to perform and eventually joined with the Hall Johnson Choir in Mr. Johnson's play, *Run Lil Chillun* (1933), choreographed by Doris Humphrey. Also in 1933, Winfield directed the ballet for the Metropolitan Opera Company's production, *Emperor Jones*. In his role of the Witch Doctor, supported by his own company, Winfield became the first Negro to dance at the Metropolitan.

> Mr. Winfield was noted for his interpretation of primitive Negro rituals. His savage dances amid jungle scenes of voodoo in the final part of *Emperor Jones* at the opera's premiere last January received critical acclaim surpassed only by that given to Lawrence Tibbett in his role as the fugitive hero . . . .[6]

Winfield was still performing the role of the Witch Doctor in *Emperor Jones* at the time of his sudden death from pneumonia at the age of twenty-seven. The manager of the Dancer's Club, of which he was an honorary member, made the following statement:

> "Mr. Winfield was the pioneer in Negro concert dancing. In that field he attained for his race an eminence comparable to that of Paul Robeson in the musical field. He achieved amazing results in such a short time."[7]

Edna Guy

Edna Guy, who assisted Winfield with the first performance of the New Negro Art Dancers, had been strongly influenced by Ruth St. Denis, having studied at Denishawn. After hearing Paul

Robeson sing, she became interested in Negro themes and began dancing to them. "Thus began the Negro 'Dance Spiritual.' She was the first to start what has since become part of many dance programs — the 'Dance Spiritual.'"[8]

Comparing her solos, "Figure from Angkor-Vat" and "Temple Offering" to her dance spirituals, Martin, the *New York Times* dance critic, wrote:

> It is not in these dances ["Angkor-Vat" and "Offering"] which echo and imitate the manner of the dancers of another race that the Negro dancers are at their best, but in those which their forthrightness and simplicity have full play. Miss Guy's group of "spirituals" and the primitive ritual dances by the group can be counted in this category.[9]

Randolph Sawyer, one of Winfield's original company, later joined the "newly formed Dance Center of Gluck Sandor and Felicia Sorel . . . Sawyer was appropriately cast and irreplaceable."[10] Through the years Sawyer also danced in a variety of Broadway musicals.

Charles Williams — Charlotte Kennedy (Hampton Institute Creative Dance Group)

While Winfield, Guy, and Sawyer were dancing in New York City, another concert group was being developed at the Negro college, Hampton Institute, in Hampton, Virginia. The group, which was known as the Creative Dance Group, was made up of Hampton students and performed in schools throughout the country. The first concert away from the Hampton campus was given in Richmond in 1925.[11] Under the leadership of Charles H. Williams, director of physical education at Hampton, and Mrs. Charlotte Moton Kennedy, the group presented in their programs a wide variety of dances based particularly on their African heritage.

Some of the dances were purely African, reconstructed by Mr. Williams from wide reading and from demonstrations by African students attending the Institute. Such dances as "Mamah Parah" (danced on stilts), "Wyomamie" (dealing with African marriage customs), and "The Fangai Man" (who served many of the same functions as the West Indian Obeah man) dealt with African matters.[12] When Margaret Lloyd, dance critic of the *Christian Science Monitor,* viewed "Wyomamie," the bride was danced by an American student, while the part of the groom was taken by a native of Liberia, Frank Roberts. She observed that compared to Robert's groom, the bride "seemed oddly sophisticated. There was more torsion to his body, more swing and sway to his movements."[13] Lloyd's comparison of native African movement to American abilities provided interesting insight into the effects of the acculturative process.

Besides the African dances, the Hampton Dance Group also used black American material. Some of the older plantation dances, such as the Juba and Cake-Walk, were choreographed for presentation. One of the most powerful compositions, entitled "Middle Passage," portrayed the horrors of the slave trade. Margaret Lloyd reported of one performance: "The program ended significantly with those devout expressions of Christian faith, those rich contributions to American music and American folklore, the Negro spirituals, in dance form."[14]

The influence of Hampton's Creative Dance Group on the development of Negro concert dance cannot be overlooked. Even though the company was composed of amateurs, most of them were majoring in physical education and would eventually be teaching in the segregated Negro schools throughout the country. With the dance training each of these company members received, their potential for creating both future programs and knowledgeable audiences of dance was obvious. Black concert dance companies were formed throughout the segregated institutions of the South, including Spellman College in Atlanta, Fisk University, Howard University, and Tuskegee Institute.[15]

Eugene Von Grona (American Negro Ballet)

At the same time that Hampton's Creative Dance Group was making its first appearance in New York City (November, 1937), another black dance group was debuting in Harlem's Lafayette Theatre. The American Negro Ballet, under the direction of Baron Eugene Von Grona, opened on November 21, 1937 to notably poor reviews. Nearly all of the reviewers felt that the

Negro was much better suited to other types of dance than ballet. While kindly remarking on the earnestness and zeal of the performers, the critic for the *New York Sun*, for example, felt that the "leaps and pas de deux . . . were singularly incongruous to these performers, honestly as they worked at them."[16]

Von Grona had worked with the dancers in the American Negro Ballet for three years prior to this premiere performance. Martin, commenting on the amount of time spent in preparation stated that:

> Not unnaturally, the performance partook considerably more of the nature of a pupil's recital than an epoch-making new ballet organization. Much of the time, indeed, it was frankly inept.[17]

Of all the critics, Martin, however, was the only one who preferred the "oversimplified" choreography of Stravinsky's "Firebird" to the other numbers on the program. The critic for the *Sun* preferred a composition entitled "Southern Episode," performed to the music of Duke Ellington and W. C. Handy. This composition was performed "with genuine finesse and consistent ensemble unity, but all of the performances were animated by the earnestness and zest which the Negro brings with him to the stage."[18]

Stark Young, reviewing the performance in an issue of the *New Republic* reported that the evening "dwindled from promise and possibility to disappointment."[19] He concluded his review with:

> The discussion of the Negro in ballet is worth more if we begin not so much with demonstration, competition, vindication, but with certain elements inherent in the Negro endowment. This point has nothing to do with the primitive, with condescension, with people of another race prescribing to Negroes what they should attempt or should stick to. It concerns only the fact that any art, in this case dancing, begins with the particular medium that that would-be creator presents, which in the Negro's case implies among other qualities, indisputably a gift of rhythm, relaxation and harmony, a narrative sense, improvisation, and vivid, free powers of the imagination.[20]

One other review, that of Joseph Pearlman, indicated a common attitude toward Negro achievements in dance. After the performance, Pearlman wrote:

Von Grona was swamped with congratulations. Through most of them ran the note of amazement at the way members of the troupe had *temporarily* abandoned the Suzy-Q and other forms of terpsichorean hotcha to go on to conquer a manner of dance expression once strange to them.[21] (Italics mine.)

While the American Negro Ballet performance was not an overwhelming success, it was a beginning. *Newsweek*, in a short article, mentioned that the troupe planned to perform on Broadway and then go on tour.[22] These plans appear not to have materialized. Langston Hughes, though, stated that the American Negro Ballet was later featured in Lew Leslie's *Blackbirds*.[23]

Wilson Williams

Although no reference to him can be found before the early 1940's, Wilson Williams must also be considered one of the forerunners of black concert dance. The sixteen-member Negro Dance Company was formed under his leadership. Williams acted as producer-director, choreographer, and dancer, with Felicia Sorel as co-director, choreographer, and dancer. Among the works presented in the first performance (January 1943) were "Breaking the Ice," choreographed and danced by Anna Sokolow, Miss Sorel's "Dance Calinda," Gluck-Sandor's "St. James Infirmary," and two of Williams' works: "Prodigal Son" and "Spring Ritual."[24]

Prior to his founding the Negro Dance Company, Williams taught dance and lectured on the Negro in dance at the Harlem branch of the YMCA. It was, perhaps, during this time that he clarified his ideas regarding the reasons for the failure of the Negro dancer and choreographer to fulfill the promise indicated by his native ability. With so much Negro influence in theatrical and social dance (including the use of Negro thematic material by Doris Humphrey, Charles Weidman, Martha Graham, and Helen Tamiris), Williams felt that the Negro should assert himself more effectively in concert dance. He identified the chief reasons for the failure to do so as:

1. The easy praise which follows the serious attempts of Negroes in any field of art, resulting in a double standard of criticism: Negro effort rather than accomplishment being overpraised.

Asadata Dafora (Horton)'s *Kykunkor*

Carl Van Vechten (Permission granted through the courtesy of Saul Mauriber, photographic
executor of the estate of Carl Van Vechten)

2. The persistent acclaim of the Negro as a natural dancer who does not need the training and strict discipline so necessary to white dancers.
3. The lack of a recognized school, to function in the manner of an Academy, to transpose the abundant native talent of the Negro dance and dancer into consciously creative channels.[25]

The minstrel stereotype of the Negro as a natural comedian-singer-dancer was recognized by Williams, and the Negro Dance Company was founded in part to eliminate this minstrel image. That Williams was at least partially successful in this attempt may be seen in the artists and performing groups following him.

Asadata Dafora (Horton)

Highlighted by a frenzied, possession-inducing Witch-Doctor dance and hypnotic drum rhythms, *Kykunkor* exploded on the New York scene in 1934. "One of the most exciting dance performances of the season";[26] "more rewarding than any other recital has been this spring";[27] "unique and excellent piece of work";[28] and "one of the most intoxicating performances I've ever witnessed":[29] these were the critics' comments about *Kykunkor*. Created and produced by Asadata Dafora (Horton), the production (termed an "opera" by its originator) had impact of such magnitude that it undoubtedly opened the door for the Afro-American in the field of concert dance. *Kykunkor* was first performed in 1934, before the advent of Williams, but Horton's influence on American Negro concert dance was of such importance that he deserves the place of honor in the discussion of the earliest pioneers.

Asadata Dafora, a native of Sierra Leone, came to New York in 1929 after having studied music in Europe. Dafora frequently used the surname of Horton, because of "the fact that his great-grandfather was taken as a slave to Nova Scotia and adopted there the family name of his owners."[30] When *Kykunkor* was first produced in New York, Dafora was forty-five years of age.

The plot of *Kykunkor*, subtitled *The Witch Woman*, dealt with a curse placed on a bridegroom (enacted by Dafora) and the attempt to remove it. The plot served primarily as a vehicle for the presentation of African instrumental and vocal music and dance, as shown by the program notes for Act III.

> The festival starts in real earnest. There is first the AGUNDA, the dance of joy; then the EBOE, the jester, dances. The BATTOO, or dance of challenge follows, then the war-dance, and then the JABAWA or festival dance.[31]

Lincoln Kirstein, in a review of the production, was most impressed with the "remarkable dancing of three male Negroes, two part Arab and one from nearer the Congo."[32] While praising the native Africans in the cast, Kirstein at the same time referred to the dances of the Afro-American women from Harlem as "innocent of much thought, monotonous and tedious to watch. . . ."[33] His most telling statement regarding the stereotype of the African and Afro-American as savage and brutal however, was, "Back stage after the performance must be a tricky place for a white man to navigate. It's not back stage to some of the performers."[34]

Kykunkor portrayed the African as a human being, thus amazing many white Americans who had never considered the black as anything but savage and animalistic. As noted in the official program, Dafora would listen to his dressing room visitors express their amazement at the thought that Africa may not be so barbaric and answer them by saying "'Barbarism? . . . but there are lynchings in this country.'"[35]

In his review of the production, Martin praised the dancing — particularly that of Abdul Assen, who played the part of the Witch Doctor. At no time did Martin infer that the Africans were savages, but he stated that Frazer's *Golden Bough* would "assume a new and more credible meaning under the impact of this extraordinary visualization of something of their content."[36] Noting that many in the cast were native Africans and that some were American-born, Martin made a statement reminiscent of Lloyd's about the movement differences between American Negroes and those of Africa. "Though this difference is frequently noticeable in the performance, there is such an air of sincerity about it all that no very severe criticism is justifiable on this score."[37]

Kykunkor was probably a success because it was exciting, colorful, and spectacular. It was a lavish production, complete with stimulating African drum rhythms, costumes, songs, and dances. Performances of this type are still enjoyed today, as evidenced by the success in the United States of national companies from Ghana, Kenya, and Senegal. *Kykunkor* could be considered the forerunner of these national companies which introduce their culture to the American public through dance.

Yet *Kykunkor* was something more. It was the first performance by black dancers on the concert stage which was entirely successful. It revealed the potential of ethnic material to black dancers, and herein lay Dafora's value as a great influence on black concert dance. It was Dafora who first experimented with African heritage thematic material, and his success caused other dancers to do the same. Martin stated that *Kykunkor* was "a revelation of the possibilities of the field"[38] and it proved to be just that.

Kykunkor proved that black dancers working with material from their own heritage could be successful on the American concert stage. Martin also, however, stated that "Negroes cannot be expected to do dances designed for another race,"[39] and *Kykunkor* demonstrated that dance done by a black person could be considered seriously as an art form, *if* the dancer performed within the restricted thematic area. Many years would pass before any Afro-American dancer could succeed outside the proscribed limits.

The successful use of an African theme in *Kykunkor* led to several imitations. The Federal Theatre Project organized an African unit, which in 1937 produced a dance-drama entitled *Bassa Moona* under the direction of Momodu Johnson. Dafora followed his own formula in a second dance-drama entitled *Zunguru* (1938). Walter Terry termed this production "untouched by the softening hands of civilization" and stated that it contained "the wildest dancing you ever saw."[40] *Zunguru* however did not have the impact of *Kykunkor*, even though it was a more mature and better developed production.

On March 7, 1937,[41] a program was presented at the 92 Street YMHA entitled *Negro Dance Evening*. It might be characterized as a program of transition. This evening of dance was co-directed by Edna Guy of the New Negro Art Dancers and included some of her Dance Spirituals. Part I on the program was listed as "Africa" and featured Asadata Dafora and some members of his company.

Part II of the program was labeled "West Indies" and featured several Haitian ceremonial dances performed by a newcomer to New York, Katherine Dunham, destined to become a leader in the establishment of Afro-American concert dance. One of the dancers was Talley Beatty, who also made his mark in the dance world. The *Negro Dance Evening* brought together the established and the rising generations, the people who opened the door and those who stepped across the threshold.

▤▤▤ THE PRIMARY LEADERS

Two great trend-setters, Katherine Dunham and Pearl Primus, arose after the earnest efforts of the early pioneers in black concert dance. Quite alike in some respects, these two women emerged to prominence in the 1940's. Their efforts were to lead to the acceptance of the black dancer as a performing artist.

Katherine Dunham

Walter Terry wrote that black dance in this country could not have emerged as it has "without the efforts of that super, black dance pioneer, Miss Katherine Dunham . . . [who captured] the love and admiration of the whole world of dance."[42] *Dance Magazine,* which belatedly bestowed upon Miss Dunham its coveted Award in 1968, recognized her as "the forerunner of the numerous fine contemporary Negro groups now emerging and developing."[43]

Dunham discovered dance in high school,[44] where she excelled in athletics — particularly basketball and track. Eventually she studied at the University of Chicago and also took classes from dancers Ludmila Speranzeva and Mark Turbyfill. It was apparently through Turbyfill that Dunham came into contact with Ruth Page, and it was in Page's West Indian ballet, *La Guiablesse* (1933) that Dunham had her first leading role.[45]

To help earn her way, Dunham gave dance lessons while

majoring in anthropology at Chicago. She chose this major because of "the strong connection between the dance, music and archaic ceremonials of a people and that people's social and economic history."[46] She also had special training in field techniques from noted anthropologist Melville Herskovits, who influenced her to choose the West Indies as the location for an anthropological investigation of Negro dance. Of this choice Dunham wrote in 1938:

> Realizing that the amalgamation of the Negro into white America has in a large measure brought about a complete lack of contact with those things which were racially his, I have recently begun an intensive study of the Negro under other less absorbing cultural contacts; in the West Indies the French, Spanish and English influence have been of far less importance than that of the American in this country. In the recreational and ceremonial dances of the island peasantry are preserved the dance forms which are truly Negro.[47]

It was through a combination of dance and anthropology that Dunham received the chance to go to the West Indies. In the abandoned store where she gave dance lessons, she also staged recitals and it was in one of these recitals that a daughter of Julius Rosenwald saw her. "Soon afterwards Katherine was dancing before the Rosenwald Committee to show them the kind of research she wanted to do."[48] Eric Fromm and Charles Johnson, members of the board of the Rosenwald Foundation were present at this performance and were influential in Dunham's receiving a Rosenwald Travel Fellowship based on her study title "Anthropology and the Dance." Dunham arrived in the West Indies in 1936 and studied the dances of the Negro in Martinique, Jamaica, Trinidad, and particularly Haiti for a period of eighteen months. Her Master's thesis, *The Dances of Haiti*,[49] was a result of this trip.

The most important product of the trip to the Caribbean, however, was the material she gathered for use in future stage productions. "It was during this visit that Miss Dunham laid the foundations for the choreography which has made her an outstanding figure in the entertainment world."[50] Working within the proscribed limits of thematic material, she opened the West Indies as an area for source material and was the leader in developing entertaining productions from authentic ethnic material.

Shortly after her return from the Caribbean, Dunham was invited to appear in the inaugural program of the New York YMHA series: the *Negro Dance Evening* presented in 1937. She was seen at this performance by Louis Schaeffer, who with Mary Hunter brought Dunham to the Labor Stage and later to the Windsor Theatre.[51] Becoming dance director for the Negro Unit of the Chicago branch of the Federal Theatre Project, Dunham staged several dances, including the dance numbers for *Emperor Jones* and *Run Lil Chillun*. One of her own dances, "L'Ag'Ya," was also produced by the Chicago branch project.[52] Of this production Hallie Flanagan wrote, "Katherine Dunham, a young choreographer of the Negro group, in 'L'Ag'Ya' dealt with folk material from Martinique, shaping with authority the native grace of our Negro dancers."[53]

In 1939 Dunham was made dance director of the New York Labor Stage, where she choreographed the dances for a musical, *Pins and Needles*. With the money she earned as dance director she not only supported nine company members brought with her from Chicago, but also presented the concert in the Windsor Theatre which was to launch her career as an internationally famous dancer.[54] This concert was entitled *Tropics and Le Jazz Hot* and opened for one night only on February 18, 1940. Beginning in the following month, it ran for ten consecutive Sundays, because of popular acclaim. The revue, subtitled *From Haiti to Harlem*, was well received by the critics. Martin wrote that the dances were "lively, colorful, humorous, and endlessly entertaining."[55] He continued with the comment that, "They are also beautifully racial and consitute the nearest thing that has yet been shown hereabouts to the basis of a true Negro dance art."[56]

"Tropics—Shore Excursion" was danced by Miss Dunham as the woman with the cigar, shown in so many of her photographs. The suite "Le Jazz Hot" was divided into three sections. The second section, entitled "Barrel House (Florida Swamp Shimmy)," danced by Dunham, was called a "truly wonderful little genre piece"[57] by Martin. The critics, and Martin in particular, were not so impressed by the final number, "Br'er Rabbit and de Tah Baby." Following this performance, the main body of "Br'er Rabbit" was discarded but the suite entitled "Plantation Dances" was extracted from it.[58]

Katherine Dunham with Vanoye Aikens

Private collection of Katherine Dunham

The critics generally praised the efforts of Dunham and dancers Archie Savage, Lili Romero, and Talley Beatty, but still offered some rather curious comments about the character of Negro dance. Martin, for example, after stating that the show was good with "sprightly and vivacious surface values," continued:

> This is quite in character with the essence of the Negro dance itself. There is nothing pretentious about it; it is not designed to delve into philosophy or psychology but to externalize the impulses of a high-spirited, rhythmic and gracious race.[59]

He also criticized the dancing of Talley Beatty for his inappropriate "serious dallying ballet technique."[60] Terry praised Dunham's choreography, complimenting her as having "retained the freshness and that quality of improvisation which we find in Negro music and which we want in the Negro dance."[61]

A revealing comment was made by Martin:

> Miss Dunham has apparently based her theory on the obvious fact so often overlooked that if the Negro is to develop an art of his own he can begin only with the seeds of that art that lie within him.[62]

Late in 1940 Dunham and her group appeared in the all-Negro Broadway musical *Cabin in the Sky*. In this production, starring Ethel Waters, Dunham played the part of the seductive Georgia Browne. From Broadway she moved on to Hollywood and made the movie *Star Spangled Rhythm* (1941). Other films which she either appeared in or choreographed include *Stormy Weather* (1943), *Casbah* (1948), *Pardon My Sarong* (1952), *Green Mansions* (1959),[63] and "the really superior Technicolor short of her own dances, *Carnival of Rhythm*."[64] She has also appeared in numerous foreign films, including *Botta e Risposta* (French, 1952), *Musica en la Noche* (Mexican, 1957), and German, Japanese, and Italian productions.

In September, 1943, Dunham and her company opened at the Martin Beck Theatre in a production titled *Tropical Revue*. Included in the revue were the familiar "Tropics — Shore Excursion," "Primitive Rhythms," "Le Jazz Hot" and the "Plantation Dances" from "Br'er Rabbit." The latter suite included dances such as the Cake-Walk, Juba, Palmer House, Pas Mala, Ballin' the Jack, and Strut.[65] The principal new composition was "Rites de Passage," about which Martin wrote, "Its movement is markedly uninhibited, and certainly it is nothing to take grandma to see, but it is an excellent piece of work."[66] Of this same composition Lloyd wrote:

> Taken seriously, it was a religious ceremonial concerning important periods of transition in human experience. But one irreverent scrivener seized with glee upon the fertility ritual as associated with marriage OR mating; and altogether the outward physicality of the work contributed to the sexational build-up that led to the show's success.[67]

Another reviewer of "Rites de Passage" called it the least successful number on the program, due in part to its "lack of restraint in the movement . . . ."[68] However, she continued, the entire revue, "goes over big with an audience that gets a kick out of sex brought into the parlor by a dancer who is obviously a lady."[69]

Danced by Dunham, Lavinia Williams, Tommy Gomez, Lucille Ellis, Syvilla Fort, Lenwood Morris, Vanoye Aikens, and Claude Marchant, among others, *Tropical Revue* was successful. On a national tour, the revue was met by receptive audiences, except in Boston, where "Rites de Passage" was banned.

In 1945 Dunham and her company opened in a musical play, *Carib Song*. The production, according to Langston Hughes, "was spoiled by a plot."[70] Miles Jefferson, a Negro reviewer for a journal called *Phylon*, noted a "hackneyed story," "interminable dances," "trite dialogue," and "music of little if any originality."[71] One of Dunham's best choreographic efforts, "Shango," came from *Carib Song*, however, so it was not a total loss.

It was also in 1945 that Dunham was involved with another project which proved more successful than *Carib Song*; this was the opening of the Dunham School of Dance in New York City. The idea for the school had been formulated as early as 1938, when she stated that her plans were:

> To establish a well-trained ballet group. To develop a technique that will be as important to the white man as to the Negro. To attain a status in the dance world that will give to the Negro

dance-student the courage really to study, and a reason to do so. And to take *our* dance out of the burlesque—to make it a more dignified art.[72]

By 1941 her plans for the school had become more concrete. She stated that she wanted a school in New York "where I can train dancers in the knowledge and use of primitive rhythms. I want to lecture on the subjects of anthropology and ethnology and dance . . . ."[73] When the school opened these ideas of Dunham's were incorporated into a curriculum which, besides dance, contained "everything from French to speech, from anthropology to playwriting."[74] A former member of the company, Syvilla Fort, was supervising director of the school and taught most of the dance classes, including those for children. Stressing Dunham technique—a "combination of classical ballet with Central European, Caribbean and African elements"[75]—the school remained in existence until 1955 when it was dissolved.

The Belasco Theatre was the scene of Dunham's 1946 production, *Bal Negre*, which many critics felt was her best revue. Martin wrote that the revue possessed "a new dignity . . . a new taste . . . ."[76] "Shango," one of the numbers from *Carib Song* was again presented with Jean-Léon Destiné in the role of the boy possessed by a snake. Other members of the company performing in *Bal Negre* included Lucille Ellis, Lenwood Morris, Vanoye Aikens, Ronnie Aul, and Eartha Kitt.[77] After touring Europe, Dunham returned to the New York stage for performances in 1950 and again in 1955. *Bamboche* was the production in 1962, which the Dunham company shared with the performers of the Royal Troupe of Morocco. The Royal Troupe consisted of fourteen dancers, singers, and musicians sent by a personal friend of Miss Dunham's, Hassan II of Morocco. Dunham Company members included Vanoye Aikens, Lucille Ellis, Hope Clarke, and Carlton Johnson. A new number, "Haitian Suite," included the undulating dance to the Damballa, Yanvalou, and Bamboche.[78]

Dunham was asked by the Metropolitan Opera to choreograph their new production of *Aida* for the 1963-64 season, thus becoming "the first Negro choreographer at the Metropolitan."[79] In 1965-66, Dunham was "technical cultural advisor to both the President and the Minister of Cultural Affairs"[80] in Dakar, Senegal. She filled the position of United States Specialist in Senegal's *First World Festival of Negro Arts*. For the past few years she has been the director of the Performing Arts Training Center, a program at Southern Illinois University, East St. Louis branch.[81]

The influence of Katherine Dunham on the Negro in the field of concert dance has been marked. Arthur Todd stated:

> Her innate sense of theatre and music, the glorious costumes and the wonderful dancers in her company, as well as her own choreography and dancing, put Negro dancing on the map once and for all and her work has since had enormous influence.[82]

Harriet Jackson wrote that "Dunham's vivid theatrical sense, choreography and costuming were to pave the way for the acceptance of the Negro dancer as an artist . . . ."[83] Martin felt that Dunham was "a superb performer and an illuminating personality, and creatively she has made an immeasurable contribution to the arts in her unfoldment of true premises of the American Negro dance."[84]

The Dunham performances undoubtedly aided in the acceptance of the black dancer in the concert field. While most of her productions were theatrical pieces rather than concert dances, they contained considerable ethnological material.

In addition to her actual performances, Dunham has provided two other contributions. The first was the training she provided for future dancers both in her company and in the Dunham School. The following people have been associated with Dunham in one way or another: Vanoye Aikens, Eartha Kitt, Lucille Ellis, Marlon Brando, Jean-Léon Destiné, Syvilla Fort, Hope Clarke, Jaime Rogers, Lavinia Williams, Pearl Reynolds, Carlton Johnson, Rudi Gernreich, Claude Marchant, Peter Gennaro, Lenwood Morris, and Talley Beatty. The noted painter Charles White was also a member of the Dunham company at one time.[85]

Through published interviews, speeches, essays, and books, Dunham has disproven many popularly held beliefs concerning the Negro. Katherine Dunham has accomplished what she set out to do: to establish a place for the Negro as a concert dancer. In her own words:

> For my part, I am satisfied to have been at the base of the awakening of the American Negro to the fact that he had roots

Katherine Dunham in "L'ag'ya"

Private collection of Katherine Dunham

260　*Black Dance in the United States*

somewhere else, to have presented dark-skinned people in a manner delightful and acceptable to people who have never considered them as persons.[86]

Pearl Primus

Like Dunham, the other primary black dance leader was also trained in anthropology and utilized ethnic material as a basis for concert presentations. Emerging to prominence in the late 1940's, Pearl Primus, however, studied the dances of Africa, creating thereby a "unique repertory of African-based movement."[87]

Of her early performances Martin wrote:

> Here, newcomer or not, was obviously the greatest Negro dancer of them all . . . besides strength and speed and elevation, her movement had a beautiful quality, a beautiful muscular phrase, and was an open channel for her inward power and her pervasive, outgoing honesty.[88]

She was born in Trinidad in 1919 and with her family moved to the United States when she was two years old. At Hunter College Miss Primus majored in biology and pre-medicine and graduated in 1940. She entered graduate school and, while attempting to find a job during the day, she "turned to the National Youth Administration for assistance. The office was also unable to find her work she wanted, so she was put into an NYA dance group as an understudy."[89] Her progress proved so rapid that she auditioned and won a dance scholarship with the New Dance Group.

Working and studying at the New Dance Group school, Primus also began research on primitive dances, partially as "a balm for the wounds inflicted by racial discrimination."[90] This research included consulting books, articles, and pictures, and visiting museums. After six months she had completed her first composition, "African Ceremonial," which she then performed for her African friends to check its authenticity. Composed as a result of her research, "African Ceremonial" was presented at Primus's first appearance as a professional dancer on February 14, 1943 at the YMHA, where she also danced "Strange Fruit," "Rock Daniel," and "Hard Time Blues."[91]

This debut at the YHMA was in a Sunday afternoon concert entitled *Five Dancers*. Of her dancing, Martin wrote, "if ever a young dancer was entitled to a company of her own and the freedom to do what she chooses with it, she is it."[92] As a result of Martin's review of her work she sought his advice, and on the basis of his encouragement, she began the serious study of dance.

Her next opportunity to perform came in April, 1943, when she was offered a position as an entertainer in the night club called Cafe Society Downtown. After ten months at Cafe Society, she left in order to study, teach (with the New Dance Group), and prepare for her first solo performance on the concert stage. One of the ways she prepared for this concert was by visiting the Deep South in the summer of 1944. While in the South, she visited nearly seventy Negro churches and lived and picked cotton with the sharecroppers. Primus's experiences in the South served as a basis for compositions and articles later published, particularly dealing with the retention of Africanisms in Southern Negro religious ceremonies.

The Belasco Theatre was the scene of Primus's Broadway debut on October 4, 1944. This concert included dances of African and Haitian origin such as "African Ceremonial" and "Yanvaloo"; dances based on the black experience in the United States, such as "Strange Fruit," "The Negro Speaks of Rivers," and "Slave Market," and lighter numbers, including "Study in Nothing," and "Hard Time Blues."[93] Edith Segal of the *Daily Worker* called the debut an "historic evening in the theatre!"[94] Segal continued:

Miss Primus has wisely gone to the rich heritage of her people
and has brought us treasures of great beauty, enhanced by
her own enormous talent.
    Pearl Primus reaches her greatest moments in her dances
of protest.[95]

Many critics agreed with Segal. Her "dances of protest" could be considered "message" dances: compositions designed to draw attention to the inequities and injustices in the lives of American Negroes. "Strange Fruit," for example, dealt with the reaction of a woman toward a lynching. "Hard Time Blues," on the other hand, was a protest against sharecropping. A protest against general ignorance of the black heritage in America,

Pearl Primus

Dance Collection, New York Public Library

Langston Hughes's poem, "The Negro Speaks of Rivers" was the basis for one of her best dances. "It is beautiful with undulating rhythms over deep-flowing currents of movement that wind into whirlpool spins."[96]

After her appearance at the Belasco Theatre, Primus expanded her company and appeared in December, 1944 at the Roxy Theatre. For this production "African Ceremonial" was rechoreographed as a group number which Martin termed not only authentic but also "definitely and legitimately exciting."[97] Following this appearance, she performed in the revival of *Showboat* and in many recitals. In 1947, Chicagoan Ruth Page invited her to play Hemsley Winfield's "Witch Doctor" role in the *Emperor Jones*, again with Lawrence Tibbett.

While performing some of her African dances at a concert at Fisk University in 1948, Miss Primus was seen by the president of the Rosenwald Foundation. Learning that she had never been to Africa, the president, Dr. Edwin Embree, arranged that she be granted the last and largest of the Rosenwald Fellowships. In her African trip of eighteen months, she visited the Gold Coast, Angola, Cameroons, Liberia, Senegal, and the Belgian Congo. In each country she performed her dances, and observed, learned, and participated in the native African dances. Accepted by the Africans, she was adopted by the Nigerians and renamed "Omowale" meaning "child returned home."

Dark Rhythm, performed at the American Museum of Natural History in May, 1952, showed the influence of Primus's travels in Africa. Included on the program were "Impinyuze," from the Belgian Congo, "Dance of Strength," from Sierre Leone, and "Excerpts from an African Journey," which included dances from Nigeria and Liberia.[98]

In 1953 Primus spent the summer studying the dance of the West Indies and it was during this trip that she met dancer Percival Borde, whom she married in 1954. Appearing as a guest artist with Borde's troupe in 1958, Primus performed two numbers, including the joyous "Fanga." Martin wrote of this performance:

> This is an unusually well unified and atmospheric presentation,
> unpretentious in manner but with a wealth of knowledge
> behind it and both skill and taste in its execution.[99]

Returning several times to Africa, Primus was named director of Liberia's Performing Arts Center in 1959. "Her job [was] to discover, restore, revive and expand African dance and allied cultures."[100] Returning to the United States after a Liberian stay of two years, Primus and Borde again went to Africa, this time under the sponsorship of the Rebekah Harkness Foundation. Between their African sojourns, they opened the Primus-Borde School of Primal Dance in New York City. Primus lectured and taught not only dance but, as a result of her doctoral studies, anthropology and sociology. At the present time, she is teaching at her alma mater, Hunter College, and has also been involved with teaching and lecturing in Harlem and Newark. A very gracious person, she is highly respected and revered by all who have come into contact with her.[101]

Of Primus's choreography and dancing, Lloyd has written:

> She presents the African, Caribbean, and American Negro
> rhythms with excellent stagecraft, but with less showmanship
> than Katherine Dunham, though she is a more powerful dancer.
> She does not glamourize her material, does not overstress
> the native pelvic movement, instinctively avoids personal
> contact with her audience. She does not over-refine her art as
> some Negro artists, inhibited by the stigma of racial inferiority,
> are wont to do. With dignity and pride . . . she sets forth the
> ancestral customs, the hopes, aims, and struggles, the inherent
> grandeur of her people. . . . The performance is rife with
> rhythmic excitements and emotional undercurrents . . . .[102]

This presentation of the African with dignity has been one of Primus's major contributions. Through her work she has helped to destroy the stereotype of the African as a savage with no culture or heritage, and has portrayed him as he really is: a human being. The research and dance of Pearl Primus have aided the American black person in developing a pride and a feeling of dignity in his ancestral roots.

> As artist, teacher and scholar, Miss Primus has successfully
> learned how to bring African traditions to life in ways that
> American Negroes can understand and accept. . . . She has
> attempted to reveal that, in a sense, African dance can be part
> of the heritage of every American.[103]

Speaking of her own life in dance, Miss Primus has said, "When I dance, I am dancing as a human being, but as a human being who has African roots."[104]

> I dance not to entertain but to help people better understand each other. . . . Because through dance I have experienced the wordless joy of freedom, I seek it more fully now for my people and for all people everywhere.[105]

Throughout her life Primus has shown a concern for the Afro-American and through her choice of dance as the means of communicating she has worked for a mutual understanding between the races. In her words:

> The dance has been my teacher, ever patiently revealing to me the dignity, beauty and strength in the cultural heritage of my people as a vital part of the great heritage of *all* mankind.[106]

Lloyd once wrote that Pearl Primus could not approve of artistic segregation: "She believes the Negro artist should be accepted as an American artist, allowed to speak as one human being to another, regardless of race."[107] And Primus added: "I'm learning to deliberately reach beyond the color of the skin and go into people's souls and hearts and search out that part of them, black or white, which is common to all."[108]

Dunham and Primus, instigators, initiators, innovators. Both were leaders toward public acceptance of the Negro as a performing artist: Dunham, with her theatrical, beautifully staged, frankly sensational concerts based on the ethnic material of the Caribbean; and Primus, with her powerful, exciting, frequently thought-provoking performances developed from African and American backgrounds. Dunham opened the stages of the American theatre for serious and artistic performances by black dancers, and Primus brought the sense of dignity, authenticity, pride, power, and beauty to those of African ancestry through the medium of dance.

Successful as these primary leaders were, they were still caught in the dilemma of the black dancer. Lois Balcom described this dilemma in an article on Primus. Written in 1944, Balcom's statements seem appropriate even today:

> The crux of the matter is not so much in what Pearl Primus, as a creative individual, gets over or fails to get over. It is what

her audience assumes that a Negro dancer is, or should be, trying to get over. . . . Her success will be judged in terms of her fulfillment of or deviation from these specifications![109]

The success of a dancer depends on whether he has lived up to the audience's expectations. If the dancer is black, the audience frequently has a preconceived notion of the type of dance he should be performing.

The dean of American dance critics, John Martin, did little to change this. He called Primus "the greatest Negro dancer of them all."[110] In his *Book of the Dance,* published in 1963, he delineated characteristics peculiar to the Negro and concluded that he was unsuitable for the ballet, since its "wholly European outlook, history and technical theory are alien to him culturally, temperamentally and anatomically."[111]

In a discussion of the "integrated" dance company, Martin wrote:

Certainly the "integrated" company is a normal artistic development, and the only problem it involves is to keep the Negro dancer from having to pretend to be what he is not and to deny what he is.

Race — exactly like sex, age, height, weight, vocal range, temperament — carries with it its own index of appropriateness.[112]

With such thinking opposing his development as a creative artist, it would seem a miracle that the black dancer ever emerged from the minstrel show-vaudeville image. But emerge he did, through the collective efforts of Winfield, Guy, Williams, Dafora, the American Negro Ballet, Hampton Institute, Katherine Dunham, and Pearl Primus.

▤▤ THE EMERGING LEADERS

The emerging leaders have built upon the foundations laid by their predecessors. Moving even farther from the accepted Negro themes than those who came before them, their most successful compositions or performances, nevertheless, have remained within proscribed limits. Experimenting with movement, design and music, the companies of these three men have been the most successful in the United States.

Talley Beatty

Talley Beatty was one of nine original Dunham dancers who traveled from Chicago to New York to perform in the YMHA's *Negro Dance Evening* in 1937. In that concert Beatty danced the part of a priest in "Yanvalou," was the featured dancer in "Carnival Dances," and starred as the fugitive in "Tropic Death," from *Swamp Suite*.[113] In 1940 he returned with her company to New York in "Le Jazz Hot," the performance which prompted Martin's complaints about his inappropriate balletic style.[114]

Anatole Chujoy and P. W. Manchester[115] reported that Beatty remained with Dunham's company for her next production, *Tropical Revue*; however, his name appeared on neither the official program nor in the reviews. Beatty may have been in the touring company of *Tropical Revue*, but Lloyd[116] made no mention of him in the Boston appearance of the company, so that, too, was doubtful.

In 1945 Beatty appeared as the dancer in Maya Deren's film, *A Study in Choreography for Camera*. Of this Lloyd wrote:

> The dancer is the Dunham-trained Talley Beatty, an excellent dancer without the aid of a camera. Under its *sorcellerie,* his leaps become phenomenal, a sort of universal wish fulfillment to navigate the air.[117]

Beatty's performance experiences were varied, ranging from musical comedies to a minstrel-ballet. In the 1946 revival of *Showboat,* Beatty shared the leading dancer role with Pearl Primus. Also in 1946 he appeared as the lead dancer in *Spring in Brazil,* choreographed by Esther Junger. Lloyd had a violent reaction to this production, writing that Junger

> . . . staged a tribal dance for the first scene and other native dances sprinkled through, as well as a Negro ballet that, gagging on the comedian's gags, I was unable to stay to see. She had former Dunham dancers Roger Ohardieno, Talley Beatty, and LaVerne French among others to work with, but whatever she did with them, it was artistically a waste.[118]

After being featured in a minstrel-ballet called *Blackface* (1946) choreographed by Caucasian Lew Christensen for the Ballet Society (later the New York City Ballet), Beatty decided

Talley Beatty in *A Study in Choreography for Camera* by
Maya Deren and Beatty

to embark on a career as a concert dancer. Chujoy and Manchester wrote that Beatty at first specialized "in dances based on Negro sources and later [embraced] a more general style, closely related, however, to jazz."[119] He formed a company of his own, and with it toured Europe and the United States for five years, presenting a program entitled *Tropicana*, based in its general pattern on Dunham's revues.[120]

When he took *Tropicana* to Boston in 1952, the *Boston Globe* reviewer stated that the Beatty company was "well trained, well coordinated," and presented a "vivid performance," while Beatty himself was a "brilliant dancer."[121] *Tropicana* was described as being "a collection of dances on Negro themes, some tracing back to Africa, others to the deep south."[122] Included was a suite of dances entitled "Southern Landscape," which gave Beatty "an opportunity for an important contribution both as a dancer and as a choreographer."[123] The second dance of the suite was a moving composition performed by Beatty called "Mourner's Bench," which Martin termed a "brilliant" solo.[124] Writing of this same solo performed at a later date, he described it as

> . . . a marvelous job, a tour de force demanding endless
> variations in control and dynamics as he moves on, around
> and under a simple long wooden seat, it is also vital in form
> and inner motivation.[125]

Beatty had grown as a choreographer. Martin wrote that maturity had brought him

> . . . a simplicity of manner, an integrity of approach and a
> sense of perspective—along with a boldness in creative
> adventure—that mark him as one of our substantial artists.[126]

One of the earliest of Mr. Beatty's works still being performed was the epic, "The Road of the Phoebe Snow." Frequently danced by the Alvin Ailey Company, it was made possible by a grant from the Lena Robbins Foundation and premiered by Beatty in 1959. Dealing with life along the wrong side of the Lackawanna Railroad, "Phoebe Snow" was described in 1969 as "a fine, tense work, strung out tautly on the music by Ellington and Billy Strayhorn, and somberly evocative of life, youth and death in the ghetto."[127] Martin wrote of the original production that the overall effect of the work was "stunning" and that the composition was "essentially classic in form and in texture,"[128] while Clive Barnes wrote in 1965 that, "'Phoebe Snow' ranks as one of the great achievements of jazz dance."[129]

The following season saw the debut of another of Beatty's works, "Come and Get the Beauty of It Hot." "Congo Tango Palace" and "Toccata" are excerpts from this suite, which Martin described as "extraordinarily beautiful . . . full of human relations and implications but essentially an abstraction. . . ."[130]

Beatty's later works focused on racial injustice, discrimination, and the inequities of the black experience in the United States. "Montgomery Variations" was premiered in 1967 in Central Park's Delacorte Theatre and was described by Barnes as

> . . . a mood study of the face of violence—tough, painful and pathetic. Mr. Beatty does not moralize, nor does he offer a story. He just paints a shriek of pain across a blank stage. It is enough.[131]

Premiered in New York in January, 1969 by the Ailey Company, Beatty's "The Black Belt," was televised nationally by National Educational Television. Powerful in impact, "Black Belt" probed and exposed the realities of ghetto life. One reviewer felt the work suffered from "explicitness," but continued that "Beatty's movement centers in the pelvic region and his Black Belt people come on strong. . . ."[132]

Besides his concert works, Beatty has staged the dance sequences for many productions. Among them are Jean Genet's off-Broadway drama, *The Blacks;* Clarence Jackson's musical, *Fly Blackbird;* the revival of *House of Flowers;* and, in 1969, *But Never Jam Today,* an Afro-American adaptation of Lewis Carroll's *Alice in Wonderland.* Recently Beatty was an artist-in-residence at the Elma Lewis School of Fine Arts in Roxbury, Massachusetts, where he worked with the school's company. He also choreographed the Broadway musical *Ari,* based on the book *Exodus.*

From his days with Katherine Dunham and his first efforts in composition, Beatty has grown into an important choreographer, and it is mainly through his choreographic efforts that his contribution to Afro-American concert dance has been made. Not always pleasant, sometimes shocking, and most of the time creating a powerful impact, his works *are* the black experience.

He has created, through dance, a portrayal of what it is to be black in America. Talley Beatty "has come through with a distinguishing and original art."[133]

Alvin Ailey

Perhaps more people have seen Alvin Ailey's dance company than any other American company, black, white, or integrated. Touring different parts of the world since their formation in 1958, they have received high acclaim wherever they have performed.

In addition to Ailey's works, his company has performed the dances of many others. The compositions of Talley Beatty in particular have been highlighted. "The Road of the Phoebe Snow," excerpts from "Come and Get the Beauty of It Hot," and the newer "Black Belt" are the works most often performed.

Born in Texas in 1931, Ailey moved to Los Angeles during his youth. Participating in athletics while attending Jefferson High School, he graduated in 1948 and enrolled in UCLA as a Romance language major. Ailey then transferred to Los Angeles City College, and in 1951 went to San Francisco State College. Early in 1949 Ailey became acquainted with the Lester Horton Dance Theatre. He served on the stage crew while a young dancer named Carmen de Lavallade was giving her first performances.[134] Joyce Trisler wrote that, "for a brief time, a young dancer appeared. He was to return after Lester's death to become a stabilizing influence in Dance Theatre. . . . His name was Alvin Ailey."[135]

It was with the Horton company that Ailey made his debut as a dancer in 1953, performing in a revue titled *Bal Caribe*. The year 1954 was important in Ailey's career; he was invited to perform at Jacob's Pillow Festival, danced in the movie *Carmen Jones*, and made his Broadway debut. Herbert Ross, the choreographer of *Carmen Jones*, remembered Ailey's dancing in the movie and invited him and Carmen de Lavallade to appear in his newest production, *House of Flowers*, opening on Broadway in 1954.[136]

Even with a stellar cast, *House of Flowers* ran only four months. Brooks Atkinson regarded the plot and music as commonplace, and wrote:

> Every Negro show includes wonderful dancing. *House of Flowers* is no exception in that respect. Tall and short Negroes, adults and youngsters, torrid maidens in flashy costumes and bare-chested bucks break out into a number of wild, grotesque, animalistic dances.[137]

Once in New York, Ailey continued his dance training with Martha Graham, Hanya Holm, Doris Humphrey, Anna Sokolow and Karel Shook. He performed with Sokolow, Sophie Maslow, and Donald McKayle and during the years 1954 to 1958 danced in several musicals both on and off Broadway. Besides *House of Flowers*, he performed in *The Carefree Tree* (1955), partnered Mary Hinkson in Harry Belafonte's *Sing, Man, Sing* (1956), and was the leading dancer in *Jamaica* (1957), starring Lena Horne. In March, 1958, Ailey and Ernest Parham presented a concert at the YMHA: Ailey's first concert appearance in New York City. Talley Beatty was featured as the guest artist. Of Ailey's dancing, Doris Hering wrote, "As a dancer, Mr. Ailey is exceptional. He reminds one of a caged lion full of lashing power that he can contain or release at will."[138]

Of Ailey the dancer, Todd wrote, "Mr. Ailey has mastered all the technique and virtuosity one could wish. He moves with a personal magnificence that is breathtaking and, for many, is the greatest male dancer in his field today."[139]

Martin considered him an impressive performer and further said:

> . . . he is strikingly handsome, with the genuine theatre artist's inborn power of projection. His technique is strong and his quality of movement is notably beautiful, like that of a svelte, nervously alert animal.[140]

The praise Ailey received as a dancer was extended to his company, the Alvin Ailey American Dance Theatre, formed in 1958. The company has retained his original concept of a total dance theatre. Ailey "believes strongly in the ballet's version of 'rep' to enlarge the experience of dancers and audiences alike."[141] Therefore, works from a wide variety of choreographers have

Alvin Ailey in "Rite" sequence from his "Cinco Latinos"

been presented. Besides the works of Ailey himself and Beatty, the company has performed compositions by Louis Johnson, Lucas Hoving, Geoffrey Holder, Paul Sanasardo, Joyce Trisler, and Pauline Koner.

The company, while integrated, is primarily composed of black dancers, because "I feel an obligation to use black dancers because there must be more opportunities for them but *not* because I'm a black choreographer talking to black people."[142] Dancers with the Ailey troupe have included, at various times, Carmen de Lavallade, James Truitte, and Joyce Trisler (all from the Horton Theatre), Dudley Williams, Miguel Godreau, Judith Jamison, Kelvin Rotardier, Michele Murray, Sylvia Waters, Renee Rose, and the lovely Consuelo Atlas. The company has proven to be an extremely hard-working, well-trained, handsome, dedicated, and pleasant group of people.[143]

Under the auspices of the U.S. Department of State, the company began its world travels in 1962 with a thirteen-week tour of Australia and the Far East. "They presented sixty performances for 146,791 people in twenty-five cities in ten countries,"[144] receiving twenty curtain calls in their Sydney, Australia, concert. Since this first tour, the group has toured extensively in the United States, Europe, and Africa. In 1966 they were the only integrated modern dance company to appear at the First World Festival of the Negro Arts in Dakar, Senegal, where they "exploded onto the stage of the Sorano Theatre and swept the audience off its feet."[145] The American Dance Theatre has been one of America's great cultural ambassadors, bringing an understanding of this country to people all over the world through the medium of dance.

In the same way that Ailey moved away from the traditional all-black company, so has his choreography parted from the proscribed thematic material. Frequently his works developed from pure movement, and even in his works based on "Negro material" the theme has usually served only as a base while the movement is quite abstract. "Revelations" was based on American Negro spirituals, yet Clive Barnes stated that "there is probably no recognisable Negro strain except in the traditional spirituals which provide the work with both its inspiration and its music."[146] Barnes continued: "What Ailey achieves in 'Revelations' is a dance statement about faith and the spirit of man."[147] Todd called the work "one of the most beautifully constructed and moving works in the repertory of any company."[148] The appeal of "Revelations" has been universal and it fulfills most completely Ailey's concept "of total 'Dance Theatre'."[149] "Revelations" was one "of those rare dance works that is a genuine religious ballet."[150]

Ailey has worked with a variety of dance techniques including jazz, classic ballet, primitive, Graham technique, and Horton technique.[151] All of these are evident in his choreography. In the dance language of jazz, Ailey composed "Roots of the Blues," "Blues Suite," and "Reflections in D." Compositions created by Ailey for the ballet include "Feast of Ashes," performed by the Joffrey Ballet, and "Ariadne," for the Harkness Ballet. He choreographed *Antony and Cleopatra* for the Metropolitan Opera in 1966 and *The River* for the American Ballet Theatre. Even though *The River* was not completed in time for its premiere performance, the part of it which was shown caused Terry to write, "A full appraisal, of course, must wait, but the Ailey dance brilliance — wonderful freshets of movement, designs to delight the eye — are already there."[152]

Two new compositions were premiered by his company in 1969-70. Performed in November, 1969, "Masekela Language" was considered Ailey's most militant piece. Of it, Anna Kisselgoff wrote:

> Characteristically for Mr. Ailey, however, its framework and message are universal rather than specific in a sectarian way. It may be about blacks. It may be about whites. It is political in a nonpolitical manner.[153]

Another work, "Streams," was premiered in April, 1970.

> "Streams" . . . contained beautiful movement for the entire company. The dancers entered in diagonal processionals, now rushing, now receding, like streams of water or the streams of history.[154]

Through his performances, his company, and his choreography, Alvin Ailey has emerged as one of the leaders in the dance. While he has utilized Negro thematic material, as have so many artists, white and black, "Mr. Ailey is, of course, a modern-dance choreographer by design and only a Negro by chance. . . . Mr. Ailey . . . employs his own choreographic technique."[155] His

Donald McKayle

Esta McKayle, from private collection of Donald McKayle

contributions to Negro performing artistry lie in the fact that he is first and foremost a creative artist. It is his blending of the black heritage with the modern dance that results in his greatness.

> It is clear that, far from being a choreographer who deals only with folk materials—in this case dance and music of the American Negro—Alvin Ailey must be recognized simply as a major creative artist of our time.[156]

Donald McKayle

Donald McKayle the dancer has been called "magnificent," while Donald McKayle the choreographer has been termed "sensitive, excitingly creative . . . [his] greatest strength is his passionate concern for his fellow man."[157] Both as a dancer and choreographer, McKayle's career has been one of discipline and excitement.

Born in New York City in 1930, he became excited about dance after seeing a performance by Pearl Primus. In his last year of high school, McKayle auditioned and won (as Primus had earlier) a year's scholarship to the New Dance Group. Studying with Primus, Sophie Maslow, William Bales, Jean Erdman, and Hadassah, McKayle also enrolled in New York City College. His debut as a professional dancer was made in the spring of 1948, at the Mansfield Theatre, in dances by Sophie Maslow and Jean Erdman.[158]

Eventually winning a scholarship to the Martha Graham school, McKayle studied with Graham and performed with her company in their Far Eastern tour in 1955-56. He also performed as guest artist with the companies of Anna Sokolow, Merce Cunningham, and Jean Erdman. Among other dance activities, he danced in Charles Weidman's *Traditions*, performed with the Dudley-Maslow-Bales troupe, and was soloist with the New York City Opera Company.[159]

In order to earn enough money to live, McKayle found it necessary at times to leave the concert field and appear on Broadway. One of the first shows he danced in was *Bless You All*, choreographed by Helen Tamiris with the assistance of Daniel Nagrin. He also danced briefly in *House of Flowers* and was dance captain for *West Side Story*. It was through his association with Nagrin, however, that McKayle received the opportunity to present his own choreography, and it has been mainly through choreographic efforts that he has made such a great contribution to Negro performing artists.

Nagrin and McKayle, along with other choreographers, formed the Contemporary Dance Group. While this group never really succeeded, the two men combined forces to present a concert at Hunter College in May, 1951, and it was at this concert that McKayle's classic "Games" was first performed.

Discussing Negro choreographer-artists, McKayle wrote that "they are not limited to nor do they necessarily exclude Negro source material."[160] McKayle's own words describe his choreography perfectly; he has certainly broken from traditional Negro thematic material and his best works are universal in scope. P. W. Manchester felt that if a word had to be chosen to describe McKayle the choreographer, that word would be "humanist." Of him, she wrote, "All his best works deal, not with abstractions, but with people; living, laughing, suffering, bitter, pitiful, protesting, superbly human beings."[161]

McKayle's first choreographic work, "Games," dealt with children, not necessarily black but living in the crowded areas of big cities. Of it McKayle wrote:

> It was a childhood memory that triggered my first dance. . . . It was dusk, and the block was dimly lit by a street lamp around which we hovered choosing a game. The street, playground of tenement children, was soon ringing with calls and cries, the happy shouts of the young. The street lamp threw a shadow large and looming—the constant spectre of fear—"Chickee the Cop!" The cry was broken; the game became a sordid dance of terror.[162]

According to Manchester, "The marvel of this work is that McKayle does not use children, he does not even use very young dancers."[163] Yet the feeling of children, their energy, imaginations, and fears are all within the work. Martin wrote that "Though ["Games"] was his initial effort, it proved to be an excellent work and has already become something of a classic."[164]

In 1952 McKayle developed "Her Name Was Harriet" and in 1953 "Nocturne," inspired by a piece of music entitled "Moondog." Of this composition he wrote:

Its basic material is pure movement, yet it is not movement in a void of mood or idea. The dance celebrates the qualities of man and woman. Man is depicted in his role of discoverer, protector; woman as inspirer. The male patterns are large, thrusting, laced with impulse, volatility, and expectation. The female movements are flowing, curved, inviting. The resulting duets are a blending of both qualities.[165]

In 1959 McKayle created "Rainbow 'Round My Shoulder," which could be termed a dance of protest. Inspired by the music and rhythms of the Southern Negro chain gangs, "Rainbow 'Round My Shoulder" was full of anger: always present was the dream of freedom and the women waiting on the outside. "It is another of McKayle's statements about life. He is reminding us of things that many of us would prefer to forget . . . ."[166]

The jazz idiom was the setting for two of McKayle's works: "District Storyville," dealing with the development of jazz in New Orleans, and "Reflections in the Park," a statement on the lives of contemporary New Yorkers.

Beside his concert dance works, McKayle has been active as a choreographer for Broadway, television, and Hollywood productions. One of his first triumphs, even though the musical itself was not, was the dance he staged for Sammy Davis's *Golden Boy*. Also to his credit was the choreography for the first of Harry Belafonte's television specials, *The Strollin' Twenties*. McKayle did the choreography for an hour TV special, *& Beautiful* (1969), and the Leslie Uggams television series.[167] He was choreographer for the movie version of *The Great White Hope* and for the Disney production, *Bed-Knobs and Broomsticks*. McKayle taught extensively in New York City, Tel Aviv, Cologne, London, Tunis, and most recently with the repertory dance group at the Los Angeles Inner City Cultural Center.

While Donald McKayle's main contributions have been choreographic, his writings have been influential in destroying some of the myths surrounding black culture. Discussing the lack of black artists in ballet, he pointed out that it was mainly in the United States that the racial stigma has been attached. In Europe, such artists as Billie Wilson, Ronnie Aul, and Ronald Frazier

> . . . have been quickly employed in ballet companies, where there are no extra-dance barriers to obscure the vision of their

real abilities — such as the most recent nonsense concerning the Negro physique or that fallacious old bromide about Negro rhythm.[168]

McKayle contended that an artist's alliance should be determined by the manner of his work. He found many American critics of the dance insensitive to the talent and quality of a dancer and often confused by the issue of race. "Some critics have discussed the work of most dance artists along the lines of their basic artistic allegiances, and then — quite separately — they have discussed the Negro dance."[169] And further:

> In the concert dance, those white choreographers that used Negro dancers as artists with no prejudgment because of color were opposed by leading critics of the press. It was perfectly all right for white performers to be orientals, Negroes, or just anything the convention of the work asked for — but for Negroes, unthinkable and lacking in "theatrical verisimilitude." Of course the Negro dancer who lived as a Negro in American society recognized this all too clearly for the sham it was and realized quite adroitly that it was much easier to take the boy out of Kentucky than it was to take Kentucky out of the boy.[170]

Three leaders — Beatty, Ailey, and McKayle — cut across the minstrel-developed image of the black man. These three men slowly and quietly began to destroy the limits placed on black dance. In their performances, companies, and choreography, they worked toward acceptance of universal values in black dance. None of these artists could have existed without those who came before, and none who have emerged since could have succeeded as well without their work.

▯:▯:▯ PRIMARILY DANCERS

There are, among black dancers, some who transcend any concept of race. These artists, because of their training, abilities, and orientation, have been able to shift back and forth from previously all-white to all-black to integrated companies, appearing equally at ease with any grouping. Such artists are in demand, not because of tokenism but because of their basic abilities.

Contrary to the opinion of some critics, the movement of

such dancers does *not* "differ from that produced by Caucasians."[171] Their dancing does *not* "release in communicative essence the uninhibited qualities of racial heritage, no matter what the immediate subject of any specific dance might be."[172] These black dancers do *not* "have to try to pretend to be somebody else."[173] Such dancers as Carmen de Lavallade, Mary Hinkson, and Matt Turney are superlative artists, never pretending to be anyone except themselves. Whether or not a composition has originated from Negro thematic material makes no difference in their ability to convince. These dancers stand out in the companies with which they perform only because of their tremendous skill.

Carmen de Lavallade

The citation of the *Dance Magazine* Award for 1966 to Carmen de Lavallade read, "Beauteous symbol of today's total dancer, she conveys the sensuous pleasure of movement with simplicity, elegance and superb control."[174]

Another product of the Lester Horton Dance Theatre, Miss de Lavallade was the company's leading dancer when she accepted an offer to perform in *House of Flowers* on Broadway. Following her work in that production, she had an eventful and varied career as a performing artist. So successful has she been that one critic termed her, "a star in the most luxuriant sense of the word,"[175] while another insisted that she was "a vision of loveliness."[176]

As a guest artist she worked with the companies of Alvin Ailey, Donald McKayle, Geoffrey Holder (her husband), Glen Tetley, and John Butler, plus the Metropolitan Opera Ballet, the Boston Ballet, and the American Ballet Theatre. "Many of the works in her repertoire were created expressly to fit her rare combination of graceful beauty and strong technique."[177]

> Watching Miss de Lavallade move—with flowing gestures of arms and fingers or taking an arabesque-like stance in lyrical slow motion or cutting the air with eager leaps—one never thinks about choreography, whether it is good or bad, for Miss de Lavallade seems to transcend mere form as she gives us the very radiance, subdued or brightly shining, of dance itself.[178]

Emory Lewis once wrote that de Lavallade, "can be sinuous and soft, all the while with great reserves of technical fire. There are few such extraordinary dancers in any generation."[179]

De Lavallade has been repeatedly praised and highly acclaimed as a performing artist, as a dancer, and an actress (with the Yale Repertory Theatre Company). She has been praised as an artist and a human being, and no reference has been found criticizing her as miscast because of race. In fact, little mention has been made of her racial heritage, a circumstance due in part to the inroads made by artists before her, in part to her outstanding talents, and perhaps in part to her beliefs about dance. In answer to a question regarding the contribution of the Negro to dance in the United States, she wrote that the black dancer works hard, and, like anyone else with talent, "when given a chance to create and develop, will give joy and beauty to the world."[180] "Dance is dance, music is music, art is art, let us all enjoy it together."[181] Of her role in the arts she stated, "The arts are my way of contributing [to civil rights]. I perform in integrated groups, and the performances are for everybody. As an entertainer my role is to give joy, not to go on marches."[182]

Mary Hinkson

A standout in Martha Graham's company since joining it in 1951, Mary Hinkson was a graduate of the University of Wisconsin. Upon joining the Graham company, she electrified dance audiences "with her superbly lyrical performance in Miss Graham's 'Canticle For Innocent Comedians'."[183] "Essentially a lyrical dancer, she excels in roles which demand fluidity of motion and tensile strength, such as Circe . . . which Miss Graham choreographed especially for her."[184] Appearing in every one of Graham's New York seasons since joining the company, she was featured in the film *A Dancer's World.*

Beside performing and teaching with the Graham company, she danced with Alvin Ailey in Belafonte's *Sing, Man, Sing,* performed for three seasons with the New York City Opera, and danced in George Balanchine's ballet *The Figure in the Carpet.* Having been on the dance faculty of Juilliard School of Music since 1952 and the faculty of the School of Performing Arts since

Carmen de Lavallade in "Bele"

Mary Hinkson as Joan the
Warrior in Martha Graham's
"Seraphic Dialogue"

1955, she has also been teaching in the Graham school since she joined the company, and is undoubtedly most well known for her work there.

With all her opportunities as a performing artist, she has never become unrealistic about the position of the black dancer in the United States. Even though she herself has not generally been categorized as a "Negro dancer," Miss Hinkson wrote that

> . . . in one way the label "Negro dancer" is realistic. Society hasn't completely eliminated racial considerations. We will have to speak of "the Negro dancer" until people are finally considered only on the grounds of their talent and merit.[185]

Matt Turney

The career of Matt Turney is similar to that of Mary Hinkson. During her study at the University of Wisconsin, where she majored in dance, she helped form the Wisconsin Dance Group, which performed in the United States and Canada.

After graduation in 1953, she also joined Graham's company and has performed in all the Graham New York seasons and tours since that time. Ernestine Stodelle wrote:

> Tall, slender Matt Turney executes difficult movements with seemingly effortless grace. Like a panther who is unconscious of the effect of its acrobatic feats, Miss Turney springs in the air, or langorously walks across the stage and the movement itself "speaks" to the senses, conveying a sense of smooth, perfectly co-ordinated natural power.[186]

Besides her work with Graham, she has made a name in concert appearances with a former company member, Robert Cohan.[187]

Others

Graham's company included at various times several other black dancers. Clive Thompson, a leading male dancer, joined the company in 1961. Thompson also appeared with Alvin Ailey, Talley Beatty, Geoffrey Holder, and Yuriko. Joining the Graham Company in 1965 was William Louther, also a member of Donald

McKayle's company. Reviewing a 1969 Graham Company performance of "Archaic Hours," Barnes wrote of Louther's "brilliant litheness" and "the more contained yet equally fascinating presence of Clive Thompson."[188]

Dudley Williams, whose most notable appearances have been with the Ailey Company, became a member of Graham's troupe in 1961. He also appeared in Broadway shows and television and was a member of the companies of Beatty and McKayle. Commenting on his performance in the Ailey company, Barnes wrote that Williams danced "with a fierce withdrawn fire" and was "technically brilliant." "Inside each step," said Barnes, "Mr. Williams seems to place a flame. His dancing is now totally individual."[189]

Black dancers have been members of a variety of modern dance companies in recent years. Among them are Carolyn Adams, a member of the Paul Taylor Dance Company; Bill Frank, appearing with the company of Alwin Nikolais; Rod Rodgers, with the Eric Hawkins Company; and Gus Solomons, Jr., a former member of the company of Merce Cunningham. More black dancers are joining previously all-white companies each year, but the process is slow in spite of the supposed liberality of the modern dance. As Dunham pointed out in 1962:

> I think that we will have to admit that with all of the progress that is being made, the field is still proportionately limited, and the young Negro dancer or aspirant has not too much to look forward to. The exceptions sound fine but they are still exceptions.[190]

▢▢▢ DANCERS IN THE BALLET

There are relatively few black dancers in the classical ballet. Martin's statement that the "European outlook, history and technical theory" of ballet are alien to the black dancer, "culturally, temperamentally and anatomically"[191] may still be held by many. The lack of black dancers in ballet cannot be blamed on Martin, however, since he was merely voicing popularly held opinions. Rather, it rests in the mythical image of the black person developed and unquestioningly believed by many white Americans.

The stereotype led Stodelle to write:

> The perfect classic Negro dancer is, however, a rarity due [to] the demands of European-dominated ballet technique. In ballet, there is an arbitrary and rigid code of proper style. That style happens to be white. African movement emphasizes, goes with, African structure.[192]

"The style of ballet is based on majesty—and this is not surprising since only royalty and nobility danced in the early ballet,"[193] said Agnes De Mille.

> Ballet is the noble way of dancing; is nobility a virtue of the white dancer alone, and not of the black? Ballet is the classical theatre dance, but have you ever seen African dances—what could be more classic than a Watusi dancer? . . . there is no difference, except color, between a black ballet dancer and a white ballet dancer.[194]

Perhaps it has been this one difference, color, which excluded the black dancer from ballet. The ballet has been based on symmetry, harmony, and "concepts of beauty and of grace";[195] and a black dancer could break up the "pretty ensemble effect— think of a corps of white swans, one of them black."[196] The concept of beauty and what is considered beautiful in the United States has been developed by the white majority. Standards in regard to the beauty of a person have been developed, and though they may be artificial, they exist nevertheless. "In this country, the standard is the blond, blue-eyed, white-skinned girl with regular features."[197] This ideal is frequently referred to as the all-American girl. The black girl, however, whose very blackness

> . . . is the antithesis of a creamy white skin . . . is, in fact, the antithesis of American beauty. However beautiful she might be in a different setting with different standards, in this country she is ugly.[198]

The few black dancers who have succeeded in ballet in the United States have approached this white standard of beauty.

There was, of course, Hemsley Winfield, performing in the ballet of the Metropolitan Opera's production of the *Emperor Jones* in 1933. However the time span between Winfield and the next featured black ballet dancer was nearly twenty years. It was not until 1951 that a black ballerina, described by Martin as "beautifully equipped physically, technically and stylistically"[199] appeared. This ballerina, who closely approximates the white ideal of beauty, was Janet Collins.

Janet Collins

The premiere danseuse of the Metropolitan Opera Ballet for four years (1951-1954), Janet Collins received her early training from Lester Horton and Carmalita Maracci. In a pattern later to be followed by her cousin, Carmen de Lavallade, Collins studied and performed on the West Coast prior to her New York debut in 1949. As so many young black dancers did, she first performed at the YMHA on Lexington and 92nd Streets. She performed two of her own compositions at her debut, a Mozart "Rondo" and two Negro spirituals. After this appearance, Martin wrote that she was "the most exciting young dancer who has flashed across the current scene in a long time. . . ."[200] He wrote that she had "a rich talent and a striking theatrical personality."[201]

One of the most interesting of Martin's comments on any black dancer appeared in this same review:

> Miss Collins happens to be a Negro, but she is not fairly to be described as a "Negro dancer." That she is aware of racial backgrounds is evident in the spirituals, but they are in every sense dances rather than an exploitation of heritage.[202]

Appearing in Cole Porter's musical *Out of This World* (1951), Collins danced the role of "Night" and was described as a "golden dancing girl." The critic went on to describe her effect:

> Janet Collins dances with something of the speed of light, seeming to touch the floor only occasionally with affectionate feet, caressing it as if she loved it and loving, wanted to calm any fears it might have that in her flight she would leave it and never come back. That she could leave it and never touch it again seems easily possible. What she does with it and in the air immediately above it is breathtaking.[203]

While still in Los Angeles, Collins had once auditioned for the Ballets Russes, where she was not accepted because of her

Janet Collins

Dance Collection, New York Public Library

race. She was told that either special parts would have to be created for her or she would have to paint her face white,[204] implying that she was unacceptable because of her color. Later in New York a special part was found for her as a dusky Ethiopian in the opera *Aïda* at the Metropolitan. She danced other roles too during her four-year reign at the Met. Beside her part as an Ethiopian captive in *Aïda*, she danced a gypsy in *Carmen*, was the leading dancer in *La Gioconda*, and led the Bacchanale in *Samson and Delilah*. During this same time period, she was studying dance, teaching at the School of American Ballet, and choreographing and performing on tours during the off-season of the Metropolitan. Miss Collins has also taught in California, mainly at the Inner City Cultural Center in Los Angeles.

Many of the reviews and feature articles about Miss Collins mention her appearance. She has been described as "cool and serene, . . . her face a pale copper oval under the sleek black hair."[205] "Her features are delicate, and regular";[206] "skin a golden tan. . . . The domed forehead, the rounded cheekbones, the features a harmony of curved forms. . . ."[207] Janet Collins fitted within the accepted concept of beauty and became the first black ballerina in the United States. She made the inroads into ballet, which would slowly admit other Afro-Americans, such as the beautiful Carmen de Lavallade, who danced some of the same roles. It is Miss Collins's belief that the black dancer has made immense contributions to the dance of America, including the ballet. However, she said, "The Negro in Ballet is just beginning to formulate. For many years he was excluded from this field."[208]

Arthur Mitchell

Since 1955, when he made his debut as a soloist, Arthur Mitchell has been "the first Negro to establish himself as a principal dancer in one of the great ballet companies of the world,"[209] the New York City Ballet. Of his debut, Martin wrote, "A casting novelty and a debut was the appearance of the talented young Negro dancer, Arthur Mitchell, in the role usually danced by Jacques d'Amboise in *Western Symphony*."[210] This was the extent of the criticism.

Dance Theatre of Harlem

New York Sunday Times, June, 1970,
from private collection of Arthur Mitchell

Arthur Mitchell

Martha Swope, New York City, from private
collection of Arthur Mitchell

291

Mitchell's appeal proved durable, however, as he created roles such as Puck in *A Midsummer Night's Dream*, and leading parts in *Agon*, *Arcade*, and *Creation of the World*. Although on a few occasions, "notably in *The Nutcracker* and *The Figure in the Carpet* — Mitchell has been specifically cast as a Negro, his color generally plays no part in his assignment in the company's repertory."[211]

After graduating from New York's High School of Performing Arts in 1952, Mitchell received a scholarship at the School of American Ballet. While studying ballet, he also continued performing as a modern dancer and appeared with Donald McKayle's company and the New Dance Group. He also danced briefly in the same *House of Flowers* in which so many other dancers made their New York start. Mitchell's entrance into the New York City Ballet, however, did not create openings for other black dancers. He still remained the only black dancer in the company as late as 1970. According to Allen Hughes:

> Possibly the most significant thing about Mr. Mitchell's success is that it is not predicated or dependent upon the fact that he is a Negro. He won his place in the New York City Ballet because he is a superior dancer . . . .[212]

Mitchell, recalling his childhood, stated:

> As a kid I was up against what every Negro kid is up against, the widespread attitude that if you're not white, blond, or blue-eyed, you're not part of things. I remember the jingle:
>
> > If you're white, you're all right,
> > If you're brown, you may stick around.
> > If you're black, stay back![213]

Even as an adult and a leading dancer, Mitchell has found his opportunities limited by his color. One of his most famous roles, in the *pas de deux* from *Agon*, was created specifically for him by George Balanchine. In this duet he partnered white dancer Allegra Kent and has danced it throughout the world. Yet he could not recreate this role for commercially-sponsored prime-time television in the United States since:

> Television stations in the South would refuse to carry the shows, and advertisers would not like that. This means quite simply that

a prejudiced minority in this country has dictatorial power over what all Americans will be allowed to see.[214]

Mitchell certainly had reasons to be bitter over the lack of opportunities for the black dancer in classic ballet. Yet it was his feeling that there were few black dancers in ballet because, "there aren't that many Negroes trained in the classics. It's not a matter of my being an exception; it's a matter of my having had more opportunities and being exposed to more."[215] He therefore set himself to remedying the situation by developing a school called the Dance Theatre of Harlem. The purpose of the school and theatre is to provide the training necessary to prepare technically sound dancers who will be able to perform if and when the doors of ballet open to them. While awaiting this time, however, Mitchell stated, "We have to prove that a black ballet school and a black ballet company are the equal of the best of their kind, anywhere in the world."[216] "It's talent and training, not the shade of your skin, that makes a ballet dancer!"[217]

The Dance Theatre of Harlem made an auspicious beginning, helped financially by a Ford Foundation Grant. Its teaching staff was composed of a variety of talented dancers, both black and white, and early performances by the group have been acclaimed by the critics. Terry called the group a "highly professional and engaging troupe."[218] Of their first extended engagement at Jacob's Pillow in August, 1970, Terry wrote that The Dance Theatre of Harlem "performed beautifully and gave pleasure to the seven sets of audiences who had traveled from near and far to see them."[219]

Speaking of his school and the future of the black classical dancer, Mitchell stated:

> Of course, I must be optimistic. How can I train young people
> if I don't keep them hoping that one day things will change?
> I'm not blind. I know exactly what's happening. It may take a
> lifetime. It's just that most prejudices are based on stupidity.
> They're not valid, and they've got to change. Finally, if the
> Negro achieves the necessary discipline and self-respect in
> the dance—or in anything—whatever he has, call it life, energy,
> or freedom, that is lacking in the puritanical society that exists
> in many parts of the country, may contribute the new blood
> needed today. This our school can help to achieve.[220]

Under Mitchell's direction, the Dance Theatre of Harlem toured the United States and the Caribbean and were artists-in-residence with the University of Cincinnati Dance Department. In its infancy the Dance Theatre rapidly achieved success. The question remains, however, as to whether Arthur Mitchell could have become a principal member of a ballet company as early as 1955 had he not fit within the accepted standards of beauty? He was described as "handsome, young and restlessly energetic";[221] "a lithe, quite dark and handsome young man who, by contrast, stands out strikingly in the company";[222] and "lean and wildly handsome, with . . . a sensational smile . . . ."[223] Mitchell could not have been mistaken for anything other than what he was—superb dancer and a committed artist.

Others

Black dancers who are members of ballet companies are very few in comparison to those in modern dance. However there are some: for example, John Jones, who has been a member of the Joffrey and Harkness companies. Jones also toured Europe as a member of Jerome Robbins' *Ballets: U.S.A.* Geoffrey Holder danced in the Metropolitan Opera 1956 production of *Aïda,* and performed the role of the dancing clown in their production of *La Périchole.* Louis Johnson appeared in Robbins's *Ballade* for the New York City Ballet. Christian Holder, nephew of Geoffrey Holder, has danced some important roles with the Joffrey Ballet. *Times Past,* choreographed by "a promising newcomer,"[224] Keith Lee, was presented during the summer season of 1970, by the American Ballet Theatre. Lee danced in Alvin Ailey's *The River* and another number entitled *Two Cities* during the same season. Sara Yarborough, daughter of Lavinia Williams Yarborough, signed a contract with the Harkness Ballet in 1968.

The list of black dancers in the ballet is a short one, but as the Dance Theatre of Harlem and the Jones-Haywood School in Washington, D.C., continue to produce trained, qualified dancers, perhaps the ballet, too, will provide the opportunities "without regard for color."[225]

◘፧◘፧◘ WEST INDIAN DANCERS

No study of black concert dancers would be complete without at least a brief review of the many natives of the West Indies who have adopted the United States as their home and performed on American stages. Their influence can be felt in the dance of this country and they are certainly to be considered as black concert artists. One of the first of the Caribbean dancers, Jean-Léon Destiné, made his debut in the United States as a guest artist of Katherine Dunham's company.

Jean-Léon Destiné

Born in Haiti in an aristocratic Creole family, Jean-Léon Destiné shocked the Haitian "elite" with his study and association with Voodoo. It was from Voodoo, inherited from black Africa, that Destiné drew inspiration to create his repertory of dances which Terry termed "purely Haitian yet brilliantly theatrical."[226] Appearing with Katherine Dunham in *Bal Negre* in 1946, Destiné danced the important role of the boy possessed by a snake in Dunham's "Shango." Forming his own troupe, Destiné "made his New York debut as soloist and choreographer in the opera *Troubled Island,* New York City Center (1949)."[227]

Destiné and his troupe toured the United States, Europe and the Far East and appeared frequently at the Jacob's Pillow Festival. Of his appearance there during August, 1970, Terry wrote that Destiné

> . . . has forged his own theatrical dance technique—and a
> brilliant one it is—from folk materials native to Haiti, from the
> French-derived social dances, and especially from the intensely
> dynamic actions born of voudoun ceremonies.[228]

Destiné was asked by the Haitian government to create and direct the first Troupe Folklorique Nationale and in 1960 was appointed cultural attaché for the Republic of Haiti in the United States. Teaching at the New Dance Group studio and New York University School of the Arts when not performing, Destiné was among the first to recognize the dances of Voodoo as great art.

Jean-Léon Destiné in "Spider Dance"

Louis Mélançon, Destiné
Afro-Haitian Dance Company,
from private collection of
Jean-Léon Destiné

Percival Borde

Robert Easton, from private
collection of Percival Borde

The unusual artistry of his presentations together with the sincerity of his convictions enable him to raise the once misunderstood and despised music and dance of Vodun to a place of respect in Haiti and throughout the world. Destiné, scholar and artist, is dedicated to the idea that greater sympathy and understanding among the peoples of the world derives from knowledge of each other's way of life.[229]

Percival Borde

A native of Trinidad with extensive education and experience in theatre and dance, Percival Borde has toured the United States and Europe with Pearl Primus, to whom he is married, and their company. According to a press release, he is "an outstanding dancer, choreographer, teacher, and lecturer, specializing in the area of Caribbean dances and their African origins."[230] Martin described him as

> . . . an excellent dancer, physically handsome and vital. He
> is light and easy of movement, with strength, admirable control
> and authority. The dances he performs here cover a wide range
> of styles — from the ceremonials of the giant Watusi of Africa,
> to the work and play dances of the Caribbean, with a poetic
> Aztec legend for good measure. He has also a personal dignity
> and an elegance that are of enormous value to an artist. . . .[231]

Beside performing, Borde has become well known as a teacher, working at the Primus-Borde school, with his wife in the New York City schools' cultural enrichment program, and with poverty-area children in a special project sponsored jointly by the Harkness Foundation and New York University. Combining African and Caribbean dance forms, he has been in demand as a teacher in mixed racial areas, leading the Bronx Community College, among others, in its first class in African and Puerto Rican dance. Borde has proven one of the most popular artists of the American Dance Symposium, where he has presented two lecture-performances entitled "The Drums of the Caribbean" and "Talking Drums of Africa." During the summer of 1970 Borde also conducted a workshop in Afro-Haitian dance at the University of Oregon. In 1969, he became the choreographer for the Negro Emsemble Company of New York.

A gracious and productive artist, Percival Borde is highly respected both as a person and as a performer. It is his feeling that many of the popular American dances were influenced by the Afro-American since "America as a whole is quick to adopt portions of the culture of any one of its peoples when it finds them desirable, interesting, and relevant to American life. . . ."[232] When asked if, in his extensive experience, he was able to identify a movement which could be termed Afro-American, he replied:

> . . . there is a caricature-concept of this idea of movement, and since this caricature is widely imitated by Americans of all ethnic backgrounds it would be impossible to detect recognizably ethnic movements if such a thing existed. It becomes impossible to differentiate between native and assumed movements in any individual.[233]

Geoffrey Holder

> To anyone who has ever watched this restless young man dance there is no need to describe the impact his long dark body, suggestive of Egyptian tribal kings, makes as it twists around a rhythm seemingly unrestricted by the usual bonds of bone and muscle, or struts in sexual insolence against the rhythm of a drum. Then there is something elemental on the stage. Something unfettered and free.[234]

Unfettered and free describes Mr. Holder as he pursues his multi-faceted career. A native of Trinidad, he has been recognized as a dancer, choreographer, photographer, singer, artist, writer, and costume designer. He even conducted a radio interview program in New York City while still engaged in his other activities.

Inheritor of his brother Boscoe's dance company in Trinidad at age eighteen, Holder staged three revues before coming to the United States, where he eventually made his Broadway debut in *House of Flowers*. Holder is married to Carmen de Lavallade, and became a leading dancer with the Metropolitan Opera Ballet in 1956. Since that time he has performed as a guest artist and also with his own company.

Probably best known in the dance world for his chore-

Geoffrey Holder in Metropolitan Opera production of "Aida"

Lavinia Williams Yarborough

Boris Bakchy, from private collection of Lavinia Williams

ography, Holder has composed many works for his wife, including the touching "Come Sunday," based on Negro spirituals. Many of his compositions are based on West Indian or African themes, including such works as "Prodigal Prince," dealing with the life of Haitian artist Hector Hippolyte; a seven-part "African Suite"; "Bele"; "Banda," the West Indian funeral dance; and "Doogla Suite." Reviewing "Doogla Suite," one critic wrote that besides being magnificently costumed by Holder, the suite, "with a piling of mass upon mass, rhythm upon rhythm, speed upon speed, and color upon color, the dancers built a crescendo of oriental-primitive movement."[235] Doris Rudko wrote that the number was "a fascinating exposition in movement terms of the genetic origins, African and East Indian, of the Doogla race."[236]

A fervent critic of the attitude in which Afro-Americans in the United States are held, Holder feels that an artist is an artist, not a "Negro" artist.

> People worry about the wrong things. This gets in the way of creativity. When I paint, I paint. I'm not a Negro painter. When I dance, I dance. I'm not a West Indian dancer, I'm not a voodoo dancer, not a ballet dancer—I'm a dancer.[237]

Lavinia Williams Yarborough

Born in Philadelphia, Miss Williams was a member of Von Grona's American Negro Ballet and American Ballet Theatre before joining the Dunham Company, with which she danced in *Cabin in the Sky* and the movies *Stormy Weather, Carnival of Rhythm, Finian's Rainbow,* and *My Darlin' Aida.* She taught at the Dunham school, and then left to tour Europe with the USO. Upon her return she replaced Pearl Primus in *Showboat.* After her marriage, she taught until 1953, when she was asked by the Haitian National Education Bureau and the Bureau of Tourism to come to Haiti to teach dance in the schools and work with the National Folklore Group.

Since that time, she has remained in Haiti, in charge of the Theatre de Verdure and director of the Haitian Academy of Classic and Folklore Dance, which she founded in 1954. At the Theatre, one of Haiti's tourist attractions, she "choreographs, teaches and directs the folk dances, most of which are based on the Voodoo ceremonials."[238] Serving as narrator, she often performs with a troupe from the Haitian Academy in the leading Port-au-Prince hotels and nightclubs.

Lavinia Williams Yarborough has been able to turn the authentic Haitian folk forms into entertaining theatrical pieces without destroying their authenticity. This she accomplishes through selectivity and a sense of timing. Because of her success in Haiti, she has taught on several of the other islands and at Jamaica's University College of the West Indies. An invitation came from the Governor of Nassau, who asked her to teach special classes stressing the ethnic origins of dance during the summer of 1970. Through extensive travel, she has clarified her beliefs and has written that:

> Every step that I have seen in America, rock and roll, etc. — I have seen in an African or West Indian dance. The twist comes from the "Coye" — Haitian dance — the "a-go-go" and "sugar-foot" from "Yenvolou" and "Spider Dance". . . .[239]

Miss Williams has contributed to black concert dance in two ways: first, by preserving the authentic folk forms of Haiti; and second, by preparing dancers, many of whom eventually perform on the stages of American theatres.

Others

What Lavinia Williams Yarborough has done for the dance of Haiti, Beryl McBurnie has done for Trinidad and Ivy Baxter for Jamaica. All three women were concerned with the preservation and perpetuation of authentic folk forms of dance and the retention of the original African dances handed down for over one hundred years. McBurnie founded the Little Carib Company as a showplace for these folk forms, while Baxter worked with a similar troupe in Jamaica. A member of Baxter's group, Eddy Thomas, who performed one season with the Martha Graham Company, was instrumental in 1962 in the founding of the Jamaican National Dance Theatre. This company should be better known. Their history and purposes are beautifully recorded in a book written by Rex Nettleford, their co-founder, artistic director, and choreographer.[240]

▣▣▣ RISING CONCERT DANCERS

Over the past few years several blacks have become publicly recognized in modern dance. Many of these are known as dancer-choreographers or dancer-teachers. In most cases, these dancers have performed first with established companies and then formed their own groups. Their dances are usually developed for their own companies but commissions and performances by other troupes are not unusual.

Working with or without Negro thematic material and with either all-black or integrated companies, these dancer-choreographer-teachers perform throughout the country, particularly on college campuses, and so probably have a greater impact than is realized. While not newcomers to dance, since many have been professionals for quite a few years, they can, nevertheless, be termed *newly found* dancers: newly-found due to the current emphasis on the black cultural heritage. They are contributing to an awareness and understanding of cultural differences by performing, composing, and teaching. They are demonstrating the universality of dance as a means of non-verbal communication, and each in his own way is communicating. In many cases the only connection the dance performed has with so-called "Negro dance" is the fact that the performer's skin is black. These are not primarily "Negro" dancers, but rather, they are human beings, dancers, and artists.

Louis Johnson

Trained primarily in ballet, Louis Johnson began his study as a youth at the Jones-Haywood School of Dance in Washington, D.C. During his last year in high school he auditioned for the School of American Ballet and was accepted and granted a scholarship, but deferred his entrance until completing high school. In a comment revealing of the bias toward black dancers in ballet, Saul Goodman wrote:

> Although Louis did not go from the School of American Ballet into the New York City Ballet Company (as do most of the school's outstanding students), he did perform with the company in Jerome Robbins' 1952 work, "Ballade."[241]

Johnson did perform, however, on Broadway in a revival of *Four Saints in Three Acts* and in *House of Flowers*, and was the lead dancer in *Damn Yankees*. Of his performing abilities, critics have stated that he was "breathtaking in virtuosity"[242] "moving,"[243] and "expert and virtuosic."[244]

It was his choreography rather than his performance, however, that brought Louis Johnson to the public eye. Showing a strong balletic background, Johnson's "Lament" was highly acclaimed at its first performance in 1955. "Lament" has been performed through the years, most recently as a part of the Ailey Company repertoire. Other well-known Johnson works are "Whisk," "Harlequin" (called by Louis Horst a "brilliant and sure-fire exhibition piece"[245]), a beautiful suite of "Negro Spirituals," "No Outlet," and "Ode to Martin Luther King." On Broadway, Johnson was assistant choreographer for the musical *Jamaica*, and choreographed *Purlie*, the 1970 musical version of *Purlie Victorious*. He has also been on the staff of the Negro Ensemble Company.

Johnson taught dance to young people in the program of the Harlem Youth Activities (Har-You Act). Participating in a symposium sponsored by the Harlem Cultural Council and Barnard College, he performed his "Ode to Martin Luther King." Speaking of this dance, he said that he did not consider himself an agent of social protest: "I'm just saying what I feel here, that a person is an artist."[246]

Rod Rodgers

Speaking of his career, Rod Rodgers has said that he "tried not to be a professional black man."[247] He has been more concerned with pure movement in an abstract sense than with a verbally developed theme. Yet his dance is Afro-American dance. Rodgers wrote:

> The dance that I do is Afro-American, simply because I am Afro-American. My blackness is part of my identity as a human being, and my dance exploration is evolving in relation to my total experience as a man. It is simply a question of what is more important in the act of creating—my total living experiences, or

Louis Johnson in
"House of Flowers"

George Lake, from private
collection of Louis Johnson

Rod Rodgers

Jack Mitchell, from private
collection of Rod Rodgers

those experiences which I consider particularly relevant to my blackness.[248]

Further:

Each dance I create has grown out of my personal experience as a black American. Each movement I explore is part of my own personal heritage. My emphasis is on exploring through my medium, experimenting with dance, trying to find fresh ways of evoking physical and spiritual images, to make new poetic comments about man's eternal beauty and pathos. My function in the Revolution will be to share my personal experience through dance, a vital and growing experience, not to show only old stereotypes or to create new ones.[249]

Growing up in Detroit, Michigan, Rodgers traveled to New York in 1962 where he studied with Hanya Holm, Mary Anthony, and Erick Hawkins, eventually joining the Hawkins Company. Awarded a John Hay Whitney Fellowship for 1965-66, Rodgers had the financial security to pursue his own creative work. He formed his own integrated company in 1966 and continued his choreography in such non-representational works as "Tangents," "Inventions," "Trajectories," and "Percussion Suite." Some of his newer works, such as "Conjuring" and "Harambee," are based on thematic material. In a review, Anna Kisselgoff wrote:

Mr. Rodgers's group work, "Conjuring," with its strong animal, almost prehistoric images, and careful structure has its own power as well. It was complemented by a softer pure-dance work, with carefully integrated movement and stick waving, entitled "Tangents."[250]

Reviewers disagree on Rodgers' choreography; the newspaper critics generally praise his work while those writing for *Dance Magazine* usually find it unpleasing.

Since 1965 Rodgers has been the director of the dance project of New York's Mobilization for Youth and also involved with lecture-performances for children with New York's Head Start program.[251] He developed a lecture-performance program entitled *Dance Poems. . . . Black, Brown, Negro* which depicts traditional dance characters and images evolving from the Afro-American experience and is directed toward adult audiences.

According to Rodgers, opportunities in dance for the black performer are still limited because of race, and though sincere efforts have been made, much of the integration is on a token basis. He suggests it is because of the shortage of males in dance that the black male has an advantage over the black female. "As a result, Negro women with limited technical or performing ability, or less than 'ideal' proportions"[252] face double discrimination, except in Negro ethnic dance. An awareness of the problems of the black choreographer in his attempt to deal with thematic material, traditional and non-traditional, was voiced by Rodgers:

> Most of the existing dance companies which are the instruments of black choreographers have placed their emphasis on traditional Afro-American material. They are exploring through their artistry the proud Afro-American heritage, and they can evoke poignant images which will encourage intolerance of racial suppression. But these images are not the only means of communicating a black consciousness. While traditional black art is playing a vital role in the awakening of a black cultural identity, now it is equally important for black artists to discourage the crystalization of new stereotype limitations by not confining themselves to over-simplified traditional images.[253]

To Rodgers: "Negro dance art, whatever form it may take, can be a celebration of the beauty and the virtue of our blackness."[254]

Eleo Pomare

They have called him angry, to which he has replied:

> I'm labeled . . . angry . . . because I will not do what they want from a black dancer. They want black exotics . . . I have something to say and I want to say it honestly, strongly and without having it stolen, borrowed or messed over.[255]

Commenting on his choreography, one reviewer stated, "At present, his failing seems partly insufficient discipline,"[256] while another wrote that frequently there appeared "undisciplined self-expression."[257] Regarding reviewers and critics, Pomare said:

> White critics are too far removed from the black experience to really criticize what we do. . . . They try to judge what I do as a black man by their own past experiences, in terms of their own values.[258]

Eleo Pomare

Eleo Pomare Dance Company,
Pacific World Artists, Inc.

The Eleo Pomare Dancers
in "Burnt Ash"

Eleo Pomare Dance Company,
Pacific World Artists, Inc.

About discipline, he has answered, "How many critics really understand the discipline it takes to erase all white influences, and yet dramatize precisely the world the black artist is struggling to escape from?"[259]

Of the classic ballet he wrote:

> They say the classic ballet is superior but they're dancing about fairies running around in gardens. They repeat these ancient, ancient rituals to death when there is so much life, so much art around them in everyday life.[260]

Commenting on the black dancer's place and his own work:

> Let's face it, the "powers-that-be" are not interested in seeing "Negroes" in any way but as rhythmic freaks about whom they say, "They certainly do have a good sense of rhythm." Well, I am not an animal and I won't tap dance or play the part of the maid. I am a human being and have the same feelings that any other human being would have. I don't want to *entertain* them.[261]

> I don't create works to amuse white crowds, nor do I wish to show them how charming, strong, and folksy Negro people are. . . . Instead I'm showing them the Negro experience from inside: what it's like to live in Harlem, to be hung-up and up-tight and trapped and black and wanting to get out. And I'm saying it in a dance language that originates in Harlem itself.[262]

Of the role of black choreographers in the United States, he says:

> Many of us are concerned with the black identity in America, defining it and probing it. The question being: if we are not Amos 'n' Andy (our old image), then who are we? I think it is our duty to destroy the old alien-created images and act as teachers and messengers to help perpetuate positive black images.[263]

> Our role is to break the ethnocentric thinking patterns which have led these people — drunk with power — to believe that theirs, although dead, is the superior art.[264]

This is Eleo Pomare. These thoughts, ideas and beliefs make up the man, and his work. Born in Colombia, brought up in

Panama and Harlem, educated at the High School of the Performing Arts, Pomare does not consider himself angry or bitter. He is, rather, "telling it like it is." Winning a scholarship, Pomare went to Germany to study with Kurt Jooss and from there to Holland, where his choreographic style was clarified. He formed his own company in 1958, toured Europe—where the group received rave reviews—and made his major New York debut in 1966. Since this debut, Pomare and his company have continued touring and have performed with the Harlem Cultural Council's Dancemobile and other projects.

Pomare's choreographic works include the powerful "Blues for the Jungle" dealing with life in the Harlem jungle; "Narcissus Rising," "Movement for Two"; a sensational solo of the psychology of a motorcycle gang member; "Cantos from a Monastery"; "Over Here"; "Climb"; "Hex"; and a suite entitled "Uptight." Affecting his choreography more than any other single thing is the black revolution, of which Pomare has been quoted as saying:

> I used to think constantly of pleasing white audiences. I used to see through blue eyes. Now, the new black consciousness, the black revolution in the streets and in the arts supports and sustains me. This new climate is allowing me to grow. I talk to black people. Instant communications. I know what I'm talking to. I'm alive.[265]

Other Dancers, Choreographers, Teachers

Another product of California's Lester Horton Dance Theatre, James Truitte first performed with the Horton group in 1951 and continued in the company for several years. In 1959 Truitte received a John Hay Whitney Opportunity Fellowship to study Labanotation for the purpose of recording Horton's technique. Joining Alvin Ailey's company in 1960, Truitte performed with and was assistant artistic director of the group until 1968. One of six dancers qualified to teach the Horton technique, Truitte has been teaching at New York City's Clark Center of the Performing Arts since 1960. An excellent teacher, Truitte handles up to seven or eight classes per week in the Horton technique

Alvin Ailey Company in "Revelations"

Jack Mitchell

at Clark Center besides his teaching at the New Dance Group Studio.

Also teaching at Clark Center and her own school is Syvilla Fort, a former member of Katherine Dunham's company. Miss Fort was Ballet Mistress for the Dunham School from 1947 to 1952. Serving as choreographer for Langston Hughes' *The Prodigal Son*, Fort composed many other works in addition to developing the Syvilla Fort technique, which she teaches at Clark Center. Her technique "has an added richness in that it is an amalgamation of Negro folklore taken from Africa, the West Indies, Haiti, and early American Negro jazz."[266] Another Dunham Company dancer, Lenwood Morris, has remained Miss Dunham's first assistant since joining her company in 1941. Primarily an exponent of jazz-swing dance, Pepsi Bethel has also taught on the excellent staff at Clark Center. Bethel has performed with the Munt-Brooks Dance Company and the Mura Dehn Jazz Ballet Company and has developed his own troupe.

An impressive dancer and excellent teacher, Charles Moore has taught Dunham technique at Clark Center, the New Dance Group Studio, and Harlem Youth Activities (Har-You Act). Moore has appeared in many dance companies, including those of Dunham and Ailey, and has performed in *Jamaica*, the revival of *House of Flowers*, *Trumpets of the Lord*, and the New York City Opera production of *Bomarzo*.

On the West Coast the two leading black teachers are Ruth Beckford in the San Francisco area and Carlton Johnson in Los Angeles. Miss Beckford, a magnificent person and teacher, has conducted most of her work in conjunction with the Oakland Recreation Department, where she specializes in Afro-Haitian dance. Johnson, one of the foremost teachers of jazz, also choreographs and dances in numerous television programs. He developed his own company, which has presented exciting programs of his work. A newcomer to California, although already established in New York, Claude Thompson has also taught Afro-Haitian dance in the Los Angeles area.

Gus Solomons, Jr., while based primarily in New York City, is also familiar to Californians through his teaching at the Long Beach Summer School of Dance and as artist-in-residence at UCLA. Mr. Solomons has studied with Graham and Merce Cunningham and performed with the companies of Graham, Cunningham, Pearl Lang, and Donald McKayle, and in the concerts of various New York choreographers.

Katherine Flowers, who studied with Dunham prior to Dunham's departure to New York, has had an interesting and varied career as a dancer, teacher and researcher. Miss Flowers was the first to present a concert program which oriented the audience to the Negro source material available in dance. One of her programs presented throughout the Midwest was entitled *Bamboula to Bop*.[267]

Throughout the United States companies led by black dancers and choreographers have appeared, many of them in connection with a sponsoring group, such as the Elma Lewis School in Roxbury, Massachusetts, where Talley Beatty, for example, organized a repertory company. Fred Benjamin, who began his dance study at the Lewis School, organized his own company under the sponsorship of Clark Center. The Inner City Cultural Center in Los Angeles developed a repertory company under the leadership of Donald McKayle, Janet Collins, and Jaime Rogers, while the Jones-Haywood School of Dance in Washington, D.C., presented several ballet performances throughout the city during the summer of 1970. Cleveland's Karamu House has been the starting place of many fine dancers and the influence of Gloria Unti's San Francisco Performing Arts Workshop has been felt.

Arthur Hall organized the Afro-American Dance Ensemble in Philadelphia, concentrating on the dances of Africa and the Caribbean. Hall's company completed two successful summers at Jacob's Pillow. Danny Duncan's Ballet Afro-Haiti, based in San Francisco and concentrating on ethnic dance, toured the West Coast, while the Watts Studio Workshop's Mafundi Dancers have also performed. Young dancer-choreographers Keith Lee, Chuck Davis, Judy Deering, and John Parks have appeared in their own works quite successfully in the New York area.

From small beginnings in the 1930's, black concert dancers have developed through the Dunham era to the present, increasing in numbers, growing in technical skill, and exerting a powerful and vital influence on American dance. In spite of the many limiting factors on their growth and development, they have persisted as a creative force, bringing the styles and rhythms of their heritage to the American concert stage.

◼︎◼︎◼︎ NOTES FOR CHAPTER 8

1. "Winfield Dead at 27; 'Emperor Jones' Dancer," *New York Herald-Tribune*. No publication given; Dance Clipping File, Schomburg Collection of Negro Literature and History, New York, n.d., n.p.

2. Edna Guy, "Negro Dance Pioneer!" *Dance Herald*, March, 1938, p. 6.

3. Langston Hughes and Milton Meltzer, *Black Magic. A Pictorial History of the Negro in American Entertainment* (Englewood Cliffs, N.J.: Prentice-Hall, Inc., 1967), p. 264.

4. John Martin, "Dance Recital Given by Negro Artists," *New York Times*, April 30, 1931, p. 27.

5. *Ibid.*

6. "Winfield Dead at 27," *New York Herald-Tribune*, n.p.

7. *Ibid.*

8. Guy, "Negro Dance Pioneer!" p. 6.

9. Martin, "Dance Recital," p. 27.

10. John Martin, *John Martin's Book of the Dance* (New York: Tudor Publishing Company, 1963), pp. 179-80.

11. Michael Lorant, "'Hampton Institute,' Negro's Unique Dancing Academy," *Dancing Times* (London), October, 1938, p. 21.

12. Michael Lorant, "The Hampton Institute, Unique Dancing Academy of American Negroes," *Ballet Today*, June, 1950, pp. 17-18.

13. Margaret Lloyd, "African Dances, American Plan," *Christian Science Monitor*, May 17, 1938, p. 8.

14. *Ibid.*

15. Dr. James Bell, numerous interviews at California State Polytechnic College, Pomona, California, 1969-1970.

16. I.K., "Negro Ballet Has Performance," *New York Sun*, November 22, 1937, n.p. John Martin earlier had said that the Negro artist is always faced by two temptations: "On the one hand he is likely, unless he is on guard, to copy the white man's art; and on the other hand it is so easy to give the white man what he chooses to believe is Negro art." John Martin, "The Dance: A Negro Art Group," *New York Times*, February 14, 1932, Sec. VIII, p. 11.

17. John Martin, "Negro Ballet Has Debut in Harlem," *New York Times*, November 22, 1937, p. 15.

18. I.K., "Negro Ballet," *New York Sun*, n.p.

19. Stark Young, "Slightly Ghosts," *New Republic*, December 8, 1937, p. 131.

20. *Ibid.*

21. Joseph Pearlman, "Harlemites Forsake Torrid 'Swing' Dances for the Modern Ballet Steps," *New York Herald-Tribune*, December 12, 1937, n.p.

22. "Harlem Under Control, Negro Ballet Gives 'Fire Bird' and Park Ave. Approves," *Newsweek*, November 29, 1937, p. 28.

23. Hughes and Meltzer, *Black Magic*, p. 264.

24. Elena Maximovna, "Negro Dance on the Scene," *Dance Magazine*, XVI (December, 1942), 24.

25. Wilson Williams, "Prelude to a Negro Ballet," *American Dancer*, March, 1940, p. 14.

26. John Martin, "Native Cast Gives An African Opera," *New York Times*, May 9, 1934, p. 23.

27. Lincoln Kirstein, "The Dance 'Kykunkor'; Native African Opera," *Nation*, June 13, 1934, p. 684.

28. John Martin, "The Dance: African Lore," *New York Times*, May 13, 1934, Sec. IX, p. 6.

29. Arthur Todd, "Four Centuries of American Dance: Part 3, The Negro Folk Dance in America," *Dance Magazine*, XXIV (January, 1950), 14.

30. "Asadata Dafora," in *Kykunkor*, Official Program. Schomburg Collection of Negro Literature and History. New York.

31. "Asadata Dafora Presents 'Kykunkor'"; Playbill, Little Theatre, 244 West 44th Street, New York, June 18, 1934.

32. Kirstein, "The Dance, 'Kykunkor,'" *Nation*, p. 684.

33. *Ibid.*

34. *Ibid.*

35. Asadata Dafora, quoted in the Official Program of *Kykunkor*, n.p.

36. Martin, "The Dance: African Lore," *New York Times*, p. 6.

37. *Ibid.*

38. Martin, *John Martin's Book of the Dance*, p. 180.

39. John Martin, "The Dance: A Negro Play," *New York Times*, March 12, 1933, Sec. IX, p. 7.

40. Walter Terry, "The Negro Dances," *New York Herald-Tribune*, April 28, 1940, n.p. Mr. Terry, in his review, commented upon American Negro dance with a statement devoid of the historical knowledge. He stated: ". . . while Africa possessed a rich store of native dances and ceremonies, the Africans in America were not *content* [italics mine] to perform the dances of their remote ancestors nor did they have a dance which was both Negro and American at the same time." This statement should be a classic in the realm of inaccuracy. It was not because the Africans were not *content* to perform the African dances, rather, they were not *allowed* to perform them.

41. All information dealing with the Negro Dance Evening was obtained from the official program of the "Young Men's Hebrew Association Major Subscription Series, 'Negro Dance Evening',", March 7, 1931, in the Theresa L. Kaufmann Auditorium, Lexington Avenue at 92nd Street, New York, found in the Dance Clipping File of the Schomburg Collection of Negro Literature and History, New York.

42. Walter Terry, "World of Dance, Black Dance," *Saturday Review*, September 26, 1970, p. 45.

43. "Awards 1968," *Dance Magazine*, XLIII (April, 1969), 34.

44. Details of Miss Dunham's early life are refreshingly written in her autobiography, *A Touch of Innocence* (New York: Harcourt, Brace and Company, 1959).

45. Margaret Lloyd, *The Borzoi Book of Modern Dance* (Brooklyn, N.Y.: Dance Horizons, Inc., 1949), pp. 250-51.

46. Katherine Dunham, quoted in A. J. Elias, "Conversation with Katherine Dunham," *Dance Magazine*, XXX (February, 1956), 17.

47. Katherine Dunham, "The Future of the Negro in the Dance," *Dance Herald*, March, 1938, p. 5.

48. Lloyd, *Borzoi Book of Modern Dance*, p. 251.

49. Katherine Dunham, "The Dances of Haiti," *Acta Anthropologica*, II, No. 4 (1947). Extensive use was made of Dunham's thesis in Chapter II of this book. For an excellent description of life among the Maroons of Accompong, see Miss Dunham's charmingly written *Katherine Dunham's Journey to Accompong* (New York: Henry Holt and Company, 1946).

50. Ralph Linton, in introduction to *Katherine Dunham's Journey to Accompong*, p. ix.

51. Katherine Dunham, *Island Possessed* (Garden City, N.Y.: Doubleday and Company, Inc., 1969), p. 245.

52. Writers' Program, Illinois, *Calvalcade of the American Negro* (Chicago: Diamond Jubilee Exposition Authority, 1940), p. 53.

53. Hallie Flanagan, *Arena* (New York: Duell, Sloan and Pearce, 1940), p. 141.

54. Richard Buckle, ed., *Katherine Dunham, Her Dancers, Singers, Musicians* (London: Ballet Publications, Ltd., 1949), p. viii.

55. John Martin, "Negro Dance Art Shown in Recital," *New York Times*, February 19, 1940, p. 21.

56. *Ibid.*

57. John Martin, "The Dance: A Negro Art," *New York Times*, February 25, 1940, Sec. IX, p. 2.

58. All information for the dances included in Dunham's 1940 performance was obtained from the *Official Playbill of Tropical Revue* (1943), in which the same dances were performed, with the addition, of course, of new compositions, at the Martin Beck Theatre in New York.

59. Martin, "Dance: A Negro Art," *New York Times*, IX, p. 2.

60. *Ibid.*

61. Terry, "The Negro Dances," *New York Herald-Tribune*, n.p.

62. Martin, "Dance: A Negro Art," *New York Times*, IX, p. 2.

63. Buckle, *Katherine Dunham*, p. viii.

64. Lloyd, *Borzoi Book of Modern Dance*, p. 244.

65. All information about the contents of *Tropical Revue* was taken from the official playbill, "S. Hurok presents Katherine Dunham and her company in *Tropical Revue*, Week beginning October 24, 1943."

66. John Martin, "The Dance: 'Tropical Revue,'" *New York Times*, September 26, 1943, Sec. II, p. 2.

67. Lloyd, *Borzoi Book of Modern Dance*, p. 246.

68. Virginia Mishnun, "Dance: Dunham 'Tropical Review,'" *Nation*, October 9, 1943, p. 416.

69. *Ibid.*

70. Hughes and Meltzer, *Black Magic*, p. 267.

71. Miles M. Jefferson, "The Negro on Broadway, 1945-1946," *Phylon*, VII, No. 2 (Second Quarter, 1946), 187.

72. Frederick L. Orme, "The Negro in the Dance," *American Dancer*, March, 1938, p. 46.

73. Dorathi Bock Pierre, "A Talk with Katherine Dunham," *Educational Dancer*, August-September, 1941, p. 8.

74. "The Schoolmarm Who Glorified Leg Art," *Ebony*, January, 1947, p. 14.

75. Buckle, *Katherine Dunham*, p. ix.

76. John Martin, "The Dance: Dunham," *New York Times*, November 17, 1946, Sec. II, p. 9.

77. All information dealing with cast and numbers in *Bal Negre* was obtained from the official playbill, "Nelson L. Gross and Daniel Melnick present Katherine Dunham in *Bal Negre*, Week beginning Monday, December 2, 1946," pp. 17-27.

78. Information regarding *Bamboche* was obtained from the official playbill, "Stephen Papich in Association with Dorothy Gray and Ludwig Gerber Present Katherine Dunham in *Bamboche*, Premiere Performance, October 22, 1962," pp. 15-22.

79. Hughes and Meltzer, *Black Magic*, p. 267.

80. "Awards 1968," *Dance Magazine*, p. 67.

81. Katherine Dunham, personal correspondence, April 1, 1970.

82. Arthur Todd, "American Negro Dance: A National Treasure," in Arnold Haskell and Mary Clarke, eds.; *The Ballet Annual, 1962* (London: Adam & Charles Black, 1961), p. 98.

83. Harriet Jackson, "American Dancer, Negro," *Dance Magazine*, XXXX (September, 1966), 40.

84. Martin, *John Martin's Book of the Dance*, p. 182.

85. Charles White, personal interviews, Altadena, California, August-December, 1969.

86. Katherine Dunham, quoted in Jackson, "American Dancer, Negro," *Dance Magazine*, 40.

87. Jackson, "American Dancer, Negro," *Dance Magazine*, 40.

88. Martin, *John Martin's Book of the Dance*, pp. 183-84.

89. "Primus, Pearl (Eileene)," *Current Biography*, April, 1944, p. 35.

90. Lloyd, *Borzoi Book of Modern Dance*, p. 269.

91. Information on Primus's early life and performances was obtained

chiefly from *Current Biography*, April, 1944, pp. 34-37; and Margaret Lloyd, *Borzoi Book of Modern Dance*, pp. 265-76.

92. John Martin, quoted in *Current Biography*, April, 1944, p. 35.

93. Edwin Denby, "The Dance," *New York Times*, October 6, 1944, p. 18.

94. Edith Segal, "Pearl Primus Thrills Broadway," *Daily Worker* (New York), October 7, 1944, n.p.

95. *Ibid.*

96. Lloyd, *Borzoi Book of Modern Dance*, p. 273.

97. John Martin, "The Dance: Current Events," *New York Times*, December 3, 1944, Sec. II, p. 4.

98. Information regarding the performance of *Dark Rhythm* was obtained from the official playbill, "The American Museum of Natural History, Central Park West and 79th Street, New York City, Thursday, May 15, 1952 at 3:30 and 8:30 P.M. Presents Pearl Primus and Her Company in 'Dark Rhythm.'"

99. John Martin, "Dance: Borde and Troupe," *New York Times*, September 29, 1958, p. 31.

100. Joseph Wershba, "The Gift of Healing Is Not Always a Medical Matter," *New York Post*, August 9, 1960, n.p.

101. During the course of several conversations with the author in January, 1970, Miss Primus mentioned many Afro-American dancers who should be contacted. In each case Miss Primus's name proved to be the magic word which opened all doors. Highest praise for Miss Primus and her work came from each of the dancers contacted. .

102. Lloyd, *Borzoi Book of Modern Dance*, p. 266.

103. David Leddick, "Everyman's African Roots," *Dance Magazine*, XXXVIII (October, 1964), 20.

104. Jackson, "American Dancer, Negro," *Dance Magazine*, 40.

105. Ric Estrada, "Three Leading Negro Artists, and How They Feel About Dance in the Community: Eleo Pomare, Arthur Mitchell, Pearl Primus," *Dance Magazine*, XLII (November, 1968), 60.

106. *Ibid.*, 56.

107. Lloyd, *Borzoi Book of Modern Dance*, pp. 273-74.

108. Estrada, "Three Negro Artists," *Dance Magazine*, 56.

109. Lois Balcom, "What Chance Has the Negro Dancer?" *Dance Observer*, November, 1944, p. 110.

110. Martin, *John Martin's Book of the Dance*, p. 183.

111. *Ibid.*, pp. 178-79.

112. *Ibid.*, p. 189.

113. All information regarding Mr. Beatty's role in *Negro Dance Evening* was obtained from the official program, March 7, 1937.

114. Martin, "Negro Dance Art Shown in Recital," *New York Times*, p. 21.

115. Anatole Chujoy and P. W. Manchester, eds., *The Dance Encyclopedia* (Rev. ed.; New York: Simon and Schuster, 1967), p. 119.

116. Lloyd, *Borzoi Book of Modern Dance*, pp. 246-50.

117. *Ibid.*, p. 352.

118. *Ibid.*, p. 232.

119. Chujoy and Manchester, *Dance Encyclopedia*, p. 120.

120. Martin, *John Martin's Book of the Dance*, p. 185.

121. K. S. Bartlett, "Talley Beatty Company in Vivid Performance at John Hancock Hall," *Boston Globe*, January 15, 1952, n.p.

122. *Ibid.* All information dealing with *Tropicana* was obtained from Bartlett's review.

123. *Ibid.*

124. Martin, *John Martin's Book of the Dance*, p. 186.

125. John Martin, "Dance: Good Job," *New York Times*, December 6, 1959, p. 18.

126. Martin, *John Martin's Book of the Dance*, p. 185.

127. Clive Barnes, "Dance: Broadway Touch," *New York Times*, January 30, 1969, p. 40.

128. Martin, "Good Job," *New York Times*, p. 18.

129. Clive Barnes, "Dance: Nothing Less Than Superb," *New York Times*, December 19, 1965, p. 19.

130. Martin, *John Martin's Book of the Dance*, p. 186.

131. Clive Barnes, "Dance: The Wizardry of Talley Beatty," *New York Times*, September 5, 1967, p. 48.

132. Marcia Marks, "Review: Alvin Ailey American Dance Theatre," *Dance Magazine*, XLIII (March, 1969), 92.

133. Martin, *John Martin's Book of the Dance*, p. 186.

134. Frank Eng, "The House on Melrose," *Dance Perspectives 31* (Autumn, 1967), 25.

135. Joyce Trisler, "The Magic and the Commitment," in *Dance Perspectives 31*, (Autumn, 1967), 57.

136. Information on Ailey's early years as a dancer and choreographer was compiled from two main sources: Saul Goodman, "Brief Biographies—Alvin Ailey," *Dance Magazine*, XXXII (December, 1958), 70; and "Ailey, Alvin (Jr.)," *Current Biography*, March, 1968, pp. 3-5.

137. Brooks Atkinson, "Theatre: Truman Capote's Musical," *New York Times*, December 31, 1954, p. 11.

138. Doris Hering, "Alvin Ailey and Company," *Dance Magazine*, XXXII (May, 1958), 65.

139. Todd, "American Negro Dance," in Haskell and Clarke, eds., *Ballet Annual 1962*, p. 101.

140. Martin, *John Martin's Book of the Dance*, p. 187.

141. Ellen Cohn, "'I Want to Be a Father Figure,'" *New York Times*, April 13, 1969, p. 35.

142. *Ibid.*

143. During a month's stay in New York (January, 1970) the author was accepted as a part of the Ailey Company, attending auditions, rehearsals, and performances as a member of the group. The author was struck by the openness and receptiveness of the dancers and the generosity of Mr. Ailey and his administrative assistant, Ivy Clarke.

144. Arthur Todd, "Two-Way Passage for Dance," *Dance Magazine*, XXXVI (July, 1962), 39.

145. Lloyd Garrison, "The Vitality of Negro Art," *New York Times*, May 1, 1966, Sec. II, p. 13.

146. Clive Barnes, "Dancing the Blues," *Spectator* (London), October 16, 1964, p. 512.

147. *Ibid.*

148. Todd, "American Negro Dance," in Haskell and Clarke, eds., *Ballet Annual 1962*, p. 101.

149. Theresa M. Franklin, "God's Velvet Shadows: Modern Dance Composition and Study of the Negro Spiritual," unpublished Master of Arts thesis, New York University, 1966, p. 73.

150. Barnes, "Dance: Nothing Less Than Superb," *New York Times*, p. 37.

151. Alvin Ailey, "African Odyssey," *Dance Magazine*, XLII (May, 1968), 53.

152. Walter Terry, "World of Dance: American Ballet Theatre: Part II," *Saturday Review*, August 1, 1970, p. 36.

153. Anna Kisselgoff, "Dance: Militant 'Masekela Langage,'" *New York Times*, November 21, 1969, p. 57.

154. Jack Anderson, "Alvin Ailey American Dance Theatre," *Dance Magazine*, XLIV (June, 1970), 79.

155. Barnes, "Dance: Nothing Less Than Superb," *New York Times*, p. 37.

156. Richard Kraus, *History of the Dance in Art and Education* (Englewood Cliffs, N.J.: Prentice-Hall, Inc., 1969), p. 237.

157. P. W. Manchester, "Meet Donald McKayle," *Dancing Times* (London), January, 1967, p. 186.

158. Saul Goodman, "Brief Biographies: Donald McKayle," *Dance Magazine*, XXXIV (June, 1960), 50.

159. *Ibid.*

160. Donald McKayle, "The Negro Dancer in Our Time," in Walter Sorell, ed., *The Dance Has Many Faces* (2d ed.; New York: Columbia University Press, 1966), p. 191.

161. Manchester, "McKayle," *Dancing Times*, p. 186.

162. Donald McKayle, "The Act of Theatre," in Selma Jeanne Cohen, ed., *The Modern Dance, Seven Statements of Belief* (Middletown, Conn.: Wesleyan University Press, 1966), p. 57.

163. Manchester, "McKayle," *Dancing Times*, p. 186.

164. Martin, *John Martin's Book of the Dance*, p. 187.

165. McKayle, "Theatre," in Cohen, *Modern Dance*, p. 57.

166. Manchester, "McKayle," *Dancing Times*, p. 187.

167. "On the Airwaves," *Dance Magazine*, XLIII (September, 1969), 7.

168. McKayle, "Act of Theatre," in Cohen, *Modern Dance*, p. 54.

169. *Ibid.*

170. McKayle, "Negro Dancer in Our Time," in Sorell, *Dance Has Many Faces*, pp. 190-91.

171. Martin, *John Martin's Book of the Dance*, p. 177.

172. *Ibid.*

173. *Ibid.*, pp. 177-78.

174. "*Dance Magazine's* Annual Award Presentations, 1966" *Dance Magazine*, XLI (May, 1967), 84.

175. Doris Hering, "Carmen de Lavallade and Her Theatre of the Dance," *Dance Magazine*, XLII (May, 1968), 31.

176. Walter Terry, "Stars Under the Stars—A Vision of Loveliness," *New York Herald-Tribune*, September 9, 1963, n.p.

177. "De Lavallade, Carmen," *Current Biography*, December, 1967, p. 8.

178. Terry, "Stars Under the Stars," *New York Herald-Tribune*.

179. Emory Lewis, cited in: "De Lavallade," *Current Biography*, p. 8.

180. Carmen de Lavallade, personal letter, April 21, 1970.

181. *Ibid.*

182. "De Lavallade," *Current Biography*, p. 9.

183. "Hinkson, Mary," program notes for the October 1964 Graham season, Dance Clipping File, Dance Collection, Lincoln Center for the Performing Arts, New York.

184. Ernestine Stodelle, "The Negro Dancer: Gift to America Beyond Value," *New Haven Register*, January 14, 1968, n.p.

185. Jackson, "American Dancer, Negro," *Dance Magazine*, 36.

186. Stodelle, "Negro Dancer," *New Haven Register*, n.p.

187. Todd, "American Negro Dance," in Haskell and Clarke, eds., *Ballet Annual 1962*, p. 102.

188. Clive Barnes, "Dance: 'Archaic Hours,' a New Graham," *New York Times*, April 12, 1969, p. 40.

189. Clive Barnes, "Dance: Broadway Touch," *New York Times*, January 30, 1969, p. 40.

190. Todd, "American Negro Dance," in Haskell and Clarke, eds., *Ballet Annual 1962*, p. 102.

191. Martin, *John Martin's Book of the Dance*, pp. 178-79.

192. Stodelle, "Negro Dancer," *New Haven Register*, n.p.

193. Agnes DeMille, *The Book of the Dance* (London: Paul Hamlyn, 1963), p. 79.

194. Arthur Mitchell quoted by Olga Maynard, "Arthur Mitchell and The Dance Theatre of Harlem," *Dance Magazine,* XLIV (March, 1970), p. 54.

195. DeMille, *Book of the Dance,* p. 81.

196. "Black Man Stars in Ballet," *Black America,* June, 1970, p. 52.

197. William H. Grier and Price M. Cobbs, *Black Rage,* Bantam Books (New York: Basic Books, Inc., 1968), p. 33.

198. *Ibid.*

199. Martin, *John Martin's Book of the Dance,* p. 179.

200. John Martin, "The Dance: Newcomer," *New York Times,* February 27, 1949, Sec. II, p. 9.

201. *Ibid.*

202. *Ibid.*

203. Arthur Pollock, "Janet Collins, Golden Dancing Girl of 'Out of This World,'" *Daily Compass,* January 23, 1951, n.p.

204. Margaret Lloyd, "The Personal Equation: New Ballerina at the Met," *Christian Science Monitor,* October 16, 1951, Sec. II, p. 9.

205. *Ibid.*

206. Morris Gilbert, "Up and Coming," *New York Times Magazine,* February 1, 1953, Sec. VI, p. 44.

207. Norma Gengal Stahl, "The First Lady of the Metropolitan Opera Ballet," *Dance Magazine,* XXVIII (February, 1954), 27.

208. Janet Collins, personal letter, March, 1970.

209. "Mitchell, Arthur," *Current Biography,* October, 1966, p. 20.

210. John Martin, "Ballet: A Homecoming," *New York Times,* November 9, 1955, p. 40.

211. "Mitchell," *Current Biography,* p. 20.

212. Allen Hughes, "'Without Regard for Color,'" *New York Times,* February 21, 1965, Sec. II, p. 11.

213. Estrada, "Three Negro Artists," *Dance Magazine,* 51.

214. Hughes, "'Without Regard for Color,'" *New York Times,* II, p. 11.

215. Joan Barthel, "When You Dream, Dream Big," *New York Times,* August 18, 1968, Sec. II, p. 22.

216. Maynard, "Mitchell & The Dance Theatre," *Dance Magazine,* 62.

217. *Ibid.*

218. Terry, "World of Dance: Black Dance," *Saturday Review,* p. 26.

219. *Ibid.*

220. Estrada, "Three Negro Artists," *Dance Magazine,* 54.

221. "Ballet Star," *Ebony,* November, 1959, p. 122.

222. Hughes and Meltzer, *Black Magic,* p. 276.

223. Barthel, "When You Dream," *New York Times,* II, p. 22.

224. Terry, "World of Dance: American Ballet Theatre: Part II," *Saturday Review,* p. 36.

225. Hughes, " 'Without Regard for Color'," *New York Times*, II, p. 11.

226. Walter Terry, *The Dance in America* (New York: Harper and Row, 1956), p. 197.

227. Chujoy and Manchester, eds., *Dance Encyclopedia*, p. 294.

228. Terry, "World of Dance: Black Dance," *Saturday Review*, p. 26.

229. "Jean-Léon Destiné," press release of The American Dance Festival, Connecticut College School of Dance, New London, Connecticut, n.d.

230. "Percival Borde," press release of Jacob's Pillow, announcing Borde's lecture, "The Dance in Africa—Past and Present," August 15, 1965.

231. John Martin, "The Dance: Borde," *New York Times*, October 5, 1958, Sec. II, p. 12.

232. Percival Borde, personal correspondence, April 15, 1970.

233. *Ibid.*

234. Allyn Moss, "Who Is Geoffrey Holder?" *Dance Magazine*, XXXII (August, 1958), 37.

235. "Geoffrey Holder and Company," *Dance Magazine*, XXXII (February, 1958), 59.

236. Doris Rudko, "Geoffrey Holder and Company," *Dance Observer*, January, 1957, p. 13.

237. Joseph Wershba, "A Dancer Says Kindness Is Killing the Negro Theater," *New York Post*, March 28, 1962, p. 50.

238. Barbard Gloudon, "High Priestess of Modern Dance," *Sunday Gleaner* (Kingston, Jamaica), September 7, 1958, p. 14. For an excellent article dealing with Miss Williams' early work in Haiti, see Lavinia Williams Yarborough, "Haiti—Where I Teach Dance," *Dance Magazine*, XXX (October, 1956), 42-44, 76-79.

239. Lavinia Williams Yarborough, personal correspondence, April, 1970.

240. Rex Nettleford, *Roots and Rhythms; Jamaica's National Dance Theatre* (New York: Hill and Wang, 1969).

241. Saul Goodman, "Brief Biographies: Louis Johnson," *Dance Magazine*, XXX, August, 1956, 39.

242. "Holder and Johnson Present Dances," *Musical America*, December 15, 1955, p. 25.

243. Anna Kisselgoff, "Louis Johnson Dance Theatre Makes Its Debut at St. Marks," *New York Times*, February 18, 1969, p. 32.

244. Louis Horst, "Geoffrey Holder, Louis Johnson and Companies, *Dance Observer*, January, 1956, p. 11.

245. *Ibid.*

246. Anna Kisselgoff, "Black Choreographers Go on Display," *New York Times*, March 17, 1969, p. 44.

247. Rod Rodgers, personal interview, New York City, January, 1970.

248. Rod Rodgers, "A Black Dancer's Credo: Don't Tell Me Who I Am," *Negro Digest*, July, 1968, pp. 16-17.

249. *Ibid.*, p. 17.

250. Anna Kisselgoff, "Black Expo Presents Dances by Eleo Pomare, Rod Rodgers," *New York Times,* April 26, 1969, p. 22.

251. For an excellent description of a Head Start performance given by Rodgers, see Marcia B. Siegel, "Starting with Dance," *Arts in Society,* IV, No. 3, The Arts and the Black Revolution II (Fall-Winter, 1968), 504-08.

252. Rod Rogers, "For the Celebration of our Blackness," *Dance Scope,* Spring, 1967, p. 7.

253. Rodgers, "A Black Dancer's Credo," *Negro Digest,* July 1968, p. 16.

254. Rodgers, "Celebration of our Blackness," *Dance Scope,* p. 10.

255. Thomas A. Johnson, "'I Must Be Black And Do Black Things,'" *New York Times,* September 7, 1969, Sec. II, p. 31.

256. "Don Redlich at Henry St. Blues Work Convinces at the 92d 'Y'," *New York Times,* October 17, 1966, p. 46.

257. Walter Terry, "Dance. Eleo Pomare," *New York Herald-Tribune,* February 6, 1961, n.p.

258. Johnson, "'I Must Be Black,'" *New York Times,* II, p. 31.

259. Estrada, "Three Negro Artists," *Dance Magazine,* 45.

260. Johnson, "'I Must Be Black,'" *New York Times,* II, p. 31.

261. Eleo Pomare, "A Letter from a Dancer," *Negro Digest,* January, 1967, pp. 47-48.

262. Estrada, "Three Negro Artists," *Dance Magazine,* 46.

263. "Eleo Pomare," *Ebony,* December, 1969, p. 100.

264. *Ibid.*

265. Johnson, "'I Must Be Black,'" *New York Times,* II, p. 31.

266. "Syvilla Fort Technique," Brochure for Clark Center of the Performing Arts, 51st Street and 8th Avenue, New York, 1968-69.

267. Official playbill, "Lincoln University Presents the Katherine Flowers Dancers in *Bamboula to Bop,* presented at Lincoln University, Jefferson City, Mo., March 17, 1952."

9
A FINAL VIEW

░▒▓▒░ The Africans danced at home in Africa and on the ships carrying them to the New World. Here, as Afro-Americans, they continued to dance, sometimes forced by the whip, and sometimes in religious ecstasy, in competition, or as entertainers.

The dances most frequently observed in the Caribbean were those of the African hip-shaking type and included the Calenda, the Chica and the Juba. Some African dance traditions were maintained in the islands, such as the John Canoe and Gombay dancers. Funeral dance customs seem to have remained close to their African origins, while wedding dances among the blacks were frequently imitative of white customs. Dance played a large role in religious observance, since the religious ceremonies developed in the New World derived in part from African beliefs. In Africa dance was meant to induce the ultimate state of religious ecstasy, "possession," an objective prominent in the New World practice of Voodoo, Shango, and Nañigo.

West Indian dance remained an influence on the dance performed by the blacks in the United States. Funeral dances, for example, were performed in the same manner here as in the islands and Africa. Traces of the Calenda and Chica were found on the plantations, and while the Juba changed from a sacred to a secular dance, it was widely known throughout the South. Other dances of African origin included those performed with containers of water carried on the head and such animal dances as the Buzzard Lope, Pigeon Wing, and Buck. A state of religious ecstasy could be achieved through the Ring-Shout, which was the Protestant counterpart of Voodoo or Shango.

While the Breakdowns and Cake-Walks were being danced on the plantation, the blacks in the North were dancing on such occasions as Pinkster Day, when a dance much like the Calenda was performed. On the levees of the Ohio and Mississippi Rivers a dance called the Coonjine developed, while in New Orleans a wide variety of dances were performed, covering the spectrum from the European social dances performed at the Quadroon Balls to the Bamboula, Calenda, and Chica of Congo Square, to the Voodoo dances held in the Bayou St. John.

Wherever black people gathered to dance, white people came to be entertained. Soon white performers were imitating the black dancers. The most famous of these early white performers was Thomas "Jim Crow" Rice. Imitating the dance and song of an old lame Negro, Rice developed the stereotype of the comic Negro which was maintained in the later minstrel shows. Though the minstrels purported to imitate the plantation Negro, the distortion was so great that by 1890 any resemblance between the Negro and his blackface stereotype was incidental. Yet in the minds of many of the minstrel audience, the real Negro was exactly that caricature, that stereotype which minstrelsy so carefully created and cultivated.

The stereotype developed by minstrelsy has been one of the greatest influences over the life of the black American. This distorted image has had both a positive and negative effect on the dance of the Afro-American. It has exerted a positive effect in that people believed the black had a natural talent for dance, rhythm and music; because of this belief the door to the entertainment world opened more readily for the black dancer. The great black dancers of the entertainment world—Master Juba, the Bohee Brothers, Williams and Walker, Bill Robinson, and Earl Tucker — were readily accepted because the stereotype allowed the Negro to entertain by dancing.

Yet even though there were strong positive effects from the minstrel caricature, the negative far outweighed any advantages gained. The stereotype restricted the black dancer to the role of an entertainer, as opposed to a serious artist. It proscribed the thematic material available for black dance and later limited the dancer to either ethnic African or West Indian material as used by Dafora, Dunham, and Primus, or to strictly Negro thematic material such as spirituals, jazz, plantation dances, and themes traditionally recognized as belonging to Negro life. Pearl Primus and Talley Beatty, in particular, have utilized this type of thematic material. The minstrel image has fostered rejection of the serious black artist when he has attempted to step outside the proscribed thematic limits.

Because the stereotype has been so all-pervasive in American life, few Americans have avoided believing in at least some part of it. Dance critics have often allowed the stereotype to influence their reviews. The function of a critic is to criticize and comment upon the *dance* performed, not to place a value judgment on the suitability of the theme based on the *color* of the performer. The critics, for the most part, have in the past done little to eliminate the stereotype but rather have fostered it by insisting that "Negro dance" was a category unto itself.

While Talley Beatty, Alvin Ailey, and Donald McKayle have broken out of the proscribed material to a certain degree, their most successful compositions still remain within the realm of "Negro" material. In the work of these three men, however, the experience of being black in America has been dramatized for white audiences and a bridge of understanding has been created.

Some dancers believe that critics have limited their aspirations by lavishly overpraising the *efforts* rather than the actual *accomplishments* of black dancers. By claiming that the Afro-American was a natural dancer and complimenting his "inherent" abilities, critics have upheld the concept that black dancers did not need the extensive training and strict discipline so necessary to white dancers. The value of discipline, however, has been shown in the work of Carmen de Lavallade, Mary Hinkson, Matt Turney, William Louther, Clive Thompson, and

Dudley Williams. These artists, all well trained and highly disciplined, have demonstrated the supreme position a black dancer may attain in the international world of dance.

The ballet world has demonstrated the strongest bias against the black dancer. The entire basis of ballet was alien to the *white's conception of the black*. The white who enslaved the black could not think of him as either noble or majestic. Neither did the white consider the black to be graceful. Black dance was considered instinctive and improvised, sometimes savage and licentious, sometimes comic, but never controlled or precise. The concept of beauty also entered into the discrimination against black dancers in the ballet and it has only been when dancers such as Janet Collins and Arthur Mitchell approached the white ideal of beauty that they have been admitted.

West Indian dancers such as Jean-Léon Destiné, Geoffrey Holder, and Percival Borde have contributed to the overall success of black concert dance. Also beginning to be seen are the rising young dancer-choreographers Louis Johnson, Eleo Pomare, and Rod Rodgers. On the West Coast Ruth Beckford and Carleton Johnson have been achieving a reputation through their choreography and teaching efforts, and new black dancers and troupes are being seen daily. The Afro-American has contributed more and has been more influential in the American dance than nearly any other factor throughout the years. The future of the Afro-American as a fresh and vital force in American dance appears to be bright, except in ballet, where the color bar seems nearly insurmountable.

Dance has the power to communicate non-verbally, to create understanding as few other arts have. Through dance the universality of man as man can be revealed. The Afro-American in the American culture is no longer the invisible man. It is time to listen to the spokesmen, the dancers, and hear their message. The black dancer is attempting to bridge the gap between black and white. He must be allowed to speak, and he must be heard.

SOURCES CONSULTED

▣▣ BOOKS

Abramson, Doris E. *Negro Playwrights in the American Theatre 1925-1959.* New York: Columbia University Press, 1969.

Abstract of the Evidence Delivered Before a Select Committee of the House of Commons in The Years 1790 and 1791, on the Part of The Petitioners for the Abolition of the Slave Trade. Printed at the Expense of the Society in Newcastle for Promoting the Abolition of the Slave-Trade, 1791.

Adams, Edward C. L. *Congoree Sketches. Scenes from Negro Life in the Swamps of the Congoree and Tales by Tad and Scip of Heaven and Hell with Other Miscellany.* Chapel Hill, N.C.: University of North Carolina Press, 1927.

Alexander, James Edward. *Transatlantic Sketches, Comprising Visits to the Most Interesting Scenes in North and South America, and the West Indies. With Notes on Negro Slavery and Canadian Emigration.* Philadelphia: Key & Biddle, 1833.

Allen, William Francis; Charles Pickard Ware; and Lucy McKim Garrison. *Slave Songs of the United States.* New York: A. Simpson and Co., 1867.

Armstrong, Orland Kay. *Old Massa's People: The Old Slaves Tell Their Story.* Indianapolis: Bobbs-Merrill Company, 1931.

Asbury, Herbert. *The French Quarter.* Garden City, N.Y.: Garden City Publishing Co., 1938.

Ashe, Thomas. *Travels in America, Performed in the Year 1806, For the Purpose of Exploring the Rivers Alleghany, Monongahela, Ohio, and Mississippi, Ascertaining the Produce and Condition of Their Banks and Vicinity.* London: B. McMillan, 1809.

Avirett, James Battle. *The Old Plantation; How We Lived in Great House and Cabin Before the War.* New York: F. Tennyson Neely Company, 1901.

Bales, Mary Virginia. "Some Negro Folk Songs of Texas." In *Follow de Drinkin' Gou'd* edited by J. Frank Dobie. Austin, Texas: Texas Folk-Lore Society, 1927.

Banting, John. "The Dances of Harlem." In *Negro Anthology,* edited by Nancy Cunard. London: Wishart and Co., 1934.

Barclay, Alexander. *A Practical View of the Present State of Slavery in the West Indies; or, an Examination of Mr. Stephen's "Slavery of the British West India Colonies." Containing more Particularly an Account of the Actual Condition of the Negroes in Jamaica: with Observations on the Decrease of the Slaves since the Abolition of the Slave Trade, and on the Probable Effects of Legislative Emancipation: also, Strictures on the Edinburgh Review, and on the Pamphlets of Mr. Cooper and Mr. Bickell.* 2d ed. London: Smith, Elder & Co., 1827.

Beals, Carleton. *America South.* Philadelphia: J. B. Lippincott Company, 1937.

Beckford, William. *A Descriptive Account of the Island of Jamaica. With Remarks upon the Cultivation of the Sugar-Cane, throughout the different Seasons of the Year, and chiefly considered in a Picturesque Point of View; Also Observations and Reflections upon what would probably be the Consequences of an Abolition of the Slave Trade, and of the Emancipation of the Slaves.* 2 vols. London: T. and J. Egerton, 1790.

Beckwith, Martha Warren. *Black Roadways. A Study of Jamaican Folk Life.* Chapel Hill: University of North Carolina Press, 1929.

————. "Christmas Mummings in Jamaica," in *Jamaica Folk-Lore.* New York: American Folk-Lore Society, 1928.

Bell, Hesketh J. *Obeah. Witchcraft in the West Indies.* 2d ed., rev. London: Sampson, Low, Marston & Company, 1893.

Bergman, Peter M. *The Chronological History of the Negro in America.* New York: Harper and Row, 1969.

Bernhard, Duke of Saxe-Weimar Eisenach. *Travels Through North America During the Years 1825 and 1826.* 2 vols. Philadelphia: Carey, Lea & Carey, 1828.

Beverley, Robert. *The History and Present State of Virginia, in Four Parts.* London: Printed for R. Parker, at the Unicorn, under the Piazza's of the Royal Exchange, 1705.

Bickell, R. *The West Indies As They Are; or, A Real Picture of Slavery: but More Particularly As It Exists in the Island of Jamaica.* London: J. Hatchard & Son, and Lupton Reefe, 1825.

Binga, Anthony. *Binga's Addresses on Several Occasions.* 2d ed. Printed by Vote of the General Association of Virginia, 190?

Blesh, Rudi, and Harriet Janis. *They All Played Ragtime. The True Story of American Music.* New York: Alfred A. Knopf, 1950.

Bond, Frederick W. *The Negro and the Drama.* Washington, D.C.: Associated Publishers, Inc., 1940.

Botkin, Benjamin A. *A Treasury of Southern Folklore*. New York: Crown Publishers, 1949.

Bradley, A. G. *Sketches from Old Virginia*. New York: Macmillan Co., 1897.

Breen, Henry H. *St. Lucia: Historical, Statistical, and Descriptive*. London: Longman, Brown, Green, and Longmans, 1844.

Bremer, Fredrika. *The Homes of the New World; Impressions of America*. Translated by Mary Howitt. 2 vols. New York: Harper and Brothers, 1853.

Brown, Alexander. *The First Republic in America. An Account of the Origin of this Nation, Written from the Records then (1624) Concealed by the Council, rather than from the Histories then liscensed by the Crown*. Boston: Houghton, Mifflin and Company, 1898.

Brown, Alexander. *The Genesis of the United States. A Narrative of the Movement in England, 1605-1616, which Resulted in the Plantation of North America by Englishmen, Disclosing the Contest Between England and Spain for the Possession of the Soil Now Occupied By the United States of America; Set Forth Through a Series of Historical Manuscripts now first printed together with a reissue of rare and contemporaneous tracts, accompanied by bibliographical memoranda, notes, and Brief Biographies collected, arranged, and edited by Alexander Brown*. 2 vols. London: William Heinemann, 1890.

Brown, Sterling A. *Negro Poetry and Drama and The Negro in American Fiction*. New York: Atheneum, 1969. [Originally published 1937.]

Brown, T. Allston. "The Origin of Negro Minstrelsy." *Fun in Black; or, Sketches of Minstrel Life, with the Origin of Minstrelsy, by Col. T. Allston Brown, Giving a History of Ethiopian Minstrelsy from 1799* compiled by Charles H. Day. New York: Robert M. DeWitt, 1874.

Bryant, William Cullen. *Letters of a Traveller; or, Notes of Things Seen in Europe and America*. New York: George P. Putnam, 1850.

Buckle, Richard, ed. *Katherine Dunham, Her Dancers, Singers, Musicians*. London: Ballet Publications, Ltd., 1949.

Buel, J. W. *Metropolitan Life Unveiled, or The Mysteries and Miseries of America's Great Cities*. St. Louis, Mo.: Historical Publishing Co., 1882.

Burwell, Letitia M. *A Girl's Life in Virginia Before the War*. New York: Frederick A. Stokes Company, 1895.

Butcher, Margaret Just. *The Negro in American Culture*. New York: Alfred A. Knopf, 1967.

Cable, George Washington. "The Story of Bras-Coupé." In *Creoles and Cajuns*, edited by Arlin Turner. Gloucester, Mass.: Peter Smith, 1965.

Canot, Theodore. *Adventures of an African Slaver. Being a True Account of Captain Theodore Canot, Trader in Gold, Ivory and Slaves on the Coast of Guinea: His Own Story as Told in the Year 1854 to Brantz Mayer*. Edited by Malcolm Cowley. New York: Albert and Charles Boni, 1928.

Carmichael, Mrs. *Domestic Manners and Social Condition of the White, Coloured, and Negro Population of the West Indies*. 2 vols. London: Whittaker, Treacher, and Co., 1833.

Castellanos, Henry C. *New Orleans As It Was.* 2d ed. New Orleans: L. Graham Co., Ltd., 1905.

Christy's and White's Ethiopian Melodies. Containing Two Hundred and Ninety-One of the Best and Most Popular and Approved Ethiopian Melodies Ever Written. Being the Largest and Most Complete Collection Ever Published. Comprising the Melodeon Song Book; Plantation Melodies; Ethiopian Song Book; Serenader's Song Book; and Christy and Wood's New Song Book. Published under the Authority of George Christy and Charles White, the Original Delineators of the Popular Ludicrous Negro Character. Philadelphia: T. B. Peterson, 185?.

Chujoy, Anatole, and P. W. Manchester, eds. *The Dance Encyclopedia.* Rev. ed., New York: Simon and Schuster, 1967.

Churchill, Awnsham. *A Collection of Voyages and Travels, Some Now First Printed from Original Manuscripts. Others Translated out of Foreign Languages, & now first publish'd in English. To which Are added some few that have formerly appear'd in English, but do now for their excellency & Scarceness deserve to be Reprinted. In Six Volumes. With a General Preface, Giving an Account of the progress of Navigation, from its first Beginning to the Perfection it is now in, etc. The Whole Illustrated with a great number of Useful Maps & Cuts all Engraven on Copper.* London: 1704, 1732.

Claiborne, John Frederick H. "A Trip Through the Piney Woods." In *Publications of the Mississippi Historical Society, IX,* edited by Franklin L. Riley. Oxford, Miss.: Mississippi Historical Society, 1906.

Clarkson, Thomas. *The History of the Rise, Progress, and Accomplishment of the Abolition of the African Slave-Trade by the British Parliament.* 2 vols. London: R. Taylor & Co., 1808.

Coleman, Stanley Jackson, ed. *Myth and Mystery in Curious Caribbean Cults.* Douglas, Isle of Man: Folklore Academy, 125 Ballabrooie Drive, 1960.

Coleman, William Head, comp. *Historical Sketch Book and Guide to New Orleans and Environs.* New York: Will H. Coleman, 1885.

Conrad, Earl. *The Invention of the Negro.* New York: Paul S. Eriksson, Inc., 1966.

Cooper, James Fenimore. *Satanstoe; or, The Littlepage Manuscripts. A Tale of the Colony.* 2 vols. New York: Burgess, Stringer and Co., 1845.

Courlander, Harold. "Dance and Dance-Drama in Haiti." In *The Function of Dance in Human Society,* edited by Franziska Boas. New York: Boas School, 1944.

——. *The Drum and the Hoe; Life and Lore of the Haitian People.* Berkeley: University of California Press, 1960.

——. *Haiti Singing.* Chapel Hill, N.C.: University of North Carolina Press, 1939.

——. *Negro Folk Music, U.S.A.* New York: Columbia University Press, 1963.

Craven, Wesley Frank. *Dissolution of the Virginia Company. The Failure of a Colonial Experiment.* New York: Oxford University Press, 1932.

Cresswell, Nicholas, *The Journal of Nicholas Cresswell, 1774-1777*. New York: Dial Press, 1924.

Crum, Mason. *Gullah; Negro Life in the Carolina Sea Islands*. Durham, N.C.: Duke University Press, 1940.

Davenport, Frederick Morgan. *Primitive Traits in Religious Revivals*. New York: Macmillan Company, 1917.

Davis, Edwin A. *Plantation Life in the Florida Parishes of Louisiana, 1836-1846 as Reflected in the Diary of Bennet H. Barrow*. New York: Columbia University Press, 1943.

Davis, John. *Travels of Four Years and a Half in the United States of America; During 1798, 1799, 1800, 1801, and 1802*. Bristol: R. Edwards, 1803.

Davis, John P., ed. *The American Negro Reference Book*. Englewood Cliffs, N.J.: Prentice-Hall, Inc., 1966.

Day, Charles W. *Five Years Residence in the West Indies*. 2 vols. London: Colburn & Co., 1852.

DeMille, Agnes. *The Book of the Dance*. London: Paul Hamlyn, 1963.

Deren, Maya. *Divine Horsemen, The Living Gods of Haiti*. London: Thomas and Hudson, 1953.

Descourtilz, Michel-Etienne. *Voyages d'un Naturaliste en Haiti, 1799-1803*. Translated by Anthony Bliss. 3d ed. Paris: Librairie Plon, Les Petits-Fils de Plon & Nourrit, 1935.

Dickens, Charles. *American Notes and Pictures from Italy*. London: Chapman and Hall, Ltd., 1892.

Donnan, Elizabeth. *Documents Illustrative of the History of the Slave Trade to America*. 4 vols. Washington, D.C.: Carnegie Institution of Washington, 1931.

Dow, George Francis. *Slave Ships and Slaving*. Salem, Mass.: Marine Research Society, 1927.

Drake, Richard. *Revelations of a Slave Smuggler: Being the Autobiography of Capt. Rich'd Drake, An African Trader for Fifty Years—from 1807 to 1857; During Which Period He was Concerned in the Transportation of Half a Million Blacks from African Coasts to America*. New York: Robert M. DeWitt, 1860.

Dunham, Katherine. *A Touch of Innocence*. New York: Harcourt, Brace and Company, 1959.

————. *Island Possessed*. Garden City, N.Y.: Doubleday & Company, Inc., 1969.

————. *Katherine Dunham's Journey to Accompong*. New York: Henry Holt and Company, 1946.

————. "The Negro Dance." In *The Negro Caravan*, edited by Sterling A. Brown, Arthur P. Davis, and Ulysses Lee. New York: Dryden Press, 1941.

Edwards, Bryan. *An Historical Survey of the Island of Saint Domingo, together with an account of the Maroon Negroes in the Island of Jamaica; and a History of the War in the West Indies. In 1793 and 1794. Also, A Tour through* the Several Islands of Barbadoes, St. Vincent, Antigua, Tobago, & Grenada In the Years 1791 & 1792 by Sir William Young. London: John Stockdale, 1801.

————. The History, Civil and Commercial, of the British West Indies; With a Continuation to the Present Time. 2 vols. 5th ed. London: T. Miller, 1819.

Edwards, Charles L. Bahama Songs and Stories. A Contribution to Folk-Lore. Boston: Houghton, Mifflin and Company, 1895.

Eppes, Mrs. Nicholas Ware. The Negro of the Old South. A Bit of Period History. Chicago: Joseph G. Branch Publishing Company, 1925.

Falconbridge, Alexander. An Account of the Slave Trade on the Coast of Africa. London: J. Phillips, 1788.

Fauset, Jessie, "The Gift of Laughter." In Anthology of the American Negro in the Theatre. A Critical Approach, compiled and edited by Lindsay Patterson. New York: Publishers Company, Inc., 1967.

Fearon, Henry Bradshaw. Sketches of America, A Narrative of a Journey of Five Thousand Miles through the Eastern and Western States of America; Contained in Eight Reports Addressed to the Thirty-Nine English Families by Whom the Author was Deputed, in June, 1817, to Ascertain Whether Any, and What Part of the United States would be Suitable for their Residence. With Remarks on Mr. Birkbeck's "Notes" and "Letters." London: Longman, Hurst, Rees, Orme, and Brown, 1818.

Featherstonhaugh, G. W. Excursion Through the Slave States, from Washington on the Potomac to the Frontier of Mexico; with Sketches of Popular Manners and Geological Notices. New York: Negro Universities Press, 1968. [Originally published by Harper and Brothers, 1844.]

Fisk University, Social Science Institute. Unwritten History of Slavery. Autobiographical Accounts of Negro Ex-Slaves. Social Science Source Document No. 1. Washington, D.C.: NCR Microcard Editions, 1968.

Flanagan, Hallie. Arena. New York: Duell, Sloan and Pearce, 1940.

Fletcher, Tom. The Tom Fletcher Story — 100 Years of the Negro in Show Business. New York: Burdge and Company, Ltd., 1954.

Flint, Timothy. Recollections of the Last Ten Years in the Valley of the Mississippi. Edited by George R. Brooks. Carbondale: Southern Illinois University Press, 1968.

Franklin, John Hope, From Slavery to Freedom. A History of Negro Americans. 3d ed. Vintage Books, New York: Random House, 1969.

Frazer, James George. The Golden Bough. A Study in Magic and Religion. 2 vols. 3d ed. New York: Macmillan Company, 1935.

Gardner, W. J. A History of Jamaica from its Discovery by Christopher Columbus to the Year 1872. Including an Account of its Trade and Agriculture; Sketches of the Manners, Habits, and Customs of All Classes of its Inhabitants; and a Narrative of the Progress of Religion and Education in the Island. New York: D. Appleton and Company, 1909.

Georgia Writer's Project. *Drums and Shadows. Survival Studies Among the Georgia Coastal Negroes.* Athens: University of Georgia Press, 1940.

Gilbert, Douglas. *Lost Chords.* Garden City, N.Y.: Doubleday, Doran and Co., Inc., 1942.

Gilman, Caroline. *Recollections of a New England Bride and of a Southern Matron.* Rev. ed. New York: G. P. Putnam & Co., 1852.

Goffin, Robert. *Jazz from Congo to Swing.* England: Musicians Press Ltd., 114 Charing Cross Rd., W.C. 2, 1946.

Goldberg, B. Z. *The Sacred Fire: The Story of Sex in Religion.* New York: Horace Liveright, 1930.

Grier, William H., and Price M. Cobbs. *Black Rage.* Bantam Books. New York: Basic Books, Inc., 1968.

Handy, W. C., ed. *Blues: An Anthology.* New York: Albert and Charles Boni, 1926.

Haskell, Arnold L. *Balletomania. The Story of an Obsession.* New York: Simon and Schuster, 1934.

Haywood, Charles. *Negro Minstrelsy and Shakespearean Burlesque.* A Reprint from *Folklore and Society, Essays in Honor of B. A. Botkin.* Hatboro, Pa.: Folklore Associates, 1966.

Hearn, Lafcadio. *Two Years in the French West Indies.* New York: Harper & Brothers, 1890.

Herskovits, Melville J. *Life in a Haitian Valley.* New York: Alfred A. Knopf, 1937.

————. *The Myth of the Negro Past.* Boston: Beacon Press, 1958.

————, and Frances S. Herskovits. *Trinidad Village.* New York: Alfred A. Knopf, 1947.

Holland, Rupert Sargent, ed. *Letters and Diary of Laura M. Towne, Written from the Sea Islands of South Carolina, 1862-1884.* Cambridge: Riverside Press, 1912.

Howard, Joseph H. *Drums in the Americas.* New York: Oak Publications, 1967.

Hughes, Langston. *The Big Sea.* New York: Hill and Wang, 1940.

————. *The Dream Keeper and Other Poems.* New York: Alfred A. Knopf, 1932.

————. *Famous Negro Music Makers.* New York: Dodd, Mead and Company, 1957.

————, and Milton Meltzer. *Black Magic. A Pictorial History of the Negro in American Entertainment.* Englewood Cliffs, N.J.: Prentice-Hall, Inc., 1967.

Hungerford, Mary Jane. *Creative Tap Dancing.* New York: Prentice-Hall, Inc., 1939.

Hurston, Zora Neale. "Mimicry." In *Negro Anthology,* edited by Nancy Cunard. London: Wishart and Co., 1934.

————. *Mules and Men.* Philadelphia: J. B. Lippincott Company, 1935.

————. *Tell My Horse.* Philadelphia: J. B. Lippincott Company, 1938.

Hutton, Laurence. *Curiosities of the American Stage.* New York: Harper & Brothers, 1891.

Irving, Washington. *Salmagundi; or, The Whim-Whams and Opinions of Launcelot Langstaff, Esq. and Others.* 2 vols. New York: D. Longworth, 1807.

Isaacs, Edith J. R. *The Negro in the American Theatre.* New York: Theatre Arts, Inc., 1947.

Jackson, Bruce, ed. *The Negro and his Folklore in Nineteenth-Century Periodicals.* Vol. IX, Publications of the American Folklore Society, Bibliographical and Special Series. Kenneth S. Goldstein, editor. Austin: University of Texas Press, 1967.

Jefferson, Thomas. *Notes on the State of Virginia; Written in the Year 1781, some what corrected and enlarged in the Winter of 1782, for the Use of a Foreigner of Distinction in Answer to Certain Queries Proposed by Him Respecting. . . .* Paris, 1782.

Jennings, John J. *Theatrical and Circus Life.* San Francisco, Calif.: A. L. Bancroft and Company, 1882.

Johnson, Guion Griffis. *A Social History of the Sea Islands. With Special Reference to St. Helena Island, S.C.* Chapel Hill: University of North Carolina Press, 1930.

Johnson, James Weldon. *Black Manhattan.* New York: Alfred A. Knopf, 1930.

Johnston, Harry H. *The Negro in the New World.* London: Methuen & Co., Ltd., 1910.

Kaigh, Frederick. *Witchcraft and Magic of Africa.* London: Richard Lesley and Co., Ltd., 1947.

Kemble, Francis Anne. *Journal of a Residence on a Georgian Plantation in 1838-1839.* New York: Harper & Brothers, 1863.

King, Grace Elizabeth. *New Orleans. The Place and the People.* New York: Macmillan Company, 1937.

Kingsbury, Susan M., ed. *The Records of the Virginia Company of London. The Court Book, from the Manuscript in the Library of Congress.* 4 vols. Washington: Government Printing Office, 1906.

Kraus, Richard. *History of the Dance in Art and Education.* Englewood Cliffs, N.J.: Prentice-Hall, Inc., 1969.

Krehbiel, Henry Edward. *Afro-American Folksongs. A Study in Racial and National Music.* 4th ed. New York: G. Schirmer, Inc., 1914.

Labat, Père. *Nouveau Voyage Aux Isles de l'Amerique.* 2 vols. Translated by Anthony Bliss. The Hague, 1724.

Latrobe, Benjamin Henry Boneval. *Impressions Respecting New Orleans. Diary and Sketches, 1818-1820.* Edited by Samuel Wilson Jr. New York: Columbia University Press, 1951.

Leach, Maria, ed. *Funk and Wagnalls Standard Dictionary of Folklore, Mythology and Legend.* 2 vols. New York: Funk and Wagnalls Company, 1949.

Leaf, Earl. *Isles of Rhythm.* New York: A. S. Barnes and Company, 1948.

Leavitt, Michael Bennett. *Fifty Years in Theatrical Management*. New York: Broadway Publishing Co., 1912.

Leigh, Frances Butler. *Ten Years on a Georgia Plantation Since the War*. London: Richard Bentley and Son, 1883.

Lekis, Lisa. *Dancing Gods*. New York: Scarecrow Press, Inc., 1960.

Levinson, André I. "The Negro Dance Under European Eyes." In *The Negro in American Theatre*, edited by Edith J. R. Isaacs. New York: Theatre Arts, Inc., 1947.

Lewis, Matthew Gregory. *Journal of a West India Proprietor, 1815-1817*. Edited by Mona Wilson. New York: Houghton Mifflin Company, 1929.

Lloyd, Margaret. *The Borzoi Book of Modern Dance*. Brooklyn, N.Y.: Dance Horizons, Inc., 1949.

Locke, Alain. *The Negro and His Music*. Washington, D.C.: Associates in Negro Folk Education, 1936.

————. *The New Negro*. New York: Albert and Charles Boni, 1925.

Loederer, Richard A. *Voodoo Fire in Haiti*. Translated by Desmond Ivo Vesey. New York: Literary Guild, 1935.

Long, Edward. *The History of Jamaica. Or, General Survey of the Ancient and Modern State of that Island: With Reflections on Its Situation, Settlements, Inhabitants, Climate, Produce, Commerce, Laws, and Government*. 3 vols. London: T. Lowndes, 1774.

Lowery, Irving E. *Life on the Old Plantation in Ante-Bellum Days*. Columbia, S.C.: The State Co., Printers, 1911.

Lyell, Charles F. R. S. *A Second Visit to the United States of North America*. 2 vols. New York: Harper and Brothers, 1849.

McKay, Claude. *A Long Way From Home*. New York: Lee Furman, Inc., 1937.

————. *Home to Harlem*. New York: Harper and Brothers, 1928.

McKayle, Donald. "The Act of Theatre." In *The Modern Dance, Seven Statements of Belief*, edited by Selma Jean Cohen. Middletown, Conn.: Wesleyan University Press, 1966.

————. "The Negro Dancer in Our Time." In *The Dance Has Many Faces*. 2d ed., edited by Walter Sorell. New York: Columbia University Press, 1966.

Mannix, Daniel P., and Malcolm Crowley. *Black Cargoes. A History of the Atlantic Slave Trade 1518-1865*. New York: Viking Press, 1962.

Marks, Edward B. *They All Sang. From Tony Pastor to Rudy Vallée*. New York: Viking Press, 1935.

Martin, John. *Introduction to the Dance*. Brooklyn, N.Y.: Dance Horizons, Inc., 1965. [Originally published, 1939.]

————. *John Martin's Book of the Dance*. New York: Tudor Publishing Company, 1963.

Metraux, Alfred. *Haiti: Black Peasants and Voodoo*. Translated by Peter Lengyel. New York: Universe Books, 1960.

Metraux, Alfred. *Voodoo in Haiti.* Translated by Hugo Charteris. London: Andre Deutsch Ltd., 1959.

Mitchell, Loften. *Black Drama; The Story of the American Negro in the Theatre.* New York: Hawthorne Books, Inc., 1967.

Montejo, Esteban. *The Autobiography of a Runaway Slave.* Edited by Miguel Barnet. Translated by Jocasta Innes. Meridian Books. New York: World Publishing Company, 1969.

Moreau de St.-Méry, De M. L. E. *Danse.* Translated by Anthony Bliss. Philadelphia, 1796.

————. *Description Topographique et Politique de la Partie Espagnole de l'isle Saint-Domingue; avec des Observations Génerales sur le Climat, la Population, Les Productions, le Caractère, & les Moeurs des Habitans de Cette Colonie, & un Tableau Raisonné des Différentes Parties de son Administration; accompagnée d'un Nouvelle Carte de la Totalité de l'isle.* Translated by Anthony Bliss. 2 vols. Philadelphia: et s'y trouve chez l'auteur, 1797-98.

Moton, Robert Russa. *Finding a Way Out. An Autobiography.* College Park, Md.: McGrath Publishing Co., 1969. [Originally published by Doubleday, Page and Co., 1920.]

Munsell, Joel. *Collections on the History of Albany, from its Discovery to the Present Time, with Notices of its Public Institutions, and Biographical Sketches of Citizens Deceased.* 2 vols. Albany, N.Y.: J. Munsell, 1867.

Myrdal, Gunnar. *An American Dilemma. The Negro Problem and Modern Democracy.* 2 vols. Harper Torchbooks. New York: Harper and Row, 1962 [Originally published 1944].

Nathan, Hans. *Dan Emmett and the Rise of Early Negro Minstrelsy.* Norman, Okla.: University of Oklahoma Press, 1962.

Neill, Edward D. *Virginia Vetusta, During the Reign of James the First. Containing Letters and Documents Never Before Printed. A Supplement to The History of the Virginia Company.* Albany, N.Y.: Joel Munsell's Sons, 1885.

Nettleford, Rex. *Roots and Rhythms; Jamaica's National Dance Theatre.* New York: Hill and Wang, 1970.

New Orleans As It Is: Its Manners and Customs—Morals—Fashionable Life—Profanation of the Sabbath—Prostitution—Liscentiousness—Slave Markets & Slavery, etc., etc., etc. Utica, N.Y.: DeWitt C. Grove, 1849.

Nichols, Thomas Low. *Forty Years of American Life.* 2d ed. London: Longmans, Green and Co., 1874.

Noble, Peter. *The Negro in Films.* London: British Yearbooks Ltd., 30 Cornhill, E.C. 3, 1948.

Northup, Solomon. *Twelve Years a Slave . . .* London: Sampson Low Son and Co., 1853.

Odell, George C. D. *Annals of the New York Stage.* 15 vols. New York: Columbia University Press, 1927-28.

Odum, Howard W., and Guy B. Johnson. *The Negro and his Songs*. Hatboro, Pa.: Folklore Associates, Inc., 1964.

Oesterley, W. O. E. *The Sacred Dance*. 2d ed. Brooklyn, N.Y.: Dance Horizons, Inc., 1923.

Ortiz, Fernando. *Los Bailes y el Teatro de los Negros en el Folklore de Cuba*. Translated by Dorothy Latasa Kiefer. Havana: Cardenas y cia, 1951.

Osofsky, Gilbert. "Harlem: The Making of a Ghetto." In *Harlem. A Community in Transition*. edited by John Henrik Clarke. New York: Citadel Press, 1969.

Ottley, Roi, and William J. Weatherby, eds. *The Negro in New York. An Informal Social History*. New York: New York Public Library, 1967.

Owen, Nicholas. *Journal of a Slave-Dealer. A View of Some Remarkable Axcedents in the Life of Nics. Owen on the Coast of Africa and America from the Year 1746 to the Year 1757*. Edited by Eveline Martin. London: George Routledge and Sons, Ltd., 1930.

Page, Thomas Nelson. *Social Life in Old Virginia Before the War*. New York: Charles Scribner's Sons, 1897.

Parkman, Dailey, and Sigmund Spaeth. *"Gentlemen, Be Seated!" A Parade of Old-Time Minstrels*. Garden City, N.Y.: Doubleday, Doran and Company, Inc., 1928.

Parrish, Lydia. *Slave Songs of the Georgia Sea Islands*. New York: Creative Age Press, Inc., 1942.

Payne, Daniel Alexander. *Recollections of Seventy Years*. New York: Arno Press and The New York Times, 1968. [Originally published in Nashville, Tenn.: A.M.E. Sunday School Union, 1888.]

Phillippo, James M. *Jamaica: Its Past and Present State*. Philadelphia: James M. Campbell and Co., 1843.

Phillips, Ulrich Bonnell. *American Negro Slavery. A Survey of the Supply, Employment, and Control of Negro Labor as Determined by the Plantation Regime*. New York: D. Appleton and Company, 1918.

Pinckard, George. *Notes on the West Indies*. 2 vols. 2d ed. London: Baldwin, Cradock, and Joy, and L. B. Seeley, 1816.

Powles, L. D. *The Land of the Pink Pearl; or Recollections of Life in the Bahamas*. London: Sampson, Low, Marston, Searle, and Rivington, 1888.

Primus, Pearl. "Primitive African Dance (And Its Influence on the Churches of the South)." In *The Dance Encyclopedia*, edited by Anatole Chujoy. New York: A. S. Barnes, 1949.

Puckett, Newbell Niles. *Folk Beliefs of the Southern Negro*. New York: Negro Universities Press, 1968. [Originally published by the University of North Carolina Press, 1926.]

Redding, Saunders. *They Came in Chains*. Phildelphia: J. B. Lippincott Company, 1950.

Roberts, W. Adolphe. *Lake Pontchartrain*. Indianapolis: Bobbs-Merrill Company Publishers, 1946.

Rourke, Constance. *American Humor.* New York: Harcourt, Brace and Company, 1931.

————. *The Roots of American Culture and Other Essays.* Edited with a preface by Van Wyck Brooks. Harvest Books. New York: Harcourt, Brace and World, Inc., 1942.

Russell, William Howard. *My Diary North and South.* Boston: T. O. H. P. Burnham, 1863.

St. John, Spenser. *Hayti or The Black Republic.* New York: Scribner and Welford, 1889.

Saxon, Lyle. *Fabulous New Orleans.* New York: D. Appleton-Century Company, 1941.

————; Edward Dreyer; and Robert Tallant, comps., Works Progress Administration Louisiana Writers' Project. *Gumbo Ya-Ya.* Boston: Houghton Mifflin Company, 1945.

Scarborough, Dorothy. *On the Trail of Negro Folksongs.* Cambridge: Harvard University Press, 1925.

Schermerhorn, R. A. *These Our People. Minorities in American Culture.* Boston: D. C. Heath and Company, 1949.

Schoener, Allon, ed. *Harlem on My Mind. Cultural Capital of Black America 1900-1968.* New York: Random House, 1968.

Schultz, Christian. *Travels on an Inland Voyage through the States of New-York, Pennsylvania, Virginia, Ohio, Kentucky and Tennessee, and through the Territories of Indiana, Louisiana, Mississippi and New Orleans; Performed in the Years 1807 and 1808; Including a Tour of Nearly Six Thousand Miles.* With Maps and Plates. 2 vols. New York: Isaac Riley, 1810.

Seabrook, W. B. *The Magic Island.* New York: Harcourt, Brace and Company, 1929.

Sketches and Eccentricities of Col. David Crockett, of West Tennessee. New York: J. and J. Harper, 1833.

Sloane, Hans. *A Voyage to the Islands Madera, Barbados, Nieves, S. Christophers and Jamaica, with the Natural History of the Herbs and Trees, Islands; to which is prefix'd An Introduction, wherein is an Account of the Inhabitants, Air, Waters, Diseases, Trade, etc. of that Place, with Some Relations concerning the Neighbouring Continent, and Islands of America.* 2 vols. London: B. M., 1707.

Smith, John. *The Generall Historie of Virginia, New-England, and the Summer Isles: with the Names of the Adventurers, Planters, and Governours from their first beginning An: 1584 to this present 1626. With the Procedings of those Severall Colonies and the Accidents that Befell them in all their Journyes and Discoveries. Also the Maps and Descriptions of all those Countryes, their Commodities, people, Government, Customes, and Religion yet knowne, Divided into Sixe Bookes.* London: I. D. and I. H. for Michael Sparkes, 1627.

Spears, John R. *The American Slave Trade. An Account of Its Origin, Growth and Suppression.* New York: Charles Scribner's Sons, 1900.

Stearns, Marshall, and Jean Stearns. *Jazz Dance. The Story of American Vernacular Dance.* New York: Macmillan Company, 1968.

Steward, Austin. *Twenty-Two Years a Slave, and Forty Years a Freeman: Embracing a Correspondence of Several Years While President of Wilberforce Colony, London, Canada, West.* Rochester, N.Y.: William Alling, 1857.

Stewart, J. *A View of the Past and Present State of the Island of Jamaica; with Remarks on the Moral and Physical Condition of the Slaves, and on The Abolition of Slavery in the Colonies.* Edinburgh: Oliver & Boyd, 1823.

Stoddard, Amos. *Sketches, Historical and Descriptive, of Louisiana.* Philadelphia: Mathew Carey, 1812.

Stroyer, Jacob. *My Life in the South.* 3d ed. Salem: Salem Observer Book and Job Print, 1885.

Sullivan, Edward. *Rambles and Scrambles in North and South America.* 2d ed. London: Richard Bentley, 1853.

Sullivan, Mark. *Our Times. The United States 1900-1925.* 6 vols. New York: Charles Scribner's Sons, 1932.

Tallant, Robert. *Mardi Gras.* Garden City, N.Y.: Doubleday & Company, Inc., 1948.

—————. *Voodoo in New Orleans.* New York: Macmillan Company, 1946.

Talley, Thomas W. *Negro Folk Rhymes.* New York: Macmillan Company, 1922.

Terry, Walter. *The Dance in America.* New York: Harper and Row, 1956.

Tillinghast, Joseph Alexander. *The Negro in Africa and America.* 3d Series, Vol. III. Publications of the American Economic Association. New York: Macmillan Company, 1902.

Todd, Arthur. "American Negro Dance: A National Treasure." In *The Ballet Annual 1962,* edited by Arnold Haskell and Mary Clarke. London: Adam and Charles Black, 1961.

Turnbull, Jane M. G., and Marion Turnbull. *American Photographs.* 2 vols. 2d ed. London: T. C. Newby, 1860.

Vandenhoff, George. *Leaves from an Actor's Notebook; with Reminiscences and Chit-Chat of the Green Room and the Stage in England and America.* New York: D. Appleton and Company, 1860.

Van Vechten, Carl. *In the Garrett.* New York: Alfred A. Knopf, 1920.

Virginia Writers' Project. *The Negro in Virginia.* New York: Hastings House, 1940.

Walsh, William S. *Curiosities of Popular Customs and of Ceremonies, Observances, and Miscellaneous Antiquities.* Philadelphia: J. B. Lippincott Company, 1898.

Warner, Charles Dudley. *Studies in the South and West with Comments on Canada.* New York: Harper and Brothers, 1889.

Weatherford, Willis D. *The Negro from Africa to America.* New York: George H. Doran Co., 1924.

Wheeler, Mary. *Steamboatin' Days.* Baton Rouge: Louisiana State University Press, 1944.

Williams, Cyrnic R. *A Tour Through the Island of Jamaica, from the Western to the Eastern End in the Year 1823.* London: Hunt and Clark, 1826.

Williams, Joseph J. *Psychic Phenomena of Jamaica.* New York: Dial Press, 1934.

————. *Voodoos and Obeahs. Phases of West Indian Witchcraft.* New York: Dial Press, 1932.

Wittke, Carl. *Tambo and Bones. A History of the American Minstrel Stage.* Durham, N.C.: Duke University Press, 1930.

Wright, Richardson. *Revels in Jamaica, 1682-1838.* New York: Dodd, Mead and Company, 1937.

Writers' Program, Illinois. *Cavalcade of the American Negro.* Chicago: Diamond Jubilee Exposition Authority, 1940.

Wurdemann, F. W. *Notes on Cuba; Containing An Account of Its Discovery and Early History; a Description of the Face of the Country, Its Institutions, and the Manners and Customs of Its Inhabitants. With Directions to Travellers Visiting the Island.* Boston: James Munroe and Company, 1844.

Wyeth, John Allan. *With Sabre and Scalpel.* New York: Harper Bros., 1914.

◼︎◼︎◼︎ PERIODICALS

"Ailey, Alvin (Jr)." *Current Biography,* March, 1968, pp. 3-5.

Ailey, Alvin. "African Odyssey." *Dance Magazine,* XLII (May, 1968), 50-53, 86-88.

Anderson, Jack. "Alvin Ailey American Dance Theatre." *Dance Magazine,* XLIV (June, 1970), 79.

Balcom, Lois. "What Chance Has the Negro Dancer?" *Dance Observer,* November, 1944, pp. 110-11.

"Ballet Star." *Ebony,* November, 1959, pp. 122-24, 126.

Barnes, Clive. "Dancing the Blues." *Spectator* (London), October 16, 1964, p. 512.

Barrow, David C. Jr. "A Georgia Corn Shucking." *Century Magazine,* October 1882, pp. 873-78.

"Black Man Stars in Ballet." *Black America,* June, 1970, pp. 52-54.

Bolton, H. Carrington. "Gombay, A Festal Rite of Bermudian Negroes." *Journal of American Folklore,* III, No. 10 (July-September, 1890), 222-26.

Bourguignon, Erika. "Trance Dance." *Dance Perspectives 35,* Autumn, 1968, pp. 5-61.

"Broadway Whispers." *American Dancer,* September, 1928, pp. 17, 30.

Cable, George Washington. "Creole Slave Songs." *Century Magazine,* April, 1886, pp. 807-28.

————. "The Dance in Place Congo." *Century Magazine,* February, 1886, pp. 517-29.

"Cakewalk King; 81 Year Old Charles E. Johnson Still Dreams of New Comeback with Dance Step of Gay 90's." *Ebony*, February, 1953, pp. 99-102, 104-06.

Cook, Will Marion. "Clorindy, the Origin of the Cakewalk." *Theatre Arts*, XXXI (September, 1947), 61-65.

Crichton, Kyle. "Peel That Apple—the Story of the 'Big Apple.'" *Collier's*, December 4, 1937, pp. 22, 48.

"*Dance Magazine's* Annual Award Presentations, 1966." *Dance Magazine*, XLI (May, 1967), 83-87.

"*Dance Magazine's* Annual Awards, 1968." *Dance Magazine*, XLIII (April, 1969), 34-37, 66-67.

DeJon, Lythe Orme. "The Gombeys of Bermuda." *Dance Magazine*, XXX (May, 1956), 32-33, 54-55.

"De Lavallade, Carmen." *Current Biography*, December, 1967, pp. 8-12.

Donahue, Jack. "Hoofing." *Saturday Evening Post*, September 14, 1929, pp. 29, 233-34, 237.

Dunham, Katherine. "The Dances of Haiti." *Acta Anthropologica*, II (November, 1947), 5-61.

————. "Ethnic Dancing." *Dance Magazine*, XX (September, 1946), 22, 34-35.

————. "Form and Function of Primitive Dance." *Educational Dancer*, October, 1941, pp. 2-4.

————. "The Future of the Negro in the Dance." *Dance Herald*, March, 1938, p. 5.

Earle, Alice Morse. "Pinkster Day." *Outlook*, April 28, 1894, pp. 743-44.

"Eleo Pomare." *Ebony*, December, 1969, pp. 94-96, 98, 100.

Elias, A. J. "Conversation with Katherine Dunham." *Dance Magazine*, XXX (February, 1956), 16-19.

Eng, Frank. "The House on Melrose." *Dance Perspectives 31*, Autumn, 1967, pp. 20-45.

Estrada, Ric. "Three Leading Negro Artists, and How They Feel About Dance in the Community: Eleo Pomare, Arthur Mitchell, Pearl Primus." *Dance Magazine*, XLII (November, 1968), 45-60.

Evans, Oliver. "Melting Pot in the Bayous." *American Heritage*, XV (December, 1963), 30-32, 49-51, 106.

"Folk-Lore and Ethnology. American Folk-Lore Society." *Southern Workman*, XXIV, No. 2 (February, 1895), 30-32.

Fortier, Alcée. "Customs and Superstitions in Louisiana." *Journal of American Folk-Lore*, I, No. 2 (July-September, 1888), 136-40.

Gannett, W. C. "The Freedmen at Port Royal." *North American Review*, CI (July, 1865), 1-28.

"Geoffrey Holder and Company." *Dance Magazine*, XXXII (February, 1958), 58-59.

Goodman, Saul. "Brief Biographies: Alvin Ailey." *Dance Magazine,* XXXII (December, 1958), 70.

————. "Brief Biographies: Louis Johnson." *Dance Magazine,* XXX (August, 1956), 39.

————. "Brief Biographies: Donald McKayle." *Dance Magazine,* XXXIV (June, 1960), 50-51.

Guy, Edna. "Negro Dance Pioneer!" *Dance Herald,* March, 1938, p. 6.

Hall, L. A. "Some Early Black-Face Performers and the First Minstrel Troop." *Harvard Library Notes,* I, No. 2 (October, 1920), 39-45.

Hansen, Chadwick. "Jenny's Toe: Negro Shaking Dances in America." *American Quarterly,* XIX (Fall, 1967), 554-63.

Hansford, M. M. "The Gombey Dance." *Dancing Times* (London), December, 1938, pp. 275-76.

"Harlem Under Control, Negro Ballet Gives 'Fire Bird' and Park Ave. Approves." *Newsweek,* November 29, 1937, p. 28.

Hering, Doris. "Alvin Ailey and Company." *Dance Magazine,* XXXII (May, 1958), 65-66.

————. "Carmen de Lavallade and Her Theatre of the Dance." *Dance Magazine,* XLII (May, 1968), 31.

Herskovits, Melville J. "African Gods and Catholic Saints in New World Negro Belief." *American Anthropologist,* XXXIX, No. 4, Part 1 (1937), 635-43.

"Holder and Johnson Present Dances." *Musical America,* December 15, 1955, p. 25.

Horst, Louis. "Geoffrey Holder, Louis Johnson and Companies." *Dance Observer,* January, 1956, p. 11.

Hurston, Zora Neale. "Hoodoo in America." *Journal of American Folk-Lore,* XLIV, No. 174 (October-December, 1931), 317-417.

Hutton, Laurence. "The Negro on the Stage." *Harper's New Monthly Magazine,* June, 1889, pp. 131-45.

Jackson, Harriet. "American Dancer, Negro." *Dance Magazine,* XXXX (September, 1966), 35-42.

Jefferson, Miles M. "The Negro on Broadway, 1945-1946." *Phylon,* VII, No.2 (Second Quarter, 1946), 185-96.

Keeler, Ralph. "Three Years a Negro Minstrel." *Atlantic Monthly,* July, 1869, pp. 71-85.

Kirstein, Lincoln. "The Dance, 'Kykunkor'; Native African Opera." *Nation,* June 13, 1934, p. 684.

Leddick, David. "Everyman's African Roots." *Dance Magazine,* XXXVIII (October, 1964), 20-21.

Lorant, Michael. "'Hampton Institute,' Negro's Unique Dancing Academy." *Dancing Times* (London), October, 1938, pp. 20-21.

————. "The Hampton Institute, Unique Dancing Academy of the American Negroes." *Ballet Today,* II (June, 1950), 16-18.

MacMillan, Dougald. "John Kuners." *Journal of American Folklore*, XXXIX, No. 151 (January-March, 1926), 53-57.

"The Magazines for June." *Nation*, May 30, 1867, pp. 432-33.

Manchester, P. W. "Meet Donald McKayle." *Dancing Times* (London), January, 1967, pp. 186-87.

Marks, Marcia. "Dance Caravan." *Dance Magazine*, XLIII (June, 1969), 94.

————. "Review: Alvin Ailey American Dance Theatre." *Dance Magazine*, XLIII (March, 1969), 92.

Matthews, Brander. "Banjo and Bones." *Saturday Review of Politics, Literature, Science and Art* (London), June 7, 1884, pp. 739-40.

————. "The Rise and Fall of Negro Minstrelsy." *Scribner's Magazine*, June, 1915, pp. 754-59.

Maximovna, Elena. "Negro Dance on the Scene." *Dance Magazine*, XVI (December, 1942), 15, 24-25.

Maynard, Olga. "Arthur Mitchell and The Dance Theatre of Harlem." *Dance Magazine*, XLIV (March, 1970), 52-62.

Mishnun, Virginia. "Dance: Dunham 'Tropical Revue'." *Nation*, October 9, 1943, p. 416.

"Mitchell, Arthur." *Current Biography*, October, 1966, pp. 20-22.

"Morals and Manners Among Negro Americans." *Atlanta University Publications*, No. 18 (1914), 1-136.

Moss, Allyn. "Who Is Geoffrey Holder?" *Dance Magazine*, XXXII (August, 1958), 36-41.

"Music. Josephine's Return." *Newsweek*, March 12, 1951, p. 82.

Nathan, Hans. "The First Negro Minstrel Band and Its Origin." *Southern Folklore Quarterly*, XIV, No. 2 (1952), 132-44.

————. "Two Inflation Songs of the Civil War." *Musical Quarterly*, April, 1943, pp. 242-53.

Nevin, Robert. "Stephen Foster and Negro Minstrelsy." *Atlantic Monthly*, November, 1867, pp. 608-16.

"On the Airwaves." *Dance Magazine*, XLII (September, 1969), 7.

Orme, Frederick L. "The Negro in the Dance." *American Dancer*, March, 1938, pp. 10, 46.

Overstreet, Harry A. "Images and the Negro." *Saturday Review*, August 26, 1944, pp. 5-6.

Pierre, Dorathi Bock. "A Talk with Katherine Dunham." *Educational Dancer*, August-September, 1941, pp. 7-8.

Pomare, Eleo. "A Letter from a Dancer." *Negro Digest*, January, 1967, pp. 46-48.

"Primus, Pearl (Eileene)." *Current Biography*, April, 1944, pp. 34-37.

Ravenel, Henry William. "Recollections of Southern Plantation Life." *Yale Review*, XXV, No. 4 (June, 1936), 748-77.

Ravitz, A. C. "John Pierpont and the Slaves' Christmas." *Phylon*, XXI, No.4 (Winter, 1960), 383-86.

Roberts, Helen H. "Some Drums and Drum Rhythms of Jamaica." *Natural History*, XXIV, No. 2 (March-April, 1924), 241-51.

Rodgers, Rod. "A Black Dancer's Credo: Don't Tell Me Who I Am." *Negro Digest*, July, 1968, pp. 14-17.

————. "For the Celebration of Our Blackness." *Dance Scope*, Spring, 1967, pp. 6-10.

Rudko, Doris. "Geoffrey Holder and Company." *Dance Observer*, January, 1957, pp. 12-13.

"The Schoolmarm Who Glorified Leg Art." *Ebony*, January, 1947, pp. 14-18.

Seldes, Gilbert. "Shake Your Feet." *New Republic*, November 4, 1925, pp. 283-84.

Shedd, Margaret. "Carib Dance Patterns." *Theatre Arts*, XVII (January, 1933), 65-77.

Sherlock, Charles. "From Breakdown to Rag-Time." *Cosmopolitan*, October, 1901, pp. 631-39.

Siegel, Marcia B. "Starting with Dance." *Arts in Society*, IV, No. 3. The Arts and the Black Revolution II. (Fall-Winter, 1968), 504-08.

Simpson, George Eaton. "The Belief System of Haitian Vodun." *American Anthropologist*, New Series XLVII, No. 1 (1945), 35-59.

Sissle, Noble. "How Jo Baker Got Started." *Negro Digest*, August, 1951, pp. 15-19.

Spaulding, H. G. "Under the Palmetto." *Continental Monthly*, IV (July-December, 1863), 188-203.

Stahl, Norma Gengal. "The First Lady of the Metropolitan Opera Ballet." *Dance Magazine*, XXVIII (February, 1954), 27-29.

Terry, Walter. "World of Dance: American Ballet Theatre: Part II." *Saturday Review*, August 1, 1970, p. 36.

————. "World of Dance: Black Dance." *Saturday Review*, September 26, 1970, pp. 26, 45.

Todd, Arthur. "Four Centuries of American Dance: Part 3: The Negro Folk Dance in America." *Dance Magazine*, XXIV (January, 1950), 14-15, 41.

———— "Four Centuries of American Dance: Dance Before the American Revolution — 1734-1775." *Dance Magazine*, XXIV (March, 1950), 20-21, 35.

————. "Four Centuries of American Dance. Negro American Theatre Dance, 1840-1900." *Dance Magazine*, XXIV (November, 1950), 20-21, 33-34.

————. "Two-Way Passage for Dance." *Dance Magazine*, XXXVI (July, 1962), 39-41.

Trisler, Joyce. "The Magic and the Commitment." *Dance Perspectives 31*, Autumn, 1967, pp. 54-65.

"Voodooism: Cuban Authorities Battle Cult Practising Kidnaping and Human Sacrifice." *Literary Digest*, January 2, 1937, p. 29.

Walker, George W. "The Real 'Coon' on the American Stage." *Theatre* (New York), August, 1906, pp. 224, i-ii.

Waring, May A. "Mortuary Customs and Beliefs of South Carolina Negroes." *Journal of American Folklore*, VII, No. 27 (October-December, 1894), 318-19

Washington, Booker T. "Interesting People. Bert Williams." *American Magazine*, September, 1910, pp. 600-04.

Watts, Richard J. "Musical Comedy and Revue Dancing—How Did It Develop?" *Dance Magazine*, II (January, 1929), 16-17, 60, 63.

Williams, Wilson. "Prelude to a Negro Ballet." *American Dancer*, March, 1940, pp. 14, 39.

Winter, Marian Hannah. "Juba and American Minstrelsy." *Dance Index*, VI, No. 2 (February, 1947), 28-49.

Yarborough, Lavinia Williams. "Haiti—Where I Teach Dance." *Dance Magazine*, XXX (October, 1956), 42-44, 76-79.

Young, Stark. "Slightly Ghosts." *New Republic*, December 8, 1937, p. 131.

▣▣▣ NEWSPAPERS

Atkinson, Brooks. "Theatre: Truman Capote's Musical." *New York Times*. December 31, 1954.

"At the Theatres: Grand—'Uncle Tom's Cabin.'" *New York Dramatic Mirror*. June 11, 1892.

"At the Theatres: Third Avenue—'Uncle Tom's Cabin.'" *New York Dramatic Mirror*. April 29, 1899.

Barnes, Clive. "Dance: Nothing Less Than Superb." *New York Times*. December 18, 1965.

————. "Dance: The Wizardry of Talley Beatty." *New York Times*. September 5, 1967.

————. "Dance: Broadway Touch." *New York Times*. January 30, 1969.

————. "Dance: 'Archaic Hours,' a New Graham." *New York Times*. April 12, 1969.

Barthel, Joan. "When You Dream, Dream Big." *New York Times*. August 18, 1968.

Bartlett, K. S. "Talley Beatty Company in Vivid Performance at John Hancock Hall." *Boston Globe*. January 15, 1952.

Bradford, Roark. "New Orleans Negro Declared Not Guilty of the Charleston." No publication given. January 3, 1926. Dance Clipping File. Dance Collection, Lincoln Center of the Performing Arts. New York.

Campbell, Robert. "Florence Mills' Life Story." *Philadelphia Tribune*. December 22, 1927.

"Cannibalism in Hayti." *New York World*. December 5, 1886.

Cohn, Ellen. "'I Want to Be a Father Figure.'" *New York Times.* April 13, 1969.

"Congo Square." *New Orleans Daily Picayune.* March 22, 1846.

Cook, Will Marion. "Letter to the Editor." *New York Times.* December 26, 1926.

"Cornshuckin' Down South." *New York Sun.* November 11, 1895.

Crowther, Bosley. "From the 'Turkey Trot' to the 'Big Apple.'" *New York Times Magazine,* November 7, 1937.

"Dance of the Voodoos." *New Orleans Times-Democrat.* June 24, 1896.

Denby, Edwin. "The Dance." *New York Times.* October 6, 1944.

"Don Redlich at Henry St. Blues Work Convinces at the 92d 'Y'." *New York Times,* October 17, 1966.

Ferris, W. H. "Writer Reviews Negro Stage For Past Forty Years; Cites Notables." *Pittsburgh Courier.* November 19, 1927.

Garrison, Lloyd. "The Vitality of Negro Art." *New York Times.* May 1, 1966.

Gilbert, Morris. "Up and Coming." *New York Times Magazine.* February 1, 1953.

Gloudon, Barbara. "High Priestess of Modern Dance." *Sunday Gleaner* (Kingston, Jamaica). September 7, 1958.

Goldberg, Isaac. "How Minstrelsy Really Began." *The Afro-American* (Baltimore). Part I: January 6, 1934. Part II: January 13, 1934.

"Grand Bal Paré." *New Orleans Moniteur.* August 22, 1807.

"The Handglass — Uncle Tom's Cabin." *New York Dramatic Mirror.* December 6, 1890.

Hearn, Lafcadio. "Levee Life." *Cincinnati Commercial.* March 17, 1876.

Hellinger, Mark. "Broadway Loves Bill Robinson." *Pittsburg Courier.* November 15, 1930.

Hughes, Allen. "'Without Regard for Color.'" *New York Times.* February 21, 1965.

Johnson, Thomas A. "'I Must Be Black and Do Black Things.'" *New York Times.* September 7, 1969.

"Josephine Baker Is Beset by More Woes." *New York Times.* March 13, 1969.

"Juba at Vauxhall." *Illustrated London News.* August 5, 1848.

Kisselgoff, Anna. "Louis Johnson Dance Theatre Makes Its Debut at St. Marks." *New York Times.* February 18, 1969.

————. "Black Choreographers Go on Display." *New York Times.* March 17, 1969.

————. "Black Expo Presents Dances by Eleo Pomare, Rod Rodgers." *New York Times.* April 26, 1969.

————. "Dance: Militant 'Masekela Language.'" *New York Times.* November 21, 1969.

K., I. "Negro Ballet Has Performances." *New York Sun.* November 22, 1937.

Lloyd, Margaret. "African Dances, American Plan." *Christian Science Monitor.* May 17, 1938.

—————. "The Personal Equation: New Ballerina at the Met." *Christian Science Monitor*. October 16, 1951.

Martin, John. "Dance Recital Given by Negro Artists." *New York Times*. April 30, 1931.

—————. "The Dance: A Negro Art Group." *New York Times*. February 14, 1932.

—————. "The Dance: A Negro Play." *New York Times*. March 12, 1933.

—————. "Native Cast Gives An African Opera." *New York Times*. May 9, 1934.

—————. "The Dance: African Lore." *New York Times*. May 13, 1934.

—————. "The Dance: Negro Art." *New York Times*. November 7, 1937.

—————. "Negro Ballet Has Debut in Harlem." *New York Times*. November 22, 1937.

—————. "Negro Dance Art Shown in Recital." *New York Times*. February 19, 1940.

—————. "The Dance: A Negro Art." *New York Times*. February 25, 1940.

—————. "The Dance: 'Tropical Revue.'" *New York Times*. September 26, 1943.

—————. "The Dance: Current Events." *New York Times*. December 3, 1944.

—————. "The Dance: Dunham." *New York Times*. November 17, 1946.

—————. "The Dance: Newcomer." *New York Times*. February 27, 1949.

—————. "Ballet: A Homecoming." *New York Times*. November 9, 1955.

—————. "Dance: Borde and Troupe." *New York Times*. September 29, 1958.

—————. "The Dance: Borde." *New York Times*. October 5, 1958.

—————. "Dance: Good Job." *New York Times*. December 6, 1959.

Nott, G. William. "Marie Laveau, Long High Priestess of Voodooism in New Orleans." *New Orleans Times-Picayune*. November 19, 1922.

Pearlman, Joseph. "Harlemites Forsake Torrid 'Swing' Dances for the Modern Ballet Steps." *New York Herald-Tribune*. December 12, 1937.

Pollock, Arthur. "Janet Collins, Golden Dancing Girl of 'Out of This World.'" *Daily Compass*. January 23, 1951.

Segal, Edith. "Pearl Primus Thrills Broadway." *Daily Worker* (New York). October 7, 1944.

Seymour, W. H. "A Voudou Story." *New Orleans Daily Picayune*. July 3, 1892.

"Sleight of Hand Artist." *New-York Journal or the General Advertiser*. No. 1266, April 9, 1767.

Stodelle, Ernestine. "The Negro Dancer: Gift to America Beyond Value." *New Haven Register*. January 14, 1968.

Terry, Walter. "The Negro Dances." *New York Herald-Tribune*. April 28, 1940.

—————. "Dance. Eleo Pomare." *New York Herald-Tribune*. February 6, 1961.

—————. "Stars Under the Stars—A Vision of Loveliness." *New York Herald-Tribune*. September 9, 1963.

"Vauxhall Gardens—Boz's Description of Juba." *Illustrated London News.* June 24, 1848.

"Vauxhall Gardens—Unprecedented Success." *Illustrated London News.* July 1, 1848.

"The Vous Dous Incantation." *New Orleans Times.* June 28, 1872.

Walton, Lester A. "Lucky Roberts Autographs Songs for the Prince." No publication given. October 17, 1926. Dance Clipping File. Dance Collection, Lincoln Center of the Performing Arts. New York.

Wershba, Joseph. "The Gift of Healing Is Not Always a Medical Matter." *New York Post.* August 9, 1960.

————. "A Dancer Says Kindness Is Killing the Negro Theatre." *New York Post.* March 28, 1962.

"Winfield Dead at 27; 'Emperor Jones' Dancer." *New York Herald-Tribune.* No date given. Dance Clipping File. Schomburg Collection of Negro Literature and History. New York.

▐▌▐▌▐▌ UNPUBLISHED MATERIAL

Federal Writers' Project of the Works Progress Administration

Federal Writers' Project. *Slave Narratives. A Folk History of Slavery in the United States From Interviews with Former Slaves.* Typewritten Records Prepared by the Federal Writers' Project. 1936-1938. Assembled by the Library of Congress Project Work Projects Administration for the District of Columbia. Sponsored by The Library of Congress. Illustrated with Photographs. 17 Volumes.

Vol. I	Alabama Writers' Project. *Alabama Narratives.*
Vol. II	Federal Writers' Project of the Works Progress Administration for the State of Arkansas. *Arkansas Narratives.* 7 parts.
Vol. III	Federal Writers' Project of the Works Progress Administration for the State of Florida. *Florida Narratives.*
Vol. IV	Federal Writers' Project of the Works Progress Administration for the State of Georgia. *Georgia Narratives.* 4 parts.
Vol. V	Slave Narratives. *Indiana.*
Vol. VI	Federal Writers' Project of the Works Progress Administration. *The Slave Narratives. Kansas.*
Vol. VII	Federal Writers' Project of the Works Progress Administration. *The Slave Narratives. Kentucky.*
Vol. VIII	Federal Writers' Project of the Works Progress Administration. *The Slave Narratives. Maryland.*

Vol. IX	Federal Writers' Project of the Works Progress Administration. *The Slave Narratives. Mississippi.*
Vol. X	Federal Writers' Project of the Works Progress Administration. *The Slave Narratives. Missouri.*
Vol. XI	Federal Writers' Project of the Works Progress Administration for the State of North Carolina. *North Carolina Narratives.* 2 parts.
Vol. XII	Works Progress Administration Writers' Project. *Slave Narratives. Ohio.*
Vol. XIII	Works Progress Administration Writers' Project. *Slave Narratives. Oklahoma.*
Vol. XIV	Works Progress Administration. *Slave Narratives — South Carolina.* 4 parts.
Vol. XV	Works Progress Administration Writers' Project. *Slave Narratives. Tennessee.*
Vol. XVI	Federal Writers' Project. *Slave Narratives. A Folk History of Slavery in the United States From Interviews with Former Slaves. Texas Narratives.* 4 parts.
Vol. XVII	Works Progress Administration Writers' Project. *Slave Narratives. Virginia Narratives.*

Writers' Program, New York (City). *The Dance.* Research Studies Compiled by Workers of the Writers' Program of the Work Projects Administration in New York City, for "Negroes of New York." New York, 1936-1940. 15 articles in one volume. Typescript portfolio. Schomburg Collection of Negro Literature and History. New York City, New York.

Young, Wilbur. "Dances Originating in Harlem." Writers' Program, New York (City), *The Dance.* Article No. 4. See previous entry.

Personal Interviews and Correspondence

Bell, Dr. James. Numerous interviews at California State Polytechnic College, Pomona, California. 1969-1970.

Engram, Carole. Personal interview. Pasadena, California. May 8, 1970.

Oswald, Genevieve. Personal interview. New York, New York. January, 1970.

Primus, Pearl. Personal conversation. New York, New York. January, 1970.

Rodgers, Rod. Personal interview. New York, New York. January, 1970.

White, Charles. Personal interviews. Altadena, California. Aug.-Dec., 1969.

Borde, Percival. Personal correspondence. April 15, 1970.

Collins, Janet. Personal correspondence. March, 1970.

De Lavallade, Carmen. Personal correspondence. April 21, 1970.

Dunham, Katherine. Personal correspondence. April 1, 1970.

Yarborough, Lavinia Williams. Personal correspondence. April, 1970.

Playbills and Programs

"The Great Callender Colossal Consolidated Colored Minstrel Festival." Playbill. Theatre Collection, Lincoln Center of the Performing Arts, New York, New York. 1887.

Kykunkor. Official Program. Schomburg Collection of Negro Literature and History, New York.

"Asadata Dafora Presents 'Kykunkor.'" Playbill. Little Theatre, 244 West 44th Street, New York City. June 18, 1934.

"Major Subscription Series. Young Men's Hebrew Association Presents 'Negro Dance Evening.'" Playbill. Theresa Kaufmann Auditorium, Lexington Avenue at 92nd Street. New York City. March 7, 1937.

"S. Hurok Presents Katherine Dunham and her company in 'Tropical Revue.'" Playbill. Martin Beck Theatre, West Forty-Fifth Street, New York City. October 24, 1943.

"Nelson L. Gross and Daniel Melnick Present Katherine Dunham in 'Bal Negre.'" Playbill. Belasco Theatre, New York City. December 2, 1946.

"Stephen Papich in Association with Dorothy Gray and Ludwig Gerber Present Katherine Dunham in 'Bamboche,' Premiere Performance." Playbill. 54th Street Theatre, New York City. October 22, 1962.

"The American Museum of Natural History, Central Park West and 79th Street, New York City, Thursday, May 15, 1952 at 3:30 and 8:30 P.M. Presents Pearl Primus and her Company in 'Dark Rhythm.'" Playbill.

"Lincoln University Presents the Katherine Flowers Dancers in *Bamboula To Bop.* Lincoln University, Jefferson City, Mo. March 17, 1952." Playbill.

Miscellaneous

Franklin, M. Theresa. "God's Velvet Shadows: Modern Dance Composition and Study of the Negro Spiritual." Unpublished Master of Arts thesis. New York University, 1966.

Borde, Percival. "Press release announcing lecture entitled 'The Dance in Africa—Past and Present.'" Jacob's Pillow Festival. August 15, 1965.

Destiné, Jean-Léon. "Press release of The American Dance Festival, Connecticut College School of Dance. New London, Connecticut." n.d.

"Hinkson, Mary." Program notes for the October, 1963 Graham season. Dance Clipping File. Dance Collection, Lincoln Center of the Performing Arts. New York.

Johnson, Charles E. and Dora Dean Johnson. Christmas Card, n.d. Schomburg Collection of Negro Literature and History. New York.

"Syvilla Fort Technique." Brochure for Clark Center for the Performing Arts, 51st Street and 8th Avenue, New York. 1968-69.

INDEX

Black Bottom (neighbor-
hood), 221
"Black-Eyed Susan," 110
Blackface, 268
Black Renaissance, 222,
223
Blacks, The, 271
Blake, Eubie, 215, 223,
228
Bland, James, 204
Bless You All, 278
Blues, 230
"Blues for the Jungle,"
310
"Blues Suite," 277
"Bobolink Bob," 141
Bohee Brothers, 204,
327
Bolero, 38
Bolton, H. Carrington, 35
Bolton, James, 85,
108–9
Bomarzo, 312
Bond, Frederick, 209,
225
Bones, 84, 86, 95, 190,
198, 211
Bonjaws, 38
Bonjour, 17, 20. *See also*
Banjo
Book of the Dance, 267
Borde, Percival, 264,
265, 296, 297–98
Boston, 82, 257, 270
Boston Ballet, 282
Botkin, Benjamin, 125,
126
Botta e Risposta, 256
Boula, 49, 53. *See also*
Drum
Bourguignon, Erika, 50
Bowery Theatre, 185
Boz, 186, 188
Bradford, Roark, 226–27
Bradley, A. G., 85
Brando, Marlon, 259

Brandy, 52
Bras de Coupé, 147
Brazil, 10, 60
Breakdown, 110, 139,
140, 186, 192, 197,
206, 326. *See also*
Virginny Breakdown
"Breaking the Ice," 247
Breen, Henry, 27
Bremer, Fredrika, 25–26,
128
"Br'er Rabbit and de
Tah Baby," 254, 256
Briggs, Vincent, 47
British settlements, 40
Broadway, 208, 210,
213, 215, 228, 236,
244, 256, 271, 272,
278, 280, 282, 304
Bronx Community
College, 297
Brother Bones, 84
Brower, Frank, 190
Brown, Alexander, 81
Brown, Fred, 95
Brown, Sterling, 184,
206, 215, 236
Bryant, Dan, 193
Bryant, William Cullen,
114–15
Bryant's Minstrels, 193,
194
Buck, 89, 93, 223, 326.
See also Buck and
Wing; Mobile Buck
Buck and Wing, 89, 90,
193, 194, 196, 204,
212. *See also* Buck;
Mobile Buck; Pigeon
Wing
Bucktowns, 145, 146
Buel, J. W., 168, 178
Bullfights, 154
Burgoyne, Ollie, 242
Burlesque, 204, 236,
258
Burlesque African Polka,
194

"Burnt Ash," 308
Burwell, Letitia, 119
Butcher, Margaret, 197,
236
Butler, Matthew, 128,
130
But Never Jam Today,
271
Buzzard Lope, 93–94,
100, 326

Cabin in the Sky, 256
301
Cable, George Wash-
ington, 158, 162–63,
164, 168, 172, 176,
178
Cafe Society Downtown,
262
Cain, Louis, 108
Cajuns, 147
Cake-Walk, 47, 91–92,
94, 108, 110, 139,
206–14, 216, 223,
245, 256, 326
Calabar River, 68
Calabash, 20, 34, 38, 80,
159
Caleinda, 24. *See also*
Calenda
Calenda, 21–24, 25, 29,
71, 95, 110, 143, 145,
147, 164, 168–69,
325, 326
Calendar, Charles, 204
California, 211, 310
Calinda, 164. *See also*
Calenda
Calypso, 36
Camaguey, 69
Camel Walk, 94, 100,
221
Cameroons, 264
Campbell, Ellen, 105
Campbell, Hettie, 92
Canada, 285
Canal Street, 147
Cannibalism, 49, 52–53

Fish Tail, 94, 100

"Fisher's Hornpipe, The," 110

Fisk University, 245, 264

Five Dancers, 262

Flanagan, Hallie, 254

Fletcher, Tom, 92, 191–92, 204, 207, 208

Fling D'Ethiope, 194

Flint, Rev. Timothy, 172, 193

Florida, 16, 83, 130, 220

Floridas, 10

Flower Dance, 128

Flowers, Katherine, 313

Flux, 8

Fly Blackbird, 271

Folies Bergères, 229, 230

Ford Foundation, 293

Fort, Syvilla, 257, 258, 259, 312

Fortier, Alcée, 173

Four Saints in Three Acts, 304

Fox Trot, 226

France, 147, 148, 153, 156, 230

Frank, Bill, 286

Franklin, Benjamin, 204–5

Franklin, Christopher Columbus, 100

Franklin, John Hope, 16, 83

Frazier, Ronald, 280

Freedman's Bureau, 122

French, LaVerne, 268

French horn, 103, 205

French Quarter, 147

French Revolution, 148

Frolic, 197

From Haiti to Harlem, 254

Fromm, Eric, 253

Funerals, 40–45, 76, 84, 103, 116, 117–19, 301, 325, 326

Gaetano, M., 154

Gamby, 18. *See also* Drum

"Games," 279

Gannett, W. C., 123

Gardie, Mme., 180

Gardner, W. J., 38, 43, 47

Garrison, Lucy McKim, 121, 147

Gede, 58

Geetchie Walk, 235, 240

Generall Histoire of Virginia, The, 81

Genet, Jean, 271

Gennaro, Peter, 259

Gens de couleur, 147, 149, 150, 153, 154. *See also* Mulattoes: Quadroons

Georgia, 83, 84, 92, 93, 94, 100, 101, 104, 105, 106, 108, 109, 115, 118, 121, 124, 138, 182

Georgia Minstrels, 196, 204, 205

Georgia Sea Islands, 83, 84, 92, 93, 95, 118, 119, 122, 214, 240

Germany, 310

Gernreich, Rudi, 259

Ghana, 251

Gibbs, Georgianna, 104–5

Gilbert, Douglas, 192

Gioconda, La, 290

Gloria, 10

Gluck-Sandor, 244, 247

Goat sacrifice, 68

Godreau, Miguel, 275

Goffin, Robert, 166

Goldberg, B. Z., 128

Goldberg, Isaac, 185

Gold Coast, 21, 35, 69, 264

Gold Coast-Niger area, 2

Golden Bough, The, 250

Golden Boy, 280

Gomba, 18, 19, 20. *See also* Drum

Gombay (dance), 34–36, 37, 71, 111, 325. *See also* Gumbay (dance)

Gombay (drum), 30, 34, 38, 158. *See also* Drum

Gomez, Tommy, 257

Goodman, Saul, 303

Goodness, Jo, 167

Goodwater, Thomas, 84

Goombay, 18, 20, 34. *See also* Drum

Gottschalk, Louis, 160–61

Gourd, 17, 20, 39, 119

Gourd rattle, 159

Graham, Martha, 247, 273, 276, 278, 283, 284, 285, 286, 302, 312

Grapevine Twist, 194

Great Nonpareil Coloured Troupe, 196

Great White Hope, The, 280

Green Mansions, 256

Green Pastures, 226

Greenwich Village, 242

Gris-gris, 147

Grona, Eugene Von, 245–47, 301

Guadeloupe, 148

Guede, 58

Guiablesse, La, 252

Guinea, 21, 30, 65

Guitar, 17, 100

Gullah, 84, 220

Gumbay (dance), 45. *See also* Gombay (dance)

Gumbé, 34, 158. *See also* Drum

Guy, Edna, 242–43, 243–44, 251, 267